Privatisation in Developing Countries

Edited by
V.V. Ramanadham

London and New York

First published 1989 by Routledge
11 New Fetter Lane, London EC4P 4EE

Simultaneously published in the USA and Canada
by Routledge
29 West 35th Street, New York, NY 10001

Reprinted 1990 (twice), 1991, 1993

© 1989 Interregional Network on Privatisation

Wordprocessed by Vibes, Brighton, Sussex
Printed and bound in Great Britain by
Antony Rowe Ltd, Chippenham, Wiltshire

British Library Cataloguing in Publication Data

Privatisation in developing countries,
   1. Developing countries. Public sector. Privatisation
   I. Ramanadham, V.V.
   351.007'2

   ISBN 0–415–03815–4

Library of Congress Cataloging in Publication Data

Privatisation in developing countries / edited by V.V. Ramanadham.
      p. cm.
   Papers prepared for the Interregional Workshop on Privatisation
  sponsored by the United Nations Development Programme (UNDP)
  at Templeton College, Oxford, during May 1987.
   Includes index.
   ISBN 0–415–03815–4
   1. Privatisation – Developing countries – Case studies –
Congresses. I. Ramanadham, V.V. (Venkata, Vernon), 1920–
II. Interregional Workshop on Privatisation (1987 : Templeton
College, Oxford) III. United Nations Development Programme.
HD4420.8.P73   1989   89–3506
338.9'009172'4–dc19   CIP

To the United Nations

the One Living Hope of Mankind

Contents

Foreword   xi

Preface   xiii

Part I: Background Material

1. Privatisation: The UK Experience and
   Developing Countries
   V.V. Ramanadham   3

2. Some Background Observations on Privatisation
   Colin Kirkpatrick   94

3. Privatisation: Macro-economics and Modalities
   Gerry Grimstone   103

4. Privatisation: Modalities and Strategies
   John Heath   118

5. Introducing Competition and Regulatory
   Requirements
   David Thompson   125

6. Some Organisational Implications of Privatisation
   Nick Woodward   133

Part II: Country Papers

7. Privatisation in Pakistan
   Riyaz Bokhari   145

8. Privatisation in India
   Y. Venugopal Reddy   178

9. Privatisation in Sri Lanka
   A.S. Jayawardene   199

10. Privatisation in Malaysia
    Ministry of Public Enterprises   216

Contents

11. Privatisation in Jordan
    Rima Khalaf   236

12. Privatisation in China
    Hua Sheng   250

13. Privatisation in Kenya
    R.W. Karanja   268

14. Privatisation in Nigeria
    John D. Edozien and S.O. Adeoye   283

15. Privatisation in Ghana
    William Adda   303

16. Privatisation in Africa
    Myrna Alexander   322

17. Privatisation in Ethiopia, Malawi and Uganda
    Roger Sullivan   352

18. Privatisation in Peru
    Felipe Ortiz de Zevallos M.   358

19. Privatisation in Jamaica, Trinidad and Tobago   378
    G.E. Mills

Part III: Concluding Review

20. Concluding Review
    V.V. Ramanadham   405

Index   433

Tables

6.1	Social and cultural context of privatisation	140
10.1	Breakdown of PEs by sectors	216
10.2	Public equity ownership of PEs in Malaysia in 1986	217
10.3	Return on capital (ROC) employed for PEs in Malaysia, 1986	219
10.4	Profitability structure of PEs in Malaysia	220
12.1	Ownership classification in terms of enterprise numbers	251
12.2	Distribution of employees in industrial enterprises, 1986	251
12.3	Industrial enterprises in 353 cities (1986) in China	252
12.4	Economic performance of different ownerships	252
13.1	Some data on state corporations	270
13.2	Loan and interest repayments by some state corporations to the Kenya government	273
13.3	Government ownership and participation in public enterprises	274
13.4	'Holding' complexes in state corporations	275
14.1	Federal public enterprises	285
14.2	The ownership pattern	285
14.3	Public-sector companies which have divested ownership from the state	286
15.1	The general structure of SOEs	306
18.1	Peruvian SOEs	361
18.2	Net profit by economic sectors of the Peruvian SOEs	361
18.3	Profitability of SOEs (1986)	364
18.4	Accumulated losses in SOEs (expressed as the reduction of net worth)	364
18.5	Accion Popular's response to a survey, 1980	368

Figures

1.1   Continuum of possibilities in privatisation   5
1.2   Comparative advantage   16
1.3   How 'A' ordinary shares may be transferred   86
1.4   How the purchase of NFC will be financed   87

3.1   Hierarchy of political desirability in
      privatisation options   106

6.1   Possible sets of criteria for a privatisation
      programme   135
6.2   Political ideology and organisational
      effectiveness   137
6.3   Distribution of income per head of population   139

20.1 Privatisation and distributional equity   422

x

Foreword

Developing countries are asking the United Nations Development Programme (UNDP) for assistance in making the most of their private sector potential. We must respond to these requests. The private sector is a potent engine for development. It can help to unleash the dynamism, creativity and talent of individuals throughout the world. Give these men and women a free hand to manage their own development and a permanent stake in that development - and they will work miracles for themselves, their communities and countries.

UNDP has a long and varied history of providing direct and indirect support to the private sector - from rural farmers to urban entrepreneurs. Recently UNDP has put increased effort into creating a better climate for private enterprise through a series of interregional, regional and national seminars where government and private sector representatives exchange views. One of the elements to emerge from these seminars has been concern about the poor performance of many public enterprises and the impact which this has on government budgets and the overall economy. Many countries are redefining the relationship between the public and private sectors either through the encouragement of private enterprises or through the selective privatisation of public enterprises.

It is in this context that I welcome the current publication, Privatisation in Developing Countries, as a UNDP-sponsored technical resource for countries considering various levels of privatisation. The UNDP Interregional Workshop on Privatisation, which was the focus of the country and background papers and the source of the material for this publication, took place at Templeton College, Oxford, UK in May 1988. The high level of participants from the academic, government and private sectors promoted the business-like debate which is reflected throughout. Our special appreciation goes to Professor V.V. Ramanadham for his highly professional work in organising the workshop and editing the resulting material. The workshop participants agreed to form a network to critically evaluate guidelines and other material on privatisation which can be made available to interested developing countries.

Foreword

This publication should therefore be seen as both the result of an effective workshop and the cornerstone of an Interregional Network on Privatisation which has the full support of UNDP.

William H. Draper III
Administrator
United Nations Development Programme
New York

Preface

This volume brings together, suitably edited, the papers prepared for the Interregional Workshop on Privatisation sponsored by the United Nations Development Programme (UNDP) at Templeton College, Oxford, during May 1988. Part I contains my basic working paper and the background material provided by the consultants. Part II codifies country experiences in Asia, Africa and Latin America, as presented by the participants in the Workshop, who represent the top levels of expertise in public enterprise matters in the different regions. Part III presents a review of the major issues of substance and aspects of experience, in the light of the documentation.

For a complete idea of the discussions and conclusions of the Workshop one may refer to the Report on the Interregional Workshop on Privatisation, distributed by UNDP.

I express my gratefulness to the contributors of the papers for their co-operation in the course of my editing obligation. I thank Mr Timothy Rothermel, Director, and Mr Philip Reynolds, of the Global and Interregional Programmes Division of UNDP for the constant support and encouragement they gave me in the conduct of the Workshop. I place on record the excellent facilities that Templeton College made available for the Workshop and the help I received from my friend Nick Woodward right through the Workshop Project.

I thankfully appreciate the kindness with which Mr William H. Draper III, Administrator of UNDP, has provided the foreword for this volume. This is undoubtedly most appropriate; for the cause of the developing countries, on which the volume focuses, is dear to the organisation he presides over.

V.V. Ramanadham
Templeton College
Oxford

Part 1

Background Material

Privatisation: the UK Experience and Developing Countries

V.V. Ramanadham*

Synopsis

I   Privatisation: The Concept and the Case
     1.   What does privatisation signify?
       (a)   Ownership measures
       (b)   Organisational measures
       (c)   Operational measures
     2.   The Case for Privatisation

II   Privatisation in the UK: An Outline

III   Inferences from UK Privatisations and the Developing Country Context

IV   Developing Countries and Privatisation
     1.   Losses and accumulated losses
     2.   Policy statements
     3.   Criteria
     4.   Implementation
     5.   Problems from the buying side
     6.   The efficiency of private enterprise
     7.   The development strategy

V   A Select List of Issues
     1.   Country experiences
     2.   Macro issues
     3.   Privatisation and the exchequer
     4.   The modalities of privatisation
     5.   Financial and legal processes of privatisation
     6.   Competition and regulation

Appendices   Numbers 1-15

*   Templeton College, Oxford

The purpose of this chapter is not to offer opinions nor canvass policies but to present analyses and suggest options. It is developed on the basis of the experience of both developed and developing countries. The chapter keeps away from direct reports on individual developing countries, since the country papers are expected to cover that task.

The chapter is in five parts. The first reviews the connotation of the term 'privatisation'; the second contains a synoptic account of the UK experience in privatisation, on which the recent publication Privatisation in the U.K. (London: Routledge, 1988) provides a detailed survey; part three contains inferences on what developing countries may learn from the UK experience; part four outlines some major issues that attempts at privatisation have raised in a number of developing economies; and the last part selectively lists the important facets of the problem of privatisation which merit the attention of the Workshop.

In preparing this chapter I had the benefit of first-hand discussion with government officials, public enterprise executives, private industrialists, stock exchange officials, and academic experts in many countries.

I   PRIVATISATION: THE CONCEPT AND THE CASE

1.   What does privatisation signify?

'Privatisation' is a term that is employed to convey a variety of ideas. (Some fifteen connotations were cited in a recent European symposium, as shown in Appendix 1.) In the UK, the idea that it most prominently suggests is 'denationalisation' (in the sense of transferring the ownership of a public enterprise to private hands). Another idea in vogue is 'liberalisation and deregulation', which unleash forces of competition.

The concept of privatisation is, in fact, far wider. It is to be understood, not merely in the structural sense of who owns an enterprise, but in the substantive sense of how far the operations of an enterprise are brought within the discipline of market forces.

Privatisation covers a wide continuum of possibilities, between denationalisation at one end and market discipline at the other. Figure 1.1 contains a diagrammatic representation of the continuum.

Figure 1.1 Continuum of possibilities in privatisation

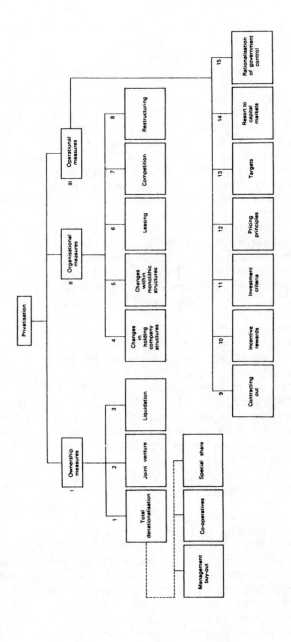

(a) Ownership measures

These are the most obvious. There can be a sale of the enterprise in full; or, private capital may be introduced in a public enterprise either through a sale of some government equity or in the course of its expansion. The larger the private equity proportion, the greater the degree of privatisation (subject to one qualification, namely, that the government's impact as a shareholder might, in practice, tend to be out of proportion to its ownership interest).

Liquidation represents the ultimate step in the arsenal of the owner. It may imply, in practice, a sale of the assets to someone that uses them again in the same activity or moves them away from their erstwhile activity. This measure is ordinarily a response to the financial failure of the enterprise.

A management buy-out is a special version of denationalisation. It represents the sale of the assets to the employees who, with appropriate loan provisions from banks, take over the ownership. This could be a co-operative, if the distinctive legal features of a co-operative society are satisfied by the organisation that buys the enterprise or the assets.

Mention may be made of the 'special share', a UK term, which signifies that the government is allotted a share in an otherwise privatised enterprise, under the arrangement that it undertakes not to participate actively in the company's directoral or management processes, except in certain extreme circumstances (e.g. where an undesirable share concentration is manipulated). This can be a helpful device in sectors where some residual public vigilance is necessary and where governmental protection of the 'national' interest is a vital consideration.

(b) Organisational measures

These can be of several kinds:

1. A holding company structure may be so revised that the government limits its control interventions to the apex level, leaving the operating companies to function under a high degree of market discipline. It is true that the very existence of a 'family' structure involves some demarketisation; but, as in the Italian IRI, substantial market freedoms can be conceded to the subsidiaries.[1] It is desirable that holding companies which operate as massive

6

controllers of subsidiaries undergo a change in organisational outlook on these lines.

2. A monolithic organisation (such as British Steel Corporation, Bharat Heavy Electricals Ltd., or Electricité de France) can be subjected to two kinds of organisational change. For one thing, it may be broken into smaller units without loss of scale economies; such units bring in certain merits of competitive behaviour. For another, the major product lines or regional operations may be converted into independent companies, though they are allowed to stay in the same family (i.e. the monolith improves into a holding company, with some corresponding reduction in centralised managerial behaviour).

3. A public enterprise may adopt the method of leasing out large chunks of its assets to the best bidders, so that it retains the benefits of ownership in the sense that it enjoys profits as per the agreement; at the same time there is some prospect of improved efficiency or lowered costs of operations on the part of the private bidder. This method can also be used as a step towards further, if not total, privatisation in ownership terms, gradually.

4. The promotion of competition is of obvious importance in ensuring results of improved efficiency, lowered cost structures and declining prices.[2] This would be possible in three ways: first, by breaking big public enterprises into less big units which have a reasonable chance of competing with one another, as mentioned earlier; second, by promoting conditions of internal competition within a large public enterprise organisation; and third, by deregulating the activities in a given sector, thereby improving the prospects of entry and exit.[3] It will then be possible for private units to establish themselves in areas where a public enterprise operates; and the more efficient units in the sector will eventually attract consumer patronage, assuming that the conditions of competition are fair.

5. In the case of certain public enterprises, restructuring would be a desirable step in bringing them under market disciplines. This can take one of two forms, or both on occasion. There can be a financial restructuring, in the sense that accumulated losses, if any, are written off and the capital composition is properly rationalised in respect of the equity-loan ratio. There can also be a basic restructuring of the functions of the enterprise such that it will be confined to a homogeneous segment of commercial activities. The rest may be hived off or transformed into

7

'projects on government behalf' or 'earmarked funds' (as in the case of Nacional Financiera's activities for promoting small-scale industry, mineral development, etc.).

(c) Operational Measures

These are the least spectacular, but very meaningful, measures of privatisation. In many circumstances and in centrally planned economies in particular, they have an important place among the options open to the government. In a mixed economy these could even constitute an appropriate first step in eventual denationalisation; and in some cases these may be all that would be necessary or desirable for a long while.

1. 'Contracting out' involves the decision of an enterprise to acquire an input across the market, instead of producing it from within itself.[4] In the process it can derive benefits of scale in the supply of the input by an outsider who organises the activity concerned in conformity with its scale economies. If the in-house provision of a given input rationalises itself into being more economical than a purchase from outside, the result is good from the standpoint of the enterprise and the consumer. The ancillary units which public enterprise in certain countries are promoting as suppliers of selected spares and parts needed by them,[5] represent a modality of privatising selected activities undertaken by public enterprises.

2. Rewards, not only to the blue-collar workers but to the white-collar employees in terms of incentives, help to introduce into public enterprises a normal and fruitful feature of the private sector.[6] Incentive payments in the shop-floor context area are quite common; but compensations for managerial motivation and proven managerial efficiency are rare in public enterprises in many countries. Once adopted, they are certain to have the effect of injecting in all employees a 'maximising' attitude. (It is worth adding here that maximising is not to be understood in terms of profit only; other agreed criteria, such as those referring to output and unit costs, are possible and in certain cases or sectors are likely to be particularly relevant. Global indices of performance respect this idea through the system of attaching to the different criteria weights considered appropriate to a given situation.[7]

3. Proper investment criteria (with qualifications for non-commercial or low-profit, yet socially desired, projects)

endow the public enterprise sector with the benefit of near-market discipline in undertaking capital expenditures.[8] They can meet the familiar criticism that public enterprises tend to over-expand, given the relatively easy money for capital expenditures from government sources. There has recently been a tendency in many countries to stiffen the financial return requirements as well as the interest rates on government capital contributions to public enterprises. If this approach were strictly followed, some similarity could develop as between private sector investments and public enterprise investments.

4.   The place of pricing principles as a step towards privatisation is not yet properly recognised, nor ensured in practice, in most countries.[9] In a competitive industry prices tend, over time, to settle at the level of costs, inclusive of a provision for self-financing; and price discriminations tend to be minimal. Every activity in the private sector does not approximate to such ideal conditions; but the normal tendency is for most enterprises to operate under such conditions in the long run, or else they invite rigorous monopoly controls. Many public enterprises, on the other hand, enjoy monopoly power in varying degrees; and neither of these price conditions seems to be satisfied. Nor is the theoretical precept of pricing in terms of the long-run marginal cost followed in practice by a vast majority of them even in the UK, as the NEDO Report in 1976 pointed out. Hence, government stipulations that elevate the pricing principles of public enterprises to their proper place in the interest of the consumer and the enterprises themselves from their long-term perspective, would rank as measures that have the flavour of privatisation in the sense of marketisation.

5.   Target-setting is a major exercise that can be employed as one proxy for the market forces in the case of public enterprise, provided the targets are so determined as to apply such pressures on managers as market discipline otherwise does. In other words, they should be formulated in a realistic manner, with allowance for any non-commercial obligations assigned to the enterprises, and aimed, broadly, at deriving the best possible outcomes from the use of resources vested in them.[10] If one were to hazard a simplistic conclusion, the absence of targets (agreed between the government and the enterprise) is probably the largest single circumstance that lets poor performance persist in the cross-section of public enterprise.

A common comment on the three preceding measures which contain the essence of privatisation (viz., investment criteria, pricing principles, and target setting) is that only a few countries have made some progress in respect of targets, investment criteria and pricing principles; but many have not satisfactorily implemented any of the three measures, even if official documents like five-year plans, budget speeches and ministerial circulars eulogise them from time to time.

6. Another measure that significantly brings a public enterprise within market discipline is to insist that it should go to the capital markets for capital funds. Obviously it can attract the funds if only the investors or lenders deem the purpose of the project concerned to be worthwhile. This is a major virtue as well as discipline in the case of private business. There is no reason why it cannot be introduced in the public enterprise sector, exception being made for non-commercial projects launched on government volition. This would be the obverse of the 'investment criteria' measure enunciated earlier, but a more powerful one in that it puts to test the investment criteria themselves.

7. We come to the last (but not least) measure of operational privatisation; namely, a drastic reform of the system of government control over public enterprise. Experience suggests that this is the heaviest factor conditioning its performance. There is a great deal of literature on this topic.[11] To cut the argument short, the suggested rationalisation can result from two routes: first, through a genuine realisation of the government not to indulge in unproductive controls, and second, through positive action under the preceding heads of operational reforms. The more expertly and comprehensively the latter are determined (e.g. investment criteria and targets), the less will be the need for constant and minute control actions from the ministries. We might describe managerial autonomy as the 'fresh-air' characteristic of private enterprise that can be 'breathed' by public enterprise managers if the system of government control is adequately rationalised; in other words, that control is a means and not an end, and that the end is the maximum contribution of the enterprise to national well-being.

2. The case for privatisation

Here we shall examine the arguments generally advanced in favour of privatisation in the sense of denationalisation.

First, many policy makers are disenchanted with the fact that a large number of public enterprises are making losses. The profit record has, no doubt, been improving over time in some countries; however, their financial performance as reflected in net profit remains disconcerting.[12] Hence, it is argued, let the enterprises move to the private sector and they will be profit-making. In this way the allocational efficiency of the investments improves.

Financial statistics extracted from the cross-section of public enterprises the world over lead many to such a conclusion; and internatonal institutions such as the World Bank and the International Monetary Fund[13] as well as major aid-givers like the USA[14], lend weight to privatisation as an urgent policy option.

While it cannot be denied that there are financial losses in the public enterprise sector, a careful analysis is needed of the anatomy of the losses - as applied to developing countries, in particular. To the extent that losses arise from the inefficiency of enterprise managers, which for some reason cannot be remedied, privatisation might erase the cause of losses; since, by hypothesis, a private enterprise works for profit and closes if losses persist.

If the losses are caused by the government's bureaucratic and unproductive control systems, and if such practices on the part of the government cannot be reformed, privatisation will remove the cause of losses; and the enterprise will raise profits.

Now we enter areas of less conclusive purport. The losses may be the result of wrong investment choices - a past event. What is needed is a restructuring of the enterprise. It is possible then that the financial situation reverses itself into one of profits.[15] Hence, current losses are not a conclusive argument for privatisation.

Again, the losses may be in the nature of 'planned losses' - a strange term with great truth, nevertheless. It refers to the 'externalities' which a private enterprise is expected to subserve. The enterprise may have been induced by the government to undertake investments and operations in the interest of achieving certain national goals of growth, regional development, workers' welfare, etc.

Distributional policies may also have been built in,

11

favouring certain consumers or workers. If the financial consequences of such external impositions are not properly compensated for by the government, the enterprise might stay in the red. In several cases the external preferences are not transparently transmitted to the enterprises; nevertheless, most public enterprise managers begin to interpret the government's inclinations and are aware of what the consequences of not doing so might be for them and the enterprise.

If the non-commercial objectives are important, and if the government decided that they be realised continuously, privatisation simply shifts the losses arising from them to the private sector but does not eliminate them. And the government will be compelled to offer subsidies to private enterprises. Perhaps they might be somewhat lower than in the pre-privatisation days, if we assume that private enterprises achieve lower cost structures.

To conclude, the 'losses' argument has to be used with extreme care if one wants to be logical; and symptoms have to be distinguished from root causes.

Second, a powerful inference is derived from the phenomenon of losses; namely, that they aggravate the problems of budget balance for the government. Since the government has eventually to finance these losses, the public exchequer is placed under strain; hence, it is argued, privatisation would be in the interest of the government. If, after providing for any subsidy payments to privatised enterprises as argued above, the net cash-flow position as between the public exchequer and the enterprises is more favourable to the exchequer than in the pre-privatisation era, privatisation would be a desirable policy, from the angle of the government budget.

Third, the government may wish to keep its borrowings under strict control. (Here the IMF conditions have a role to play.) And the chances of public enterprises receiving the required funds for expansions from the government are slim. Hence, it is argued, if they are privatised, private investors and lenders supply the funds and the investment programmes can be undertaken.

This 'public sector borrowings requirement', meticulously followed in the UK, is self-evident. But it does not explain two things. If the government allows public enterprises, even if on a selective basis, to go direct to the capital markets, the investment funds can be gathered without straining the public exchequer. (We assume that the investments are justified on commercial grounds if the capital markets adequately respond; where they are justified on non-commercial grounds, the government has to step in, in any case.) Further, the idea of 'crowding-out' (e.g. that public borrowings leave correspondingly less for private investments) needs careful examination. If it is assumed that an investment is deemed necessary for the economy on commercial or non-commercial grounds, it makes little difference in aggregates whether it is undertaken in the public or private sector. There is a feeling in some countries that privatisation will make increasing proportions of bank credit available to private enterprises. True, in terms of arithmetic; what needs noting is that, foreign capital incomings apart, the national pool of investable resources is given and that what is required is a careful cost-benefit analysis of investment projects. If it is shown convincingly that such an analysis is bound to be defective in the case of public enterprise, the argument for privatisation gains in strength.

Fourth, in the factual context of certain countries, it can be argued that the original objectives with which a public enterprise was established have been achieved, or that no efforts, through public aids, are any longer necessary in pursuing them; hence, it can be privatised. Where experience justifies this line of thinking, the argument for privatisation is strong and can be applied to several cases of widely proliferating public enterprise sectors.

Fifth, certain public enterprises have been adopting input and output policies which have dubious, if not negative, value from the angle of income distribution. For example, low prices are offered, which benefit, even if indiscriminately, the richer sections of the population; high wage benefits accrue to workers who are not the poorest in the economy, and so on. If the enterprises are privatised, the new managers will be under no impulse to continue such non-commercial policies; thus, it is argued, privatisation would be a step in the direction of reducing anti-distributional effects.

Where the facts are clear enough to lead to the above conclusion, there can be no quarrel. But a few questions need to be considered. Is it not possible to minimise the alleged anti-distributional outcomes of public enterprise operations? Are there no distributionally justified elements in their operations which might be lost under privatisation?

How certain can we be that the operations of a privatised enterprise enjoying monopoly power do not have any anti-distributional implications? If in the context of a given industry (e.g. transport or electricity) there is public preference for offering certain distributional benefits through enterprise operations, what arrangements will be necessary between government and a privatised enterprise to put that preference into effect and how complex will they be? The privatisation of sports facilities in the UK brings out some of these points conspicuously.[16] It should also be noted here that in countries where the differences between private benefits and social benefits accruing from an enterprise activity are high, the argument for privatisation has to be probed beyond its face value.

Sixth, a large public enterprise implies that senior civil servants are constrained to expend a great deal of their time and energy in dealing with its problems. Two consequences follow: their main responsibilities in the departments tend to be ill-attended; and their involvement in public enterprise matters tends to be less than competent. Increasing their numbers does not solve the problem (since many items float up to the top desk, in any case); the more senior civil servants, the higher the centralisation. Privatisation, it is argued, minimises the problem.

This argument is far from simple. It has several qualifications:

(a) Certain organisational and operational modalities mentioned in the previous section can have the effect of minimising civil service work on public enterprise.

(b) Privatisation will be accompanied by a distinctly new regulatory culture, again bringing in the civil service problem through the back door.[17]

(c) While the literature plentifully documents and criticises the great variety of interrelationships that exist between civil servants (or ministers) and public enterprises, we do not have an adequate idea of what kind of interface exists between civil servants and private enterprise owners and managers in developing countries. Massive programmes of privatisation are likely to introduce new dimensions into these relationships, based on fact or suspicion.

I shall now look at a positive and intrinsically significant argument for privatisation. Where a public enterprise loses its comparative advantage it is preferable to privatise it (or 'co-operativise' it). As long as public enterprise is a superior means of making a contribution to the national well-being, it should be preferred to other forms; but when it has a comparative disadvantage in this respect, it should be re-organised into a private enterprise. This, strictly, would be a non-ideological approach.

The comparative advantage is to be measured in terms of the commercial returns, social returns, and a desired trade-off between them both. To operationalise this approach ideally, one needs to quantify these items, and for this one needs to have comparative data for private enterprise in 'similar' operations. The first condition itself is difficult to achieve, but agreed judgements are helpful, which would be no more demanding than in the context of cost-benefit appraisals of projects. The second condition presumes the comparability of the enterprise situations under comparison. In many cases where comparable private enterprises do not exist, the likely results of their operations -- if they were to come into existence at the point of time in question - have to be forecast or speculated upon. Thus, judgemental and forecasting limitations apply to the concept of comparative advantage; but these apply to any project feasibility analysis which looks into events that do not exist yet. In any case, the approach itself would be commendable and would keep one from excessive reliance on deficits as an argument for privatisation, or on symptoms as against root causes, to repeat an earlier phrase. Deficits may represent a version of the loss of comparative advantage on the part of a public enterprise; but again, they may not. And there may well be cases of loss of comparative advantage even where a public enterprise makes profits; a private enterprise might, perhaps, do better or be more consumer-oriented.

While I do not wish here to go deeper into a full discussion of the technical aspects of the concept of comparative advantage,[18] some further annotation of the conceptual level may be of use. Looking at Figure 1.2, assume that, over time, the commercial-cum-social benefits of a public enterprise per unit of investment or capacity are represented by curve B, and those of a comparable private enterprise by curve B1. Up to the point T on the time-scale, the comparative advantage is in favour of the public enterprise; beyond that, it is in favour of private enterprise. The X-axis may also be understood to represent size of output or capacity set up in the industry concerned, which may be a function of the developments in its demand and supply conditions.

Figure 1.2: Comparative advantage

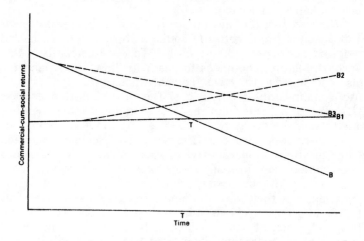

The reasons why curve B is above B1 up to point T range over a variety of factors, such as the high initial costs of establishing the technology and the operations, the low price levels and profit rates permitted in the early stages, and the needs of large, lumpy, and slow-yielding investments - all of which dampen private entrepreneurship in the initial stages, and contribute to the comparative advantage of a public enterprise. As these conditions change in the course of time, or as the transactions organised by the enterprise expand and create external economies in the sector concerned, private enterprise may begin to gain an edge over public enterprise - not necessarily because it is intrinsically more efficient, but for two strong reasons:

(a) The social-returns element in the comparative advantage of a public enterprise generally weakens over time in several sectors of activity.

(b) Public enterprise, as an institution, is exposed to certain intrinsic costs, which can be a constant drag on its performance.

There can be gradual changes in the relativity of the two curves B and B1. For instance, significant declines in market imperfections can raise B1 to B2. On the other hand, the effective application of non-ownership measures of privatisation to a public enterprise, including, in particular, the rationalisation of public controls, can raise B to B3, by improving the determinants of its performance. The point of time at which the comparative advantage of a public enterprise may be 'inferior' is therefore indefinite, and it is of course enterprise- and sector-specific. The important point is that governments should begin to think on these lines, so that the development strategy that ought to treat an organisational form as a means and not an end in itself bears fruit.

One thing has to be scrupulously kept in mind: not to raise the public enterprise curve B or depress the private enterprise curve B1, by creating unfair conditions of competition as between private and public enterprises - not totally uncommon in certain countries. For that would amount to a cosmetic improvement but would not represent anything of substantive value for the economy.

In concluding this section, it may be noted that governments have several practicable options ranging over a wide spectrum. The exact modality of privatisation is a function of the circumstances of the country and of the enterprise in question. The same modality need not be followed in all cases in the country. Where a major change such as ownership transfer through denationalisation or divestiture is the most appropriate, other measures would be inferior palliatives and should not be resorted to purposelessly. On the other hand, where non-denationalisation measures can work in significantly marketising a public enterprise, they should be tried genuinely.

II   PRIVATISATION IN THE UK: AN OUTLINE

The UK experience in privatisation has been considered by many as a success story. This part seeks to present a synthesised survey of it, scanning an extensive mass of facts.

(1)   The public corporations sector accounted for 11.1 per cent of Britain's gross domestic product at factor cost[19], and this was about a third of the public sector's aggregate proportion of gross domestic product (GDP). The 'nationalised industries' category had a total investment of about £5,000 million and employed some 1.5 million people

17

in that year. In the main they are concentrated in five sectors: energy, transport, communications, iron and steel, and shipbuilding.

There are significant variations among them in size of investment, amount of turnover, capital-employee ratio and capital-turnover ratio. In 1981-2 eight industries had capital investment figures below £100 million, and two about £1,000 million in historic terms. Five had an employee force below 10,000 while seven employed more than 100,000 each; and so on. The investment figures neither reflect the replacement values of the assets nor give a clue to the capital write-offs effected in several cases over the years.

(2) The policies of privatisation have been two-pronged. Essentially, first, there is denationalisation, or the return of a state-owned corporation or industry to free enterprise. Second, deregulation has been pursued in certain sectors, which brings in the benefits of competition, whether with continuing public enterprises, or among privatised and other enterprises in a given sector. For example, the government deregulated long-distance coach services, increased competition on air routes within the UK and between certain European countries, deregulated telecommunications and suspended the Post Office monopoly of time-sensitive and valuable mail.

The political support gained for these policies is worth noting. The uninterrupted spell of governmental power which the Conservative party has enjoyed since 1979 is a major factor in the UK's pursuit of privatisation measures.

(3) The case for privatisation in the UK may be excerpted from three sources: (a) as assembled from official sources; (b) as argued in a government document with reference to the water industry; and (c) as claimed in the Conservative Manifesto 1987.

(a) As assembled from official sources:

> (i) Privatisation will enhance economic freedom:
> 'The consumer is sovereign in the private sector. In the public sector he is dethroned by subsidy or monopoly.' (Sir Geoffrey Howe, July 1981)
> (ii) Privatisation will increase efficiency:
> 'Nationalised industries are immunised from the process of spontaneous change which competition and fear of bankruptcy impose upon the private sector.' (Sir Keith Joseph, January 1980)

(iii) Privatisation will ease the problem of public sector pay:
'Where nationalised industries have the nation by the jugular vein, the only feasible option is to pay up.' (The Ridley Report, 1978)

(iv) Denationalisation will reduce public sector borrowing:
'Why should they [nationalised industries] be a demand on our resources?...Why shouldn't they contribute to the nation's resources instead of being a drag on them?' (Adam Butler, December 1979)

Source: David Heald and David Steel, 'Privatising public enterprise: an analysis of the government's case', in John Kay, Colin Mayer, and David Thompson (eds.) Privatisation and Regulation - The UK Evidence (Oxford, 1986) pp. 64-75.

(b) As argued in a White Paper (Cmnd 9734, HMSO, London, 1986):

Why Private Ownership?
The Government believes that the privatisation of the water authorities will benefit their customers and employees, and indeed the nation as a whole, in the following ways:

(i) The authorities will be free of Government intervention in day to day management and protected from fluctuating political pressures.

(ii) The authorities will be released from the constraints on financing which public ownership imposes.

(iii) Access to private capital markets will make it easier for the authorities to pursue effective investment strategies for cutting costs and improving standards of service.

(iv) The financial markets will be able to compare the performance of individual water authorities against each other and against other sectors of the economy. This will provide the financial spur to improved performance.

(v) A system of economic regulation will be designed to ensure that the benefits of greater efficiency are systematically passed on to

19

customers in the form of lower prices and better service than would otherwise have occurred.

(vi) Measures will be introduced to provide a clearer strategic framework for the protection of the water environment.

(vii) Private water authorities will have greater incentive to ascertain the needs and preferences of customers, and to tailor their services and tariffs accordingly.

(viii) Private authorities will be better able to compete in the provision of various commercial services, notably in consultancy abroad.

(ix) Privatised authorities will be better able to attract high quality managers from other parts of the private sector.

(x) There will be the opportunity for wide ownership of shares both among employees and among local customers.

(xi) Most employees will be more closely involved with their business through their ownership of shares, and motivated to ensure its success.

(c) As claimed in the Conservative Manifesto, 1987:

Over a third of the companies and industries which used to be owned by the State has been returned to free enterprise. Productivity and profitability have soared in the newly privatised companies.

It is no mystery why privatisation has succeeded. The overwhelming majority of employees have become shareholders in the newly privatised companies. They want their companies to succeed. Their companies have been released from the detailed controls of Whitehall and given more freedom to manage their own affairs. And they have been exposed to the full commercial disciplines of the customer. Even former monopolies now face increased competition.

Competition forces the economy to respond to the needs of the consumer. It promotes efficiency, holds down costs, drives companies to innovate and ensures that customers get the best possible value for money.

Source: The Next Moves Forward, the Conservative Manifesto 1987, pp. 35-7.

(4) There have been some forty-three cases of privatisation since the 1977 offer of government shares (to the extent of 49 per cent) in British Petroleum, as listed in Appendix 2.[20] Some have been piecemeal transfers to the private sector: e.g. British Petroleum Co. Ltd, British Aerospace, Britoil, Associated British Ports, Cable and Wireless, British Telecommunications, Unipart, British Leyland Trucks, and Istel; in some of these the government still holds some shares (representing a minority holding). Several transfers have been total in nature and at one stretch (e.g. British Gas and British Airports Authority) except for the government holding of one 'special share' and sufficient shares to satisfy the entitlements to loyalty bonus. Many have been public sales, but several have been in the nature of private sales, including management buy-outs, as indicated in Appendix 3.

(5) Different techniques of public sale may be inferred from the privatisation measures.

(i) Offer for sale at a fixed price (e.g. Associated British Ports Holdings plc's first issues in 1983, British Telecommunications plc in 1984 and British Gas plc in 1986).

(ii) Sale by tender, with the minimum price fixed (e.g. Associated British Ports Holdings plc's second issue in 1984, British Petroleum Company plc (including 1983 issue) and Enterprise Oil plc in 1984).

(iii) Offer for sale and sale by tender (e.g. BAA plc in 1987 at a fixed price of 245 pence; also tender applications were accepted 'in full' and at the price tendered, in descending order of the prices tendered).

(6) Public sales have been underwritten. Overseas share offers have also been underwritten by overseas companies and, in the case of British Telecommunications plc, by the Bank of England also. The underwriting commissions and costs of sale varied widely from case to case (e.g. between 0.5 per cent of gross proceeds in the case of Rolls-Royce plc and 13.6 per cent in the case of the first issue of Associated British Ports Holdings plc in 1983). Full details of the underwriting arrangements are given in Appendix 4; and column 5 of Appendix 5 indicates the details of costs of sale.

(7)   There are several aspects of share allotment which merit notice. First, some importance has been attached to the allotment of shares to 'small' applicants, in line with the government's policy of widely spreading share ownership among individuals.[21] Allotments were characterised by some kind of rationing (e.g. in the case of BAA plc, those who applied for up to 1,000 shares were allotted 100 shares and those who applied for more were to receive nothing).[22]

Second, limits were placed on individual share-holdings (e.g. not more than 15 per cent of the voting shares - see Appendix 6). In several cases, limits were imposed on the proportion of foreign share holding (e.g. 25 per cent in the case of British Airways plc and 15 per cent in the case of Rolls-Royce plc).

Third, special terms of offer were formulated in the case of the employees (and pensioners) of a privatised enterprise. Details, which show variations from case to case, are indicated in Appendix 7. Broadly, they got some 'free shares' at government expense; free 'matching shares' (usually placed in a trusteeship scheme); and preferential consideration in the case of allotment. (See Appendix 8 for full details, by way of illustration, of the special arrangements for employees and pensioners, in the context of share allotments by BAA plc).

Fourth, the idea of loyalty bonus for 'individual' shareholders has been introduced. A free share for a specified number of shares, say ten, 'held continuously' for roughly 3 years would be given, within a limit (e.g. 500 shares in the case of British Gas plc and 200 in the case of BAA plc). (See Appendix 9 for details.) The government also retained a sufficient number of shares to meet its obligation to offer the loyalty bonus shares in the course of time.

(8)   While selling a public enterprise, the government retained a 'special share' in some cases. The special share has significance essentially in entitling it to act in circumstances that appear to violate restrictions on share holding or transfer more than 50 per cent interest in voting rights to any person(s) or dispose of a material part of the assets or involve voluntary winding up of the company. (Appendix 10 gives a full picture of the rights attached to the special share - a unique experiment in the UK - with reference to two enterprises namely Britoil and British Steel.) In some cases no provision has been made for the special share (e.g., BAA plc). (See Appendix 11 also.)

(9)   The management buy-out technique, followed in a

few cases, is an interesting experiment. A full account of it with reference to National Freight Corporation, a conspicuous case, is presented in Appendix 12. It deserves close study, in view of the glamour widely attached to employee ownership under privatisation.

(10) Major privatisations have been followed by the institution of new arrangements for public regulation (e.g. OFTEL in the case of British Telecom plc and OFGAS in the case of British Gas plc). In the case of BAA plc, airport charges and operational activities are subject to review by the Monopolies and Mergers Commission on a reference by the Civil Aviation Authority (CAA): 'trading conditions' may be imposed by the CAA; the government has the power to limit the number of Air Transport Movements at any airport having spare capacity; and the Secretary of State can make rules for distributing air traffic among airports and in respect of aircraft noise.

(11) It would be interesting to close this survey with a brief narration of a very recent episode of privatisation: the BP share offer in October 1987. The government offered its remaining shares in British Petroleum Co. Ltd at 330 pence per share (the down-payment would be 120 pence a share, the second instalment of 105 pence due in August 1988 and the third one of 105 pence due in April 1989). About mid-October, the share markets had serious trouble and the prices of BP shares sank to 287 pence and to 259 pence by the end of October. The underwriters were exposed to severe cash problems - calculated at about £800 million. There was great pressure from many quarters, including the American underwriters and the British Labour Party, on the government to postpone the offer. But the government went ahead with the flotation, inventing, however, a novel arrangement. The Bank of England would buy back any BP share (subscribed for during this offer and partly-paid) at a price of seventy pence for 2 months (the period might be extended). This served as the 'floor' protection for the allottees and relieved them of loss, if they chose to sell their shares, from a fall in the share value in the market below seventy pence. The share subscribers, it may be remembered, have a loyalty bonus entitlement, and are promised a full dividend on the partly paid shares.

(The appendices cited in this section should be of particular interest to those concerned with privatisation transactions.)

III INFERENCES FROM UK PRIVATISATIONS AND THE DEVELOPING COUNTRY CONTEXT

This section has a two-fold focus. It builds on the preceding factual survey, highlighting the ways in which certain problems raised by privatisation have been met and the several unresolved questions. An attempt is also made to look at the situation of developing countries in the context of each major point of inference from the UK experience.

(a) To start with, the concept of privatisation has been implemented in the UK essentially through denationalisation.

There are at least two reasons why in developing countries the concept of privatisation has to be pursued in the sense of a 'continuum' comprised of three options: ownership, organisational, and operational changes.

(i) The numbers involved are large: for example, India has more than 250 public enterprises at the central level and a much larger number at the level of the state governments; Kenya had 234 public enterprises in 1982;[23] Sri Lanka had 114 in 1986,[24] and Malaysia about 900.[25]

(ii) Several enterprises need to be prepared for denationalisation first, even where that option has been decided upon.

(b) There are some unique points about the privatised enterprises in the UK. The nationalised industries have not been assigned a significant developmental role (except for such sporadic cases as the National Enterprise Board). Their objectives have been predominantly commercial, and their role as an income-distribution tool has been minimal. Further, the socio-political climate on 'efficiency' has undergone a noticeable change over the last decade or two. Here is an apt, illustrative observation:

> There has been an enormous change in the content of the idea of efficiency. In the post-war era efficiency and growth had a social purpose. Through policies to promote full employment and the welfare state, the benefits of growth were meant to be widely spread. In the late 1980s profitability is the vital measure and purpose of efficiency. Companies are not in business for social purposes, they are not even in business to make products, they are in business to make profits.[26]

There is, in addition, the subtle conservative notion that labour in the nationalised industries holds the nation to ransom and that the power of the trades unions should be exorcised.[27] (Needless to say, developing countries present a quite contrasting picture.)

(c) A strong argument has been advanced in the UK that the government's control relationships with public enterprises have been so unsatisfactory - tending towards undesirable interferences - that 'the dead head' of Whitehall (changed into 'the itchy fingers' by R.H. Smethurst),[28] could only be removed through privatisation. The Morrisonian 'arm's length' relationships have long proved unworkable,[29] and came to be fashioned from time to time on an exigent and ad hoc basis.

The government public-enterprise interface in developing countries is, on the whole, far less satisfactory.[30] Whether that could be an equally powerful reason for the UK version of privatisation, is, however, a difficult question. A recent official observation from Thailand has illustrative value: 'Privatisation in Thailand is more about raising efficiency than transfer of ownership'.[31]

(d) The processes of implementation of privatisation in the UK reveal a triangular conflict situation. The three related factors are (i) the government's anxiety to make a flotation successful per se: (ii) the government's interest in raising sizeable sales proceeds; and (iii) the objective of promoting competition in the sector of operations concerned. These factors may be broadly categorised, respectively, as: a political objective; the exchequer objective; and the efficiency objective.

The first objective seems to have been achieved, by and large, barring the recent stock exchange impacts on the 1987 BP share offer; and the privatisation wagon rolls on without deceleration.

When we come to the second objective, we face problems of analysis. There is some evidence to suggest that the offer prices were relatively low in the early cases (see the comments of the National Audit Office with reference to British Airways,[32] and the comments of the Committee of Public Accounts.[33] The interests of the public exchequer (i.e. the tax payer) have been subordinated to the 'prime objective', namely, the successful sale to the private sector. In the event, 'maximisation of the proceeds of sale, while extremely important, was a secondary consideration',[34] and the Committee of Public Accounts repeatedly emphasised

25

'the importance of seeking a satisfactory return to the tax payer by maximising the proceeds from the sale of the company.[35] The fact that terrific over-subscriptions have been the general rule is of some significance in this context, though it has been argued that they only reflected the high elasticity of demand for shares within a small range of pricing.

It is the third objective that is the least satisfactorily met - a point we shall consider in the next sub-section. Suffice it to note at this stage that the first two factors, along with the objective of providing a wide spread of ownership, stood in the way of an efficiency-oriented transfer of a public enterprise to the private sector.

The lessons for developing countries are as follows:

(i) There has to be clarity on the importance of improving the marketisation of enterprise behaviour, in any scheme of divestiture.

(ii) Extreme care is necessary in fixing the price at which a public enterprise is to be sold to private parties.[36]

(e) Let us turn to the basic issue of competitive efficiency as a product of privatisation in the UK. 'Competition is an extraordinarily efficient mechanism',[37] provided enough competition follows. It has not followed yet,[38] with minor exceptions (in bus transport - even here, not fully at all).[39] The reasons are as follows:

(i) Privatisation has left the pre-privatisation sizes and monolithic organisations undisturbed (e.g. British Telecom, British Gas and British Airways). Even BAA plc remains just as large as a single 'holding' complex. And now attempts are being made to explore ways of introducing some degree of competition (for example, through Mercury Communications having won the right to compete with British Telecom in pay-phone business).

(ii) The 'innocent barriers' as well as the 'strategic barriers' to competition and entry are proving real, even in bus transport dominated by 'National Express' in many areas.

(iii) The major enterprises have been privatised as single entities so as to attract public interest in the flotation of a potential monopoly and also to avoid attitudinal confrontation with the top management of the enterprises who little liked the parcelling out of an empire. The latter factor has attracted the description of being 'the self-interested influence of nationalised industry management'.[40]

There are several points of interest for developing countries in this area:

i.   On grounds of economies of scale the intrinsic scope for introducing competition in many sectors of privatisable activity may be more limited than in the UK.
ii. Constraints on entry and exit are likely to be more severe.
iii. Technical skills in establishing the logicality of a contemplated break-up of a gigantic enterprise (e.g. an electricity board or a heavy electricals corporation) are not likely to be sufficiently abundant.

(f) Since competition, the engine of efficiency, is still to roll off by itself, a progressively growing complement (or surrogate in a partial sense) has been in evidence in the shape of public control or regulation. (Note the November 1987 reference of British Gas by OFT to MMC[41]). Besides, doubts are expressed on the adequacy of the regulatory mechanism as applied to a powerful industry.[42]

The problems posed by the practical limits to competition in the privatised industries[43] merit the serious attention of developing countries. They will have more sectors to deal with, perhaps with less of experience and technical skills in regulation. (In many countries there are no direct parallels to such British institutions as OFT and MMC.) It will be long before circumstances of oligopoly give place to real competition in more areas than in the UK.

(g) The UK privatisations are credited with promoting wide share ownership in the country. Some nine million, out of a population of about 57 million, now hold shares. It is claimed that a capital-owing democracy is evolving, with one in every five adults holding shares.

A few comments would be in order.

(i) Whether the numbers will stay on, if not increase, in course of time, after the loyalty bonus periods run out, is not clear. There have been substantial reductions in the numbers of small shareholders in some cases; for example, in British Aerospace plc the number fell from 44,062 to 3,279 within a year after flotation, in the 0-99 shares category; from 81,558 to 12,849 in the 100-499 shares category; and so on.[44]

(ii) The small shareholders, in the aggregate, account for a very small percentage of the equity capital of the privatised enterprises (except for the management buy-outs). Skewness in corporate ownership, therefore, does not seem to have been forced down by privatisation.

(iii) It is doubtful if owning a few shares in one or two obviously profitable, utility-type companies, which the privatised enterprises broadly represent, is a convincing symptom of entrepreneurship on the part of the small shareholder, though one may argue it is the beginning.

These issues gather greater significance in developing countries, where share ownership is very highly skewed. It is said of Pakistan that all shares are held by 200 families.[45] In Kenya disenchantment has often been voiced at the reversion of many enterprises taken over by the indigenous businessmen back to the Asians. To take an example from the developed world, Italy, it is feared that 'privatisation could lead to a further concentration of economic power in the hands of a few families.[46] On the whole, the average small shareholder in most developing countries would be less talented in investment-portfolio management, would face far higher transaction costs when selling or buying shares,[47] and might be under more frequent pressures of economic circumstances to dispose of his holdings, unless the government steps in with 'financial public enterprise' continuously to offset these problems.

A further question which developing countries may face concerns the propriety of bonus and low-price incentives on share offers during privatisation. In an economy where the likely beneficiaries are bound to be an infinitesimal proportion of the population, doubts can arise on the equity of such measures on macro grounds.

(h) An allied issue refers to the UK practice of concessional treatment of the workers and pensioners in the allotment of shares. This might be happening in the private sector too. But there is an asymmetry. In the private sector, the decision is for the owners whether and what kind of benefits to give the workers; whereas, in the case of a public enterprise, it is the taxpayer's equity that is offered on soft terms (or gifted away) to the workers.

This point would be of far greater substance in developing countries, where the workers in public enterprise are clearly in far higher income brackets than the vast majority of the people - i.e. the rural, landless agricultural labour, the artisans, and the considerable numbers without employment. (For example, 43 per cent of the people live below the poverty line in Nepal, and a slightly smaller percentage in India.)

Once this issue is out of the way, the UK experiment of involving a majority of the workers of a privatised enterprise as shareholders is worth emulation, though its success as a full-fledged entrepreneurial change will be limited to relatively small enterprises with high labour intensity.

(i) The UK privatisations emphasise the importance attached to 'marketing techniques' in the sale of the enterprises. For instance:

(i)   Attention has been paid to promoting co-operation on the part of the management and the workers of an enterprise slated for privatisation. The National Freight Corporation 'buy-out' transaction illustrates this.

(ii) Care has been taken to involve 'small' applicants, through preferential allotments, 'loyalty bonus' shares, and graduated payments towards the share price, yet with proportionately high dividend benefits from the beginning (e.g. in the October 1987 BP share offer, and in the earlier British Gas share offer).

(iii) Different kinds of pricing and selling channels have been adopted so as to attract a variety of potential applicants, domestic (small and institutional) and foreign.

(iv) Advice has been taken from a number of merchant banks and the Bank of England, as to the techniques of selling, the prices to be fixed, the timing of the share offer, and the parcelling of it among major potential categories of applicants. (At times the major adviser and the major underwriter happened to be the same. A potential conflict of interest may have been implicit in such an arrangement.)

(v) Media publicity has been well planned; and the sheer logistics of applying for shares greatly simplified. One could act easily through many of the bank and building society offices, and even borrow from them most of the money payable on application.

An interesting chart covering the steps in privatisation is shown in Appendix 13.

Developing countries would gain from a close study of all these aspects, once a decision is made to denationalise an enterprise. (Decisions on foreign equity pose unique problems; for example, Ivory Coast and Senegal are relatively permissive, while Mexico is relatively hesitant.[48]

(j) Many of the privatisations in the UK have been preceded by some kind of preparation.

(i) Enterprises came under the rigorous impacts of market surrogates like targets, performance aims, and most prominently, external financing limits.

(ii) Redundancies of labour have been consistently and systematically dealt with (e.g. British Airways).

(iii) Several enterprises have been financially restructured, through capital write-offs and fresh cash injections.

(vi) Certain ad hoc measures, calculated to improve the prospect of success of privatisation, have been taken. For example, in the case of British Aerospace plc, 'the Government had been advised very strongly by its merchant bank advisers that a reduction in distributable reserves would reduce the attractiveness to the market of the company which was to be floated; it therefore decided not to require the £55m to be paid'.[49] This was the sum due to the government from that company.

Another instance is the government's offer of £47 million towards the Pension Fund liability of the National Freight Consortium, which reduced the net cash incomes to the public exchequer from a possible £53.5 million to £6.5 million; this made the 'management buy-out' easy.

(v) With privatisation round the corner, the general direction of public enterprises has been towards accelerating organisational and operational changes that pushed them nearer to the market place - a smooth path towards eventual privatisation. The Jaguar case aptly illustrates this phenomenon.[50] What is happening in British Rail is also interesting. Easily separable, non-core activities (such as hotels and Sealink) have been hived off; and many inputs will be acquired across the market if in-house supply proves more expensive.[51] For example, about two years prior to privatisation, BAA plc was engaged in internal changes that decentralised operating behaviour and introduced the element of least-cost acquisition of inputs.

(vi) The government has refrained from using public enterprises as tools of social policies.

There are several lessons here for developing countries. Their public enterprise portfolio is so heterogeneous, in terms of technical efficiency, profit efficiency, accumulated losses, and employee motivation, that far-reaching restructuring would be necessary in most cases, just to improve their performance, prior to a decision on divestiture. The privatisation programme is likely to take a very long time in developing countries; and in several cases the non-ownership options would remain more practicable for quite some time. Recent changes in the organisational structures in Argentina,[52] and actual additions to public enterprise investment in Brazil,[53] 'with private sector investment remaining sluggish', evidence the point.

It would be purposeful for developing countries to note that several changes, productive of efficiency, which have occurred after privatisation, did not in fact need privatisation as a pre-condition: for example, the alteration of the monolithic BAA into a holding-company structure, the introduction of 'market versus in-house' decisions on input acquisitions and involvement in foreign business transactions. With minor changes in the Act in some cases and none in others, these could have been achieved in the pre-privatisation regime. The lesson is, therefore, that a developing country does not have to assume that every desirable step in marketisation is only possible through divestiture. Conversely, privatisation will not automatically bring about all desirable marketing changes, as the UK experience suggests.

(k) Brief reference needs to be made to the unique price control technique that UK privatisations have adopted.

An 'RPI minus X' formula has been preferred to a system of profit control. Briefly, it takes the given price structure for granted and permits changes in line with the retail price index, but to a smaller extent as set by the 'X factor'. The 'X factor' implies that improved productivity or cost economy should keep the price rise below the RPI trend. This attractive formula has several qualifications, into which I do not propose to go at this point.[54]

In view of its wide use in the UK and claims of superiority over the 'fair rate of return' approach of America, it is worthwhile for developing countries to take a close look at the formula for its applicability to their conditions.

(i)   A fundamental asymmetry in the situation arises from the fact that the pre-privatisation price level in the UK has been the product of years of target setting and financial restructuring exercises.

(ii) The price-and-output conditions of nationalised industries in the UK have, for about a decade now, been under MMC investigations, the like of which have been lacking in developing countries.

(iii) Developing countries have far less knowledge than the UK, on the order of investments that each of the many privatisable enterprises will need in the near future. The permissable price level, it may be appreciated, eventually has to be a function of the permissable investment returns.

(1)   The major privatisation measures in the UK, involving public corporations, called for the initial legal step of conversion into the company form with an equity structure. Then the flotation followed; and where a special regulatory apparatus was felt necessary, provision was made for it in the privatising legislation. Several matters, including the 'special share' were left to the articles of association, which Parliament would not be concerned with while passing the Act.

In so far as the public corporations in developing countries are concerned, the legal step, first of all, would have to be similar. However, many of their public enterprises are already in the company form.

What may therefore be necessary in their case will be to pass an overall Act, dealing with cross-sectional questions such as:

(i)   the extent of shareholding that a single shareholder is permitted to hold;
(ii) the extent of any government shareholding;
(iii) any version of the UK's 'special share';
(iv) the limits of foreign ownership;
(v)   any special forms of accountability to the consumer or the public either over a transitory period or all along (e.g., in the case of electricity supply); and
(vi) any deviations from the provisions of the Companies Act, for a transitory period or for a far longer period. Ideally, these should be minimised.

If necessary, the Act may have schedules (differently under these different heads), listing the companies to which a provision applies; and the minister may be allowed to make changes from time to time and lay a statement before parliament. In this way issues that tend to be of a policy nature in developing countries will rightly attract Parliament's attention.

(m) In conclusion, what lessons does the UK experience offer developing countries with reference to the concept of comparative advantage as the basic guideline on privatisation? In the UK, the nationalised industries have been seen as organisations meant predominantly for commercial or profit efficiency; and popular opinion has swung towards private enterprise on this ground.

The decisional process cannot be equally simple in developing countries. There will be need to apply the concept of 'comparative advantage' before deciding on divestiture or denationalisation. The following factors have to be taken into account:

(i)   Many of the public enterprises have a 'public' element in them;[55] and their comparative efficiency has to be judged in socio-economic terms.
(ii) This has to be judged after allowing for the organisational and operational measures of marketisation within the limits of possibility in the country's circumstances. In other words, the present state of losses of an enterprise cannot invariably be taken as reflecting its intrinsic loss of comparative advantage.
(iii) Even a divestiture programme takes so long that priorities have to be set on the ground of loss of comparative advantage (i.e. those which have lost it should merit privatisation earlier than others).

33

The UK experience in privatisation is rich. The experiments have been interesting and some techniques somewhat ingenious. Privatisation has been a governmental commitment, the pace has been swift and determined, and the logistics have been articulated to make privatisation a success per se. But it is not clear that the right answers to ensure the efficiency of the privatised industries have yet been found.

A discerning study of the UK experience would be rewarding for developing countries - not on what to denationalise or for concluding that denationalisation is the only modality of privatisation - but in understanding what may be done while implementing a divestiture decision and, in some respects, what not to do, consistent with their own social ethos. In particular, it would be useful to grasp the nature of preparation that preceded a prospectus or share offer. The UK experience suggests that privatisation is a much harder exercise than nationalisation itself and in developing countries calls for more difficult decisions than in the UK.

IV   DEVELOPING COUNTRIES AND PRIVATISATION

The aim of this section is to analyse the problem of 'privatisation' in the experience of developing countries. (It represents a highly condensed version of the original draft. Many details are to be found in the country papers.)

1.   Losses and accumulated losses

As mentioned in Section I, the poor financial results of public enterprises have precipitated the concern of governments towards privatisation. The following excerpt from Nigeria's Structural Adjustment Programme (July 1986-June 1988) contains a typical reflection of the concern.[56]

> Government investment in this sector is over N23 billion (N8 billion equity and N15 billion in loans), but the returns thereon are less than N500 million annually. The Government is thus clearly not receiving a fair return on its investment outlay, when it continues to pay interest charges and principal on the huge loans. Also, as much as 40 per cent of the Federal Government's non-salary recurrent expenditure and 30

per cent of its capital investment budget has gone to support public enterprises.[57]

But how exactly does privatisation help in this respect? In analysing this issues, let us deal separately with accumulated loss and current losses, which have different purport for the privatisation argument.

(a) Accumulated losses: Appendix 14 contains data on the accumulated losses sustained by public enterprises in India, Sri Lanka, and Nepal. They refer to 112 out of some 250 enterprises of the central government and 34 out of 56 of one state government - Karnataka - in India; 11 out of 16 enterprises intended to be converted into public limited companies in Sri Lanka; and all public enterprises in Nepal. These losses were about 30 per cent of the equity plus long-term loans figure in the case of the Indian Central Government enterprises in 1985-6; 66 per cent of the share capital of all public enterprises in Karnataka; and many times more than the value of the fixed assets of the 16 enterprises in Sri Lanka.

These losses are a fait accompli; and privatisation does not relieve the government of the budgetary impacts of these losses. If they are written off, and the enterprises concerned are financially restructured, the result will be for the public exchequer to accept the amounts concerned as a continuing public debt whose prospect of being serviced by public enterprises is legally annulled. If, on the other hand, the government, for any reason, fights shy of undertaking an open measure of write-off, it will derive from privatisation a price that reflects the loss in the net worth of the enterprise which the figure of accumulated losses signifies. Since that price will fall short of the public debt that corresponds to the government's investment in the enterprise, the public exchequer will continue to bear the burden of debt-servicing on the amount of shortfall.

Under either strategy, privatisation does not eliminate the financial impacts of accumulated losses. An interesting course of action recently taken in Sri Lanka illustrates the point. The accumulated losses have been isolated in the case of the four textile enterprises recently brought under management contracts; and the government issued bonds to the banks (e.g. the People's Bank) to the extent of RS400 million to be paid over a 10-year period. Corresponding debt-servicing obligations are included in its annual budgets.

As a first step in proper policy decision, the aggregate of accumulated losses has to be computed in a technically expert manner. Attempts at restructuring have no doubt been commenced (e.g. in Kenya). But the scale and pace of implementation in this area fall far short of the desideratum in most developing countries.

The financial restructuring has to go beyond the figure of accumulated losses. There may have been causes of wrong investment and excess capacity. The capital structure of the enterprises has to be adjusted (downward) for such errors (not to do so will only delay and complicate the privatisation). The capital write-offs implicit in this process entail the same kind of continuing debt-servicing burdens on the public exchequer as the write-offs of accumulated losses do. Privatisation, by itself, does not eliminate them.

My discussions in developing countries indicated dissimilarities in government responses towards the idea of restructuring and write-offs. Some officials thought that it would be politically difficult to go through a write-off and that the result could be left to privatisation to achieve through a low price. Some felt that the latter was less preferable, as it might offer room for public suspicion about the genuineness of the sale transaction and the price. The basic requirement in this connection is strength of political will which can convince the government and the public of the technical logicality, if not imperativeness, of financial restructuring.

(b) Current losses: As argued in Section I: (i) interest charges incurred in financing accumulated losses, (ii) interest charges and costs of maintenance in connection with the capital outlay attributable to wrong investment decisions including excess capacity, and (iii) planned losses continue to be borne by the public exchequer in one way or another even after privatisation. It is the operating losses, as distinct from them, that it can hope to be free from. It is, therefore, essential to undertake a rigorous analysis of current losses under the four categories, so that no false hopes are raised in the public mind about the extent of financial relief that the public exchequer derives from a given measure of privatisation.

The figure of loss as shown in the accounts may often be in need of recomputation in terms of economic costs. An illustrative exercise is made below for Royal Nepal Film Corporation.

	Rs
Loss in 1987-8, as per books	2.63 lakhs
Add cost of equity capital, not met, at 12 per cent on Rs274 lakhs	+32.88
Deduct interest charges incurred in financing accumulated loss of Rs594 lakhs, at 12 per cent	-11.28
Recomputed loss	24.23

This is not the end of the exercise. There is, in this case, a policy loss - traceable to its statutory objectives of promoting culture. The amount is indefinite but may be taken as represented by the government's cash grant of Rs8 lakhs during the year. While this is likely to repeat itself, even if in a higher or lower figure, in the government budgets, the recomputed loss traceable to the enterprise management comes down to Rs16.23 lakhs. This, prima facie, is what the public exchequer may hope to eliminate through privatisation.

There is one last step in the analysis. This figure of loss refers to the current organisational and operational circumstances of the enterprise. Several of these are high-cost oriented (e.g. under-utilised labour, the lack of a colour laboratory, deficiency of working capital, and the non-ownership of a cinema house). None of these can be asserted as elements of intrinsic inefficiency of the current public enterprise management, and they can all be removed by the government pursuing desirable non-ownership measures. It is on the assumption that such measures materialise that the comparative advantage of this enterprise as a public enterprise needs evaluation. The Rs16.23 lakhs loss cannot be taken as a conclusive index of its state (or lack) of comparative advantage.

2. Policy statements

There are wide differences among developing countries in the official enunciations of privatisation policies (as is amply illustrated by the country papers). For instance, Nigeria's approach is uniquely comprehensive in its coverage, classifying public enterprises under five heads: (i) to be fully privatised; (ii) to be partially privatised; (iii) to be fully commercialised; (iv) to be partly commercialised; and (v) to remain as public institutions.[58]

The first category is the clearest; under the second, as Chief S.O. Falae observes, 'with Government still holding substantial equity in the enterprise, the much dreaded abuses of private capitalism can be checked and controlled'.[59] The third category retains the control consequences of government ownership; while the fourth, in addition, creates difficulties concerning ex ante quantifications of government subsidisation.

Reference may be made to the Government's policy on public enterprise in Nepal,[60] announced in 1985, visualising divestment of 49 per cent of the government's shares. The policy has gradually been explained in terms of a three-fold categorisation:

(i) Enterprises with 'social' objectives not to be privatised (e.g. National Electricity Authority); similarly enterprises with high revenue potentiality, such as sugar and tobacco.

(ii) Enterprises in which the government will retain majority shareholding for policy reasons (e.g. to regulate credit).

(iii) Other enterprises to be divested from.

Just to indicate the variety of government approaches, the preference for 'structured liberalisation' in India may be mentioned.

3. Criteria

It goes without saying that in most cases the criteria for privatisation in the sense of denationalisation have not been derived from a specific evaluation of the comparative advantage of the public enterprise concerned. Several results ensued. First, the criteria have varied from country to country. Second, what appear to be proxies for the comparative advantage criterion do not invariably have that value. Third, periodic changes easily occur in the listing or otherwise or an enterprise as a candidate for denationalisation, partly on grounds of bureaucratic or political preferences.

Illustrative references to the criteria contemplated in some developing countries are helpful. In Pakistan, an enterprise making losses and marked by relatively simple technology would be a candidate fit for privatisation while one that earns a profit of 25 per cent or above on capital outlay is outside the list. The underlying idea seems to be heavily public-exchequer-oriented. In contrast, Sri Lanka's criteria envisage that the first group of enterprises selected for privatisation should be 'visibly profitable', though one or two losing ones may also be brought into the list. The 'ease of sale' should be a major consideration. Enterprises in 'sensitive' sectors like plantations, ports, and petroleum should not be privatised, while those of a 'peripheral' nature should be.

This last criterion seems to be implicit in Kenya's approach and in Nigeria's categorisation. The Task Force on Divestiture of Government Investments, set up in 1983 in Kenya, was expected to identify public enterprises which were public-sector oriented, providing public goods and services, and those which were private-sector oriented. The Working Party on Government Expenditures recommended, in 1982, that public enterprises should be classified under four heads:

(i)   Those whose retention as government enterprises is essential to accelerated and equitable national development and the regulation of the private sector.

(ii) Those whose objectives have been achieved and should be discontinued.

(iii) Those whose functions could be absorbed by parent ministries.

(iv) Those whose functions would be more efficiently performed by the private sector.[61] (The underlining is mine). There are clear traces of the comparative advantage criterion here.

The Nigerian categorisation has the implication that the enterprises in the first category have lost their comparative advantage as public enterprises. But it is not clear if the listings under the other categories rest on proven continuance of comparative advantage in favour of public ownership.

The Nepalese approach has the flavour of sectoral demarcations. For example, privatising cement is a tough decision to take since cement tends to be considered a 'basic' sector in the small-country economy of Nepal. In contrast, the view is expressed in some quarters of Sri

Lanka that, since the sizes of basic industries that the local markets justify would be too small to make them economical, it might be a good idea to depend on imports; hence there would be no compelling need for government investment in such sectors.

The privatisation criteria, on the whole, tend to compromise between the exchequer perspective of giving up losses and holding on to profits, and national development strategy implying a preference for public investments in certain sectors.

4. Implementation

The question follows: how well have privatisation policies been implemented in developing countries?

Preparatory efforts have been well devised in several countries like Kenya, Nigeria, Ghana, Pakistan, and Sri Lanka, as the country papers show. In some of them, the enterprises to be privatised have been identified (e.g. some eighteen in Sri Lanka and twelve in Pakistan). However, actual privatisation has not been fast enough. For instance, Sri Lanka has been struggling with the first three candidates chosen for privatisation - State Distilleries Corporation, United Motors Ltd, and Ceylon Oxygen Ltd. No decision has yet been finalised on certain limited privatisations such as Himal Cement in Nepal. Very little has been achieved in India, to cite another example, at least at central-government level.

A variety of reasons explain the lag between policy enunciations and implementation. Those on the buying side will be considered in sub-section 5 below. The difficulties on the selling side are as follows:

1. In deciding to offer for sale an enterprise or several enterprises, the governments have had to reckon with three serious problems:

    (i) Strong opposition from the work-force can be illustrated by the Indian experience. The 1986 all-India convention of unions in the public sector called for a 'halt to the policy of privatisation of the public sector'.[62] In the famous Scooters India Ltd context, the unions produced an interesting argument - namely, that the enterprise incurred losses entirely on account of gross mismanagement and the government's wrong policies and that it was starved of technical know-how and finances.[63] It was the unions' view that these defects should be rectified rather than privatise the company. The Indian National Trades Union Congress, in fact, pressed for the nationalisation of the textile industry, in March 1988.[64]

(ii) <u>Political opposition</u> can again be illustrated by the Indian experience, all major opposition groups in the Upper House of the Indian Parliament staged a walk-out on 7th March 1988, protesting that the privatisation proposed for Scooters India Ltd was 'only a first step in handing over sick public sector units to the private sector'.[65]

(iii) <u>Fear of economic concentration</u> can be explained under three heads:

(a) Wealth concentration. Already there is a disconcerting skewness in the ownership of industrial shares in developing countries; and it is feared that the already large shareholders would be the first and the most likely to benefit from privatisations. For example, shares are 'closely' held - and <u>private</u> limited companies are the more common form in Nepal;[66] we hear the fear expressed there of 'familyisation' through privatisation. While there are no accurate data, in Sri Lanka about 70 per cent of all shares are believed to be held by 2,000 persons. It is said that in Pakistan some 6,000 persons hold 80 per cent of all shares.

A heavy concentration in share ownership was revealed by the Reserve Bank Studies in India. In the higher size-range of above Rs50,000 of share ownership, less than 0.4 per cent of the total number of shareholders in the sample companies studied held about 70 per cent of the total paid-up capital in 1978.[67]

(b) Income concentration. Partly as a result of wealth concentration, and also through enterprise policies favouring high-income managerial groups and capital-owners, the conditions of income skewness can deteriorate.

(c) Monopoly power. It is likely under the small-market and technology-deficient conditions of many developing countries that several privatised enterprises can enjoy significant powers of monopoly; and public regulation may be too ineffective.

2.   In deciding on the sequence of privatisation programmes, governments are unclear on several important issues:

(i)   Whether an enterprise is to be privatised fully at one go or the process is to be phased out.

(ii)   Whether there should be some permanent public holding of equity in the enterprise and whether this should represent a majority share or a minority share.

(iii)   Further to (ii), whether the public holding should be in the hands of the ministries or vested in a public sector corporation (like an Industrial Development or Investment Corporation).

(vi)   Whether it is desirable to concentrate on the sale of losing enterprises, to begin with, or of profitable enterprises, or of both.

(v)   Whether it is useful to undertake privatisations, sector after sector.

3.   It has not been easy to decide on whether privatisation through denationalisation is preferable in a given case or in a category of cases to the adoption of non-ownership options of policy (e.g. 'commercialisation', to use the Nigerian term). The problem is not one of indecision; in developing countries there is a great deal to be achieved by placing public enterprises on a reformed or restructured commercial footing before valid and far-reaching decisions are taken on transferring their ownership to private hands - if efficiency rather than denationalisation were considered to be the objective.

5.   Problems from the buying side

Developing countries present serious problems regarding the buyers of privatised enterprises. These may be reviewed under five heads: (a) aggregate buying capability; (b) the price; (c) who buys? (d) the buyer's preference for a joint venture; and (e) the preparation of the buying interest and habit in the community.

(a)   Aggregate buying capacity.   Reliable information on whether the private investors have funds enough to buy privatised enterprises is not available in most countries; but there is a general feeling that it is on the low side. (The

Economist Intelligence Unit's observation with reference to Ghana that there is a shortage of local funds and there is no organised capital market applies to several other developing countries as well.)[68]

There have been cases of over-subscription to capital issues in Nigeria, Nepal, and others, in recent years. But these represent relatively small magnitudes, as against the probable demands of privatisation on the investment markets. The recent buoyancy of subscriptions to public sector bonds in India has to be understood in terms of the qualifying facts that they offer guaranteed interest - not a risk dividend - at high rates, tax-free in many cases; and they are easily saleable. The five-year bonds issued by the Water and Power Development Authority, a huge public enterprise in Pakistan, are similar in character; moreover, they are bearer bonds, with no questions asked.

In several countries the potential investor has ample choice of investment; and this is becoming wider with gradual liberalisation of investment and licensing controls. From the investor's angle, therefore, how attractive is the buying of shares in public enterprises, many of which have been 'inefficient' profit-wise, probably run-down in equipment, deficient in the production function and overmanned? He would, in general, be averse to buy these problems, unless the price was right - my next point.

(b) The price. I am not concerned here with irregularities in fixing the price of the enterprise under privatisation, but shall look at the technical aspects.

First, the buyer approaches the price question from the angle of the future earning power of the enterprise. If the government sticks to the value of the assets at historic or replacement cost, there will be protracted negotiations between the buyer and the seller; and the government, for various reasons, may stand back in the end. Estimating the future earning capacity of the enterprise in question calls for important and, often difficult, assumptions. For instance, allowance has to be made for the good results of relief from government controls that the privatised enterprise will enjoy; the net revenue prospects have to be estimated, as may be relevant to a new regime that will not automatically derive the benefits of governmental protection - in market monopoly, in securing inputs, in tariff conditions, etc.; and there has to be some knowledge about the nature of public regulation that will be applied to a privatised unit, for that can have an impact on its net

43

earnings.

Second, the buyer would be reluctant to take over the loans of the enterprise on sale - an issue repeatedly raised in my discussions in Pakistan. The relevant point here is, not that loans exist, but that they are probably not represented or supported by revenue-raising assets on the other side of the balance sheet. The problem resolves itself if the government undertakes a financial restructuring, as argued earlier in this part. It is where it does not that the buyer's approach appears to be an impediment in concluding the sale transaction.

Third, among the enterprises chosen for privatisation there would be some whose performance might have been low on grounds of the 'leaning curve' but would, in the future, be under the beneficial effects of its past developmental expenditures, technological and otherwise, bearing fruit. Not to give full weight to this consideration would amount to passing on a silver platter a business that is potentially profitable.

Fourth, the technical aspects of the price deter-mination should be entrusted to a non-ministerial agency, though the finalisation of the total figure due on the sale of an enterprise and of the price per each of the shares into which it may be divided, would be a prerogative of the government. In some countries there are agencies that have some experience in this area. Nigeria is an interesting case. The Securities Exchange Commission has been engaged for a long time in determining share prices in the context of indigenisation. Its techniques of evaluation generally led to relatively low prices which may have agreed with the national ethos by offering the foreign sellers low prices. If repeated in the context of privatisation, the methodology would cause adversity to the government (i.e. the taxpayer) while the investing groups reap the benefits. Besides, the emphasis has to be on the future earning power, subject to the qualifications mentioned above, rather than on the valuation of assets as such.

Last, it would be relevant to say a word on the underwriting costs of privatisation. The higher these are, the lower would be the net price proceeds that the government gets. And in many developing countries underwriting is not an easy task, the more so in the case of the innumerable loss-making enterprises. There has been a thinking in Pakistan in favour of entrusting underwriting to the Investment Corporation of Pakistan and the National

Development Finance Corporation. Both being in the public sector, the profits of the underwriters derived from the high underwriting commissions will stay in the public sector. This advantage will be real if the underwriting enterprises develop a mechanism for speedy unloading of the shares they may have had to take up initially. In any case, where there are no plentiful facilities for underwriting other than through such organisations, the idea is worth implementing. Nepal is another example: here the Capital Development Fund, which exists without any distinctive status under the Securities Exchange Centre Ltd, Nepal Industrial Development Corporation (NIDC), and the government, can be promoted into a full-fledged underwriting agency; or NIDC can itself take up underwriting. The profits of underwriting will remain in the public sector, assuming, once again, that the financial costs of holding shares would not be excessive.

(c) Who buys? Some of the reasons for the serious lag between government policy inclinations towards privatisation and actual implementation are derived from the complexities surrounding the question of who the buyer is likely to be. In most countries there is preference for a wide spread of shares; at the same time, practical considerations weigh in favour of somewhat opposite modalities. In Nigeria, for instance, the Securities Exchange Commission's supervision of allotments results in no individual holding more than 5 per cent of a company's share capital. There is a strong investor view that the limit should be changed to at least 10 per cent, so that a 'core' group of owners with management interest and influence may come into being. The recent episode of Himal Cement in Nepal provides another interesting illustration.

The idea of selling the shares to the workers has no doubt crossed the minds of many governments. Some suggested during my discussions in Nigeria that the government should encourage banks to offer easy credit to workers to buy shares. Such a measure eventually involves the public sector in financial enterprise while the basic aim is to reduce its financial involvement. Apart from this, the amounts of capital involved in denationalisation measures are bound to be so large that, even if all workers become shareholders, they may together account for a minor portion of the total capital of the enterprise, as the UK experience shows.

The basic problem is one of the workers' ability and/or willingness to defer current consumption and go in for saving and investment. In the low-income countries, where large numbers live at subsistence level and many below the poverty line, this is a tough problem. Could the bonus payments made by a public enterprise, such as Bharat Heavy Electricals Ltd in India -- there are not many such anyway - be offered as shares, so that the employees become sizeable owners of the enterprise? Yes, in theory, although perhaps not in practice - for they have consumption commitments already, or they would sell away the share-property at the slightest pinch of need. If restrictions are placed on share transferability, their very acceptance of the scheme can be doubtful, for several good reasons.

Finally, social attitudes in some countries operate against certain classes of buyers - certain groups or tribes in the country or non-indigenous nationals, either all or some.

The foreign buyer is a special case. Different countries have different degrees of permissibility of foreign capital, with qualifications concerning the sector of activity, proportion of ownership, and technology considerations. The governments of developing countries are, on the whole, under opposite pulls: to admit foreign capital gives greater guarantee of progress in privatisation - for example, in Ivory Coast as against Mexico; but it raises fears of foreign ownership, especially in areas that seemed to call for an active government role not so long ago.

(d) The buyer's preference for a joint venture. Does the buyer want the government to continue to hold some equity in a privatised enterprise? There can be no uniform answer.

In Pakistan and Sri Lanka there was a strong view on the side of the investors that partial ownership by the government might constitute a vehicle of undue interference and control and affect the efficiency of the enterprise. A suggestion has been put forward that the government should take non-voting shares or that the government's 'block' should be below the proportion of equity - 25 per cent in Sri Lanka, for example - which entitled the shareholder to block a special resolution.

On the other hand, the view is widely held in countries like Kenya and Nigeria that some equity holding by the government would instil confidence in the investor. In fact, in so far as the foreign investor is concerned, there is clear preference for a joint venture with the government (e.g. in Ivory Coast, Ghana, and Kenya). That would give him the guarantee of securing the needed protections from the government.

Joint ventures with majority or minority ownership by the government are likely to be a major aspect of privatisation programmes in developing countries for a long time to come. Even today, there are many such schemes in countries like Ghana - where the government has a majority stake in 181 enterprises and a minority stake in 54;[69] and proposals are afoot for some equity interest remaining under state control, for a wide scale of public participation and for limited foreign ownership in Morocco.[70]

The success of this modality varies from situation to situation

(i) Where the enterprise has fully or almost fully commercial functions, the ownership interests of the government and its partners, local or foreign, coincide. In fact, the government might be tempted to increase its proportion of the lucrative equity unless it prejudices the very making of profit.

(ii) Where the enterprise operates in a sector that warrants some degree of 'administered' approach from the government, the government as part owner begins to intervene; and the results can be unpredictable.

Where the partner is a foreigner, the terms of the joint venture agreement call for competent, rigorous scrutiny, in order to plug all available avenues of exploitive behaviour and excessive repatriation on the part of the foreign investor - this is easier said than achieved. (Kenya is currently examining its joint venture contracts, with UNDP assistance.)

Where an enterprise is eventually nominated for full privatisation, the government ought not only to refrain from managerial interferences that prejudices it but adopt proper strategies of phased release of its shares, making sure that these are widely spread and avoiding any depression of share value in the process. Expert advice from underwriters and merchant bankers would be helpful.

At this point reference may be made to the extensive progress of the joint venture modality of privatisation at the State Government level in the Federal structures of Nigeria and India. It appears, in the Nigerian context, that privatisations can be faster at state level than at federal level because:

(i)   They involve smaller-sized enterprises, on the whole;
(ii) Questions of ethnic concentration in ownership would be subdued since the buying clientele might largely be from within the state;
(iii) Techniques of 'an ownership core' or a management contract can be experimented with more easily since the scale of concentration of economic power, in consequence, is likely to be small and perhaps amenable to prompt control. Appendix 15 provides interesting information on the privatisation efforts in the State of Imo.

In India, too, joint ventures are an expanding category at state-government level. In fact, may potential investors look at these as a convenient device for securing: licences from central government; site, water, electricity, and other facilities from state government; and finance from the public sector financial institutions. Some state governments, including the communist government of West Bengal, aim to attract private capital through joint venture arrangements so as to promote industrial development in their own states, for which adequate financial assistance may not be forthcoming from central government. It is interesting to note that the official environment at state level seems to be more favourable to privatisation than it is at central level. As observed by the Bureau of Public Enterprises of the State of Karnataka:

> A time has come when some hard discussions need to be taken in regard to the need for the private sector to have a presence in certain areas of production and operation in which there is already a strong presence of the private sector. The scarce resources of the State government need not be invested in areas of consumer market in which it would merely be doing what the private sector is already doing much better ... The State will do well to disinvest from such areas of public enterprises - before it has to do so by sheer weight of persistent and accumulated losses. Such investment does not, in any case, stand any test of socio-economic justification".[71]

The underlining is mine, and is intended to emphasise the concept of comparative advantage, which should be the main argument in the privatisation debate.

(e) The preparation of the buying interest. The interest of potential buyers of privatised enterprises has to be stimulated in developing countries through (i) measures for encouraging the development of stock exchanges; (ii) the provision of effective information on the objectives and programmes of privatisation in their proper time-frame; (iii) schemes that attract and appeal to the small investor; and (iv) measures that reduce the transaction costs for the small investor.

The Privatisation Commission of Sri Lanka plans to initiate a proper programme of enlightening the potential investor. The Securities Exchange Centre Ltd of Nepal intends to develop a programme to promote shareholder culture. These are examples of developments, good in themselves and helpful in the proper implementation of privatisation measures. But the best inducement to investor interest comes from the successful working of the privatised enterprises (the partly privatised ones in particular). There are examples already of difficulties in this respect in some developing countries.

6.   The efficiency of private enterprise

There is a body of opinion in many developing countries to the effect that the assumptions of efficiency on the part of private enterprise and of its entrepreneurial dynamism call for rigorous scrutiny. Hence, it is argued, the benefits of privatisation are likely to be less real than in developed economies. The following are among the reasons why such a view has developed.

First, it is not necessarily through 'efficiency' (e.g. technical efficiency) that several private enterprises make profits in developing countries. They operate under conditions of monopoly or oligopoly derived in one way or another. In a large number of cases the total supply on the part of an industry falls short of the demand for its products, so much so that the producers and sellers have opportunities of making good profits. Many enterprises enjoy the benefits of tariff protection. The infant industries argument is stretched far too long. Barring exceptions, technology development has, in general, been far less evident in the private sector than in the public sector (e.g. in India, where the motor-car industry is a commonly cited illustration of this).

Second, many private enterprises are 'sick', particularly

in countries like India where some 130,606 units were identified as 'sick' in 1986, with an outstanding bank credit of RS4,655 crores, which was about 15 per cent of the total bank credit to industry (689 among them are large units).[72] The textile mills there are a familiar example and a large number of them have been taken over by the government and constituted into a public sector holding company called National Textile Corporation Limited. (There are interesting descriptions of how 'the project is made sick from the time it is born' through a variety of questionable practices on the part of the 'sponsors of the project'.[73])

Third, how private are private enterprises in developing countries? They depend on financial institutions (in the public sector) for a predominant part of their capital. (India and Pakistan illustrate this phenomenon conspicuously.) The loan proportion in their capitalisation is high and a major part of it is traceable to those institutions (the share subscriptions by the latter are not equally large,[74] though there are provisions in many of the loan agreements for the conversion of loans into equity at their discretion).

Fourth, the segment of equity investments in the total capital procured by private enterprises is relatively low. The 1986-7 figures for India indicate that they accounted for about a fifth of the total. The entrepreneurial interest, as against the fixed-income interest, is not high yet.

Fifth, there are the familiar comments that tax evasions occur in some cases of private, but not public, enterprise and that, on the whole, it tends to impose more social costs on the community than public enterprise does.

Sixth, there is a vague suspicion in official quarters (e.g. in India and Pakistan) that, in some cases, the main interest of the bidders for a privatised enterprise lies in the property value of the site, in particular. They may 'cannibalise' the equipment (which might already be in a somewhat dilapidated condition) and treat the transaction as a real-estate deal. The workers would then lose their jobs and the industrial activity as such would go out of existence, at least from the erstwhile location.

Last, it is relevant to refer at this point to a particular aspect of the country's development strategy. The investing interest of private entrepreneurs will be inclined more towards the light and technologically simple industries, the more so if large chunks of their financial resources get progressively sucked into the public exchequer. Who will take care of the more basic and difficult industries - the 'core' as termed in some countries? The government may have to use the incoming cash resources for its own new investments in such directions. Thus, an investment rotation at government level tends to take place. There will be a change in the industrial composition of the public sector; and perhaps the less profitable or slow-yielding investments will occupy a relatively high proportion, as the others get progressively privatised. It may take a long time before capital markets and entrepreneurial interests develop in favour of such projects in the private sector in developing countries.

Some illustrative data may be offered from Pakistan. The provisions for public investments in industry have gradually declined in the recent years - from RS 1597 million in 1984-5 to RS362 million 1987-8; and the percentage of the public sector in the total investments in industry in the country declined from 49 per cent in 1982-3 to 9.5 per cent in 1987-8. A large part of the Sixth Plan target for private investment (of RS63 billion) has been achieved. However, most of it went into light industry: for example, into textiles and agro-based industries (about 60 per cent) with cement and engineering accounting for about 10 per cent each.

7.   The development strategy

In theory, liberalisation intensifies the market forces, strengthens the environment for competition, and offers good results of operations even on the part of enterprises that are not privatised. There are practical limitations which assume importance in developing countries.[75] Basically these are incidental to the development strategy that the government adopts. With a plan for development in which a 'core' is postulated, liberalisation does not adequately marketise certain segments of enterprise operations; and 'administered' pricing and other features originating in their case will have spread effects over a large part of the economy. If the 'core' includes investment financing or financial/intermediation, the consequence would be severe.

It is widely believed in Nepal that the declaration by His Majesty that by the year 2000 the basic needs of the people must be fully met might obligate the public sector to undertake or continue to undertake the production of certain essential goods and services. In theory this may not be necessary; but in the conditions of Nepal many think that it would be.

Limits to the good effects of liberalisation also emerge by another route. In most developing countries there are scarcities of water and electricity, as well as import licences and capital. They limit market freedoms and develop oligopolistic conditions. The regulatory hand of the government is impelled to move in constantly and, often, rigorously. If liberalisation meant that imports would come in so as to compel domestic production to be cost-effective and competitive, two difficulties would present themselves. It is almost certain that in most developing countries there are not enough foreign exchange resources to try the experiment on a large scale; and local industry would run the serious risk of gradual extinction.

We may conclude this section by posing a practical question: how effective or unqualified would liberalisation be in its application to the input and output policies of enterprises - ranging over investment, pricing, product mix, employment and exit, in each of the following cases?

(a) Where there is only one public enterprise in a given sector, fully owned by the government.

(b) Where there are a few public enterprises in a given sector.

(c) Where there are public and private enterprises in a given sector.

(d) If a public enterprise monopoly is partly owned by the government, and partly by private investors: (there can be three sub-divisions here, depending on whether the latter are local or foreign or both.)

(e) If the government's ownership is partial in most or all cases in situation (b).

(f) If a public enterprise in situation (a) or (b) is under a management contract.

(g) Where there are only private enterprises in a given sector - all domestic or all foreign or a mixture of both domestic and foreign ownership.

The foregoing categorisation refers to the composition of a sector. Apart from this, the nature of the sector itself has an influence on the degree of liberalisation.

Whatever the precise answer in a given case to start with, the aim should be to let liberalisation operate genuinely in favour of the maximum possible alignment of the market forces. Perhaps much more of this is possible even in the first category - i.e. (a) - than obtains today in many countries, if only the organisational and operational modalities of privatisation were adopted. And if large-scale denationalisations are not possible in the immediate context, these other options entailing varying degrees of liberation ought not to be overlooked or delayed - in the hope, or under the pretext, of eventual denationalisation.

A word, in conclusion, on the device of a management contract either as an alternative or as a first step to the denationalisation of an enterprise. The outlook on it is somewhat heterogenous among developing countries. In Nigeria the experience of the Airways with the management contract system is generally considered unfavourable. In Sri Lanka, on the other hand, four textile mills have been entrusted to private hands under management contracts; in fact all of them are foreign companies, reputed in the industry. The companies seem to have turned around. In India it is reported that suggestions in favour of managing contracts produced a hostile reaction in Parliament. Doubts concerning the system arise partly because of the sad experience that some countries like India have had with the 'managing agency' system and partly because of the technical weakness of many developing countries in formulating beneficial joint venture contracts with foreigners. This handicap must be minimised if the device should be attractive to developing countries and prove an important modality of privatisation, which in a large number of cases might involve the influx of foreign capital and foreign management skills.

V   A SELECT LIST OF ISSUES

The purpose of this section is simply to list the facets of privatisation which merit being included within the comprehensive range of discussions at the Workshop. It is indicative and by no means exhaustive.

1.   Country experiences

(a)   The relationships between a country's socio-economic circumstances and the thinking on privatisation; and the role of such circumstances in the translation of the thinking into action.

(b)   Similarities   and   dissimilarities   among   developing countries in respect of privatisation policies and implementation.

(c) Any perceptible or unique regional distinctions.

(d) Differences in the role of foreign assistance in the fruition of privatisation policies in different countries.

2. Macro issues

(a) The distributional impacts of privatisation.

(b) Skewness in the ownership of corporate share capital.

(c) Techniques of share allotment.

(d) The attitudes of:

- labour in public enterprises
- managers of public enterprises
- civil servants concerned with public enterprises

(e) Liberalisation: its relationship with privatisation.

(f) Foreign ownership of capital.

(g) Industrial sickness: impacts on privatisation policies and programmes.

(h) The financial dependence of private enterprise on public financial institutions.

(i) The state of efficiency of private entrepreneurship in the country.

(j) Capital markets and stock exchanges.

(k) The strategy of national development planning.

(l) Foreign assistance in privatisation programmes.

3. Privatisation and the exchequer

(a) The relationship between the impacts of public enterprise on the public exchequer and the privatisation policies.

(b) Criteria of privatisation and their impacts on the exchequer.

(c) Selling profitable enterprises.

(d) Maximising the sales proceeds.

(e) Costs of restructuring public enterprises before privatisation.

(f) Costs of redundancies of labour.

(g) Waivers of dues to the exchequer from public enterprises.

(h) Utilisation of cash incomings on sale of enterprises.

(i) Arrangements for any subsidies to a privatised enterprise.

(j) Continuing involvements of the exchequer in financing small and worker shareholders.

4. The modalities of privatisation

(a) The concept of "continuum" and its relevance to developing countries.
(b) Different methods of denationalisation: full, partial with majority equity in government hands, and partial with minority equity in government hands.
(c) Leasing and management contracts.
(d) Management buy-outs.
(e) Co-operatives.
(f) Revisions in the organisational structure of the enterprise under privatisation.
(g) The role of the special share for the government.

5. Financial and legal processes of privatisation

(a) Conversion of public corporations into companies.
(b) Legal problems concerning 'original' owners.
(c) Valuation of the enterprise.
(d) The capital structure.
(e) Fixing the share values.
(f) Different techniques of offer of shares or enterprises to the private sector.
(g) Costs of underwriting.
(h) Loyalty bonus in share allotments.
(i) Preparation for privatisation: the balance sheet and the prospectus.
(j) Time-frame of privatisation - with reference to an enterprise or sector, or in the aggregate.
(k) Any special legal provisions to govern certain privatised enterprises.

6. Competition and regulation

(a) The scope for competition in a given sector.
(b) Deregulation before, during, or after privatisation.
(c) The needs of regulation of a privatisated enterprise.
(d) Patters of regulation. In particular: prices; profits; and outputs (quality, mix, etc.).
(e) Conditions for efficient monopoly control.
(f) Government interface with privatised enterprise and its managerial culture.

'Country experiences' aim at building a total picture of the privatisation situation in each country; while the discussions on issues seek to delve into each substantive issue critically.

NOTES

1. V.A. Marsan (1986) 'Instituto per la Recostruzione Industriale', in V.V. Ramanadham (ed.) Public Enterprise: Studies in Organisational Structure, London: Frank Cass.
2. Several recent writings in the UK have emphasised this point.
3. As in bus transport in the UK.
4. Most nationalised industries (e.g. British Rail) are actively pursuing this technique.
5. The annual volumes of Public Enterprise Survey, issued by Bureau of Public Enterprises, Government of India, provide extensive information on this aspect.
6. Pakistan's experiments in the evaluation of performance, accompanied by the employee's eligibility to a profit bonus, are interesting in this context.
7. See A.M.H. Bennett's (1988) paper on evaluation in the thematic issue, of ICPE's Journal of Public Enterprise.
8. This was the familiar theme of a White Paper (Cmnd 7131, HMSO, London, 1976).
9. Emphasis was placed on proper pricing principles of public enterprises by a White Paper (Cmnd 3437, HMSO, London, 1967); but there is no evidence that these, as commended, have been scrupulously followed by the nationalised industries in the UK.
10. Reference may be made to target-setting practised in the UK since the early 1960s and the technique of contract de programme followed by France.
11. For some recent evidence, see the Thirty-second Report of the Committee on Public Undertakings (of the Indian Parliament) on Accountability and Autonomy of Public Undertakings, New Delhi, 1987.
12. For a recent illustration, see Economic Survey of Nepal, 1986-7, p.19. Gross profit as a percentage of capital employed was -2.6 inn 1984-5 and 1.4 in 1985-6, Kathmandu, 1987.
13. Structural Adjustment Agreements of many countries illustrate the point.
14. See the US State Department's communication to US AID Missions in 1986.

15. There are several instances of capital restructuring undertaken in the UK public enterprise sector, which helped produce improved accounting results in subsequent years (e.g. British Railways Board, British Steel Corporation, National Freight Corporation, and National Bus Company).

16. 'Local authorities will retain control over policy decisions on the use of the facilities and, most importantly, will retain control over pricing'. (Financial Times, London, 1 July 1988).

17. See R.G. Smethurst, 'Privatisation and regulation'; John Hatch, 'Privatisation and the consumer'; and George Yarrow, 'Regulatory problems in the electricity supply industry', Seminar on Privatisation, Templeton College, Oxford, September-December, 1987.

18. See V.V. Ramanadham (1984) The Nature of Public Enterprise, Chapter 14 London: Croom Helm. See also his IDL Chemicals Endowment Lecture on 'The comparative advantage of public enterprise', delivered at Osmania University, Hyderabad, India, March 1988.

19. Nationalised Industries in Britain (1982) London: HMSO p.27.

20. The source of basic financial data for this section is Privatisation: the Facts, Price Waterhouse (London, 1987).

21. 'After eight years of Conservative Government... one in every five British adults now owns shares... Only the Americans remain ahead', says the Conservative Manifesto, 1987, p.16.

22. John B. Heath (1988) 'Privatisation - the case of BAA plc', in V.V. Ramanadham (ed.) Privatisation in the UK, London: Routledge.

23. Working Party on Government Expenditures (Nairobi, 1982).

24. Public Enterprise Division, Ministry of Finance, Colombo.

25. 'Privatisation in Malaysia', paper presented by Ministry of Public Enterprises at the Interregional Workshop on Privatisation, Oxford, May 1988.

26. Charles Leadbeater, The Policies of Prosperity, Fabian Society, no. 523 (London, 1987).

27. For instance, 'Public sector trade unions have been extraordinarily successful in gaining advantages for themselves in the pay hierarchy by exploiting their monopoly collective bargaining position. Herbert Morrison's dreams of employee responsibility are a caricature of the true position.' (John Moore, 'Why Privatise?' London,

1 November 1983).

28. See John Heath, 'Privatisation: the case of BAA plc'; John Hatch, 'Privatisation and the consumer'; and R.H. Smethurst, 'Privatisation and regulation', papers presented at the Seminar on Privatisation at Templeton College, Oxford, September-December 1987.

29. See the National Economic Development Office, A Study of UK Nationalised Industries: Their Role in the Economy and Control in the Future (London: HMSO, 1976).

30. Recent evidence comes from an Indian government-commissioned policy paper which speaks of 'too many back-seat drivers', and concludes that 'greater freedom for the public enterprises is central to reform' (Financial Times, London, 25 November 1987, 'Survey on India', p.xiv).

31. Financial Times, London, 2 December 1987, 'Survey on Thailand', p.17.

32. British Airways 'may have been under-valued and under-priced when it was floated for just under £900m'. 'The opening premium of 44 pence on the partly paid price of 65 pence and 55 pence on the fully paid share of 125 pence was worth an extra £300m'. (As cited in The Times, London, 22 July 1987).

33. 'The price was over-cautious. It... seems likely that the taxpayer could have benefited further from the sale'. (Third Report from the Committee of Public Accounts, Session 1985-86, Sale of Government Shareholding in British Telecommunications plc, p.xii (35, HMSO, London, 1985).

34. Seventeenth Report from the Committee of Public Accounts, Session 1983-84, Sale of Government Shareholdings in Publicly-Owned Companies, p.vi (443, HMSO, London, 1984).

35. Thirty-first Report from the Committee of Public Accounts, Session 1984-85; Incorporation of Royal Ordnance Factories, p.vii (417, HMSO, London, 1985).

36. The Economist Intelligence Unit has some interesting comments on the selling and sale prices of public enterprises with reference to Guinea. 'The process within the government appears to be moving very slowly ... and offers considerable scope for corruption. The task of determining the sell-off price for these enterprises is notoriously difficult, and easily susceptible to manipulation by vested interests, both Guinean and foreign', (Country Report, no.4, 1987, London).

37. John Moore, 'Why Privatise?' (London, 1 November 1983).

38. 'When the test comes, it is far from clear that the Government's free-enterprise instincts are anything like as committed to competition as they are to private enterprise'. David Heald, 'Will the privatisation of public enterprises solve the problem of control?', Public Administration 63 (1) Oxford, 1985.

39. See David Thompson (1988) 'Privatisation: introducing competition opportunities and constraints', in V.V. Ramanadham (ed.) Privatisation in the UK, London: Routledge.

40. The Times, London, 22 May 1987.

41. The MMC report has since been presented.

42. With reference to British Gas, it has been observed that 'the regulatory framework hardly seems adequate to control such a powerful and dominant industry'. Katherine Price, 'Privatising British Gas: is the regulatory framework adequate?', Public Money 6 (1) (London: June 1986) p.19.

43. George Gardinier, MP, observed at the Conservative Conference in Blackpool, 'The experience of British Telecom and British Gas tells us never again to turn public monopolies into private ones', The Times (London, 7 October 1987).

44. Tenth Report of Public Accounts, Session 1981-82, Sale of Shares in British Aerospace: Sales of Government Shareholdings in other publicly owned Companies and in British Petroleum Ltd: Postponement of Payments, p.15 (189, HMSO, London, 1982).

45. Overseas Development Institute, Briefing Paper (September 1986).

46. 'Privatisation, Italian style', Financial Times (London, 28 September 1987).

47. Even in the UK 'private investors ... will continue facing difficulty in finding a reasonably-priced broker to carry out smaller equity transactions'. The 'minimum dealing charges' may be £20.00 - 'expensive if you have only a few hundred pounds worth of shares'. Teresa Hunter, The Guardian (London, 5 December 1987) p.25.

48. Economist Intelligence Unit, Country Report, Mexico, no. 4, 1987, p.9 (London).

49. Tenth Report of Public Accounts, Session 1981-82, op cit, p. vi.

50. David Chambers, 'Managing Operations and the Relevance of Privatisation', in V.V. Ramanadham (ed.), Privatisation in the UK, (London, 1988).

51. For example, since the adoption of competitive

tendering, orders for locomotives and coaches worth some £420m have been placed and the private sector has won over £200m worth of them. Also privately owned wagons are about 30% of all wagons running on the BR system (British Railways Board, Annual Report and Accounts, 1986-87, p.9, (London 1987).

52. 'The organisational changes include the establishment of a state holding company, which is to agree with the executive (via the Interministerial Committee) production and investment targets'. Economist Intelligence Unit, Country Report, Argentina (no. 1, 1987, pp.13-14, London).

53. Economist Intelligence Unit, Quarterly Economic Review of Brazil, no.1, 1986, pp.11-12, London.

54. See Dieteur Helm, 'RPI minus X and the newly privatised industries: a deceptively simple regulatory rule', Public Money (1) London, June 1987.

55. For a full discussion of the 'public' and the 'enterprise' elements in the concept of public enterprise, see V.V. Ramanadham (1984) The Nature of Public Enterprise, Part I, London.

56. Also, see - for Nepal - Economic Survey 1986-1987 p.21 (Kathmandu).

57. Structural Adjustment Programme for Nigeria (July 1986 - June 1988), p.13 (Lagos, 1986).

58. Ibid.

59. Nigerian Management Review, p.107 (Lagos, December 1985).

60. Decisions taken by the Cabinet on May 1985 regarding public enterprise.

61. Working Party on Government Expenditure, Report and Recommendations of the Working Party, p.43 (Nairobi, 1982).

62. The Hindu, p.10 (Madras, India, 30 January 1988).

63. Ibid.

64. Deccan Chronicle (Hyderabad, India, 9 March 1988).

65. Deccan Chronicle (Hyderabad, India, 8 March 1988).

66. A 1984-1985 Study by the Securities Exchange Centre Ltd (Kathmandu).

67. Reserve Bank of India, Survey of Ownership of Shares in Joint Stock Companies as at the end of December 1978 (Bombay, 1983).

68. The Economist Intelligence Unit, Country Report on Ghana, Sierra Leone and Liberia, no.4, p.14 (London,

1987).

    69. Ibid, p.15.

    70. The Economist Intelligence Unit, Country Report on Morocco, no.1, p.15 (London, 1988).

    71. Bureau of Public Enterprises, State of Karnataka, Public Sector Enterprises, Sixth Annual Report (Bangalore, India, 1985).

    72. Reserve Bank of India, Annual Report 1986-1987, p.82 (Bombay, 1987).

    73. The Nation, 25 December 1987 (Lahore, Pakistan).

    74. For instance, shares and stocks were 3.5 per cent of the total investments of Industrial Development Bank of India in 1986 (September), as against its loans and advances which amounted to 85.9 per cent, Reserve Bank of India Bulletin (Bombay, March 1987).

    75. For instance, "the new drug policy measures announced in India in December 1986 and the new Drug Price Control Order promulgated in 1987 are held as major landmarks in the deregulation of the industry ... A closer look ... gives cause for concern and rethinking, whether deregulation has, after all, been truly liberal enough". K. Jayaraman, 'Drug Policy: Liberalisation in Reverse Gear?', (Economic Times, 3 February 1988, Bombay).

APPENDIX 1   The many senses of privatisation

(As inferred from international discussion on economic theory, by Professor Theo Thiemeyer, Chairman of the Scientific Commission of CIRIEC)

1. Transfer (sale) of public assets (firms, parts of firms - 'partial privatisation') or individual assets to private persons.
2. Transition to private law legal forms.
3. Transfer of individual public supply tasks to private persons (e.g. contracting out); also functional privatisation.
4. Transition to private business management in the sense of profit-oriented management.
5. Extension of the margin of autonomy for the management of public enterprises.
6. Debureaucratisation, in the sense of freeing from formal provisions and administrative instructions.
7. Decentralisation, in the sense of the delegation of authority to decide, plan, and act.
8. Aligning the conditions under which public enterprises act on those which apply to private firms.
9. Promotion of competition by market processes (or market-like systems of incentives).
10. Dismantling of such state monopolies as are justified by referring to the traditional argument of 'natural monopoly'.
11. Adaptation of wages and working and employment conditions to those applicable to the private sector: privatisation of jobs.
12. Unilateral reduction of the nature and scope of public services.
13. Privatisation of public resources.
14. Privatisation of public revenue: conversion of revenues from public investments into private profits; or private access to public capital and its revenues.
15. Denationalisation: pressures of international competition; increasing activity in foreign markets; take-over of capital shares and rights of disposal by foreigners.

Source: Annals of Public and Co-operative Economy, April-June 1986.

APPENDIX 2: Privatisation and sales proceeds

Enterprise	Year	Gross proceeds £million
British Petroleum	1977	564
British Petroleum	1979	290
Fairey	1980	?
Ferranti	1980	?
British Aerospace	1981	150[a]
Cable and Wireless	1981	224[b]
Amersham International	1982	71[c]
National Freight Consortium	1982	7
Britoil	1982	549
Associated British Ports	1983	22
British Rail Hotels	1983	45
International Aeradio	1983	60
British Petroleum	1983	566
Cable & Wireless	1983	275
Associated British Ports	1984	52
British Gas - Wych Farm	1984	80
Enterprise Oil	1984	392
Jaguar	1984	294
Sealink UK	1984	66
Inmos	1984	95
British Telecom	1984	3,916[d]
British Aerospace	1985	551[a]
Brooke Marine	1985	0.1
Yarrow Shipbuilders	1985	34
Britoil	1985	449

Appendix 2: cont.

Enterprise	Year	Gross proceeds £million
Vosper Thorneycroft	1985	18.5
Cable and Wireless	1985	933[e]
Swan Hunter Shipbuilders	1986	5
Hall Russell	1986	?
Vickers Ships and Engineering	1986	60
British Airways Helicopters	1986	13.5
British Gas	1986	5,434[f]
National Bus	1986/7	?
Unipart	1987	30
Leyland Bus	1987	4
British Airways	1987	900
Royal Ordnance	1987	190
British Leyland Trucks	1987	Nil
Rolls-Royce	1987	1,363[g]
DAB	1987	7
Istel	1987	26
BAA	1987	1,284

			£million
a	Including amount raised for		
	British Aerospace 1981		100
	1985		188
b	Including amount raised for Cable and Wireless		35
c	Including amount raised		
	for Amersham International		6
d	Including amount raised for BR Telecom		1,290
e	Including amount raised for Cable and Wireless		331
f	Including amount raised for British Gas		2,286
g	Including amount raised for Rolls-Royce		283

APPENDIX 3: Private sales

Enterprise (1)	Year (2)	Gross proceeds £million (3)	Management buy-out (4)
1. British Shipbuilders' warship yards	1985-6		
Brook Marine Ltd		0.1	Yes
Yarrow Shipbuilders Ltd		34	
Vosper Thorneycroft Ltd		18.5	Yes
Swan Hunter Shipbuilders Ltd		5	Yes
Hall Russell Ltd		_a	
Vickers Shipbuilding and Engineering Ltd		1	
2. British Technology Group Holdings	1978-4	95	
3. National Bus Company	1986-	0.1	Yes
4. National Freight Company	1982	7 (net)	Yes
5. Rover Group:			
Unipart		30[b]	Yes
Leyland Bus		4	Yes
British Leyland Trucks		None (merger)	
DAB		7	Yes
Istel		26	Yes
7. Sealink UK Ltd	1984	34	
8. International Aeradio	1983	60	
9. British Rail Hotels	1983	45	
10. British Gas Onshore Oil Assets (Wych Farm)	1984	80[c]	
11. British Airways Helicopters	1986	13.5	
12. Royal Ordnance	1986-7	11+190	

a not available.   b Plus a further £15 million if profit targets are achieved and £7 million if the expected stock market flotation succeeds.   c Plus £135 million when production reaches 20,000 barrels per day; British Gas will also receive 40 per cent of production profits after the buyers recover their investment and production reaches 23 million barrels.

Source: For Appendices 3-7, 9, and 11: <u>Privatisation: The Facts</u>, Price Waterhouse, London, 1987.

APPENDIX 4: Some instances of underwriting arrangements

1. Amersham International plc, 1982
All shares, except those reserved for employees: fees of £1.732 million.

2. Associated British Ports Holdings plc
First Issue 1983:   All shares: at a commission of 1.675 per cent.

Second Issue 1984:   All shares: at 0.525 per cent of the striking price plus 1.25 per cent of minimum tender price.

3. BAA plc 1987
Competitive underwriting bid: at 0.05311 per cent of the fixed price.

4. British Aerospace plc
First Issue 1981:   All shares: at 1.75 per cent

Second Issue 1985:   All shares: at 0.425 per cent

5. British Airways plc
First Issue 1987:   Competitive bids: at 0.111 per cent (non-employee share offers only)

Overseas offers: 1.575 per cent

6. British Gas plc 1986
Competitive bids: at 0.175 per cent (3,230 million shares in UK)

Overseas: 1.65 per cent (795.5 million shares)

7. British Petroleum Co Ltd
First Issue 1977:   All shares

Second Issue 1978:   All shares: 1.375 per cent

Third Issue 1983:   All shares: 1.375 per cent

8. British Telecommunications plc 1984
2,597 million shares (UK): At 0.375 per cent

Overseas: 415 million shares: 1.25 per cent plus further commissions of between 2.5 per cent and 3.75 per cent plus advisory services and reimbursement of certain expenses.

9. Britoil plc
First Issue 1982: 255 million shares: at 1.55 per cent
Second Issue 1985: 194.5 million shares (UK): at 0.425 per cent.
24 million shares (Canada): at 1.8 per cent.
24 million shares (Europe): at 1.8 per cent

10. Cable and Wireless plc
First issue 1981: All shares: at 1.75 per cent
Second issue 1983: All shares: at 1.375 per cent
Third issue 1985: 146.1 million shares (UK): competitive bids at 0.2625 per cent
Japan: 8 million new shares: 2.5 per cent
Canada: 4.8 million new shares: at 1.8 per cent

11. Enterprise Oil plc 1984
All shares at minimum tender price: at 1.55 per cent

12. Jaguar plc 1984
All shares: at 1.75 per cent

13. Rolls–Royce 1987
789.7 million shares excluding employee/pensioner reservations: competitive bids at 0.061 per cent

Claw–back clause

(i)   Included in:
BAA plc, British Gas plc, Cable and Wireless plc, and Rolls-Royce plc
(ii) Triggered in:
British Gas plc and Rolls-Royce plc.

APPENDIX 5: Some data on public offers under privatisation

Enterprise	Date of sale	Share price as percentage of offer price		Cost of sale as percentage of gross proceeds	Over-subscription (times)	Price/earnings ratio
		On day of issue	One week after issue			
(1)	(2)	(3)	(4)	(5)	(6)	(7)
1. Amersham International plc	1982	132	135	-	24	18.9
2. Associated British Ports Holdings plc	1983	-	-	13.6	34	9.1
Associated British Ports Holdings plc 2nd issue	1984	-	-	1.9	1.9	11.3
3. BAA plc	1987	-	-	-	0.4	15.3
4. British Aerospace plc 1st issue	1981	114	119	2.7	3.5	5.2
British Aerospace plc 2nd issue	1985	-	-	3.3	5.4	6.9
5 British Airways plc	1987	168	168	9.7	10 a	13.1
6. British Gas plc	1986	125	129	3.0	1.7b	9.7

Appendix 5: cont.

7. British Petroleum Co. Ltd	1977	123	126	–	4.9	18.2
British Petroleum Co. Ltd 2nd issue	1979	–	–	2.4	1.5	6.5
British petroleum Co. Ltd 3rd issue	1983	–	–	1.6	1.3	10.4
British Petroleum Co. Ltd 4th issue	1984	–	–			
8. British Telecommunications plc	1984	185	185	4.9	3	9.4
9 Britoil plc 1st issue	1982	81	74	2.3	27%	11.9
Britoil plc 2nd issue		–	–	3.3	10	5.0
10. Cable and Wireless plc 1st issue	1981	117	118	3.1	5.6	13.3
Cable and Wireless plc 2nd issue	1983	–	–	1.8	70%	16.4
Cable and Wireless plc 3rd issue	1985	–	–	13.4c	2	16.4
11. Enterprise Oil plc	1984	100	101	2.8	37%	8.3
12. Jaguar plc	1984	108	107	1.9	8.3	6.9
13. Rolls-Royce plc	1987	168	168	0.5		9.0

a   Applications received for 7,800 million shares as against 720.2 million of total issue.
b   Applications received for 6,600 million shares as against 4,025.5 million issued.
c   Costs borne by the company only.

Columns 3, 4 and 5 are calculated by the author from the source data.

APPENDIX 6:   Restrictions on share ownership

1.   Amersham International plc 1982
No person to have an interest in 15 per cent or more of the voting shares.

2.   BAA plc 1987
Similar.

3.   British Aerospace plc 1981 and 1985
Foreign-held shares not to exceed 15 per cent of the issued shares conferring voting rights.

4.   British Airways plc 1987
No more than 25 per cent of the shares to be owned by non-UK nationals. No one person to have interest in more than 15 per cent of the issued shares.

5.   British Gas plc 1986
No one person to have interest in 15 per cent or more of the voting shares.

6.   British Telecommunications plc 1984
Similar.

7.   Cable and Wireless plc 1985
Similar.

8.   Jaguar plc 1984
Similar.

9.   Rolls-Royce plc 1987
Foreign-held shares not to exceed 15 per cent of the voting shares. Until January 1989 no one person to have an interest in over 15 per cent of the voting shares.

APPENDIX 7: Some instances of special terms of share offer to employees

1. Amersham International plc

(i) 35 shares free, at the Government's expense.
(ii) The Government matched, one for one, purchases by employees up to 350 shares per employee (with a maximum of 217,700 shares): these shares are held in the Amersham Share Participation Scheme.
(iii) Preferential consideration in allotment (up to 2.5 million shares).

2. Associated British Ports Holdings plc
First issue 1983
(i) 53 free shares for each eligible employee, at the Government's expense.
(ii) Matching shares up to 225 per employee: held by the Trustees of Associated British Ports Employee Share Ownership scheme.
(iii) Preferential consideration up to 3 per cent of the issued capital, less (ii).
Second issue 1984
Preferential consideration up to 1,000 shares per employee.

3. BAA plc 1987
(i) 41 free shares per employee.
(ii) Matching shares up to 111 per employee.
(iii) Preferential consideration up to 4,082 shares per employee/pensioner.

4. British Aerospace plc
First issue 1981
(i) 33 free shares per eligible employee.
(ii) Matching shares up to 600 per employee.
(iii) Preferential consideration up to 2.5 per cent of the issue capital.
Second issue 1985
Preferential consideration up to 10,000 shares per employee, within 2 per cent of the issued share capital.

5. British Airways plc 1987
(i) 76 free shares per employee.
(ii) Matching shares (two for one) up to 120 per employee.
(iii) Up to 1600 shares by each employee under the priority offer were offered at a discount of 10 per cent.

6. British Gas plc 1986
(i) 52 free shares per employee (56 for a pensioner).
(ii) Matching shares (two for one) up to 111 per employee.
(iii) 10 per cent discount on 1,481 shares per employee purchased under the priority arrangements.

7. British Petroleum Co Ltd
First issue 1977:
Preferential consideration
Second issue 1978:
(i) Preferential consideration up to 137 shares per employee.
(ii) Matching shares, one for one.
Third issue 1983:
Preferential consideration up to 250 shares per employee.

8. British Telecommunications plc 1984
(i) 54 free shares per employee.
(ii) Matching shares, two for one, up to 77 per employee.
(iii) 10 per cent discount for up to 1,600 shares per employee purchased under the priority arrangements.

9. Britoil plc
First issue 1982
(i) Free shares of the value of £60 per each eligible employee.
(ii) Matching shares, one for one.
(iii) Preferential consideration up to 11,500 shares per employee.
Second issue 1985
Preferential consideration up to 10,000 shares per employee within 3 per cent of the issued share capital.

10. Cable and Wireless plc
First issue 1981
(i) Preferential consideration within 5 per cent of issued share capital.
(ii) 285,833 free shares to Cable and Wireless Employee Share Schemes.
Second issue 1983
(i) Preferential consideration up to 1,000 shares per employee.

Third issue 1985
Preferential consideration up to 5,000 shares per employee (2,500 per pensioner) within 15 per cent of issued share capital.

11. Enterprise Oil plc 1984
Preferential consideration up to 13,500 shares per employee.

12. Jaguar plc 1984
15 per cent of issued share capital reserved for employees.

13. Rolls-Royce 1987
(i)   41 free shares per eligible employee.
(ii) Matching shares, two for one, up to 88 per employee.
(iii) Priority reservations of 5,882 shares per employee (pensioner) up to 5 per cent of the issued share capital; 10 per cent discount on 1,176 shares out of this.
(iv) A total of 10 per cent issued share capital reserved under the above arrangements.

APPENDIX 8:   BAA plc

SPECIAL ARRANGEMENTS FOR EMPLOYEES AND PENSIONERS

The Directors and eligible employees and pensioners of BAA and eligible employees of BAI are being offered the opportunity to apply for shares under the Offer in accordance with the following special arrangements:

(a) the "Free Offer", under which each employee of BAA who is eligible (being resident in the United Kingdom on 8 July 1987 and having been in continuous employment with BAA from 1 January 1987 until 8 July 1987 and throughout that period having been contracted to work eighteen hours or more per week) will be offered by HM Government, free of charge, 41 Ordinary shares;

(b) the "Matching Offer", under which each eligible employee (as described in paragraph (a) above) will be offered the right to purchase, at the fixed price (payable in full on application), 82 Ordinary shares and will also be offered by HM Government, free of charge, two shares for each share so purchased; and

(c) the "Priority Offer", under which each person who on 8 July 1987 is both resident in the United Kingdom and is:

   (i)   a Director or an employee of BAA, or
   (ii) an employee of BAI, or
   (iii) in receipt of a pension from BAA or the BAA plc Pension Scheme

   may apply at the fixed price (payable in two instalments) for up to 4,082 Ordinary shares in priority to public applications, but subject to the rights to reject or scale down described below.

All shares acquired by employees free of charge under the Free Offer and the Matching Offer will be vested in BAA Trust Company Limited, as trustee of the BAA Employee Share Ownership Scheme, and will be subject to the restrictions on dealing described in paragraph 7 of Section 8.

Overall limits
All valid applications received under the Free Offer and the Matching Offer will be met in full. Not more than 2,025,000

Ordinary shares will be allocated under these Offers. A total of 25 million Ordinary shares (representing 5 per cent of the Company's issued Ordinary share capital) has been reserved for applications under the Priority Offer. In the event of excess demand under the Priority Offer, applications under the Priority Offer may be subject to scaling down in such manner as the Secretary of State thinks fit.

To the extent that applications are not accepted on a priority basis as a result of scaling down, they will be treated as applications for fixed price shares under the Offer without priority. The Secretary of State reserves the right to reject any application under the Priority Offer.

Source: BAA: Offer for Sale, 1987, p. 84.

APPENDIX 9: Some instances of loyalty bonus

1. BAA plc 1987

One for every ten shares held by individuals continuously until 31 July 1990, subject to a maximum of 200 shares.

2. British Airways plc 1987

Similar - until 28 February 1990, subject to a maximum of 400 shares.

3. British Gas plc 1986

Either bill vouchers worth up to £250 per person or one bonus share for ten held continuously for three years subject to a maximum of 500 shares.

4. British Telecommunications plc 1984

Either bill vouchers worth up to £216 per person or one bonus share for ten held until 30 November 1987, up to a maximum of 400 shares.

5. Britoil plc, 1982

One share for every ten retained by individuals until 30 November 1985.

APPENDIX 10:   The special or golden share: Britoil

> Excerpt from the Seventeenth Report from the Committee of Public Accounts (1984) <u>Sale of Government shareholdings in publicly-owned companies</u> (From annex: letter from HM Government)

ARTICLES OF ASSOCIATION

The Articles of Association of the Company contain, <u>inter alia</u>, provisions to the following effect:

(a)   The Special Share

(i)   The capital of the Company includes the Special Rights Preference Share of £1. The Special Share may be held only by or transferred only to the Secretary of State for Energy or any successor ("Secretary of State") or another Minister of the Crown or the Solicitor for the Affairs of Her Majesty's Treasury. The registered holder for the time being of the Special Share ("Special Shareholder") may require the Company to redeem the Special Share at its nominal amount at any time.

(ii) The Special Shareholder shall be entitled to receive notice of and attend and speak at all General Meetings and meetings of the holders of voting shares but except in the circumstances referred to in (iv) below, the Special Share shall carry no right to vote at such meetings. Each of the following proposals shall be deemed to be a proposed variation of the rights attaching to the Special Share:

> (1)   The alteration or removal of, or alteration of the effect of, all or any of certain specified Articles, being the Articles setting out certain definitions; the rights attaching to the Special Share; the right to convene Extraordinary General Meetings; the right to call for a poll at General Meetings; the special voting rights attaching to the Special Share referred to in (iv) below; the loss, in certain circumstances, of the voting rights attaching to shares; Government Directors; the maximum and minimum number of Directors; the powers of the Directors to manage the business of the Company; the right of a Director the vote in respect of resolutions of the Board concerning certain matters in which he is interested; the right of a Government Director to vote in respect of resolutions of the Board

concerning matters in which the Crown may be interested; the right of the Directors to appoint additional Directors with a maximum of two such Directors in any period between one Annual General Meeting and the next following Annual General Meeting and the proceedings of the Directors including the quorum at Board meetings.

(2) The voluntary winding up or dissolution of the Company.

(3) The issue of any shares with voting rights not identical to those of the Ordinary Shares.

(iii) On a return of assets in a winding up of the Company, the Special Shareholder shall be entitled to repayment of the capital paid up on the special Share in priority to any payment to other members. The Special Share confers no further right to participate in the profits or assets of the Company.

(iv) In certain circumstances special voting rights attach to the Special Share as follows:

(1) In the event of any Director becoming aware of any facts which might lead to the Board taking the view that a person (being interested in shares in the Company) either alone or jointly with other persons (such joint parties being referred to as "relevant persons") who are, or would pursuant to the provisions of section 66 and/or section 67 of the Companies Act 1981 be taken to be, interested in any shares in the Company in which that person is interested, has obtained or is attempting to obtain, directly or indirectly, control over the Board or its composition, he shall forthwith give written notice thereof to the Board setting out the relevant facts and the Board shall forthwith transmit a copy of such notice to the Special Shareholder. The Board shall as soon as possible thereafter consider the contents of such notice and shall forthwith inform the Special Shareholder in writing of the Board's views thereon.

(2) (a) If there are, in the opinion of the Special Shareholder, reasonable grounds for believing that any person or relevant persons has obtained or is attempting to obtain, directly or indirectly, control over the Board or its composition, the Special Shareholder, whether or not he has received any notice pursuant to the above provision, shall give written notice to the Board that he believes that

there are such grounds, specifying them.

(b) From and after delivery of such notice:

(i) the Special Share shall, if voted against the resolution on a poll, on any resolution to appoint, re-elect or remove any Director, have a total number of votes which (when added to the total number of votes which may be cast on such poll in respect of all the voting shares registered in the names of the Secretary of State) is one more than the total number of votes which may be cast on such poll in respect of all the voting shares which are not registered in the name of the Secretary of State; and

(ii) the provisions contained in the Articles as to Directors retiring by rotation shall be deemed to be amended so that all of the Directors for the time being other than the Government Directors shall retire from office at each Annual General Meeting.

(c) The Special Shareholder shall upon the cessation of the grounds giving rise to such notice inform the Board in writing of the withdrawal of such notice whereupon the provisions described in b(i) and (b)(ii) above shall cease to apply provided that the Special Shareholder shall be entitled to give any further such notice at any time or times thereafter when the relevant circumstances apply, whereupon those provisions shall again apply.

(d) The provisions of this sub-paragraph (2) shall not apply during any period when the Special Share has the special votes attaching to it described in sub-paragraph (3) below.

(3) If any person or relevant persons:

(a) makes an offer (whether or not conditional) for shares of the Company with a view to any person or relevant persons becoming beneficially interested in shares carrying more than 50 per cent of those voting rights which are exercisable in all circumstances at General Meetings and ignoring for this purpose the voting rights attaching to the Special Share described in sub-paragraph (2) above or this sub-paragraph (3), or

(b) is entitled to exercise, or is entitled to control the exercise of, more than 50 per cent of those voting rights exercisable in all circumstances at General

Meetings and ignoring for this purpose the voting rights attaching to the Special Share described in sub-paragraph (2) above or this sub-paragraph (3): (Provided that for the purpose of this provision no person shall be taken to be entitled as aforesaid by reason only that he has been appointed a proxy to vote at a particular General Meeting or at any adjournment of that meeting or has been appointed by a corporation to act as its representative at any such meeting or at any adjournment of that meeting)

the Special Share shall, from the date on which either of such events first occurs until any such offer has lapsed or closed or the person or relevant persons ceases to be entitled as aforesaid, as the case may be, have in respect of any resolution of the Company in General Meeting on a poll, a total number of votes which (when added to the total number of votes which may be cast on such poll in respect of all the voting shares registered in the name of the Secretary of State) is one more than the total number of votes which be cast on such poll in respect of all the voting shares which are not registered in the name of the Secretary of State. In addition the Special Shareholder shall have the right to require the Directors forthwith to proceed to convene an Extraordinary General Meeting and provisions in the same terms as section 132 of the Companies Act 1948 and the Article setting out the right to convene Extraordinary General Meetings shall apply to such right.

(v) In the Articles the expression "voting shares registered in the name of the Secretary of State" means voting shares for the time being registered in the name of the Secretary of State, voting shares registered in the name of any nominee of the Secretary of State as notified in writing to the Board by the Secretary of State, voting shares registered in the name of any other Minister of the Crown, voting shares registered in the name of any nominee of any such Minister as notified in writing to the Board by such Minister and voting shares registered in the name of the Solicitor for the Affairs of Her Majesty's Treasury; "voting shares" means the Ordinary Shares and any other shares for the time being in the capital of the Company having attached thereto voting rights identical to those attaching to the Ordinary Shares.

Excerpt from the prospectus of British Steel plc, November 1988

PART VII: RELATIONSHIP WITH HM GOVERNMENT

Shareholding

Following the Offer for Sale, HM Government will hold no Shares in the Company except the Special Share described below and any Ordinary Shares reserved under the Free and Matching Offers (see section 6(i) and (ii) of 'Additional Information' in Part XI) but not taken up under the UK Public and Employee Offer; any Shares not taken up will be sold in due course.

Restriction on ownership of shares

HM Government will hold the Special Share (described in section 2(ii) of 'Additional Information' in Part XI). Certain matters, in particular the alteration of specified Articles of Association (relating to or affecting limitations which prevent a person or persons acting in concert from having an interest in 15% or more of the issued Ordinary Shares), will require the prior consent of the holder of the Special Share. The Special Share, which may only be held by a Minister or other person acting on behalf of HM Government, does not confer any right to vote at meetings but entitles the holder to attend and speak. The Special Share may be redeemed at par at any time prior to 31 December 1993 by agreement between the Directors and the registered holder and unless so redeemed will be redeemed at par on that date.

PART XI

(ii) The Special Share

The Special Share may be redeemed at par at any time prior to 31 December 1993 by agreement between the Board and the registered holder for the time being of the Special Share ('the Special Shareholder') and, unless so redeemed, will be redeemed at par on that date.

The Special Share may only be held by and transferred to the Secretary of State, another Minister of the Crown, or any person acting on behalf of the Crown.

The Special Shareholder is entitled to receive notice of,

and to attend and speak at, any general meeting or any meeting of any class of shareholders, but not to vote at such a meeting. The Special Share confers no right to participate in the capital or profits of the Company, except that on a winding-up the Special Shareholder is entitled to repayment of £1 in priority to other shareholders. Each of the following matters is deemed to be a variation of the rights attaching to the Special Share and is only effective with the consent in writing of the Special Shareholder:

(a) the amendment, removal or alteration of the effect of certain definitions (relating primarily to the Special Share) in the Articles, of the Article relating to the Special Share, or of the Article relating to the limitation on shareholdings (referred to in paragraph (x) below);

(b) the creation or issue of any shares in the Company with voting rights or the variation of any voting rights attached to any shares in the Company, in each case not being shares comprised (or shares which would, following such issue or variation, be comprised) in relevant share capital (as defined in section 198(2) of the Act) of the Company, provided that there is excluded from this sub-paragraph (b) the creation or issue of, or variation so as to give rise to, (1) preference shares only carrying the normal right to vote in certain specified circumstances and (2) shares which do not constitute equity share capital (as defined in section 744 of the Act) and which, when aggregated with all other such shares, would (on the assumption that such shares carry the right to vote in all circumstances) carry the right to cast less than 15% of the votes capable of being cast on a poll at any general meeting; or

(c) a proposal for the voluntary winding-up or dissolution of the Company.

APPENDIX 11: UK enterprises in which the Government holds a special share

---

1. Amersham International plc

2. BAA plc

3. British Aerospace plc

4. British Gas plc

5. British Petroleum Co. Ltd

6. British Telecommunications plc

7. Britoil plc

8. Cable and Wireless plc

9. Enterprise Oil plc

10. Jaguar plc

11. Rolls-Royce plc

   Private sales

12. Sealink UK Ltd

APPENDIX 12: Privatisation of the National Freight Corporation

The National Freight Corporation (NFC), the largest road haulage organisation in the UK, was converted into the National Freight Company Ltd under the Transport Act 1980, as a first step towards privatisation, with all shares resting in the Government. In 1982 a staff-management 'buy-out' was effected, the first such measure of privatisation; and the new private-sector enterprise was named the National Freight Consortium plc.

This note seeks to highlight the salient features of an undoubtedly novel experiment carried out successfully in the UK. It might be of interest to other countries with reference to certain sectors of activity where conditions of predominant labour intensity in the production function present themselves.

First, the privatisation sought to involve the employees as owners. It was not a 'participation' scheme, but was meant to give them a sense of belonging.

Second, those entitled to buy shares included the NFC employees, families, and pensioners - about 40,000 in all. Some 10,000 of them bought shares - many of them for the first time ever. They were offered 'A' shares up to 82.5 per cent of the issued capital of £7.5 million. The balance was given to banks as 'A' shares, considering their provision of loan capital and working capital to NFC.

Third, 'B' shareholders would appoint a director, not subject to re-election on the principle of rotation, as long as they held at least 5 per cent of the issued capital. They also had the right to veto any large increase in the issued 'A' share capital, lest the 'A' shares should become too large a proportion of the total. The share capital could be raised by 2 per cent each year to accommodate new eligible members of NFC.

Fourth, in order to bring about the widest possible share ownership, no single person or family was allowed to hold more than 100,000 shares; and an Employee Loan Scheme was established by NFC, with £3 million provided by Barclays, for offering interest-free loans up to £200 to enable NFC employees to purchase the shares. They could repay over a year through wage deductions.

Fifth, there would be no stock market quotation or sale for 5 years. However, to assist transfers between willing buyers and willing sellers, the Share Trust would conduct transfer transations at certain times of the year at prices published in reasonable advance. Figure 1.3 explains the mechanics of 'A' share transfers.

Sixth, the NFC would be bought from the Government at £53.5 million. The Government would pay NFC about £47 million towards NFC Pension Funds. The full financial arrangements for the privatisation are illustrated in Figure 1.4.

Seventh, the financial record of NFC prior to privatisation was not good. No dividends were paid. The profit forecast of £4.3 million, presented in the prospectus, included profits accruing from the sale of properties; and a dividend of 10.7p per share was predicted. A fully subscribed share of 100p had, in effect, an asset back-up of 516p. The major factor that assured the success of the buy-out scheme was the employee confidence created by the team of top managers as well as directors; and this was strengthened substantially by the fact that banks were willing to offer loans to take up 'A' shares. Confidence in recovery of business conditions in favour of NFC was also an important consideration.

Last, but not least, the falling interest rates at the time constituted a favourable background for the entire transaction in which there was a high gearing.

In conclusion, the seven factors considered by Mr Peter Thompson, Chairman and Chief Executive of NFC plc, as essential to the success of the NFC buy-out scheme were:

(i) participative management style;
(ii) high quality communications;
(iii) first class consultation machinery with trade unions;
(iv) profit-oriented remuneration;
(v) this concept must extend to wage earners to replace quality-related bonuses;
(vi) ability to measure profitability in relatively small units; and
(vii) a work force which, given the opportunity to do so, is prepared to take a share in the business.

ACKNOWLEDGEMENT

This appendix draws substantially on <u>The National Freight Buy-Out</u> by Sandy McLachlan.

Figure 1.3: How 'A' ordinary shares may be transferred

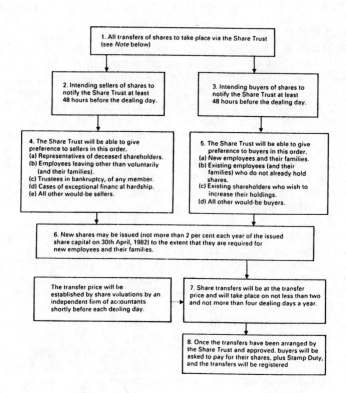

1. All transfers of shares to take place via the Share Trust (see *Note* below)

2. Intending sellers of shares to notify the Share Trust at least 48 hours before the dealing day.

3. Intending buyers of shares to notify the Share Trust at least 48 hours before the dealing day.

4. The Share Trust will be able to give preference to sellers in this order.
(a) Representatives of deceased shareholders.
(b) Employees leaving other than voluntarily (and their families).
(c) Trustees in bankruptcy, of any member.
(d) Cases of exceptional financial hardship.
(e) All other would-be sellers.

5. The Share Trust will be able to give preference to buyers in this order.
(a) New employees and their families.
(b) Existing employees (and their families) who do not already hold shares.
(c) Existing shareholders who wish to increase their holdings.
(d) All other would-be buyers.

6. New shares may be issued (not more than 2 per cent each year of the issued share capital on 30th April, 1982) to the extent that they are required for new employees and their families.

The transfer price will be established by share valuations by an independent firm of accountants shortly before each dealing day.

7. Share transfers will be at the transfer price and will take place on not less than two and not more than four dealing days a year.

8. Once the transfers have been arranged by the Share Trust and approved, buyers will be asked to pay for their shares, plus Stamp Duty, and the transfers will be registered

Note: These arrangements are not obligatory in the case of transfers on death or bankruptcy or between an employee or pensioner and certain members of his/her family. Such transfers should, however, be notified to the Share Trust.

Figure 1.4: How the purchase of NFC will be financed

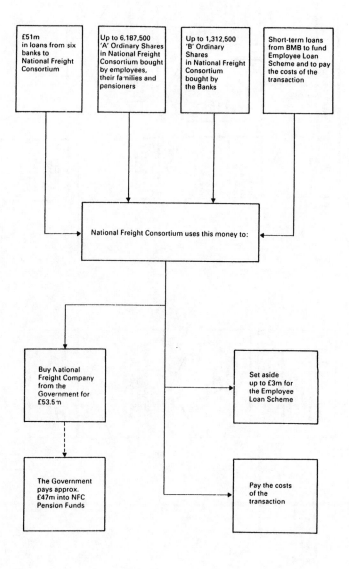

£51m in loans from six banks to National Freight Consortium

Up to 6,187,500 'A' Ordinary Shares in National Freight Consortium bought by employees, their families and pensioners

Up to 1,312,500 'B' Ordinary Shares in National Freight Consortium bought by the Banks

Short-term loans from BMB to fund Employee Loan Scheme and to pay the costs of the transaction

National Freight Consortium uses this money to:

Buy National Freight Company from the Government for £53.5m

Set aside up to £3m for the Employee Loan Scheme

The Government pays approx. £47m into NFC Pension Funds

Pay the costs of the transaction

APPENDIX 13: Outline of typical steps to privatisation*

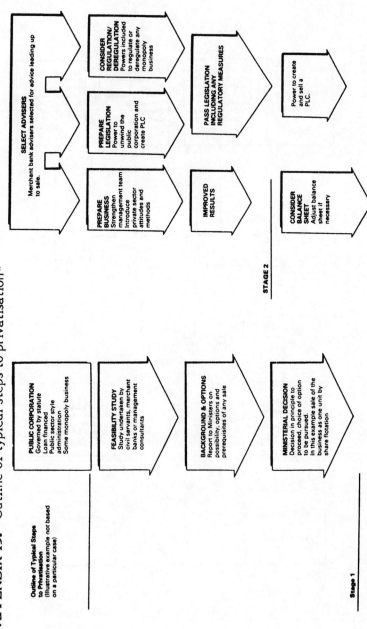

Outline of Typical Steps to Privatisation
(Illustrative example not based on a particular case)

PUBLIC CORPORATION
Governed by statute
Loan financed
Public sector style administration
Some monopoly business

FEASIBILITY STUDY
Study undertaken by civil servants, merchant banks or management consultants

BACKGROUND & OPTIONS
Report to Ministers on possibility, options and prerequisites of any sale

MINISTERIAL DECISION
Decision in principle to proceed, choice of option to be pursued.
In this example sale of the business as one unit by share flotation

Stage 1

SELECT ADVISERS
Merchant bank advisers selected for advice leading up to sale.

PREPARE BUSINESS
Strengthen management team
Introduce private sector attitudes and methods

PREPARE LEGISLATION
Power to unwind the public corporation and create PLC

CONSIDER REGULATION/DEREGULATION
Powers included to regulate or deregulate any monopoly business

IMPROVED RESULTS

PASS LEGISLATION INCLUDING ANY REGULATORY MEASURES

CONSIDER BALANCE SHEET
Adjust balance sheet if necessary

Power to create and sell a PLC.

STAGE 2

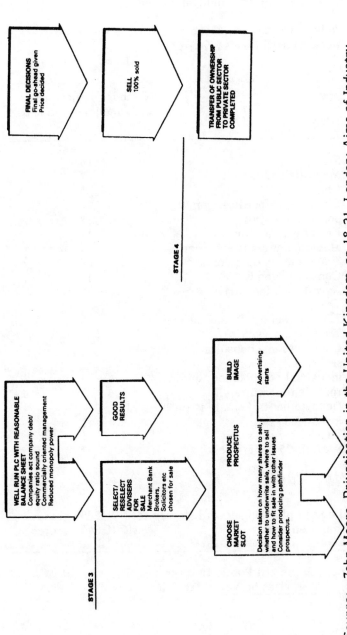

STAGE 3

WELL RUN PLC WITH REASONABLE BALANCE SHEET
Companies act company debt/ equity ratio sound
Commercially oriented management
Reduced monopoly power

GOOD RESULTS

SELECT/ RESELECT ADVISERS FOR SALE
Merchant Bank
Brokers,
Solicitors etc
chosen for sale

CHOOSE MARKET SLOT
Decision taken on how many shares to sell, whether to underwrite sale, where to sell and how to fit sale in with other issues
Consider producing pathfinder prospectus.

PRODUCE PROSPECTUS

BUILD IMAGE
Advertising starts

STAGE 4

FINAL DECISIONS
Final go-ahead given
Price decided

SELL
100% sold

TRANSFER OF OWNERSHIP FROM PUBLIC SECTOR TO PRIVATE SECTOR COMPLETED

Source: John Moore, Privatisation in the United Kingdom, pp.18–21, London: Aims of Industry

* With acknowledgement to HM Treasury

APPENDIX 14: Data on accumulated losses

A. India: Central Government enterprises with accumulated losses (1985-6)

(Rs lakhs)

Sector (1)	Number of enterprises with accumulated losses (2)
1. Steel	4
2. Minerals and metals	7
3. Coal	4
4. Chemicals, fertilisers, and pharmaceuticals	17
5. Heavy engineering	11
6. Medium and light engineering	9
7. Transportation equipment	9
8. Consumer goods	12
9. Agro-based industries	3
10. Textiles	14
11. Trading and marketing services	8
12. Transport services	3
13. Contracts and consultancy services	3
14. Industrial development and technical consultancy	4
15. Development of small-scale industries	1
16. Tourist services	1
17. Section-25 companies	2
	112

Total equity plus long-term loan capital	Rs2794 crores
Accumulated losses	Rs843 crores

Source: Bureau of Public Enterprises, Government of India, Public Enterprises Survey, 1986-7 (New Delhi)

B. India: State of Karnataka (March 1986)

Sector (1)	Total number of enterprises (2)	Number of enterprises with accumulated losses (3)	Total share capital in the sector (Rs crores) (4)	Total accumulated losses in the sector (Rs cores) (5)	Total accumulated (5) as a percentage of (4)
1. Sectoral development	15	12	66.3	7.9	11.9
2. Weaker section development enterprises	2	2	17.0	1.5	8.8
3. Service enterprises	7	4	11.8	21.0	178.0
4. Marketing enterprises	4	-	5.9	-	-
5. Production enterprises	22	12	228.6	165.6	72.4
6. Organisations under special statute	4	2	162.2	117.4	72.4
7. Deemed government companies	3	2	7.8	13.8	176.9
Totals	56	32	499.6	327.2	65.5

Source: Bureau of Public Enterprises, State of Karnataka, Bangalore, India.

C. Sri Lanka: Cumulative losses (1986)

Enterprises to be converted	Cumulative losses as a percentage of fixed assets
Ceylon Plywoods Corporation	17.9
Ceylon State Hardware Corporation	391.2
National Paper Corporation	19.0
State Distilleries Corporation	-
State Mining and Mineral Development Corporation	-
British Ceylon Corporation	242.2
British Ceylon Milling Corporation	282.2
Ceylon Extraction Co. Ltd	483.4
Ceylon Oxygen Ltd	-
Colombo Commercial Co.	39.7
Essential Oil (Ceylon) Ltd	-
National Textiles Corporations:	
Mattegama Mill	9.9
Pugoda Mill	3.9
Thulhiriya Mill	21.1
Veyangoda Mill	429.5
United Motors	-
Total	1395.2

Source: Public Enterprise Division, Government of Sri Lanka.

D. Nepal: Cumulative deficits of public enterprises

At the end of 1985-6	Rs 1.35 billion
As percentage of the government's investments in share capital	30

Source: Economic Survey, 1986-7, p.35 (Kathmandu)

APPENDIX 15: Some instances of privatisation through joint ventures in the state of Imo in Nigeria

a. Aluminium Extrusion Ltd (35 per cent a private company, 35 per cent state government and 30 per cent private individuals).

b. International Glass Industries Ltd (fully owned by the government; when it is in full steam, private capital will be invited).

c. Raisin and Peanuts Co. (A private company will take up management by taking about 40-50 per cent equity. The balance, initially with the government, will eventually go to individual subscribers.)

d. NSW Tyre Factory, Cardboard Packaging, and Integrated Aluminium Products: the government is contemplating action with the Securities Exchange Commission and ICON merchant banks, to float bonds first and, when the companies are on stream, to float shares also. The bond holders will have the first option to buy the shares; and also to convert bonds into shares.

e. Progress Bank: 20 per cent to be given to the public. The management is given to private hands, though the government appoints directors. It is a very profitable enterprise.

f. IMO Modern Poultry Co.: an Israeli firm, which set it up, is given management powers for five years.

g. SOCFINCO: a Dutch company, is given a management contract - an exception still - for Adapalms.

2

Some Background Observations on Privatisation

Colin Kirkpatrick*

MACRO ISSUES

The economic case for privatisation is more commonly made in terms of its impact on micro, or enterprise, level performance. Here, however, we simply draw attention to the fact that much of the pressure for privatisation stems from macro level concerns.

The size of the public sector

It is widely held that the public sector has become too large in many less developed countries (LDCs). The World Bank's 1981 report on economic prospects in sub-Saharan Africa ('Berg Report') concluded that:

> It is now widely evident that the public sector is over-extended, given the present scarcities of financial resources, skilled manpower, and organisational capacity. This has resulted in slower growth than might have been achieved with available resources, and accounts for the present crisis. (World Bank, 1981, p.5).

Although it is frequently made, the argument that the public sector in LDCs is 'over-extended' and requires 'rolling-back', as a general proposition is empirically unproven. Evidence to support the hypothesis of an inverse relationship between macroeconomic performance and the size of the public sector is lacking. Nunnenkamp (1986) was unable to detect any statistically significant cross-country relationship between the relative importance of the public enterprise

* Professor, University of Bradford

94

sector in LDCs (as measured by their output and investment shares) and various in GDP and gross fixed investment, the level of industrialisation, the growth in employment). Kirkpatrick (1986) found a negative, but statistically insignificant correlation between the share of public enterprise output in GDP, and growth in income in the 1970s, for a sample of twenty-three LDCs.

A variant of the argument that public sector growth adversely affects economic growth performance is found in the 'crowding-out' hypothesis. Here, it is argued that public sector investment can lower private investment if it utilises scarce resources that would otherwise be available to the private sector, where, for example, public sector investment is financed by taxation or debt issue which is paid for from the private sector's investable surplus. This hypothesis was tested by Blejer and Khan (1984) using pooled cross-section data for twenty-four LDCs over the period 1971-79. They reported that the effect of aggregate public sector investment on private investment was consistent with the crowding-out hypothesis, but the substitution coefficient between public and private investment was very small and not significantly different from zero. When public invest-ment was disaggregated by type, it was found that an increase in the infrastructural component of government capital formation raised private investment, presumably since it enhanced the possibilities for private investment activity. Increases in other kinds of public investment were found to have some crowding-out effect, but the degree of substitution between public and private investment was significantly less than unity.

The size of the public sector per se does not have a significant bearing on the performance of the sector or the economy. What matters is the effectiveness with which resources allocated to the public sector are utilised.

Fiscal impact of public enterprise sector

The public enterprise sector in LDCs has frequently failed to generate an investable surplus and instead has created a budgetary burden for the public sector. The overall deficit - defined as the difference between current plus capital expenditure and revenue plus receipts of current transfers and of non-government capital transfers - of public enterprises in LDCs averaged almost 4 per cent of GDP in the mid-1970s, as compared to an average of 1.7 per cent in the industrial countries (Short, 1984). If government current transfers are excluded from receipts, the LDC average rises to 4.6 per cent. Furthermore, the public enterprise overall deficits in LDCs have increased in recent years, by 2.5 per cent of GDP between the late 1960s and the mid-1970s. Overall deficits for public enterprises are not undesirable per se, and it may be appropriate to run deficits to finance investment needed to expand marketable output. Nevertheless, it is relevant to note that the degree of self-financing appears to be low: comparing current and capital account balances suggests that if receipts of current government transfers are excluded, the self-financing ratio of state enterprises amounted to only 10 per cent in the mid-1970s, in those developing countries for which data were available.

Public enterprise deficits have been financed either from borrowing by the state enterprises in domestic and international financial markets or from central government transfers. In the mid-1970s, for those developing countries for which a breakdown of sources of finance is available, it appears that about 25 per cent of the state enterprises' deficits were met by direct foreign borrowing. In the period 1976-78, state enterprises accounted for one-third of all international borrowing by LDCs (World Bank, 1980). A further 60 per cent of the overall deficit was financed from central government and the banking system, the remaining 15 per cent being covered by other domestic borrowing.

These financing demands have a direct effect on macro-economic variables and performance. Where the public enterprise sector can borrow from the central bank, there will be an immediate impact on domestic credit and money supply. Where transfers from government are used, the overall public sector deficit is increased. When foreign borrowing occurs, the debt ratio is raised. In some LDCs, in an attempt to relieve the burden on the state budget, public enterprises have been required to raise funds for investment and working capital directly from the domestic commercial bank sector. At the same time, governments have often directed the commercial banks to grant loans to the public enterprise sector on preferential terms.

The precise effect of these financing requirements on macro-performance will vary from country to country, but their magnitude suggests that in many LDCs the public enterprise sector's financial deficit will contribute significantly to inflation and balance of payments difficulties. A concern with the impact of the public enterprise sector financial deficit on macro-stability is reflected in the priority given in the International Monetary Fund's stabilisation programmes to improving public enterprise financial performance. In a survey of ninety-four IMF-supported adjustment programmes in developing countries during the period 1980-4, it was found that sixty-eight of the programmes included policy recommendations relating to non-financial state enterprises, aimed mainly at improving financial performance (IMF, 1986a). Indeed, the current attention given to the financial position of the public enterprise sector in LDCs probably relates more to the macroeconomic consequences of large budget deficits than to a concern with profitability as an indicator of enterprise performance.

Distributional impact of the public enterprise sector

Public enterprises in LDCs are often expected to pursue social objectives, which can range from subsidising particular consumer groups, assisting certain regions, and creating or maintaining employment. Thus, in addition to economic and financial performance, consideration must be given to the public enterprise sector's performance in fulfilling 'non-economic' objectives.

In many LDCs the public enterprise sector is seen as an important instrument to promote income redistribution. While economic theory would suggest that distributional objectives should be pursued through the use of the fiscal system, in practice LDC policy makers typically operate in a 'second-best' environment in which limitations on the use of tax and subsidies measures require them to pursue their redistributive goals by employing other, less direct instruments. The public enterprise sector, therefore, is frequently used to create employment, to assist employees through the payment of higher wages and benefits, and to benefit consumers by subsidising the price of public enterprise outputs.

Has the public enterprise sector been an effective means for advancing redistributive objectives in LDCs? While acknowledging the difficulties in identifying the distributional impact of the public enterprises, critics would argue that they have not served to redistribute income (IMF, 1986a; Jones, 1985). Employment opportunities have been lessened by the adoption of capital-intensive technology in production, improvement in employees' wages and employment conditions have created a privileged labour elite, subsidies on output have failed to reach the lowest income group thereby benefiting the better-off, and price controls on foodstuffs have disadvantaged poor rural producers.

The empirical evidence appears to support the view that public enterprises have failed to realise their redistributional goals, and, in some circumstances, have produced perverse results. In Zambia, stringent price controls on refined oils and fats produced by publicly-owned agro-based enterprises and up subsidising large industrial users, wholesalers, and affluent urban dwellers (Ayub and Hegstad, 1987). In Bangladesh, some 75 per cent of the public enterprise sector's manufactured output was subject to price control. In almost all cases the administered ex-factory price was set at a level significantly below the market clearing price, giving rise to windfall gains at the distribution and retailing stages, where market prices ranged from 80 per cent to 400 per cent above the official price (Sobhan, 1983).

Killick (1983) indicates that public enterprises in Africa have been associated with the accelerated Africanisation of industrial employment, and that this has had distributional consequences since it has resulted in a shift in the total wage bill from foreigners towards nationals. However, this process may worsen the interpersonal distribution of income within a country if a high proportion of the occupations formerly undertaken by foreigners were highly paid.

COUNTRY EXPERIENCES

Few countries have been immune from the worldwide interest in privatisation. As the Financial Times observed recently, 'if political ideas could be copyrighted like popular novels, Mrs Margaret Thatcher's Government would today be well on the way to achieving a runaway international bestseller.

Despite widespread interest, however, the actual pace of privatisation in LDCs appears to be slow. A recent survey covering the post-1980 period found that partial or total sale of public enterprises had occurred in only fifteen developing countries (excluding Chile and Bangladesh) and covered fewer than 100 enterprises. In most cases the privatised firms were small in terms of asset value and employment, and had previously been in private ownership (Berg, 1985). A recent World Bank report estimated that for low-income African countries, no more than 5 per cent of public enterprises had been privatised or closed down in the 1980s (World Bank, 1986, p.2).

Rather more progress has been made in the deregulation and liberalisation aspects of privatisation, with measures relating to the reform of the public enterprise sector becoming an increasingly important element in the conditions attached to World Bank and IMF lending programmes. Of the ninety-four IMF-supported adjustment programmes in LDCs during the 1980-4 period, the majority contained policy recommendations relating to non-financial state enterprises (IMF, 1986a). Sixty-one per cent of programmes contained provisions for reducing subsidies to public enterprises and introducing prices that would cover operating costs while at the same time making a reasonable contribution to capital maintenance and new investment. Twenty-seven programmes curtailed current transfers to state enterprises, and eleven specified sub-ceilings on credit to state enterprises. More than a quarter of the programmes contained intentions for the divestiture of enterprises to the private sector. Twenty-five programmes included measures aimed at improving managerial efficiency and autonomy.

A similar concern with measures aimed at improving public enterprise performance is evident in the World Bank's lending programme. Mosley (1988) established that of the forty Structural Adjustment Loans introduced in twenty-one LDCs between 1980 and 1986, some 73 per cent did call for some action in the area of 'public enterprise financial performance'. In 62 per cent of the programmes there was a requirement for deregulation of pricing or licensing legislation. A detailed examination of the programmes shows that the emphasis in the Bank's recommendations has been on deregulation and competition, rather than on divestiture.

Why has the pace of privatisation in LDCs been slow? A variety of factors can be suggested, some relating to practical problems of implementation, others reflecting reservations as to the repercussions that might follow from the adoption of a programme of privatisation.

The experience in developed countries has shown that, even where there is a sophisticated financial infrastructure, it is difficult to establish the appropriate market value for the enterprise assets. The problems of valuation and public sale are compounded in developing countries where the capital market is insufficiently well-developed to handle large equity sales. The absence of a well-developed financial system means that divestiture will have to be made by direct placement with local or foreign interests large enough to handle the transaction. The government may be unwilling, however, to have its assets transferred to certain groups of potential buyers, if it results in a further concentration of wealth. In some countries, it will be politically unacceptable to sell enterprises to wealthy racial minority groups. Similar objections may be raised to increased ownership by foreign interests.

The economic rationale for widespread programmes of privatisation is not yet firmly established, and there may be legitimate doubts as to the economic gains of privatisation. Divestiture may do little to improve the economic performance of the enterprise if it simply transfers the ownership from public to private sector. The fiscal benefits may also be limited if, for example, tax and subsidy concessions are offered as an inducement to the sale of loss-making enterprises. If market protection is offered as a further incentive to buyers, the economic gains from increased competition are sacrificed for budgetary gains. (Mansoor, 1988).

There is an unwillingness to accept the current policy priorities of the international agencies, and the accompanying cohort of international merchant banks and managerial consultancy firms. As Heals (1988) comments; 'at present there seems to be a striking combination of aggressive ideology and of what, if taken at its face value, can only be described as naive managerialism'. Fashions change, and there is a certain irony in the aid agencies' current advocacy of denationalisation for the public sector enterprise which they were instrumental in establishing in the 1960s.

The resistance from interest groups that stand to lose from privatisation is likely to form a powerful political constraint. This opposition will come from the labour force employed in the public enterprises who fear job losses, and opportunity for patronage will be reduced. Where liberalisation is threatened, further resistance will come from those groups who currently enjoy the protected economic rents created by the system of regulations and controls. The opposition by various sectional interests that are threatened by privatisation may well be more immediate and more vocally expressed than the anticipated longer-term benefits from greater economic efficiency.

REFERENCES

Ayhub, M.A. and Hegstad, S.O. (1987) 'Management of public industrial enterprises', World Bank Research Observer, 2 (1), 79-101.

Berg, E. (1982) 'Divestiture of state-owned enterprises in LDCs', report prepared for the World Bank, November 1985.

Blejer, M. and Khan, M.S.M. (1984) 'Government policy and private investment in developing countries', IMF Staff Papers, 31, 379-403.

Heald, D. (1988) 'The relevance of UK privatisation for LDCs', in Cook, P. and Kilpatrick, C. (eds) Privatisation in Less Developed Countries, Brighton: Wheatsheaf Press.

International Monetary Fund (1985) World Economic Outlook, Washington DC: IMF.

International Monetary Fund (1986) Fund-supported Programs, Fiscal Policy and Income Distribution, Occasional Paper 46, Washington DC: IMF.

Jones, L.P. (1985) 'Public enterprise for whom? Perverse distributional consequences of public operational decisions', Economic Development and Cultural Change, 33 (2), 333-47.

Killick, T. (1983) 'The role of the public sector in the industrialisation of African developing countries', Industry and Development (UNIDO), no. 7, 57-88.

Kirkpatrick, C. (1986) 'The World Bank's views on state-owned enterprises in less developed countries: a critical moment', Rivista Internazionale di Scienze Economiche e Commerciali, 33, (6-7), 685-96.

Mansoor, A. (1988) 'The fiscal impact of privatisation', in Cook, P. and Kirkpatrick, C. (eds) Privatisation in Less Developed Countries, Brighton: Wheatsheaf Press.

Mosley, P. (1988) 'Privatisation, policy-based lending and World Bank behaviour', in Cook, P. and Kirkpatrick, C. (eds) Privatisation in Less Developed Countries, Brighton: Wheatsheaf Press.

Nunnenkamp, P. (1986) 'State enterprises in developing countries', Intereconomics, July/August, 186-93.

Short, R. P. (1984) 'The role of public enterprises: an

international statistical comparison', in R.H. Floyd, C.S. Gray, and R.P. Short, Public Enterprise in Mixed Economies, Washington DC: IMF.

Sobhan, R. (1983) 'Distributive regimes under public enterprise: a case study of the Bangladesh experience', in F. Stewart (ed.) Work, Income and Inequality: Payment Systems in the Third World, London: Macmillan, pp. 138-67.

World Bank (1980) Borrowing in International Capital Markets, 1979, Washington DC: World Bank.

World Bank (1981) Accelerated Development in Sub-Saharan Africa: An Agenda for Action, Washington DC: World Bank.

World Bank (1982) Financing Adjustment with Growth in Sub-Saharan Africa, 1986-90, Washington DC: World Bank.

3

Privatisation: Macroeconomics and Modalities

Gerry Grimstone*

In the UK nearly half of the previously state-owned industrial sector has been privatised since 1979. More than £25 billion has been raised for the Exchequer, over 600,000 workers have been moved to the private sector, and the proportion of people who own shares has more than trebled.

Why has privatisation in the UK proved so successful and why is it now studied so closely by so many countries worldwide? It is because deliberate care was taken to design a programme that was not only achievable but was also a popular success. Much attention has been paid to both macro-economics and modalities. No privatisation programme can proceed in a meaningful sense unless it advances national objectives and takes full account of local sensitivities. Politics are often more important than finance.

THE UK PRIVATISATION PROGRAMME'S OBJECTIVE

The original rationale of the programme was primarily economic, as nationalisation had not been a success in the UK. Privatisation was heralded by the incoming Conservative Government in 1979 as being the only way to bring lasting improvements in economic performance.

As presently organised, the UK programme, in common with other programmes elsewhere, has the following key objectives: to increase efficiency through competition, deregulation, or other means; to raise finance which can be used to fund other expenditure priorities, to reduce borrowing, to reduce taxation, or any combination of these;

* Director, Schroders, London

to encourage employees to own shares in the company in which they work; to boost the level of share ownership in the general economy; to strengthen the capital market; and to gain domestic and international prestige.

Judged by these objectives, the UK programme has clearly been successful. Seventeen major companies and a number of smaller enterprises have been sold. The performance of privatised companies has improved; for example, the profits of British Aerospace have trebled, those of Cable and Wireless are up sevenfold, Amersham International's have doubled, Jaguar's are up by a third and the National Freight Consortium's have increased sevenfold. The combination of freedom from statutory and bureaucratic constraints, strong balance sheets, progressive elimination of internal inefficiencies, and generally favourable economic conditions have done wonders for the companies concerned.

Although the commercial and political arguments in favour of privatisation now seem clear-cut, it was easy for opponents in the early stages of the UK programme to argue that, financially, the programme was misjudged. Was the government 'selling the family silver' to fund current expenditure? Was there a case, in a narrow financial sense, for keeping profitable industries in state ownership? It was not clear that selling profitable industries would, in the longer term, be of financial benefit if the proceeds from selling equity were ignored. However, subsequent work indicated that a continuing cash benefit to the Exchequer was likely to be produced by a combination of the following: increased tax payments by companies (as their profitability increased once they were freed from government constraints); interest savings on debt not borrowed by the government (as a result of selling equity); dividends from residual shareholdings where these have been temporarily retained; and the funding of future investment by requirements by the private sector rather than by the state. Privatisation could be justified on financial grounds alone.

IT TAKES TWO TO TANGO

Establishing the objectives of a privatisation programme is of little use if they cannot be put into effect. It is occasionally forgotten by those attempting to administer a privatisation programme that, unlike nationalisation, privatisation is a two-way process. Governments may want to sell a company but someone else must also want to buy it if the transaction is to be brought to a successful conclusion.

Methods of sale in the UK privatisation programme have been determined by the programme's overall objectives and by practicalities. Because of the desire to spread ownership widely, public offerings of shares are the preferred choice if they can be achieved. Failing this - and a public offering is a severe test for a company - employee buy-outs have been welcomed provided that the funds are available and the company's cash flow can support the necessary leverage. The most difficult sales to bring to a popular conclusion are sales to corporate purchasers, particularly if overseas buyers are involved. The politics of privatisation are such that domestic investors normally have to be given preference although minority sales overseas can be an important factor in bringing an otherwise domestic sale to a successful conclusion.

In practice, therefore, a hierarchy of political desirability can be established, which coincides, fortuitously, with the level of capital market sophistication that is necessary to bring the sales to a conclusion. This hierarchy is demonstrated diagrammatically in Figure 3.1. The public offering represents the acme of privatisation achievement. For countries with undeveloped capital markets, overseas trade sales may be the only option even if undesirable politically. Whether or not privatisation on such terms is desirable is a matter for debate.

ORGANISING A PROGRAMME

A key initial step in assembling a privatisation programme is to create the right organisational structure within the public sector. Nationalised industry policy in the UK has always been the responsibility of HM Treasury. Nationalised industry White Papers are presented to Parliament by Treasury ministers, and the co-ordinating mechanism responsible for advising on nationalised industry policy is chaired and serviced by Treasury officials. The reasons for this are not hard to fathom. Whilst it was appropriate for individual sponsor departments, such as Transport and Energy, to be responsible for the day-to-day sponsorship of individual nationalised industries, these departments were

Figure 3.1: Hierarchy of political desirability in privatisation options

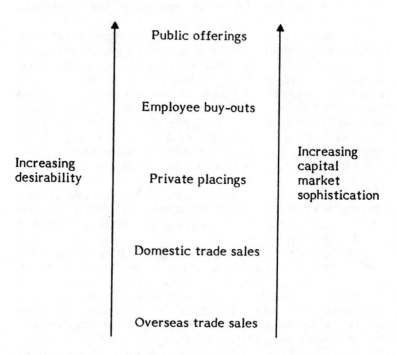

not happy to see any one individual sponsor department exercising overall control. It made sense for the Treasury to seek to occupy the central policy vacuum that this created, both because of the nationalised industries' public expenditure impact and their effect on macro-economic policies. Controlling both policy and the purse-strings put the Treasury in a dominant position. Because privatisation policy was seen as an adjunct of nationalised industry policy in its early days, it was natural for the Treasury to take on responsibility for privatisation policy and the overall co-ordination of the programme. At least, that was the way it seemed to Treasury ministers and officials.

In practice, this approach produced clear benefits. The natural nexus between the Treasury and the Prime Ministers' Policy Unit could be used to good advantage; the Treasury's desire for revenue, whilst not unduly emphasised in public would sustain the programme's momentum; and the

Treasury's innate abilities could be deployed to advance a policy that was central to the government's thinking. It was also clearly beneficial to create a small caucus of officials at the centre who would be involved in each and every privatisation. This eased technology transfer between departments and helped to overcome the inertia that tended to seize sponsor departments when privatisation threatened to break up much-loved bureaucratic fiefdoms. It also allowed discipline and cohesion to be maintained. Given that the market viewed the sales as a programme, it behove the government to do so likewise.

ACHIEVING SUCCESSFUL PRIVATISATION

This is a long and complex process. Three separate strands of activity can be identified: legal and constitutional changes; re-orienting a company's business, systems, and management towards the private sector; and selling a company. The necessary steps may take 2-3 years to complete and tight central control and co-ordination is necessary if a series of sales is to be completed.

An important initial task is to identify candidates, to ascertain what changes are necessary if they are to operate as successful private businesses, and to decide how and when they should be sold. Although some 'window-dressing' may be desirable, it is a foolish vendor who creates a company whose performance is not sustainable. It is possible that a company would get away with this ploy once, but not twice! The credibility of the programme must be established early on if momentum is to be sustained and investor interest generated. This points to doing the easiest sales first (e.g. selling companies trading on the fringes of the public sector, which already have the necessary private-sector orientation. To take industries out of the heart of the public sector and to re-orient them is a lengthy process. For example, preparing the water and electricity industries for total privatisation will take over 3 years, despite all the skills available in the UK.

THE PRICE RIGHT?

Having determined in outline terms the method of sale and its structure, those conducting the privatisation will, at some point, need to advise the vendor on likely proceeds and, in due course (unless a competitive auction is held) to set a price. A competitive auction will mean that a demonstrably fair market price is obtained but this is not always as clear-cut as might be expected. As well as naming a price, bidders will often hedge it around with various conditions which may or may not be easy to value. If the management of the company concerned are participating themselves in the bidding process, the prospective bidder might be concerned that the management have an unfair advantage and thus may not want to bid. If management do bid, but are unsuccessful, the result might be demoralisation and a damaged business. In some cases, management teams taking part in a competitive auction are given a defined price preference (say 5 per cent), and this may cause a non-management prospective bidder to wonder whether this justifies the time and expense of making a bid.

Pricing a privatisation of shares is never easy, especially if there are not market analogues already in existence. Conventional pricing techniques in tne London market normally involved establishing likely earnings (e.g. the profit attributable to future shareholders), and applying a multiple to these earnings based on a review of analogues tempered by a judgement of likely investor perceptions. Traditionally, there is an understanding that a well-judged flotation will go to an immediate after-market premium of 10-15 per cent. Where no analogues are available, a certain amount of imaginative thinking will be needed. Provided a reasonably secure stream of dividends can be identified, a yield-based valuation can sometimes provide a useful insight. Techniques such as the Capital Asset Pricing Model or the Dividend Discount Model are rarely robust enough to be of any use, disappointing though this might be to business-school graduates.

With a conventional offer for sale on the London Stock Exchange, the price is fixed at the beginning of the offer period and investors thus know what price they will pay for the shares if any are obtained. If, with the benefit of hindsight, the set price proves to be wrong, the vendor (or the underwriters) will suffer. In contrast, the tender offer allows the market to set the price. A minimum tender price is laid down and investors tender for shares at that price, or whatever higher price they would be prepared to pay.

The price at which the vendor decides to clear the offer is known as the striking price, which is generally the common price paid by all investors. This is then determined in light of the subscriptions. In order to get a band wagon going, which is an essential feature of a successful tender, the minimum tender price has to be set low enough to attract the market and this price will generally be lower than would be achieved in a fixed price offer. The tender will be underwritten at the minimum tender price; this is, of course, good news for the underwriters. If the tender is successful, higher eventual proceeds might be obtained for the vendor but at some penalty to the after-market.

The problems with a tender are twofold: it requires not only that prospective investors make a judgement about whether or not they wish to buy the share, but also that they decide what price to pay. This added complexity tends to discourage amateur investors and the method is not therefore suited for shares which are intended to have a wide popular appeal. The apparent accuracy in pricing which results also tends to deflate the performance of shares in the after-market and this discourages speculative buying. Although this may appear desirable, a certain amount of excitement and market interest is always necessary, as boring sales are rarely successful.

It may be rational for a vendor conducting a series of sales to seek to maximise advantage over a period of time rather than in relation to individual sales. In practice, if a government is planning a series of sales, it is unlikely to be in its interest to price a privatisation issue to the last penny, if by so doing the risks of the offer failing are materially increased. The single offer will be achieved in these circumstances but the rest are likely to suffer disproportionately.

IS IT A PROPER UNDERWRITING RISK?

One of the marginal consequences of the 1987 BP sale, apart from securing for the United Kingdom Treasury a guaranteed stream of privatisation revenue over the next 3 financial years, is that it has brought to the fore the role of the underwriter in the London market - a role in the past which has not been well understood by vendors and even by some underwriters themselves.

The underwriting process in London generally works as follows. An issuing house, or group of houses, ('the lead underwriters') enter into a binding agreement to acquire, in certain circumstances, a number of shares at a given price.

On behalf of the bank, brokers to the issue then lay off that risk to a greater or lesser extent by passing it on to a group of so-called 'sub-underwriters' who are prospective long-term holders of the shares (e.g. pension-fund managers). The issuing house then offers the shares to investors; if the shares are not taken up, they then pass to the sub-underwriters. In a typical private-sector transaction, the lead underwriter is paid a commission of 0.5 per cent, the broker 0.25 per cent, and the sub-underwriter 1.25 per cent.

The government in the UK has been successful in driving down underwriting commission rates for privatisation in the London market to a level where a dispassionate observer could conclude that the transactions were effectively risk-free and thus not worth underwriting. As part of this process, the 1985 sale of Cable and Wireless shares, which Schroders conducted for the government, introduced the first-ever underwriting competition to the London market. The price of the shares on offer was set by the government, and lead underwriters were invited to bid - to underwrite the offer at whatever commission they considered appropriate. At the time, this was seen as an extremely radical development and led to the lead underwriters' commission being reduced to 0.2625 per cent (the lowest ever achieved).

Having held one competition, the government, understandably got a taste for more. The circle of banks invited to participate was progressively widened and some banks thought that bidding low for what they thought was a risk-free transaction was a cheap way of acquiring the prestige that seemed to be associated with having their name on the front page of the prospectus. One eventual consequence of this driving down of rates was that the commission paid to the lead underwriters for the BP sale amounted to the princely sum of £18,000 per £100 million pound of risk insured. When the world's biggest ever share sale coincided with the world's biggest ever slump in share prices, it is no wonder that some houses squealed that this was not 'a proper underwriting risk' and sought to have the underwriting agreement terminated. If it had been, the future underwriting of privatisation issues would clearly not have been justifiable, and the City of London's reputation as a financial centre would have been damaged.

The imprudent behaviour of some finance houses on the BP sale (in assuming a greater risk than they were prepared to stand by) raises the question of whether the vendor and its advisers were prudent in adopting the offer structure that they did. It also brings to the fore the inherent conflict that exists between a merchant bank acting as both adviser to government and as lead underwriter. At times of extreme tension, no man can happily serve two masters and it is very probable that the roles of adviser and underwriter in future British privatisation will be split, as is now being done in some major forthcoming European privatisations. Advisers' remuneration will need to be adjusted accordingly.

ACHIEVING SUCCESS

What makes a successful privatisation is not easy to define. An after-market premium is a good thing, provided that it is not too large. Millions of shareholders are desirable, provided that their applications are not so sealed-down in terms of shares distributed per person as to be meaningless. Overseas sales are welcome if they make the domestic offering 'successful'. In practice, demand for privatised equity can be categorised as follows: employees' demand; domestic retail demand (i.e. from the general public); domestic institutional demand; and overseas institutional demand.

Unless the domestic institutions (e.g. pension funds and insurance companies) are keen to participate, the sale is unlikely to be achievable. Yet, if their participation is too great, the political benefits of spreading ownership amongst employees and the general public will be lost. Additionally, in an efficient capital market such as London, little is to be gained by establishing a 'round-table' core of investors as has been done in France (the 'noyau dur'). Selecting such a favoured group is a recipe for political and other antagonisms. The ideal is an offer structure which segments the sale into defined portions and attempts to keep the element of unsatisfied demand in each portion, particularly amongst the domestic institutions (who are the most likely buyers in the after-market if left short of sales). The general public may like shares, but what they want are shares which go to a premium. The right answer is complicated by the fact that the only demand which matters is that which manifests itself in applications for the shares which are to be sold.

Even using sophisticated market research techniques, this demand is very hard to predict in advance and thus an offer structure is needed which is flexible enough in its allocation across segments to cope with changes in the anticipated demand. We developed a method of doing this, called 'flexible clawback', which involves allocating shares provisionally to institutions at the beginning of the offer period, thus creating a perceived shortage, promoting demand in the retail sector, then 'clawing back' the shares that had been provisionally placed with institutions, depending on the demand that materialises in the retail sector in order to reallocate them to the retail sector.

Another innovation has been the 'partial tender', whereby shares are offered at a fixed price to the retail sector but with a margin tendered to institutions who bid, and pay, whatever price they choose, provided it is at or above the fixed retail price. This technique both promotes wider share ownership (through making the retail offer as simple as possible) and increases marginal proceeds for the vendor (albeit with some effect on the immediate after-market).

CAPITAL-MARKET EFFECTS

Privatisations are an order of magnitude greater than previously-contemplated transactions and this has led to profound capital-market effects. Two main positive impacts can be distinguished: privatisation can lead to a widening of the capital market by introducing new investors both domestic and international; and it can lead to a deepening of the market by introducing mature companies with a strong market position.

Both these effects, which are inter-related, are clearly advantageous. As an illustration of the first effect, privatisation in the UK has clearly led to personal savings being switched into the stock market from other forms of investment. The sale of British Telecom in 1984 was the first privatisation anywhere in the world specifically designed to have widespread popular appeal. Prior to this, there were many who doubted that the British general public could be taught to buy shares via privatisation. The proportion of shares owned by the general public was decreasing, so attracting even 50,000 people to a privatisation offer was reckoned to be good going. Yet the British Telecom sale attracted around 2.2 million applicants, about half of whom had never before owned shares.

How was this done? The British Telecom sale was five times larger than any sale that had previously been attempted and was the first to be marketed on a wide scale to the general public. It had been clear for some time that existing share-selling techniques were not capable of creating a new breed of shareowners. Stockbrokers generally were happiest selling shares to their existing clients and, in consequence, if shares were to be sold widely, new distribution channels needed to be created. The vendor would have to go over the heads of the normal intermediaries both by motivating a more lively salesforce than traditional stockbrokers and by selling direct to prospective shareholders. No vendor was more suited than the government to take on the challenge.

Why was it so popular? British Telecom combined features of both a utility and a high-technology business which made it ideally suited to inexperienced shareholders. The sale was advertised widely in both the press and television, and generous commissions were paid to financial intermediaries. At the government's expense, small shareholders were given the added attraction of a one-for-ten free loyalty bonus issue of shares if they held their shares for more than three years, or alternatively, were given discounts on their telephone bills. The sale captured the public's imagination, proved with the benefit of hindsight to be significantly under-priced, and was both a popular and political success. It marked the emergence of popular capitalism in the UK and showed that the largest privatisation, if properly handled, could be successfully absorbed by the capital market. Prior to the sale of British Telecom £500 million raised in a single transaction was reckoned to be a fair price. The British Telecom sale raised nearly £4,000 million, paid by instalments over a 3-year period.

Privatisation can deepen as well as widen a country's capital market. This arises because often it is the dominant businesses that were previously nationalised and brought into state ownership. They were brought into the state sector because of their position in the economy, their strategic importance, or their size and market dominance. It is these very characteristics which, on privatisation, enable them to give depth to a stock market and to provide ballast to what may have otherwise been an unduly speculative environment. The experience of the UK and other countries is that privatisation - contrary to the original expectations of economists and others - can create its own market capacity. There are a number of reasons for this.

First, the equity that is being sold is normally of good quality and represents an attractive investment opportunity. Purchasers gain comfort from the fact that the vendor is a government and have learnt by experience that governments are risk-averse when it comes to privatisations. Success is valued highly, which is no wonder, given privatisation's invariably high profile.

Second, a government that is raising finance by selling equities will borrow less for a given public sector financial deficit than it would do otherwise. A government's total demand on the capital market may therefore be unchanged by a privatisation programme. The equity of utilities that hold a dominant market share, either via operating a natural monopoly or otherwise, can closely resemble debt in its financial characteristics and thus may be accommodated in that portion of an investor's portfolio previously reserved for fixed-income securities.

Third, and this point is often overlooked, even a single privatisation may create a company that is a material component of a stock market's index. Those investors who attempt to match their portfolios to the main constituents of a country's capital market must buy privatised equity if they are to maintain their relative position. Some privatised equity - for example, that of a national electricity or telecommunications equity - also gives good exposure to the totality of economic development in a particular country and this may be valued by an investor.

Fourth, it should also be remembered that governments who are selling equity become interested in the operations of the equity market and, implicitly or explicitly, take steps to strengthen the market. Traditionally, of course, governments only operated in the debt market whereas the equity market tended to be left to market practitioners. This is now no longer the case in countries which are pursuing successful privatisation policies. It is also true that the same political philosophy, which produces privatisation is also likely to encourage market liberalisation and deregulation. Privatisation and the growth of London as an international financial centre have gone hand in hand.

Despite the large proceeds raised from privatisation sales in the UK in the last 5 years, the total net issues of ordinary shares in London have reached record levels. It is clear that despite the heavy demands that privatisation has placed on the London market, private issuers have not suffered. New capital-raising has reached record levels. There has been no crowding-out of private investment by government sales and this is important if the overall success of a privatisation policy is to be maximised.

In order to achieve capital market benefits, a sophisticated marketing programme must be created to maximise interest from all classes of investors. This will normally be extremely cost-effective. Not only can such a campaign benefit the proceeds and commercial image of the company that is being sold but it can also provide an opportunity to project a country's general economic development and financial status. Many countries would like to have a privatisation programme. Few can assemble sufficient determination, expertise, and credibility to achieve one.

PROTECTING THE NATIONAL INTEREST

The significance of some of the companies which have been sold by the UK and other governments was such that privatisation would not have been possible if steps had not been taken to secure the national interest. Determining the national interest has to be done on a case-by-case basis but in some cases the government has required certain stipulations (e.g. a company's continued independence to be guaranteed, chief executives to be British, and foreign ownership to be restricted in companies where defence or security interests are at stake). In the case of natural monopolies which have been privatised, it has been important also to ensure that customers' interests are fully protected.

It has proved possible to build in safeguards to protect these important requirements in ways that are fully compatible with United Kingdom and European law. No special legal framework has needed to be created in order to do this. Where necessary, specific restrictions have been written into privatised companies' Articles of Association and, in order to ensure that these restrictions cannot be varied after privatisation, a 'special' or 'golden' share has been created to protect those Articles regarded as essential. These special shares, which are similar in virtually all respects to a single £1 share in the companies, carry no rights other than in relation to the specified Articles. They are held by the relevant minister and the practical effect is that the protected Articles cannot be changed in future except with the government's consent. It is a technique which has since been copied by other countries world-wide. The privatisation of 'natural monopolies' such as domestic telecommunications, gas, electricity distribution, and water services, would not be possible without the development of specific regulatory regimes designed to encourage efficient operations and protect customers from exploitation. Licensing systems have been developed that aim to encourage competition where this is practical and, by imposing controls on prices, to increase productive efficiency. Licensing requirements or specific subsidy arrangements may also impose specific social obligations on companies. For example, British Telecom is required by its licence to maintain the Fire, Policy, and Ambulance emergency free-dialling service and to provide rural phone-services and call-boxes. These services are then cross-subsidised by British Telecom's other services and are the quid pro quo for British Telecom being allowed to run a monopoly.

PRIVATISATIONS ARE NOT JUST
FINANCIAL TRANSACTIONS

Privatisations are unlike all other financial transactions. The differences arise because of size, political sensitivities, investor interest, and the complexity of privatisation's objectives. In summary, the UK privatisation programme has been successful because the critical participants in the programme were identified early on and dealt with in the most satisfactory fashion. Key groups normally include the following: the general public as taxpayers, customers and voters; the employees of the firm being privatised; the management of the firm being privatised; prospective investors; commentators and opponents of privatisation.

Fair pricing (which balances the needs of the taxpayer and the investor), voucher offers for customers, free shares for employees (not least to negate Trade Union opposition), retaining the privatised company's corporate structure, widespread distribution of shares, full disclosure of information, and careful attention to detail, may all be necessary if a successful sale is to be achieved. In political terms, few policies can claim the benefit of privatisation and be so attractively presented in terms of privatisation's ability to increase industrial efficiency, raise money, boost ownership amongst employees and the wider general public, and carry domestic as well as international prestige. Provided the relevant interested groups are clearly identified at an early stage, and are satisfied, everybody seems to win.

What lessons are to be learned from all this? First, privatisations are not merely financial transactions, and opportunities will be lost if they are treated as such. Second, the case for the programme must be argued effectively and enthusiastically. Third, involving employees and the general public to the greatest possible extent not only helps provide market capacity but can create genuine popular success. This is, of course, only the beginning of the process and for privatisation to be a long-term phenomenon, not just the sales but the companies which are created must be successful. Only time will tell to what extent this will be achieved.

4

Privatisation: Modalities and Strategy

John Heath*

COUNTRY EXPERIENCES

In all countries there appear to have been two distinct phases in the development of state enterprises. In the first phase, most commonly there has been an initial period when wholesale nationalisation and the growth of state enterprises were seen as being politically appropriate, usually as the best way to bring about economic development and growth. This was sometimes associated with the achievement of independence from a colonial power. The second phase was the realisation that major problems had arisen in the management of state owned enterprises - problems of efficiency and of technological change which led to major financial crises. In most countries these became so severe and so threatening to government finances that something had to be done. There is a new phase today - privatisation. However, there are differences among countries because political attitudes vary widely and because of cultural factors.

The range of stated problems experienced by developing countries can be summarised as follows:

1. 'A private sector which is not thought to be behaving well' (not in accordance with national plans for example) (e.g. India, Pakistan).
2. 'Inadequate or no capital market' (e.g. Pakistan, Jordan).

* Formerly Professor of Economics at London Business School and Member of the British Airports Authority

3. 'The problem of accumulated losses' especially where there are foreign loans involved (e.g. Pakistan, Ghana).
4. 'Too many permits and controls' - such as investment sanctioning procedures, access to foreign exchange, or price control (e.g. Pakistan, India).
5. 'Obligations carried through to the private sector' (e.g. Ghana where employees of state-owned enterprises who are declared redundant may be entitled to 10 years' salary).
6. 'Inappropriate requirements' (e.g. the requirement in Jamaica that a significant part of the price of hotels being privatised should be paid in foreign exchange was thought to have been a factor in the privatisation failure; in Pakistan enterprises must first be offered to their former owners).
7. 'Public enterprises became the most important instrument of economic policy' (e.g. India).
8. 'Constitutional and legal issues' (e.g. India, Malaysia, Ghana, Nigeria).
9. 'Absence of political will' (e.g. China, Ethiopia, Peru).
10. 'The absence of an appropriate framework of commercial law' (e.g. Mauritania).
11. 'Market miscalculations' (e.g. in Jamaica, the Cement offering was thought to have been less than fully successful for this reason).
12. 'Depressed state of the economy and a current unfavourable climate for foreign investment' (e.g. Jordan).
13. 'Minister, managers, unions or employees may be in opposition to privatisation (one or more groups) (e.g. Pakistan, Nigeria, Kenya, Jordan).
14. 'Cumbersome and bureaucratic procedures to achieve the sale of a public enterprise (e.g. Pakistan).
15. 'Lack of systematic information about public sector enterprises (e.g. India, Malaysia, Ghana).
16. 'Previous attempts at privatisation were unsuccessful' (e.g. Ghana).
17. 'Conceptual lack of clarity about the issue of privatisation' (e.g. Peru, and earlier in Ghana).

MODALITIES OF PRIVATISATION

The range of opportunities for privatisation is very wide. This is well illustrated in Chapter 1 of this book (see Figure 1.1 on p.5 and Appendix 1). Three categories of privatisation were identified in Chapter 1: ownership measures; organisational measures; and operational measures.

In this chapter I comment on the principal opportunities and discuss the question of choice. Broadly one can think of a range of privatisation opportunities in terms of the degree of ownership, control, management or operations which is foregone by the government.

First, privatisation can operate at many levels. The lowest form of privatisation may involve no more than introducing good business practice in state enterprises through the engagement of a manager or a consultant from the private sector. This is probably the lowest boundary of the term 'privatisation'. Only a slightly higher level might involve minor operations being undertaken by the private sector - cleaning or catering in a state organisation, for example. AT the other extreme, the highest level of privatisation would be the sale of 100 per cent of the equity in an enterprise to private sector purchasers with no special powers over it being retained by the government. (General powers over the private sector, through companies' legislation for example, would be unaffected.) Ownership, control, management, and operations would be entirely given up by the government.

There are also many intermediate levels. For example: contracting out the management of a whole enterprise; contracting out the management and operations of a major activity, such as street cleaning in Kingston, Jamaica; the sale of a minority of the equity in a state enterprise to private sector purchasers (in all such cases ownership and control would be retained by the state); ownership might be foregone through the sale of equity but some special controls retained, through a regulatory body, such as the Office of Telecommunications in relation to that industry in the UK. While there is, therefore, a broad sense of a range of privatisation modalities, there is no smooth continuum. Indeed there can be combinations of measure relating to ownership, control, management and operations.

Moreover, for communication purposes, 'privatisation' has political overtones of capitalism which in some countries may inhibit the development of policies which favour market and competitive solutions to the problems of state enterprise. 'Marketisation' may be a more politically neutral term, or the notion of a 'public enterprise reform programme', as described in Chapter 16. In any event, it is important for clarity of communication to describe in appropriate terms what is being meant.

Second, there are different <u>degrees of change</u>, comparing the level of private sector involvement at a starting point with that at the finish. There is no easy way of measuring these levels, especially where there are combinations of factors, and there is probably little point in trying.

Third, privatisation can be <u>undertaken in stages</u>. Lower-level changes can be introduced first, experience gained, and if the results are satisfactory, more radical changes can then be made. For example, some shares can be sold, to test the market and to learn about the appropriate share price. A management contract may prepare the enterprise for complete privatisation, through improving its profitability and therefore its attractiveness to the market. A privatisation programme can thus be developed and modified with experience.

This wide breadth of choice suggests the need for a policy on privatisation, especially where the government holds a large portfolio of enterprises. Such a policy would be a political act of considerable importance. The first stage in developing a policy would be to define the government's <u>aim or purpose</u>. Why is privatisation being considered? What are its hoped-for consequencies? By way of example, the latest proposal for privatisation in the UK relating to the electricity supply industry may be cited. In a White Paper in February 1988 the government stated its specific aims as follows:

1. Decisions about the supply of electricity should be driven by the needs of customers.
2. Competition is the best guarantee of the customers' interests.
3. Regulation should be designed to promote competition, oversee prices and protect the customers' interests in areas where natural monopoly will remain.
4. Security and safety of supply must be maintained.
5. Customers should be given new rights, not just safeguards.
6. All who work in the industry should be offered a direct

stake in their future, new career opportunities and the freedom to manage their commercial affairs without interference from government.

In effect, the government is proposing to replace the discipline on management imposed by the Department of Energy with (1) the discipline of the market where competition can be introduced, and (2) the discipline of a separate regulatory body (to be called 'The Office of Electricity Supply') where monopoly will remain. Competition will be introduced in two ways: by splitting the Central Electricity Generating Board into two separate generating companies, with a separate company to manage the National Grid, and by encouraging the developing of private sector power stations. The notion of 'success' in privatisation should refer to achieving these ultimate aims. Generally, however, success is seen in terms of achieving the transfer to the private sector - 'a successful flotation' - and these two aspects should be distinguished.

THE NEED FOR A STRATEGY

The next stage would be to formulate an explicit strategy for the development of privatisation, identifying the criteria of choice, setting priorities, drawing up a programme and a timetable. Many countries had started the process with a high level government committee of inquiry which produced a rationale for privatisation and criteria for selection, as the basis of political commitment (the clearest examples are in Pakistan, Kenya, Ghana, Nigeria, and Malaysia. Generally, these gave high priority to loss-making enterprises while reserving to the public sector enterprises variously described as 'commanding heights', 'core industries', 'apex industries', or those 'essential for public welfare'. They had the lowest priorities for privatisation. Generally the public utilities were in this category.

A committee of inquiry has a different function from a committee of implementation , although the former group may be made responsible for the latter function also. Implementing privatisation is a highly specialist activity, and to be successful many different experts will be needed. Some may be consultants with experience in privatisations elsewhere. In order to learn the lessons of experience there has to be information collected systematically and analysed.

122

A strategy or privatisation by stages will depend upon suitable feedback from earlier endeavours.

In terms of where to start, circumstances vary so much that only general statements can be made. The first suggestion would be to start with the easiest situations - for example, enterprises where the state has only a minority share ownership and where there are willing buyers. The second suggestion would be to start with situations where privatisation is likely to be able to demonstrate success. These might be situations where there are already well run state enterprises and co-existing private-sector companies, such that extra competition would be beneficial. But the privatised companies must operate under exactly the same rules and obligations as those already in the private sector. They must not receive special low-interest loans (for example, to help them be successful), nor must they be required to employ their existing workforce. The third suggestion would be to endeavour to create a competitive situation. Privatisation by itself may do very little: competition has the most powerful impact. So there may have to be structural adjustments - splitting a large company into several parts, for example - prior to privatisation itself. Leaving this until after privatisation may be too late.

Having said that, the impact of privatisation even in a monopoly should not be underestimated if there is effective leadership at the top to commercialise the organisation and to take advantage of new opportunities. It is crucial to ensure that the leadership in the privatised organisation, especially the personal qualities of the chairman and the chief executive, is of the best. Poor leadership will not lead to the benefits which privatisation should, in principle, provide. It is also important to avoid being too ambitious. Any high-level privatisation, if it is to be successful, is complex and time-consuming. In the UK, the least satisfactory schemes, from a public interest point of view, were those which were rushed - the privatisation of British Gas is an example. If the circumstances are clearly not right it may be better to wait.

Given the wide scope of state ownership in some countries and the enormous number of enterprises which could in principle be privatised, and given that some enterprises are considered unsuitable for privatisation, many countries will continue to have a state enterprise sector for many years. Alongside privatisation, therefore, there should

123

be policies to improve the performance of state enterprises. If such policies were successful, governments would then have an option: continue holding these enterprises in the public sector, or privatise them. With improved performance through the commercialisation of state enterprises and in other ways, privatisation would not only be easier but also more successful. So, improving the performance of state enterprises could also be seen as part of their preparation for privatisation.

5

Introducing Competition and Regulatory Requirements

David Thompson*

A government which plans to privatise a public enterprise faces two important policy questions which must be determined prior to the more proximate issues (e.g. financial restructuring) concerned with the sale:

(a) Should the competitive structure of the industry be re-shaped?
(b) Should the newly privatised firm be regulated?

In some cases, the answers to these questions will be straightforward. Where the enterprise operates in markets which already have a significant number of competitors (domestic or international) then there will generally be no public policy advantage in continued regulation of the firm; market forces can be relied upon to regulate its operations. In the UK, the privatisation of National Freight provides a good example. This was a loss-making subsidiary of the public-sector British Rail. It operated in the highly competitive road-haulage market. Privatisation - achieved through management buy-out - has been followed by significantly improved performance. In many cases, however, the privatisation candidate will be a monopoly supplier. The privatisation strategy will need to consider whether the monopoly should be kept intact - or whether the enterprise's markets should be liberalised. The question of how to regulate the privatised monopoly will also require consideration.

* Formerly of the Institute for Fiscal Studies

COMPETITION AND REGULATION

Most economists are agreed upon the important role which competitive markets play in inducing enterprises to operate efficiently. The theory of competitive markets shows that, under familiar conditions, both productive and allocative efficiency are achieved: allocative efficiency - supplying a range of goods and services which match consumers preferences at prices which reflect the costs of supply; and productive efficiency - supplying goods and services at minimum efficient cost.

The theory is supported by empirical experience, which has analysed the introduction of competition into markets where previously it has prohibited, and has compared the experience of otherwise similar markets, in some of which competition is restricted and in some of which it is not (for reviews, see: Bailey, 1986; Millward, 1982; Yarrow, 1986; and Domberger and Piggott, 1986). Policy initiatives in the UK provide some recent examples. The liberalisation of long distance ('express') coach services prompted significant reductions in fares, and improvements in the quality and frequency of services (see Jaffer and Thompson, 1986). The introduction of competitive tendering for refuse collection in some parts of the UK has resulted in cost levels which are 20 per cent lower (when the characteristics of each area and the type of service provided are standardised) compared with areas where tendering has not been introduced (see Domberger et al., 1986).

However, there are significant constraints which may prevent the introduction of competition in sectors where public enterprises operate. These constraints may be economic, political or institutional in nature. Economic constraints arise because, typically, these are sectors where the conditions which underpin the theory of competitive markets do not hold; in other words, these are sectors which are subject to market failure. This assessment suggests that the tasks of regulation can be divided into two parts: promoting competition where it is feasible; and preventing the abuse of monopoly power where it is not. This characterisation is clearly over-simplified and, in practice, the two tasks overlap. The first involves identification of the economic constraints on competition and the development of policies to minimise their effect. The second task involves identification of the potential abuses of market power and the formulation of regulatory controls to inhibit these abuses.

THE ECONOMIC CONSTRAINTS ON THE INTRODUCTION OF COMPETITION:

These can usefully be divided into three types. Probably the most important is the existence of natural monopoly. Natural monopoly arises where the technology of production in an industry means that production is carried out most efficiently by a single firm. The distribution networks for gas, electricity, and water are all relevant examples. In the case of many natural monopolies, a potential entrant to the market will face significant 'sunk' (i.e. irrecoverable) costs of entering the market. In these circumstances, the possibility of competitors entering the market is sufficiently remote, even where entry is not statutorily prohibited, and the threat of entry will not be sufficient to induce incumbents to operate efficiently; in other words, the natural monopoly is not 'contestable'. It can be noted, in passing, that this is not true of all natural monopolies; for example, a network of airline services may be provided most efficiently by a single supplier. However, the sunk costs of entry may be sufficiently low that the single incumbent is constrained from acting monopolistically by the threat of entry by airlines operating adjacent networks. This possibility underlies the current debate on the wave of airline mergers in the USA which has followed deregulation (see Levine, 1987, for an extensive discussion).

The second group of constraints arises where there is a divergence between the private interest which competitive markets achieve and the public good. This might arise where there are important benefits or costs which are external to the private decision maker; environmental pollution and traffic congestion are two relevant examples. Or importance may be placed on ensuring that the less well-off are able to afford particular commodities; energy and housing are particular examples.

The third group of constraints is one common to all competitive markets. In general, a firm's self-interest is best served by restricting competition - through collusion with rivals, the take-over of competitors or discouraging market entrants - rather than by its enhancement. The machinery of competition policy (in the UK, the Office of Fair Trading, the Restrictive Trade Practices Court, and the Monopolies and Mergers Commission) is tasked with the prevention of such anti-competitive action. The particular relevance to privatisation policy is that recently privatised enterprises are likely to be especially powerful competitors - by virtue of their established status - and the containment of anti-competitive action is likely to prove even more difficult than in other sectors of the industrial economy (see Thompson, 1988, for a discussion in relation to the de-regulated market for express coaching in the UK).

Minimising Competitive Constraints

The existence of natural monopoly, where this is associated with high entry costs, is a powerful constraint on the introduction of competition. Typically, however, natural monopoly is characteristic of only a part of the activities of a public enterprise. The electricity supply industry provides a good example. The <u>distribution</u> of power has obvious characteristics of natural monopoly; however, this is far less clearly the case for the <u>production</u> of power, whilst the sale and maintenance of electric appliances is clearly a competitive activity. Nevertheless, whilst this latter market is indeed competitive in the UK, with participation by the public sector electric companies, the first two activities have, until recently, both been statutory public sector monopolies.

The policy response which this immediately suggests is the separation of natural monopoly and potentially competitive activities. This raises several difficult issues, however. Typically, there will be reasonable claims that economies of scope exist between the activities in question (i.e. that they are provided more efficiently in combination by a single supplier). How far should these scope economies be sacrificed in order to enhance competition? How adversely will competition be inhibited if the activities are not separated? These questions can be seen to underlie an important part of the UK privatisation debate (e.g. in relation to the restructuring of the electricity industry upon privatisation or in relation to British Airways' take-over of its main UK rival - British Caledonian).

The existence of external benefits and costs, or of distributional concerns, provides a less serious constraint on the introduction of competition. In many cases, a policy solution will be provided by an appropriately designed tax or subsidy, or by the implementation of regulatory standards which specify required qualities of the product, or which require the provision of information to consumers. For example, concern to ensure the provision of public transport services to remote rural areas (where demand, and hence profit opportunities, are low) could be reflected in the suppression of a market in public transport to allow the provision of unprofitable services. Effectively, this was the UK policy up to 1986. An alternative approach, implemented through the de-regulation of bus services in 1986, would be to hold competitive tenders to operate loss-making routes at minimum public subsidy.

Anti-competitive action by incumbent firms is, as already noted, a policy concern common to many sectors of the industrial economy. Particular advantages which have benefited incumbents in recently deregulated markets in the UK are:

(a) a product name established in the regulated area;
(b) a vertical integration of deregulated activities with other activities where the sunk costs of entry are high; and
(c) financial strength arising from the common ownership of deregulated activities and activities where competition is limited.

In many cases, the latter two advantages flow from the common ownership of natural monopoly and potentially competitive activities (although this is not always the case, as is illustrated by express-coach deregulation). Again, the policy solution which this immediately suggests is the separation of ownership; this again raises questions on foregone economies of scope and the significance of common ownership in inhibiting competition.

REGULATING MONOPOLY

However successfully the first task of regulation - promoting competition - is carried out, there will remain many areas of monopoly. The objective of regulating the possible abuse of monopoly can perhaps best be thought of as an attempt to mimic the outcome which would result were competition to be feasible; In other words: preventing prices being raised above costs to monopoly levels; preventing sub-standard service levels being provided; preventing inefficient cost performance.

The most extensive experience with the regulation of private utilities arises in the US, where private ownership in sectors, (such as water, gas, and electricity) is common. The weaknesses of the typical method of regulation - rate-base or rate-of-return regulation - are familiar. Rate-of-return regulation puts a ceiling on the prices which the monopoly utility is allowed to charge each year; the ceiling is computed so as to cover the utility's costs and to provide for a fair rate-of-return on capital. This regulatory tool is evidently effective in preventing prices being raised above costs; but it is apparent that it is ineffective in securing efficient cost performance. Effectively, management has no incentive to improve performance; whatever action is taken, the utility's profits will be no greater (nor less) than the 'fair' return on capital. Furthermore, because profits are constrained to a specified rate of return on assets, there is an incentive toward over-capitalised methods of production. Empirical analysis of rate-base regulated utilities has shown that these weaknesses in incentives are reflected in poor performance in practice. (Averch and Johnson, 1962, provided the classic analysis of rate-of-return regulation; Crew and Kleindorfer, 1979, provide a more recent survey).

The perceived weaknesses of rate-of-return regulation have led to a search for more effective methods. In the UK, the recently privatised utilities - British Telecom, British Gas, and the British Airports Authority (BAA) - are all subject to a similar regulatory framework. Central to this is what has become known as the 'RPI-X formula'. Developed by Professor Stephen Littlechild to regulate British Telecom (BT), the formula places a ceiling on the prices charged by the utility (or a designated bundle of what are regarded as its monopoly activities) over a period of 5 years. During this period, the prices of the bundle of products can be increased by an amount which is not greater than the increase in the Retail Price Index less X per cent. The value of X in the formula is specified in relation to the anticipated scope for reduction in real costs over the 5-year period. In the case of British Telecom, X has been set at 3; in the case of British Gas, at 2; and in BAA at 1. The differing values of X reflect the different impact of technological change in each sector as well as perceptions on the scope for productivity improvements.

In principle, the RPI-X formula overcomes the adverse incentives associated with rate-base regulation. Under the RPI-X formula any enterprise which is able to out-perform expectations over the 5-year period, is able to retain the additional margin of profits, whilst an enterprise which

130

underperforms would be expected to have a poor profit record. Associated with the RPI-X formulae in each industry are statutory provisions which prohibit the charging of excessive or predatory prices for individual products <u>within</u> the overall RPI-X ceiling. These provisions apply equally to the more competitive products not governed by the formula. In each sector, a specific regulatory authority is tasked with overseeing compliance with the formula and implementing the statutory provisions precluding anti-competitive pricing.

The proper test of whether the RPI-X framework proves a more successful method than rate-base regulation will lie in the performance of newly privatised enterprises. It is too early yet to reach even a preliminary verdict, but there are some areas of concern.The effectiveness of the RPI-X approach will be determined both by whether the value of X can be set independently of the enterprise's actual performance record, and whether, in this case, under-performance results in sanction in the capital markets. The near-monopoly status and associated financial strength of BT, British Gas, and BAA do not give strong grounds for optimism on either count.

One potential policy solution is horizontal divestment analogous to the break-up of AT&T in the United States. This would provide for competitive sources of information to both regulators and shareholders, and would reduce the financial commitment of a hostile acquirer to more manageable proportions (See Vickers and Yarrow, 1985, for a discussion). However, horizontal divestment clearly raises the issue of whether significant economies of scope would be foregone.

REFERENCES

Averch, H. and Johnson, L. (1962) 'Behaviour of the firm under regulatory constraint', <u>American Economic Review</u> 52, 1052-69.

Bailey, E.E. (1986) 'Price and Productivity change following de-regulation: the US experience', <u>Economic Journal</u>, March.

Crew, M.A. and Kleindorfer, R. (1979) <u>Public Utility</u> Economics, London: Macmillan.

Domberger, S., Meadowcroft, S.A. and Thompson, D.J. (1986) 'Competitive tendering and efficiency: the case of refuse collection', <u>Fiscal Studies</u>, 7 (4) 69-87.

Domberger, S. and Piggot, J. (1986) 'Privatisation policies and public enterprise: a survey' Economic Record 62, 145-162.

Jaffer, S.M. and Thompson, D.J. (1986) 'De-regulating express coaches: a re-assessment', Fiscal Studies, 7 (4).

Levine, M.E. (1987) 'Airline competition in de-regulated markets: theory, firm strategy, and public policy', Yale Journal on Regulation.

Littlechild, S.C. (1983) Regulation of British Tele-communications' Profitability, London: Department of Industry.

Millward, R. (1982) 'The Comparative Performance of Public and Private Enterprise' in Lord Roll (ed.) The Mixed Economy, London: Macmillan.

Thompson, D.J. (1988) 'Privatisation: introducing competition - the opportunities and constraints', in V.V. Ramanadham (ed.) Privatisation in the UK.

Vickers, J. and Yarrow, G. (1985) Privatisation and the Natural Monopolies, London: Public Policy Centre.

Yarrow, G. (1986) 'Privatisation in theory and practice' Economic Policy, 2, 323-64.

6

Some Organisational Implications of Privatisation

Nick Woodward*

COUNTRY EXPERIENCES

Some common themes seem to emerge from the diverse
country experiences in privatisation. But first a word of
caution. There is a tendency, particularly at the macro
level, to use aggregate quantitative indices as measures of
improvement, and as targets - words such as growth,
productivity, foreign exchange earnings, and so on, which
derive from the shorthand of economics and nestle happily
in the reports of aid agencies. but these are surrogate,
though important, measures of social and economic welfare:
growth may be achieved with adverse distributional effects,
productivity at the cost of social cohesion, and so on. The
benefits of economic development need to be carefully
weighed in the context of national or regional cultures.
There may indeed be an inverse relationship between
economic development and cultural development. This is not
an argument against growth or change, only a caution to
look behind and beyond the figures which define growth as a
surrogate measure of economic and social welfare.
    The first common theme that emerges from most
country experiences is a recognition of the 'administrative/
political' constraints deriving from public ownership upon
aspects of enterprise performance. In Chapter 12 Professor
Sheng expresses it well: as an attempt to unfetter the
shackles of a kind of feudal bureaucracy, so as to make
enterprises more responsive to customers, an initiative
consistent with his country's cultural and political
traditions. Aspects of performance, productivity, and
financial viability follow. What is fascinating is that many

* Fellow, Templeton College, Oxford

large private-sector organisations, operating in competitive markets, with shares publicly traded, also have very much the same concern - the need to drive through customer sensitivity, flexibility, and responsiveness to change, under the constraints of organisational inertia. There is something extremely important here about aspects of organisation and management, which goes beyond concern with ownership structures, environmental conditions, and so on.

Second, and related to the first theme, there is a tendency to talk about 'management' as if it were a factor of production - good management skills and techniques. Business schools, particularly those operating in an instrumental US tradition, tend to advertise their capability of transforming students into managers through the acquisition of techniques, skills, and knowledge. Of course these matter. Indeed, one can specify a minimum level of appropriate capability in areas such as marketing, operations management, finance/accounting, and so on, which most commercial organisations would require. But there is a further aspect of organisation which is fundamental, but goes beyond these skills and techniques - the matter of co-ordination and integration, which provides a sense of mission, of purpose, and of common values. If one asks why there has to be 'organisation' and presents a simple model, this will be clear. Organisation is needed, at a fundamental psychological level, to make sense of apparent chaos - the child's organisation of perception, of experience, etc., through learning and education. In the case of social organisation, the benefits of specialisation are acquired by task, by competence, and by knowledge, as eloquently proposed by Adam Smith in the case of pin manufacture. But this specialisation produces differentiation: by function, by status, and by place. If the solution to this separation is seen as a matter of further specialisation by appropriate experts (whether corporate planners, strategists, organisational designers, or even general managers) then one may end up where one started - with organisational chaos, even though this chaos may be structured, orderly, and bureaucratically proper. What is needed is a rebuilding of the roots of organisation, in the sense of common purpose and common task, which is transmitted at the operational level into clarity as to service, quality, and so on - a clarity which drives and unites the organisation, up and down the hierarchy, and across its functional separations. This aspect of 'management' goes far beyond technique. It is particularly important in many state enterprises which are characterised by size, by diversity of function, and by geographical dispersion. In this respect, large private-sector organisations face similar problems. Though a competitive environment may make them more responsive, the challenge of management remains.

The third point is perhaps less abstract, but also points to a common theme. All the presentations seem to recognise that some operations are more saleable than others, and some are more amenable to marketisation than others. This can be expressed graphically, as in Figure 6.1, which suggests that there may be a set of criteria which might guide a privatisation programme.

Figure 6.1: Possible sets of criteria for a privatisation programme

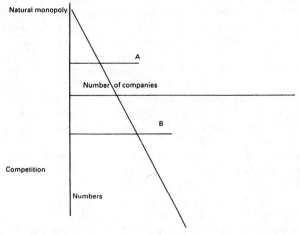

Some activities do not fall naturally under public management, for they are characterised by smallness, freedom of entry, need for local response, change, experimentation - activities such as shops, hotels, small manufacture. At the other extreme, activities with degrees of natural monopoly require some form of regulation, whether legal or structural. There may be different classifications (e.g. between points A and B in Figure 6.1), according to local conditions, and national policy and politics (e.g. banking), but at least Figure 6.1 suggests a classificatory scaling device which might unite many of the presentations and perhaps contribute to our thinking.

FURTHER COMMENTS

The standard model of privatisation as articulated by economic thinking in a western tradition goes something like this. Government, in the form of administrative bureaucrats and of politicians, is bad at running businesses. Therefore, such businesses, in the name of allocative and productive efficiency, must be privatised - subjected to the disciplines of competition, of consumer choice, and of financial discipline mediated through some kind of capital market - and monopolies must be regulated appropriately. This then comes close to some kind of alignment of privatisation with capitalist free-enterprise ideology.

There is evidence of various levels of discontent with the performance of state enterprise. Thus privatisation of street cleaning in Kingston, Jamaica, has been demonstrably successful, and even the most socialist of any subsequent governments would renationalise this activity at its peril - so long as the current arrangement continues to deliver its current levels of service, cost, and effectiveness. Yet we have an opposite case in India of a cartel of tyre manufacturers conspiring to maintain high prices, with subsequent state-inspired initiative to increase competition or counteracting power. Clearly, private enterprise does not ipso facto solve all problems. It was for this reason - deep suspicion of the motives and behaviour of profit-motivated businessmen - that Adam Smith advocated the virtues of competition. It is ironic that one of the institutes in this country which advocates free enterprise - the Adam Smith Institute - brings businessmen together. One of this choleric Scots economist's tags goes like this: 'any two businessmen meeting together will be conspiring against the consumer'. He would have looked askance at an Institute, even in his name, which brought such rapacious fellows together. His advocacy of enterprise was based on concern for the consumer - not for businessmen's interest, and his theoretical work was rooted in a deeply pessimistic view of human nature,

Similarly, but without necessarily echoing Adam Smith's pessimism, one of the issues which unites all the authors in this book is a concern for the consumer, and this concern is translated into a concern for organisations' maintenance of market responsiveness, openness to technological change, and so on. This concern is not ideological in the traditional sense. I illustrate this in Figure 6.2.

136

Figure 6.2: Political ideology and organisational effectiveness

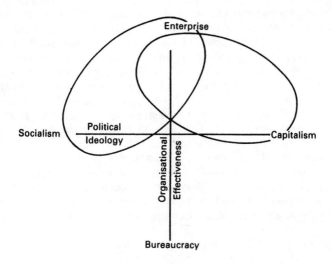

Perhaps the words used in Figure 6.2 are not ideal. We will, however, for want of better words, stick with these, since we would all agree on their connotations as 'ideal-types'. Wherever we, or our governments, appear on a scale of political ideology, we are united in our concern for organisational effectiveness in our enterprise, whether public or private. This then enables us to work on some interesting opposites. One of the dominant themes in the history of UK nationalised industries is government intervention for political purposes, perhaps mediated through Civil Service bureaucracy. There are, typically, fundamental differences between the requirements of political activity and those of running organisations in the sense of getting things done in a consistent and coherent manner. These can be characterised as opposites, as follows:

Politics	Enterprise/Organisation
Concern for short-term	Concern for long-term
Ambiguity	Clarity and consistency
General expressions of policy	Action
Processes	Results

This list is not exhaustive, nor mutually exclusive. Many companies have political activity at the top which shows resemblances to public political activity - particularly in multi-divisional companies, and some politicians have clear and actionable programmes of reform. But the contrast is illuminating in principle, since it suggests that politics and enterprise, in the good sense in which to use it, do not mix well. The policy implication is that, typically, one needs mechanisms, procedures, and structures, which enable enterprises to conduct their consumer-oriented, long-term activities, isolated in some degree from the short-term, inconsistent pressures which might otherwise be exerted upon them by the powerful political dimension.

One word of caution, however, consumers are not homogeneous, and will embody regional, large/small, rich/poor, and other differences. Likewise, enterprises are not homogeneous, and combine many potential interests - employees, shareholders, management, directors, functional specialisms, and so on. This is the source of a major management problem referred to earlier.

Finally, if we still feel that each country situation is uniquely different, there is a way forward. Within the set of state enterprises we could rank all on a scale from successful to unsuccessful; this scale would, of course, use different dimensions (finance, service delivery, etc). If we take the outstanding ones and look for what factors underlie success we may find that these factors lie on the 'enterprise' dimension of our previous matrix. We can then ask how we can change, galvanise, or restructure the rest, so as to bring them closer to that level of performance, building constructively from the experience of the successful.

DISTRIBUTIONAL IMPLICATIONS

Let us look at the issue of 'distributional implications', building from the viewpoint that privatisation is a means to an end, not an end in itself; the end depends on the cultural and social context.

But, first a small point about words. If one pictures the world and all its variety as an uncategorised mass, then our frameworks and words help us to categorise, define, and operate. But these frameworks and words are not things in themselves. They may be useful, enlightening, inspirational; or constraining, deadening, and depressing. In the same way our measures and conceptual frameworks may be useful or constraining - they are models and surrogate indices. We need constantly to have a sense of their fitness and use relative to the complex phenomena they selectively reflect. The danger then for us, as analysts and policy makers, comes when the words and measures become the reality - ends in themselves. For then we run the risk of becoming emperors without clothes.

Let us look at some of the classifications we use. Figure 6.3 illustrates a classic economics distribution graph of income per head of population. Curve A may represent a typical subsistence economy, with a development strategy of moving through time to curve B. If income matters, then nearly everyone will be better off: but, recognising the classic problem of interpersonal utility, many may feel worse off. In addition, the fabric of society may be falling apart with urbanisation, the old stability may be lost, and so on.

Figure 6.3: Distribution of income per head of population

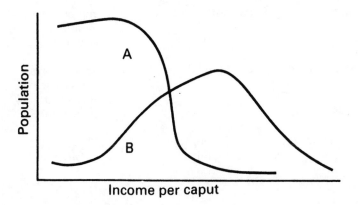

Let us then consider some other classifications. Table 6.1 is an example of one possible representation. This scheme is neither comprehensive nor exclusive, nor well thought through, but we will use it to make a point about the political aspects of privatisation. Politics is the articulation of differences, representing interest groups; and also, typically for those in power, the articulation through rhetoric of commonality and common experience - of a nation, a people, or whatever. The appeal is always to the

Table 6.1: Social and cultural context of privatisation

Social classification	Academic discipline	Implied Personal concern (?)
Income	Economics	Wealth, consumption
Class/status	Sociology	Social differentiation
Rural/urban	Sociology	Style of living: meaningful work (?)
Geographical regions (north/south, plains and mountain)	Demography/ geography/sociology	Lifestyle: local interest and culture
Tribal/cultural/ religious	Cultural/social anthropology	Sense of place and purpose: meanings and symbols
Indigenous/exogenous	Multiple	Social status via wealth; access to power, etc.
Male/female; old/young, etc.	Demography/ sociology	Change/ stability etc.

implied personal concern, at the emotional level, perhaps combined with interest. Now if privatisation is seen merely as a matter of structural change, of efficiency and productivity, to the neglect of the 'social and cultural context', articulated in the left hand column, then privatisation may well fail. All local contexts are particular and different, but one may find the above table a help in analysing the social/cultural context of privatisation measures.

In this respect, a change in organisational context, so that a privatised company seems genuinely to serve a particular group of consumers, may help to energise and transform its own internal culture. conversely, in some of the large public utilities/services in the UK, concern has been expressed about the possible loss of the public-service ethos when privatisation occurs. Ironically this kind of ethos, the sense of commitment, is exactly what many private-sector companies are seeking through programmes of 'cultural change'. The organisation cannot be seen in economic terms, in isolation from its cultural context. Take the case of 'efficiency'. Japanese companies, for good historical reasons, seem highly productive, transforming inputs into outputs with little loss. Some UK companies, particularly in the 1960s and 1970s, seemed to have low productivity, low output, and poor efficiency. This was not, however, a matter of complete loss in the transformation process. If there were leakages - through theft of time and material (a form of inefficiency) into the local community, then in various subtle ways the local community benefited. Without wishing to advocate this, one can suggest that many Japanese companies have extremely strong boundaries, providing their employees with a powerful sense of identity, but with a thin community outside. In the UK there is a strong tradition of private individualism, and companies' boundaries are often thin, with employment as a source of income, not identity, and much private energy and initiative is devoted to the private pursuits which make for strong communities - in all kinds of leisure activities. It is unwise, therefore, to ignore context, and it should always be borne in mind that our focus of analysis determines our perceptions and conclusions.

Part II

Country Papers

7

Privatisation in Pakistan

Riyaz Bokhari

THE PUBLIC ENTERPRISE SITUATION

The status and relative roles of public and private sectors in Pakistan have been determined largely by the political leanings of the government of the day in four distinct phases. During 1948-58, the country saw the creation and development of an aggressive public industrial sector in close relationship with private industry. In the next phase, lasting up to 1971, the role of the public sector shrank somewhat, and there was a distinct shift in favour of the private sector. The period 1972-7, however, saw a complete reversal of this policy. The concept of government controlling the 'commanding heights of economy' was introduced, and wholesale nationalisation of many establishments in basic industrial and other sectors was carried out. Subsequent to 1977, the declared policy has been to contain the public sector and to restore the confidence of the private sector it had enjoyed in the 1970s.

Aggregate performance

There are nearly 250 separate enterprises (holding companies as well as their subsidiaries) under the federal government of Pakistan. These range from departmental organisations (like the railways, post offices and telegraph and telephone departments) at one end of the scale, to companies in which the government holds an equity interest (not necessarily as a majority shareholder) at the other. All these enterprises had a total capital investment of about Rs87 billion with a net retained earning amounting to Rs23.6

* Auditor-General of Pakistan

billion on 30th June 1985. The dividend payments during 1984-5 amounted to Rs2.66 billion, or 2.41 per cent of the investment. They also had loans of Rs61.6 billion from the federal government, on which interest amounting to Rs3.7 billion (or nearly 6 per cent) was paid during the same year.

The four provincial governments have nearly eighty enterprises - departmental undertakings such as workshops, factories, and printing presses, as well as development authorities or corporations with a total investment of nearly Rs3.2 billion. Most of these have had substantial accumulated losses.

As per the Federal Finance Ministry's annual report on government-sponsored corporations, covering practically all public enterprises (except railways; Water and Power Development Authority; Karachi Port Trust; Port Qasim Authority; post offices; telegraph and telephone departments) the total assets stood at Rs510 billion in 1985-6, of which Rs353.6 billion were accounted for by commercial banks, development financial institutions and insurance, and the remaining Rs156.4 billion by other corporations. They recorded a turnover of Rs135.3 billion during the year. Fifty-nine of these corporations earned a pretax profit of Rs10.34 billion, and the remaining fourteen made losses amounting to Rs4.38 billion during 1985-6. Thus the overall (net) pre-tax profit amounted to Rs5.96 billion; the profit after tax amounted to Rs3.08 billion.

Financial institutions, Pakistan International Airlines, and corporations engaged in energy production and distribution were very profitable. The enterprises engaged in commerce, manufacturing, and mining displayed very low or negative returns on assets.

The value added (gross market value at domestic prices) calculated as the sum of profit before tax, salaries/wages, depreciation and interest by these corporations, accounted for 4.87 per cent of the GNP for 1985-6. They employed more than 231,000 persons or 0.81 per cent of the total labour force. If the figures pertaining to the railways, post offices, telegraph and telephone departments, and the Water and Power Development Authority are also taken into account, the percentages would rise to 7.47 per cent for value added and nearly 2 per cent for labour employed.

The sectoral spread of the public enterprises, along with the severe accumulated losses in the manufacturing, construction and railway activities, is shown in Appendix 1 on p.164-5.

Size, structure, ownership pattern, and profitability

Appendices 2-4 (on pp. 166-8) show the spread of public enterprises over different levels of (original) capital outlay, the extent of holding company interest (equity ownership) in subsidiaries, where applicable, the general structure of direct federal government ownership of the holding corporations/controlling units themselves, and their profitability (accumulated loss) structure.

About a fourth of the total number of subsidiaries had less than 50 per cent of equity holding by their parent company/organisations. Almost a similar pattern exists in respect of the holding companies themselves. Only between 20 per cent and 35 per cent of the enterprises yielded more than a 15 per cent return (after tax) during the four years 1982-3 and 1985-6. Thirty-five of the enterprises had accumulated losses which exceeded their capital and another fourteen had eroded more than 50 per cent of their equity capital by 30th June 1986.

Divestitures

Disinvestment of government interest in public enterprises is not a recent development. Over the years, disinvestment or sale of government shares in enterprises was undertaken for various reasons. Appendix 5 (on pp. 169-72) gives a list of such enterprises, of which the majority are in the manufacturing sector. (It does not include the hundreds of small units which were denationalised during 1977-8 shortly after their nationalisation.)

THE THINKING ON PRIVATISATION

The background

The acts of nationalisation and performance of public enterprises had become such controversial issues that one of the first acts of the new regime in 1977 was to undertake reviews of the performance, policies, and organisational structures of these enterprises, and also to consider ways and means of reviving production by improving the investment climate for the private sector, which had been paralysed by the fear of further nationalisation and by constantly eroding profit margins. It was also found that the bulk of industrial development had been directed to the public sector, but had contributed little to growth of output and exports. The sector had inherited a productive apparatus that was not efficient but to which unjustifiably high expectations had been attached at the time of nationalisation. The leadership which came into power in July 1977 generally believed in the sanctity of private property.

In order to establish its credibility with private investors, the government promulgated the 'Transfer of Managed Establishment Order' in September 1978 which empowered it to transfer shares or proprietary interests of the establishments nationalised under the Economic Reforms Order of 1972 to persons in whom the management or ownership was vested immediately before the takeover. The previous owners were debarred from making any claim for compensation of any nature against the government and provision was made for assumption by it of the net losses incurred after the take-over until transfer back to the previous owners. Not many owners took advantage of this enactment, perhaps because the transfer was a complicated affair subject to formal audit, accounting of liabilities at the time of take over, and the valuation of new assets created during the period of public management. The processes involved in denationalisation were so long drawn out, and the financial valuation so unattractive that very few enterprises were demanded by and handed over to the previous owners.

The government might perhaps have accepted the demand of the private sector/previous owners to transfer the enterprises to them through a sweeping law in the same manner as they were taken over. However, during the period of public ownership and management, another vested interest, that of the workers and lower/middle management, had gained power and developed a sort of 'proprietary' stake in these enterprises. They vehemently opposed any general move of wholesale denationalisation.

Keeping in mind that a sweeping denationalisation would create unrest and serious labour problems, the government considered two other directions to reactivate the private sector in pursuance of its general policy of restoring market mechanism and to use this sector as the engine of growth. All ten industrial sectors reserved for public-sector investment in the Economic Reforms Order were opened up to the private sector, and a law was promulgated which provided that industrial units could not in future be arbitrarily taken over by the government.

At about this time, the World Bank noted that the problems faced by Pakistan's economy required that the balance of its industrial strategy be shifted more in favour of export-oriented, labour-intensive industries where investment quickly yields increases in output. This would depend not only on a slowing down of public-sector investment in basic (long-gestation-period and capital-intensive) industries, but also on a revival of private sector investment and continued growth of small-scale industries. Government procedures for and control over private investment required to be further streamlined; conditions conducive to improved labour-management relations had to be created and availability arranged of more foreign exchange for private investment. It was also suggested that the possibility of joint ventures between public and private capital might be explored.

Main considerations for privatisation

During the 1980s, the tilt towards higher rates of investment by the private sector and for privatisation has been justified by political leaders, government officials, and most of the Press on a number of overlapping considerations, such as the following:

(1) Continuing with such public enterprises as register losses year after year does not strengthen government policies in the social sector. To the extent that the failure to earn satisfactory returns on investment in public enterprises limits the government's capacity to extend the coverage of essential services, there is an implicit subsidisation of some sections of the population at the expense of others. If the benefits are available only to small (often the more affluent) sections of the population, the long-term objectives of social policy are not achieved.

(2) The government would like to remove all unnecessary controls and interventions; 'under the dark shadow of such controls, corruption breeds and public interest is brazenly sold'. Popular capitalism fostered by deregulation and privatisation should be recognised as a superior method of achieving the country's social and economic objectives with equity.

(3) Good and efficient management has become not only necessary for greater profitability but essential for survival itself. Whatever incentives are provided to public-

sector managers, endeavours to improve performance will remain constrained by difficulties of attracting and retaining able managers and skilled manpower within public-sector enterprises. The government must consider a systematic divestment of at least the smaller public enterprises because they require a disproportionate share out of the limited resources of competent management while contributing only a small share to the total public-sector production. Furthermore, privatisation of some units has had the effect of altering the climate in most of the remaining units in which the workers become more willing to change inefficient work practices.

(4) One of the principal objectives of the current Five-Year Plan (1984-8) is to achieve a rapid development of selected industries in which Pakistan has a competitive advantage. Private sector is expected to play the leading role in this development strategy. This is now a central part of the strategy for development, and the government has to provide adequate infrastructure essential to support private-sector growth.

(5) While some recovery in production can be obtained by improving the efficiency of existing enterprises, the achievement of sustained industrial growth will require further investment. Given the continuing limits on resources there is little scope for government to finance more than a small proportion of the required investment. A compelling reason for the government to disinvest is that 'sell-offs' raise money - which is good for politicians who want to cut taxes or not raise them despite yawning deficits in their budgets.

(6) As part of its strategy of shifting investment priorities away from large projects with long gestation periods towards smaller, more rapidly yielding undertakings, the rate of investment in public industry is expected to decline. The bulk of future investment in public industry can be expected to take the form of balancing, modernisation and rehabilitation, together with some minor expansions. This strategy will free scarce public resources for the financing of necessary investments in high-yielding, short-gestation projects, particularly in the agricultural, water, and energy sectors, towards improvements and extensions of the infrastructure, and for increased expenditure on improving basic social services. It will also allow an increased diversion of domestic credit to finance private investment.

(7) Although government economic policies have been successful on many fronts, savings rates have consistently lagged behind expectations. In the context of the government's declared objective of introducing Islamic concepts into economic management, interest rates have not been, and seem unlikely to be, used as a major policy tool for mobilising private savings through the banking system. Until alternative mechanisms are developed, the chief method for inducing private savings appears to be through the creation of opportunities for private investment.

(8) There is one fundamental need everywhere - the need to increase efficiency in the production and distribution of goods and services. Experience in industrialised western markets has shown that efficiency is possible only in a general environment of decentralised decision-making, distribution, and investment. Private firms are free to do things that are unacceptable in the public sector: one company can merge with another or take over a firm; a privatised firm can diversify into new fields of activity and compete with existing private companies, raise funds through borrowing or equity issues unfettered by public expenditure controls, and generally evade political interference. The World Bank and the International Finance Corporation see themselves as partners with the private sector in the economic development of the Third World and they are determined to strengthen that partnership. The main planks of the economic policies embraced by the government since 1977 have to a large extent been determined by this thinking, although it should be fairly obvious that the deregulation and privatisation measures were not adopted entirely at the insistence of the IMF and the World Bank. They coincided with the desires and aspirations of the entrenched socio-economic groups in the country.

On the whole, there appears to be a general consensus that the motive underlying the rejuvenated faith in the private sector is the government's need to supplement resources at its command.

ACTIONS IN PRIVATISATION

Early disinvestments

The first period (up to 1970) of disinvestments related mostly to the operations of the Pakistan Industrial Development Corporation (PIDC), and privatisation was restricted to those industrial units or projects which had been set up and successfully operated by PIDC itself. A couple of its jute and paper mills in East Pakistan (now Bangladesh) were disinvested during the 1960s. Other disinvestments during this period are included in the lists in Appendix 5 on pp. 169-72. The primary consideration was not to get rid of any loss-making public enterprise but rather to stimulate private-sector investors to take an interest in expanding the industrial base of the economy. How far these disinvestments also contributed to strengthening the power relationships underlying the political and social system of the times remains a subject of research and debate.

Denationalisation during 1977-83

The second phase of disinvestment or denationalisation of taken-over units took place immediately after the change of regime in 1977. First, all the rice-husking units were denationalised during 1977-8 under an ordinance, the object of which was to repeal an earlier Act promulgated by the previous regime to provide for their take-over. Similar ordinances were promulgated in respect of flour mills and cotton-ginning establishments which had also been taken over by the government in 1976. The thinking about these disinvestments had started towards the last days of the previous regime itself. The ordinances providing for the repeal of the previous act empowered the government to deliver possession of a taken-over establishment to the previous management. In order to protect the financial interests of PIDC, which had been set up earlier to manage and operate these units, the ordinance provided that no claim or legal proceedings arising out of the return of an establishment would lie again the government or PIDC. A provision was also made to pay compensation for the loss of interest on the amount determined as payable under the nationalisation Act. The terms and conditions of service of all full-time employees under the previous management and those who had been employed by PIDC were to be protected.

The second stage of this denationalisation relates to the period up to 1982-3. During the Fifth Five-Year Plan (1978-83), the status-quo in the new public/private sector relationship was maintained. Partial denationalisation and a demarcation of private-sector investment areas were undertaken. Several incentives were introduced (tax holiday, exemption from customs duty, accelerated depreciation, and export rebates) with the object of arresting the declining trend of private investment. Between 1977 and 1983, private-sector projects involving an investment of Rs46.4 billion were sanctioned. This amount was more than double the investment approved during the previous 17 years.

Two loss-making units in the light-engineering sector and a steamship company were returned to their previous owners during 1978-80, under the provisions of a presidential order, which provided that all persons employed in the transferred establishments would continue in such employment without any change in their terms and conditions. The units transferred under this Order to their previous owners were subjected to special audits by independent auditors and the values of assets and liabilities as at the date of transfer were recast.

Privatisation since 1983

The third phase of disinvestment relates to the period after 1983. The Sixth Five-Year Plan (1983-88) adopted privatisation as a philosophy, limiting the role of the government as a facilitator of the private initiative and as investor of the last resort; the central theme of the Plan was deregulation and privatisation. A number of measures had been initiated earlier by the new regime to 're-instil the virtues of endeavour, enterprise, discipline, and efficiency'. Reviews of the working and management of public enterprise were carried out by committees with wide-ranging terms of reference and, after considering their reports, the Cabinet decided to rationalise and consolidate the management of the public sector and to reduce its size to economically viable proportions. Noting that there were a number of uneconomic and non-commercial (industrial) entities which were running into financial losses, it was agreed that mergers of companies/units, regrouping of corporations, and financial restructuring of individual public enterprises should be carried out after a thorough review. A standing committee of the Cabinet, on Reorganisation of

Pakistan

State (Industrial) Enterprises, was set up to oversee the implementation of these decisions. The number of (holding) corporations was reduced from eleven to eight through mergers, and a number of chronically sick enterprises, which after rehabilitation were not likely to become viable, were earmarked for closing down or liquidation. A programme of financial restructuring of enterprises was drawn up and implemented after detailed studies.

Out of the federal-government public enterprises, four units belonging to PIDC were disinvested after 1983, mostly because of continuing losses and inefficient operation. Another enterprise under the Ministry of Industries was liquidated for similar reasons. An inefficient and loss-making foundry/pipe making unit was closed down and liquidated. Similarly, a small fertilizer project, the machinery for which had been imported but not installed for a number of years, was also liquidated. In the provincial public sector, three sugar and three textile mills were disinvested in view of their losses.

The national airline had set up small hotels and tourist inns in the inaccessible northern areas of Pakistan, and it was decided to dispose of them to private-sector operators for better management in 1984. Another such subsidiary in the Province of Sind was also sold in 1986. Negotiations for the transfer of these units were held with selected parties which had shown interest in their purchase and efforts were made to obtain the highest price for the assets handed over to the buyers.

Three units (cigarette manufacturing, textiles looms, and marble mining and processing), which had been set up by a federal-government corporation for developing backward areas, were found to be incurring heavy losses. It was decided to lease these units to private parties in 1981-2. However, this arrangement did not work satisfactorily and it was decided to close down their operations during 1985-6. The management of two other joint ventures with government majority shareholding has been entrusted to private sector partners. Negotiations are being held to adopt this arrangement for two more joint ventures.

There are fifteen more federal-government enterprises (see part C of Appendix 5, on p. 172) which have been considered for disinvestment/liquidation from time to time, but as yet it has not been possible to finalise the 'disinvestment package' for various reasons.

Over the years, out of nearly 350 public enterprises of

the provincial and federal governments, 30 units have actually been disinvested/liquidated and another 20 are under various stages of consideration for disinvestment. In denationalisations carried out during 1977-83, whereas the consideration and conditions of return, sale, or transfer were arrived at through direct negotiations with the previous owners, the process of later privatisations was initiated by inviting bids from interested parties. The total purchase consideration involved in the disinvestment packages finalised after 1983 adds up to more than one billion rupees. The procedure followed in one of the cases is briefly described, by way of illustration, in Appendix 6 on pp. 173-5.

In all cases of loss-making public enterprises, substantial amounts of loans from nationalised banks are outstanding. The banks' aggregate credit exposure in public enterprises stood at Rs42 billion on 30th June 1987; as much as Rs14 billion was caught up in sick or defunct enterprises. Any proposal to disinvest, close down or liquidate an enterprise is, therefore, a matter of great concern to the creditor banks. The Pakistan Banking Council (PCB), which administers and controls the nationalised banks, feels that it must be fully associated with the process of disinvestment. It has drawn up, in consultation with the government agencies concerned, a standardised and comprehensive procedure (see Appendix 7 on pp. 176-7) for adequately dealing with the different stages of disinvestment - namely, preparation of sale, advertisement, and standard-offer proformas, bid evaluation, establishing bidders' creditworthiness, final negotiations with the responsive parties and, finally, the drawing up of a standard disinvestment package. Offers are invited for fixed assets and current assets are matched against current liabilities on the basis of a joint audit carried out by auditors appointed by the sellers and buyers.

Other measures

The process of actual closing down, disinvestment, or sale of inefficient public enterprises has the indirect effect of improving the overall efficiency of the remaining units taken together. The government has been taking a number of imporant steps to improve the operating environment of these enterprises with the object of enabling them to play a more effective and positive role in national development.

These measures (i.e. decentralisation of management decisions, rationalisation of target setting, performance evaluation and bonus-payment procedures, the sale of some enterprises to private owners, and the closure of several plants) have begun to yield results, and there has already been an encouraging improvement in the profitability and efficiency of many public-sector enterprises.

As regards sick units, it has been declared that the government has no intention of either closing down a factory or selling it unless appropriate arrangements have been made for the workforce. At the same time, the government cannot allow a drain on public resources to go on for ever. It was in pursuance of this line of thinking that the workers of two loss-making units were offered either alternative jobs in other units or generous termination-of-service benefits ('golden handshake') in 1984 pending the sale of the assets of the units. Unfortunately due to litigation with ex-owners, it has not been possible to dispose of the units so far.

A new industrial policy statement was issued by the government in July, 1984. It confirms its commitment to a mixed economy in which the private sector is the engine of growth while the public sector acts as investor of last resort.

The areas open to the private sector have been widened, together with safeguards against arbitrary government acquisitions. Investment sanctioning procedures and a number of bureaucratic regulations are being streamlined. Incentives have been introduced to encourage investment and exports by private sector. A programme of import liberalisation has been implemented to increase the availability of industrial raw materials and capital goods.

The process of privatisation is not restricted to loss-making public enterprise only. While presenting the budget for 1985-6, the Finance Minister announced that the government had decided to sell a part of the shares, valuing Rs2 billion, of profitable units to the general public. A disinvestment committee was to formulate the policy which would govern the sale of these shares. The objective was stated to be not to enhance the wealth of a few rich families but to bring about a widespread participation by the general public in the ownership of public enterprises. Unfortunately, it has not been possible to implement this proposal due to some problems but it has not been abandoned.

There has been progress in liberalisation in a number of areas. For example: (a) liberalisation of investment sanctioning and removal of twelve categories of industries from the 'specified list'; (b) deregulation in matters of manufacture and pricing of cement, edible oils, tractors, and nitrogenous fertilizers; (c) rationalisation of natural gas prices; (d) the opening up of high quality (basmati) rice, edible oil, and fertilizers to private-sector marketing; (e) allowing the private sector back into rice and cotton exports; and (f) more flexible management of the exchange rate to assure international competitiveness. These changes together with the derationing of wheat and flour and opening up of nitrogenous fertilizer imports to the private sector have all been viewed as positive steps, although the view is sometimes expressed that the deregulation policies are being thwarted by the (public-sector) loan/credit giving agencies.

It is estimated that as a result of all these measures, private sector investment during the Sixth Five-Year Plan (1983-8) would record a much higher rate of growth (57.5 per cent) over the previous plan period than that expected to be achieved by public-sector investment (31.3 per cent). The draft Seventh Five-Year Plan (1988-93) envisages a continuation of this trend, although the total figures of private sector investment (Rs265.7 billion) would still be much less than those proposed to be earmarked for public sector (Rs367.8 billion). The difference in allocation is perhaps most marked in the manufacturing sector; against an investment of Rs18 billion during the current plan period, the public sector is to be allocated Rs9.52 billion (i.e. a fall of 47 per cent) during the next 5-year period, while private sector investment is expected to grow from about Rs62 billion to Rs91 billion (i.e. an increase of 47 per cent).

The private sector is to be attracted to intersectoral and regional priority areas and, with appropriate policy environment, into the social sectors of health and education also. The draft Seventh Five-Year Plan also envisages an important role for the private sector in electricity generation, telecommunications, and roads. To overcome its resource constraint the government has already announced a policy for the induction of private sector in power generation based on oil and indigenous coal. A new pricing formula has been announced to attract investment in hydrocarbon exploration. The mode of financing for highway development programmes will be broadened by offering to

157

the private sector such sections of the national highway as cannot be financed by the public sector.

The Water and Power Development Authority (WAPDA), the Oil and Gas Development Corporation (OGDC) and the Telegraph and Telephone departments are estimated to have drawn Rs100 billion from the government during the Sixth Five-Year Plan period. These are to be 'cast out' of the government budgets and will be required to 'raise their own funds to meet their requirements' during the next plan period. WAPDA has already floated government-guaranteed 13.5 per cent (tax-free) bearer bonds (5 years) to raise Rs2 billion for the purpose of financing its power development programme. This is the largest bond issue ever floated by a public body and preliminary reports indicate that as much as Rs3.02 billion worth of these bonds have been taken up. The share of the public in the total subscription is reported to be larger than that of the public and private sector companies and corporations. The bonds have been listed on the stock exchanges and are expected to help in developing a broad-based and diversified capital market in the country.

PROBLEMS ENCOUNTERED

The process of privatisation has been proceeding both at the broad macro level of the economy (through efforts at deregulation and creation of a climate favourable to private investment) and at the level of individual public enterprises (through efforts at sale/disinvestment or exposing them to the pressures of market discipline). However, frustration is felt by the planners when the individual private sector entrepreneurs do not 'behave' in consonance with the perceived overall interests of the economy, or even of the private sector as a whole, but choose to place their own short-term gains above all other considerations by exploiting loop-holes or oversights in the privatisation processes. This can lead to inequities in the distribution of national wealth and generate tensions which might result in a policy swing.

Deregulation

Private investment has expanded, but has not entirely followed the priorities stipulated in the national develop-ment plans. The new investment has mostly gone into import substitution and consumer-goods industries which enjoy higher protection, require less capital and yield high margins of profit within a comparatively short span of time. The development of export-oriented and basic-engineering industries has, by and large, been neglected. Furthermore, industrial investment has not moved towards the less industrialised regions.

Views have been expressed from time to time that excessive controls at almost every stage of investment and operation of projects have been acting as formidable deterrents to the expansion of private sector activity (e.g. in matters affecting company formation, investment sanctioning, imports and access to foreign exchange). There is a need for further streamlining of procedures and reduction in the discretionary powers of government functionaries and investment bankers if a continuing and self-sustaining expansion of the private sector is to be quickly achieved. Inadequacies of infrastructure (including water, gas, electricity, roads, and telecommunications) have also been responsible for serious bottlenecks in private-sector expansion. The problem is compounded when attempts are made to tie investment sanction/credit limits to backward areas where these facilities do not exist, and/or the supplying agencies do not find it economic to provide services/connections to individual project sites.

Disinvestment of individual enterprises

In the disinvestment/privatisation of individual units, progress has not kept pace with the government's own plans. The private sector has not been eager to purchase non-profitable enterprises at the indicated prices. Potential buyers usually have alternative opportunities and they may be interested only in the best-performing public enterprises with low-risk and high-profit potential. Public enterprises located in less-developed areas on social welfare consider-ations are necessarily less efficient; and the inadequacy of infrastructure does not make them attractive to the private sector. Moreover, doubts about markets inhibit private bids in the case of enterprises whose viability depends on full utilisation. Besides, ministries, enterprise managers, and labour unions are often reluctant to give up control over a public enterprise.

Procedures for according final approval are cumber-some - there are far too many tiers and bodies to be consulted for advice or for protection of genuine or imaginary interests. But delays in decision only add to losses, further reducing the net worth. Cases have been reported in which the final approval to the 'disinvestment package' arrived at after long and tedious negotiations was withheld, apparently because the purchasing party was not acceptable on political considerations.

In the case of denationalisation of a taken-over unit, the law requires that it should first be offered for sale to its previous owners. They may not even qualify on grounds of credit worthiness or managerial competence. This legal lacuna is now being taken care of by an amendment in the law, without which there cannot be much progress in cases which are sub-judice.

CONCLUSIONS

From Pakistan's experience, for a group of public manufacturing units, a sophisticated system of setting targets and monitoring and evaluation of performance is being developed. It is indeed a pity that this concept has not yet been extended to the rest of the manufacturing sector, nor been adapted for other sectors, in order to achieve better value for money invested in borderline enterprises which could be 'turned around', rather than treating them as hopeless cases for which the only remedy is disinvestment.

The government is now clearly committed to an overall policy of gradual privatisation of the economy - through deregulation, and 'opening up', and selective disinvestment. However, the relevance of the public sector and the necessity for its efficient management and healthy-growth are not denied; this should not be obscured by the present emphasis on private-sector expansion, particularly because of the proposed infrastructural expansions in the public sector.

An intriguing sidelight has been that there is no move to denationalise taken-over commercial banks or to set up investment banks or financial institutions in the private sector. It is difficult to judge at this stage whether this is because of the attractive profits earned for the government by this sector year after year, or that there is a continuing desire on the part of government to retain a controlling device which may have to be employed in case the deregulation process for private-sector investment gets out of hand due to unforeseen developments.

In conclusion, the share of public enterprises in the total, gross fixed-capital formation (which was about 48 per cent in 1977-8) fell to 37.5 per cent by 1986-7.

REFERENCES

Auditor-General of Pakistan (1987) Federal Government Investment and Loans in Public Enterprises, Lahore.

Clausen, A.W. (1985) 'Promoting the private sector in developing countries - a multilateral approach'. Extracts from an address to the Institute of Directors, Pakistan and Gulf Economist, Karachi, April 6-12.

Economic Advisor's Wing, Finance Division, Government of Pakistan, Economic Survey, 1985-86.

────── Economic Survey, 1986-87.

────── Government Sponsored Corporations, 1984-85 and 1985-86.

Experts Advisory Cell, Ministry of Production, Government of Pakistan, Public Sector Industries - Annual Reports: 1983-84; 1984-85; and 1985-86.

Government of Pakistan (1972) Report on 31 Industrial Establishments taken over in January, 1972, Islamabad.

Hague, Irfan-ul (1988) 'Privatisation of economy - the factors that have kept the pace slow', Economic and Business Review, Dawn, January 16-22.

Hasan, Muzaffar (1988) ' "WAPDA" bearer bonds', editorial in Pakistan and Gulf Economist, March 12-18, Karachi.

Jafarey, V.A. (1987) 'Deregulation and economic discipline', an address by the Governor, State Bank of Pakistan, Karachi, November, 1987.

Kardar, Shahid (1987) The Political Economy of Pakistan, Lahore: Progressive Publishers.

Khan, Abud Hafeez (1986) 'Disinvestment - who isn't making up the mind?', Pakistan and Gulf Economist, January 4-10, Karachi.

Mahmud, Ayesha (1986) 'Disinvestment of public sector industries' The Economic Review, May 1986, Karachi.

Medhi, Istaqbal (1987) The Role of the Public Sector in Developing Countries: Pakistan, Yugoslavia: The International Centre for Public Enterprises.

Ministry of Finance, Government of Pakistan (1984) 'Fiscal policy in Pakistan - a historical perspective (Budget Speeches 1947-8 to 1984-5), Islamabad.

—— Budget Speeches 1985-6, 1986-7, and 1987-8.

Ministry of Industries (1983) Private Investment in manufacturing. A study in the restoration of confidence, Islamabad.

Planning Commission, Government of Pakistan, The Fifth Five-Year Plan (1978-83).

—— The Sixth Five-Year Plan (1983-88).

—— Draft of the Seventh Five-Year Plan (1988-93).

Secretary for Industries, Government of Pakistan (1984) 'Elements of new industrial policy', paper read at a seminar organised by the Karachi Chamber of Commerce and Industry.

State Bank of Pakistan, Annual Reports 1985-86 and 1986-87.

Wertzel, Lawrence H. (1988) 'Why privatisation will not always work', Economic and Business Review, Dawn, February 27 - March 4, Karachi.

World Bank, World Development Report 1987, and other annual reports on Pakistan.

Zaheer, Hasan (1985) 'Pakistan experience in public sector industrial management', Pakistan Institute of Management, Karachi.

APPENDIX 1: Public enterprises in Pakistan - numbers and capital outlays (in millions of rupees)

S.no.	Sector and sub-sector	No. of enterprises in the sector/sub sector
	(1)	(2)
1.	Communications: mass media	4
2.	Communications: post and telecommunications	2
3.	Construction and engineering	9
4.	Consultancy, research, and training	5
5.	Electricity	3
6.	Financial institutions: central bank	1
7.	Financial institutions: commercial banks	5
8.	Financial institutions: development banks and other financial institutions	14
9.	Financial institutions: insurance	4
10.	Manufacturing	11
11.	Mining and quarrying	3
12.	Oil and gas	13
13.	Printing and publishing	3
14.	Trade and commerce	6
15.	Transport: air transport	1
16.	Transport: ports and shipping	3
17.	Transport: rail transport	1
18.	Transport: road transport	4
19.	Water	3
20.	Other services	5
		100

No. of separate units	Federal government investment in the enterprises on 30th June, 1985			
	Capital	Retained earnings	Accumulated losses	Total (5+6-7)
(3)	(4)	(5)	(6)	(7)
4	1,235	317	13	1,539
6	5,168	10,889	840	15,217
9	1,871	172	3,698	(1,655)
5	703	19	-	722
3	6,366	11,656	-	18,022
1	100	6,150	-	6,250
5	374	722	-	1,096
16	617	899	-	1,516
4	60	467	-	527
117	16,645	2,664	4,704	14,605
3	292	91	6	377
21	9,009	783	1,838	7,954
4	661	280	111	830
8	402	815	199	1,018
12	990	1,754	-	2,744
4	3,928	2,062	532	5,458
3	13,227	-	3,696	9,531
4	2,472	162	847	1,787
3	21,544	232	-	21,776
19	1,327	8	3	1,332
251	86,991	40,142	16,487	110,646

APPENDIX 2: The general structure of public ownership in the holding companies controlling units

S. no.	Extent of public equity ownership (1)	Number of public enterprises (holding companies) (2)
1.	100%	60
2.	50-100%	9
3.	25-50%	14
4.	Less than 25%	8
	Total	91

APPENDIX 3: Profitability structure of public enterprises

A: Pretax profits related to capital

S. no.	Return before tax on capital (1)	Number of enterprises			
		1982-3 (2)	1983-4 (3)	1984-5 (4)	1985-6 (5)
1.	Above 20%	51	67	68	47
2.	15-20%	11	13	18	12
3.	10-15%	20	24	14	17
4.	5-10%	19	23	20	15
5.	0-5%	28	26	30	31
6.	Negative	68	53	49	73

B: Pretax profits related to total assets

S. no.	Return before tax on capital (1)	Number of enterprises			
		1982-3 (2)	1983-4 (3)	1984-5 (4)	1985-6 (5)
1.	Above 20%	6	11	20	13
2.	15-20%	5	8	11	6
3.	10-15%	9	21	19	17
4.	5-10%	31	32	28	20
5.	0-5%	78	81	72	66
6.	Negative	68	53	49	73

APPENDIX 4: Number of enterprises with accumulated losses

S. no.	Accumulated loss as a percentage (1)	1982-3 (2)	1983-4 (3)	1984-5 (4)	1985-6 (5)
1.	More than 100%	32	32	29	35
2.	50-100%	20	21	12	14
3.	25-50%	7	3	10	8
4.	0-25%	15	20	17	15
		74	76	68	72

APPENDIX 5: List of public enterprise units which were disinvested (wholly or partially from time to time)

A: Disinvestment involving sale or transfer of more than 50 per cent shareholding

S.no.	Year of disinvestment	Name of project/unit	
1.	1955–9	Jauharabad Sugar Mills	
2.	1961	Talpur Textile Mills	
3.	1961–3	Sethi Straw Board Mills	
4.	1962	DDT Factory, Nowshera	PIDC projects
5.	1964	Bawany Sugar Mills	
6.	1964	Crescent Jute Products	
7.	1964–5	Adamjee Paper Board Nowshera	
8.	1964–5	Bannu Woollen Mills	
9.	1978	Lahore Engineering & Foundry Ltd	Nationalised units returned to original owners
10.	1979	Nowshera Engineering Co. Ltd	
11.	1979	Synthetic Chemicals	A federal-government project
12.	1980	Pan Islamic Steamship Co. Ltd	Nationalised unit returned to original owners
13.	1981	Samundari Sugar Mills	
14.	1981	Bahawalpur Sugar Mills	Provincial-government projects
15.	1982	S.D.A. Corn Complex	

A: (cont.)

S.no.	Year of disinvestment	Name of project/unit	
16.	1982	Pakistan Fertilizer Co.	Federal-government projects
17.	1983	Northern Foundry	
18.	1983	Pakistan Garment Corp.	
19.	1984	Bannu Sugar Mills	PIDC unit
20.	1984	Rakaposhi Inn	Subsidiaries of Pakistan Inter-national Airlines Corporation Ltd
21.	1984	Hunza Hotel	
22.	1984	Swat Hotel	
23.	1986	Inter Pak Hotel	
24.	1985–6	Pasroor Sugar Mills	A provincial-government project
25.	1986	Tarbela Cotton and Spinning Mills	PIDC units
26.	1986	Al-Libas International Ltd	
27.	1987	Mehran Flocking Industries	
28.	1988	Paras Textile Mills	Provincial-government projects
29.	1988	Ghazi Textile Mills	
30.	1988	Harappa Textile Mills	

Note: The disinvestment packages in respect of a sugar mill, three cold storages, and a leather tannery (all provincial-government projects) have been approved, but the assets have not yet been handed over to the purchasers.

B: Disinvestments involving sale or transfer of less than 50 per cent shareholding by PIDC

S.no.	Year of disinvestment	Name of project/unit	Total cost of project	Face value of transferred shares
			(millions of rupees)	
1.	1959-65	Charsadda Sugar Mills	13.83	4.60
2.	1961	Model cotton-ginning factory, Mirpurkhas	0.75	0.05
3.	1963-9	Zeal-Pak Cement, Hyderabad	39.60	2.10
4.	1966	Model cotton-ginning factory, Sultanabad	0.50	0.005
5.	1966	Model cotton-ginning factory, Sargodha	0.90	0.01
6.	1969	Sui Gas Transmission	37.80	1.51
7.	1969	Sui Northern Gas Pipelines	177.70	1.68
8.	1969	Harnai Woollen Mills	6.0	0.075

Pakistan

C. Federal Government enterprises which have been considered for disinvestment from time to time but final decisions not taken for various reasons

---

1. Larkana Sugar Mills

2. Pak Iran Textile Mills Ltd   (presently closed down)

3. Shahdadkot Textile Mills   (presently closed down)

4. Quaidabad Woollen Mills

5. Pakistan PVC Limited

6. Domestic PVC Limited

7. Trailers Development Corporation

8. Pioneer Steel Mills

9. Special Steels of Pakistan   (presently closed down)

10. Karachi Pipe Mills

11. Quality Steel Works

12. Spinning Machinery Company of Pakistan

13. Textile Winding Machinery Company

14. Punjab Vegetable Ghee Mills   (presently closed down)

15. Khyber Vegetable Ghee Mills   (presently closed down)

APPENDIX 6: Brief description of the procedure followed for the disinvestment of a public enterprise in 1985-6

The Tarbela Cotton Spinning Mills (Private) Ltd had been set up by the Pakistan Industrial Development Corporation (PIDC) during 1980-1 at a cost of nearly Rs142 million primarily for the rehabilitation of Tarbela Dam evictees. It provided direct employment to nearly 1,400 workers and officials, and helped create multiple job opportunities in allied service industries. However, it was not a profitable enterprise and had accumulated a loss of nearly Rs38 million by June, 1983. A proposal was made to disinvest the unit, and the National Development Finance Corporation (NDFC) was asked to invite and examine bids for its sale or lease. According to the examination carried out in July 1983, the net worth (i.e. the value of fixed and current assets reduced by current and long term liabilities) according to historical costs was estimated at a mere Rs7 million but, if the assets were revalued (mainly land) at current market prices, the net worth was estimated at Rs40 million. Examination and analyses of the cash flow and the terms of long-term loans indicated that if the unit were to be disinvested, at about Rs94 million for its fixed assets, PIDC would recover its net equity investment and loans; it will not make any further loss. However, if a buyer could be found at Rs142 million, there would be a net gain to PIDC after recovery of its accumulated losses. Two or three parties were interested in buying the unit but they did not offer acceptable terms (not more than Rs58 million for fixed assets) and the matter had to be deferred.

Further losses were incurred during 1983-4 (Rs26 million) and 1984-5 (Rs34 million) causing considerable erosion of equity even after adjustment of some losses against capital reserves and a comparison of figures of assets and liabilities depicted a negative net worth. All the traditional indices of financial health of a company fell within disappointing ranges and were deteriorating over the years. Overall production was a bit higher during 1984-5 but the sales revenues were poor, due to a slump in the market caused by the withdrawal of an export refinancing scheme on cotton yarn and by severe (energy) load-shedding. The company's contribution to the national economy, in terms of gross value added at factor cost, declined from Rs8.3 million in 1983-84 to Rs2.1 million in 1984-5. The gross savings of the company in terms of retained earnings and reserves plus depreciation had become negative (and worked out to Rs27.52 million on 30th June 1985). The figure of social surplus, in terms of public profit at current prices, was also negative (at Rs16.4 million).

In view of continuing losses, the disinvestment proposal was revived in 1985. On the basis of the provisional balance sheet as on 30th June 1985, bids were invited through the Press in July/August 1985. In response, four bids were received, and a disinvestment negotiation committee was then set up (headed by a senior officer of the Ministry of Production) to evaluate these bids. As a result of negotiations, an offer amounting to nearly Rs110 million was found to be the highest. An offer for sale of the unit as a corporate entity was issued in May 1986 and, after acceptance of the broad terms of sale, an agreement was signed and possession handed over in July 1986.

The agreement provided that the enterprise would be handed over to the purchaser as a corporate entity. Cash consideration for the transfer of shares was to be determined on completion of a joint audit by independent auditors to be nominated by PIDC and the purchaser. A down payment (25 per cent of provisional cash consideration) was received before the agreement was signed - the balance was payable in three, equal, yearly instalments, with interest on an agreed rate on the unpaid balance. The joint audit included a 100 per cent physical verification of all the current assets, and inventory sheets of stocks, raw materials, stores, and spares were prepared and initialled/countersigned by the auditors/management. A verification of current liabilities towards banks and financial institutions was also carried out, and it was noted that the Pakistan Banking Council (PBC) had agreed to waive off penal interest levies on outstanding loans.

The sale agreement provided for the sale and transfer of 400,000 fully paid up shares of Rs100 each in the capital of the company for a total price of Rs11.762 millions at the rate of Rs29.405 per share. The liabilities of the company pertaining to foreign aid and the government's cash development loan were 'deleted'. PIDC agreed to ensure that the services of all the officers of the company were terminated and their service benefits duly settled before handing over the possession of the assets of the company to the purchaser. As regards the unionised staff/ workers, the parties to the agreement noted that they would be governed by their existing terms and conditions in accordance with the law. The agreement also noted that PBC and NDFC had confirmed that PIDC and the federal government would stand absolved from all liabilities of loans outstanding against the company.

APPENDIX 7: Salient features of procedures devised by the Pakistan Banking Council (PBC) for the disinvestment of loss-making public enterprises

Subsequent to the government's policy decision to disinvest (under a standard procedure) some of its loss-making public sector enterprises, Pakistan Banking Council (PBC) has prepared comprehensive proformas of sale advertisements and bid documents so as to standardise the disinvestment process. Accordingly, sale advertisements are usually vetted by PBC prior to their appearance in the national press. The offers are invited for fixed assets and current assets are matched against current liabilities on the basis of a joint audit carried out by auditors of the seller and buyer jointly.

Subsequent to receipt of offers, PBC is advised of complete particulars of the bids and the bidders' existing banking relationships. While nationalised commercial banks are asked to provide reports about the bidders' credit worthiness, the offers are evaluated in terms of their net current worth. Upon receipt of complete information about the bidders' credit credentials from banks, the party with the highest offer and essentially positive credit references is cleared for purchase of the unit under sale (in terms of standard disinvestment policy parameters chalked out by the PBC). However, PBC reserves the right to reject even the highest offer in case the bidder's credit worthiness is found to be doubtful.

The salient features of the above disinvestment parameters are:

i) The qualified bidder should make an immediate cash down-payment of 10 per cent of the aggregate offer for fixed assets on receipt and acceptance of a 'letter of intent for sale' from the holding corporation. However, in some cases the above condition has been relaxed to a 5 per cent immediate cash down-payment, the balance of 5 per cent being payable within one year (with a mark-up at 14 per cent on the outstanding sum). The outstanding balance is covered through a bank guarantee to the satisfaction of the banks.

ii) The cash down-payment should be utilised first towards reduction of superior credits of the unit under disinvestment. Similarly, all future payments by the buyer should be applied first towards settlement of priority charge holders' claims.

iii) For purchase consideration of the 90 per cent balance, the buyer should assume superior credits of the unit repayable in 10 years, inclusive of 2 years moratium for the principal amount only.

iv) Besides providing security in the form of assets of the unit, the buyer should provide additional collateral, such as personal guarantees, cross corporate guarantees, etc., to banks.

v) In addition to the above, considering the sponsor's low equity stance and to minimise banks' future risks, the buyer is asked to place shares of the unit along with duly verified blank transfer deeds under pledge with banks.

vi) To ensure viable operation of the unit under new management, the buyer cannot declare a cash dividend until the unit achieves a debt equity ratio of 60 : 40.

vii) The banks should arrange the working capital and balancing, modernisation, and rehabilitation fund needs of the unit under disinvestment, on merit.

However, it is worth mentioning here that progress in disinvestment has been exceptionally slow, because of cumbersome procedures which have been adopted by the government, and clearance of sale at many tiers. Furthermore, under the existing laws, a public-sector enterprise should first be offered for sale to its previous owners, who may not even qualify for purchase; this legal lacuna has also slowed down the disinvestment process. PBC, in this connection has time and again made recommendations to the government for setting up a high-powered committee consisting of professionals from PBC, National Development Finance Corporation, Ministry of Finance and other concerned Ministries. This committee, with the assistance of other financial institutions and consultants, if required, should arrange quick disposal of loss-making public-sector enterprises through public bidding.

Furthermore, the government has shown reluctance in working out a modus operandi for settlement of the unassumed portion of bank loans for units which have been disinvested to the private sector. This indecision on the government's part, due to application of interest, is resulting in an escalation of unsecured bank loans.

8

PRIVATISATION IN INDIA

Y. Venugopal Reddy*

THE PUBLIC ENTERPRISE SITUATION

Developments with reference to public enterprise in India
consist of four phases. The first phase may be called the
'commanding heights' phase, lasting from 1950 to the mid-
1960s. The second phase saw the nationalisation of banks
and general insurance, along with the evolution of the
concept of a joint sector in industry. The third phase began
in the late 1970s, lasted up to the mid-1980s, and was
characterised by a review of approaches to planning and the
role of public enterprises. A set of policies (termed the New
Economic Policy) emerged by the mid-1980s, ushering in the
fourth phase.

In order to appreciate the totality of the public-
enterprise situation in the country it is at first necessary to
divide the economy into an organised and an un-organised
sector (which is totally private). Even in the organised
sector, a sub-division can be made between the public and
private sectors. In the public sector one can distinguish
between government-departmental enterprises and non-
departmental enterprises. While for some parameters,
existing information can be classified on the above basis, for
some others it is not possible. As an illustration,
employment in the organised sector is presented in Appendix
1 on p.192.

* Director General, Public Enterprises Management Board,
Andhra Pradesh, India

THE PUBLIC SECTOR

Only 10 per cent of the workforce is in the organised sector, although 7 per cent out of this 10 per cent is in the public sector. Within the public sector, nearly two-thirds of the employees are in community, social, personal services, transport, storage, and communications, etc. If the manufacturing sector alone is taken into account, the number of employees in the private sector (including the non-corporate elements) is more than two and a half times the number in the public sector. The share of the public sector in net domestic product has doubled over a 20 year period. More importantly, the non-departmental enterprises in the public sector which previously contributed to a mere 1.3 per cent of national income, today contributes to nearly 10 per cent of it. In terms of capital stock, while the non-financial autonomous corporations and companies account for about 45 per cent of the total in the public sector, Indian Railways account for about 9 per cent and Irrigation and Power (which are in the government sector) account for 39 per cent. In fixed capital formation, the share of the public sector rose rapidly from a little over 20 per cent in the early 1950s to nearly 50 per cent in the 1960s; subsequently, it dropped to slightly below 50 per cent.

The share of non-departmental enterprises in the public sector has been rising rapidly and is now around one and a half times greater than that in departmental enterprises. However, in terms of share in the total net savings, the public sector, which was over 20 per cent in the 1960s, is now showing a downward tendency. The large amount of savings in the private sector is mostly from household savings. In recent years, private corporate sector has contributed about the same level of savings as the public sector.

Public enterprises account for over 90 per cent of the national income in banking and insurance, telecommunications, railways, mining and quarrying (mainly coal); and these are essentially in the realm of central government. In electricity, gas, and water supply also, public enterprises account for over 90 per cent; but these enterprises are mostly in the state sector. Forestry and transportation (other than national railways) also have public enterprise elements and are in the state sector. In terms of investments, the investments in the public sector have been growing faster, accounting for about half of the total investments; in terms of income, however, these investments account for around one fifth. Most recently, an increasing proportion of public-sector investments has been drawn from household savings.

Public enterprises dominate the organised sector. Of the 100 leading Indian companies, 42 government companies have a paid-up capital of over Rs 14,000 crores, while the other 58 (non government) companies have a paid-up capital of only about Rs1,200 crores. The private corporate sector has been contributing around 3 per cent out of the total savings of over 18 per cent.

Public Enterprises

For the purpose of analysis, it is useful to differentiate between different sets of public enterprises in India:

(a) Departmental enterprises (e.g. railways, telecommunications, Door Darshan (TV), All India Radio, and irrigation works;
(b) Manufacturing (most of which has a company form);
(c) The financial sector;
(d) The state-level public enterprises, of which electricity and transport are the dominant ones. Some promotional undertakings can also be found in this sector;
(e) The joint sector: i.e. companies in which the governments (state and federal) or the government companies hold equity but together do not have more than a 50 per cent (these are generally not analysed as part of the public-enterprise sector);
(f) the co-operative sector, particularly at state level: though co-operatives are supposed to be based on principles of voluntary association, government support is so large that governments tend to exercise as much control over them as over public enterprises, and even view them as part of the public-enterprises sector. But this paper, as do many academic works generally, excludes this from analysis.

There is an intricate mechanism of administered prices, with linkage of outputs and inputs of some public enterprises (e.g. coal for electricity boards, National Thermal Power Corporation (NTPC) power to Electricity Boards, etc.) making it extremely difficult to identify the enterprises operating in competitive and non-competitive environments.

Sick units, if taken over, are large in number, but small in terms of capital. Certain organisations like the Food Corporation of India and the State Trading Corporation more or less perform agency functions for the government on the basis of agreed margins.

The gross tangible assets of public enterprises (central financial and non-financial enterprises, railways, power, irrigation, ports, telegraphs and telephones, road transport and several departmental enterprises) was Rs 1,103,000 million by March 1983. Gross fixed capital formation in public enterprises was Rs 14,489 crores in 1981-82, as against Rs 15,227 crores in the private sector. In 1986 the return on capital form the public enterprises sector as a whole was 12.54 per cent. If the petroleum sector is excluded, this would drop to 7.56 per cent, and if sick mills which have been taken over are excluded, this would improve to 8.30 per cent. The corresponding return on capital for comparable private-sector enterprises is only 13.65 per cent, just 1.11 per cent more than public-sector enterprises. The position of accumulated losses of public enterprises is distressing. There are more enterprises which have been running under losses continuously for 5 years, there are some whose net worth has been totally eroded, and there are still others where the per-worker emoluments are more than the value added per worker.

If we adopt the recommendations of the Arjun Sen Gupta Committee, and differentiate these enterprises into core and non-core sectors, it clearly emerges that the non-core sector accounts for a minor part of investment and losses. It is clear that the enterprises covered by the Bureau of Public Enterprise (BPE) are a mixed bag, though the dominance of a few enterprises in select sectors is very evident (i.e. the top ten, in terms of investment or turnover, account for over two-thirds of the total). The unitwise investment ranges from thousands of crores to some two crores of rupees. The holding-company structure has been adopted for select industries, such as coal, steel, textiles, and jute.

In terms of ownership most of the public enterprises have 100 per cent equity held by the government or government companies. Yet another interesting aspect is that in a number of sectors like steel, cement, and fertilizers, public enterprises co-exist with private enterprises. Financial support, whether in terms of equity or debt, has almost invariably been provided by the government

181

through its budgetary channels (except in the very recent past). For working capital requirements, the public enterprises have to approach the commercial banking channels. However, in the recent past, some enterprises have been permitted to go to the open market for raising bonds; in most cases these provide tax concessions, thereby helping public enterprises to raise revenues at less than market rates, while at the same time providing higher-than-market yields to richer segments of bond-holders. Internal cash generation for the public enterprises as a whole is impressive, though much of it accrues in selected sectors.

The position regarding the financial sector is difficult to assess in terms of standard indicators of profitability. By the very nature of their activities (excluding banking in the informal and small sector), the functions of financial intermediaries are virtually a monopoly of the public sector.

State-level enterprises:

The position regarding state-level public enterprises is difficult to assess, since consolidated data have not been collected by any agency. Recently, the Institute of Public Enterprise in Hyderabad started collecting this information. However, for more detailed analysis, Andhra Pradesh has been used here as a representative state. There are four categories of enterprises:

(a) the most dominant are the state electricity boards and the road transport corporations.
(b) Statutory corporations such as the state finance corporation and the Industrial Development Corporations come next. They are of an essentially promotional-cum-developmental nature, engaged in providing consultancy, equity, debt, infrastructural development, etc., for industry.
(c) A number of welfare- and weaker-section-financing organisations, which are also registered as companies.
(d) A very narrow manufacturing sector, invariably registered under the Companies Act and subjected to the same regulatory discipline as the private sector, except that equity and special debt arrangements may be extended from time to time by the concerned state government. The ownership pattern is more varied.

Overall, the returns on investments are found to be particularly low in most of the state-level public-enterprise sectors, though the relatively large elements of social obligations discharged by the three major units, (i.e. electricity, Road Transport Corporation (RTC) and welfare organisations have not been duly quantified. Interestingly, units in public utility and promotional/welfare organisations are making profits while many commercial units make losses. The net worth is also eroded in some cases.

THINKING ON PRIVATISATION

A set of policies, broadly described as the New Economic Policy, have been enunciated, which broadly coincide with the policy framework of the Seventh Five-Year Plan that commenced in 1985. The policy involved, inter-alia, elements of deregulation of private industry, liberalisation, and autonomy to public enterprises (including emphasis on market culture). In the Indian context, these measures, along with the introduction of competitive elements (domestic and international), direct access to open market funds, redefining of the government/public-enterprise and public-enterprise/market relationships, and larger recourse to techniques of contracting out and franchising, are not considered as privatisation. Only disinvestment or divestiture is treated as privatisation.

There are three streams of thinking on disinvestment:

(a) There are a few who consider even disinvestment in a 'non-government company' as privatisation.
(b) The second more popular stream believes that allowing private participation in equity of government enterprises, to reduce its equity stock proportionately but not below 51 per cent, is privatisation.
(c) The third stream, where there is a virtual unanimity, defines privatisation to mean a change in ownership and control of a government company to a situation where the government is left with a minority share-holding or no share-holding.

The more important reasons to re-examine the scope of functioning of public enterprises can be listed as follows;

(a) budgetary strains on the government, resulting in inadequate availability of resources to public enterprises;

183

(b)   financial losses in a number of public enterprises; and
(c)   concern with the level of 'efficiency' in public
      enterprises - efficiency being defined to include cost,
      quality of products/services, and technological develop-
      ment.

The major facets of the thinking in the context of
privatisation can be summarised as follows:

(a)   The Prime Minister of India, while indicating that there
      is no move to adopt privatisation as a policy, has in
      some fora (1986-88) expressed dissatisfaction at the
      existence of public enterprises in non-core, non-priority
      sectors;
(b)   The Seventh Five-year Plan (1985-90) emphasises the
      need to introduce market elements and develop capital
      markets to help funding of public enterprises. It does
      not envisage disinvestment;
(c)   A number of government-appointed expert committees
      which have gone into the working of physical controls,
      public financial institutions, monetary policy, trade
      policy, fiscal policy, etc., have emphasised competition
      as an important element but have not suggested
      privatisation.
(d)   The Dr Arjun Sen Gupta Committee, however, examined
      the issue of public enterprises, largely confining its
      attention to the enterprises covered by the Bureau of
      Public Enterprise. The Sen Gupta committee
      specifically considered involving private investments in
      the equity of public enterprises but dismissed it as not
      desirable. The possibility of some public enterprises
      raising funds form the public through the sale of shares
      was also considered by the Committee. It was felt that
      only companies which were performing well would be in
      a position to raise funds from the capital market
      through the sale of shares, which they could do as well
      by raising deposits or floating non-convertible deben-
      tures. While the raising of loans involves a fixed
      liability, the Committee felt that selling shares may
      create problems of ownership without giving the public
      enterprise any particular advantage. Closure and
      liquidation of non-viable, loss-making units in the non-
      core sector has, however, been suggested (but no action
      has been taken on this, as yet).
(e)   A body consisting of the chief executives of public

enterprises in India Standing Conference of Public Enterprises (SCOPE) has recommended, at its annual Conference in January 1987, that up to 49 per cent of the shares of select public enterprises should be made available to the public and to the workers, and that these should be allowed to be traded in the stock markets;

(f) Public sector union workers as a whole went on strike in January 1987. One of the reasons was opposition to privatisation policies; they reiterated the stand in a muted strike in March 1988;

(g) Among academicians and journalists, while there is a large measure of support for introducing competitive elements and deregulation as well as redefining the objectives and scope of public enterprises, there have been very few voices in favour of large-scale privatisation. Few authors tended to support SCOPE's approach and a few wanted the government to rid itself of peripheral activities (like running hotels). However, of late, eminent academicians have been openly discussing the potential advantages of pruning the public-enterprise sector through privatisation in the limited context of the fiscal crisis;

(h) Private corporate industry has been critical of public enterprises and regulation but has not come out openly with convincing offers for purchasing equity in public enterprises;

(i) There is no major political party which has come out openly in support of large-scale privatisation. Yet there are occasional voices (even within the Council of Ministers) in favour of privatisation.

ACTIONS IN PRIVATISATION

There have been sporadic cases of units in the non-core sector where disinvestment took place, giving controlling interest to the private sector. A greater role for joint ventures in areas hitherto reserved for public enterprises is to be encouraged. Recently, however, there have been some cases (under the case-by-case approach) of privatisation. For instance:

(a) A decision was announced in Parliament despite opposition from with and without to transfer a 100 per

cent government-owned, two-wheeler unit-running at a loss (due to obsolete technology in a competitive market), having no serious public purpose, and needing Rs 200 million to revive it (Scooters India Ltd) - to a large, private-sector, two-wheeler manufacturer.
(b) Another announcement was to close down and sell a cycle-market unit which was taken over from an industrial house as a sick company and run in the public sector for over a decade.
(c) A proposal is under consideration to close down two loss-making divisions (Project Engineers India Limited and Bharat Tanneries) of a central-government enterprise located in the State of West Bengal, and with a corporate office in the State of Uttar Pradesh.
(d) A proposal to sell to private industry the controlling interest in two public-sector units in the State of Andhra Pradesh (one in two-wheeler and the other in four-wheeler automobiles) is under active consideration (i.e. by converting them into joint-venture units).
(e) The Finance Minister of India, in his budget speech of 1988, announced that 5 per cent of capital issues will be reserved for employees, for which banks will also render assistance.
(f) More generally, the national government and the governments of some states, it is reliably learnt, are examining (on a case-to-case basis), the possibilities of divesting part of government investments in selected, non-core, loss-making public enterprises.

It can thus be concluded that actions on privatisation in India are: (a) on a case-by-case basis; (b) restricted to loss-making non-viable units; (c) in competitive sectors where the private sector is already dominant; and (d) includes conversion into joint ventures.

PROBLEMS AND PROSPECTS

In view of the historical background of public enterprise in India, it is inconceivable that privatisation in this country will be accepted by society as an end in itself, since there is no consensus in favour of market solutions and property rights, nor are these considered as prime-movers for much needed social and economic change. The real issues centre on the alleviation of poverty and the upgrading of technology in a highly differentiated society of continental dimensions. This implies that privatisation will have to be viewed essentially as the best possible means of achieving pre-determined ends, and ensuring that it does not distort the parameters of such ends.

Social and equity issues:

The more significant issues relating to the social dimensions of the problem may be presented as follows:

(a) Public enterprises in India are symbols of the process of building the nation.

(b) In Indian society the pressure from most of the people is not towards less government, but towards more efficient government, and a far larger coverage of welfare measures, those being defined in an entirely different way from developed countries.

(c) There is serious concern in the public at large with the dangers of concentration of economic power in some business houses.

(d) In the absence of an automatic safety net in terms of unemployment insurance, the burden of retrenchment of works will be unbearable for the workers.

(e) Middle-level management and, to some extent, the bureaucracy itself are also important forces in resisting efforts towards privatisation.

(f) The size and extent of the private corporate sector is comparatively small and its track record, in terms of performance, has not generated enough faith from the public that the private corporate sector will be able to take over the responsibilities of public enterprises in any large measure (and perform better).

(g) The private sector itself has been hesitant in seeking a transfer of ownership from the large public enterprises.

(h) On the equity issues, most of the departmental units in the Government of India (such as railways) have important implications. Similarly, the financial sector has been in the forefront in emphasising priority-lending to weaker sections. In the state sector, both road-transport and electricity undertakings have equity implications. It is conceivable that society will be supportive of the privatisation of such enterprises (which would affect the poorer sections).

In these circumstances the compulsions of the political economy of India would indicate that the consideration of privatisation would relate to limited areas (i.e. non-core manufacturing and select parts of the service sector).

Macro–economic aspects:

Some of the more important aspects are described below:

(a) Given the geo-political considerations, it is unlikely that India can opt for an export-led growth strategy or a highly open economy. Even if it does, it will have to be phased over the medium term. Inviting overseas investments would also be on a limited scale and on a selective basis.

(b) There is a large degree of consensus that competition, particularly in the domestic arena, should be encouraged. However, a mere transfer of ownership of a public enterprise does not necessarily ensure this. The track record of the private sector shows that competitive forces cannot, as a matter of routine, be assumed.

(c) In the macro-economic environment based on comprehensive planning, the distinction between public enterprises and the private corporate sector appears very thin. The entry conditions are restricted even in the private sector, and term loans are contributed by public financial institutions which have their representations on the Board. Equity is also held in substantial measure by government-owned industrial promotional institutions. Thus, again in terms of ownership, the distinction is thin. The price environment is often controlled in many important activities. It is only in the consumer-goods sector that some competition in the private sector can be perceived. The overall regulatory framework makes the operating environment of the private corporate-sector quite close to that of the public sector. The exit conditions are also as rigid, in the sense that the real threat of the medium and large private sector going out of business is non-existent. (Recently however, a Sick Industries Act applicable only to private industry has come into force, which provides a statutory framework for closures, liquidation, etc., if the whole net worth is eroded. Even so it is the financing institutions in the public sector which continue to play a dominant role in this process.

(d) In terms of skilled manpower, financial practices, and
even overall efficiency, data have not unequivocally
established the perceivable superiority of private
enterprises over public enterprises.
(e) If socio-economic transformation is not desired widely
and privatisation is viewed purely as a means to achieve
predetermined ends, the allocative aspects of investment will continue to be determined by public policy
rather than by market forces. In such a situation the
scope for allocative efficiency through privatisation is
restricted.

Financial issues:

An essential prerequisite for privatisation is the capacity of
the private sector, in particular capital markets, to absorb
the divestiture of ownership from the public sector. less
than 1 per cent of the population have an equity stake in the
corporate sector. The participation in capital markets is
highly skewed in favour of selected urban centres and in
favour of large holdings by small numbers. Most of the
trading in stocks takes place in selected centres and various
stock exchanges are not effectively linked with each other.
There is a large presence of public financial institutions in
the equity markets. The private corporate sector itself has
large dependence on finances from public financial
institutions. There is also a genuine fear of the crowding-out
effect when public enterprises divest (even the issue of
bonds by public enterprises is upsetting the markets).

Thus, in financial terms, if privatisation is a means of
obtaining finances for the government, the first step will be
the privatisation of the private sector (i.e. selling of
government shares held in the private, corporate sector).

Regulation issues:

In respect of the activities of public utilities or potential
monopolies, the prospects for privatisation should take into
account several regulation issues. To the extent that
economic change is attempted through structural transformation, allocative efficiency becomes an important
aspect of public policy. Simplistic formulae like RPI-X will
not suffice.

There is virtual unanimity in the country that the present
regulatory administration in matters of industrial licensing

has led to inefficiency, on a large scale. Hence, the assumption that regulated private enterprise in a monopoly situation results in greater economies than in public enterprise would be a heroic one to make. Reconciliation of complex sets of interests (regional, linguistic, caste, etc.), so essential in the functioning of utilities, will be a highly iterative process. The transaction costs involved in regulating a private enterprise may exceed the possible advantages of transferring the ownership and management from the public to the private sector.

Legal issues:

There are some unique considerations in the Indian context. The written Constitution of India provides fundamental rights which can be upheld in law. In fact, public enterprises are often treated by courts as an arm of the government. The limitations imposed on public enterprises by such legal provisions cannot be easily removed by mere change of ownership. The protection in law that the workers have originally acquired may have to be continued even after any change in ownership, resulting in a reduction in the potential benefits of privatisation.

Innovative mechanisms (e.g. the 'golden share' in the UK, which implies control by the government without a proportionate stake in the equity), could be a subject matter for review by the courts, in terms of its compatibility with the constitutional provisions.

CONCLUSIONS

The privatisation debate in India has to be viewed in the context of serious concern with the low levels of efficiency in public enterprises, the problem of financial resources of the government and inadequate competitive elements. It has not been established that the efficiency of public enterprises cannot be improved or that private enterprises cannot be improved or that private enterprises can be more efficient through a simple process of transfer of ownership. Indeed the disenchantment with public enterprises is not matched by enthusiasm for private enterprises in India. Introduction of competition requires decisions far beyond privatisation. Large areas of the existing public enterprises involving huge investments, monopolistic units and public utilities are not amenable for privatisation.

If the objective is purely obtaining financial resources, privatisation of the existing private sector (i.e. selling of shares held by the Government and public financial institutions in the joint sector) would yield more returns. This does not mean that privatisation in terms of a greater role for private enterprise, through increased recourse to methods such as contracting and franchising of hived-off items, will not occur. At the same time, measures like management contracts (given the large pool of managerial skills in the public sector) and debt-equity swaps (given the relatively low level of foreign debt) do not appear relevant to Indian conditions.

The role of co-operatives as an alternative to public and private sectors may be emphasised in the Indian context. It would, however, be unrealistic to proceed on the assumption that the issue of privatisation will not take an important place in future debates on economic policies. However, privatisation by itself will be only one issue in policy changes, the other and more important issues being the relations between: government and industry; government and public enterprise; public enterprise and market forces; and government and market forces.

APPENDIX 1: Employment in the organised sector: public and private, as at September 1983 (in lakhs)

	Public Sector		Private Sector		Total	
	Number	Percent	Number	Percent	Number	Percent
Agriculture, hunting, etc	4.76	2.0	9.22	3.8	13.98	5.8
Mining and quarrying	8.94	3.7	1.13	0.5	10.08	4.2
Manufacturing	16.66	6.9	44.56	18.5	61.22	25.5
Construction	11.23	4.7	0.64	0.3	11.87	4.9
Electricity, gas, water, etc.	7.23	3.0	0.38	0.2	7.61	3.2
Wholesale and retail trade, etc.	1.19	0.5	2.73	1.1	3.92	1.6
Transport, storage and communications	28.52	11.9	0.59	0.2	29.11	12.1
Financing, insurance, real estate, etc.	8.82	3.7	2.09	0.9	10.91	4.5
Community, social and personal services	78.97	32.8	12.84	5.3	91.81	38.2
Total	166.32	69.2	74.18	30.8	240.50	100.0

Note: Individual figures in columns/rows may not necessarily add up to total due to rounding off.

Source: Ministry of Labour, Employment Review: July-September 1983 (extracted from Commerce Year Book of Public Sector 1984–5).

APPENDIX 2: Net profits/losses of some major sections of the public sector not covered in the central government public enterprise (BPE) survey, 1984-5 (in Rs crores)

1.	Railways	-266
2.	Posts and telegraph	122
3.	Departmental commercial enterprises of the state governments	
	Forests	455
	Mines and minerals	36
	Irrigation projects	-392
	Multi-purpose river projects	-106
	Dairy development and industries	-19
	Power, road, and water transport services etc.	-119
4.	State electricity boards	-1,123[a]
5.	State road transport corporations	-149
	Total net profits/net losses	-1,761

a   commercial losses

Source: CMTE, Economic Intelligence Services. 'A Statistical Review of Central Government Enterprises', 1984-85, April 1986, P.IV.

APPENDIX 3: Financial data on central government public enterprises in India (in crores)

(1)	1977-8 (2)	1978-9 (3)	1979-80 (4)	1980-1 (5)
1. No. of enterprises	155	159	169	168
2. Capital employed	12065	13969	16182	18207
3. Gross margin (surplus before depreciation interest and tax)	1489.16	1765.82	2054.66	2400.89
4. Depreciation and DRE	574.49	694.59	825.50	983.06
5. Gross profit	914.67	1071.23	1229.16	1417.33
6. Interest	755.13	886.18	1004.03	1399.15
7. Pre-tax profits (5 minus 6) after setting off losses of loss making units	159.53	185.05	225.13	18.68
8. Percentage of gross margin to capital employed	12.34	12.64	12.70	13.19
9. Percentage of gross profit to capital employed	7.58	7.69	7.60	7.79

Source: Extracted from Government of India: Bureau of Public Enterprises, Public Enterprises Survey, vol. 1, 1986-7.

1981–2 (6)	1982–3 (7)	1983–4 (8)	1984–5 (9)	1985–6 (10)	1986–7 (11)
188	193	201	207	211	214
21935	26526	29851	36382	42965	51931
4012.16	5184.49	5770.54	7386.21	8270.27	9893.54
1375.79	1719.75	2205.14	2758.40	2982.99	3381.89
2654.37	3464.74	3565.40	4627.81	5287.28	6511.65
1629.71	1922.74	2085.81	2529.20	3114.62	3416.31
1024.66	1542.00	1479.59	2098.61	2172.66	3095.34
18.29	19.54	19.33	20.30	19.25	19.05
12.10	13.06	11.94	12.72	12.31	12.54

APPENDIX 4: Public enterprise (PEs) in Andhra Pradesh

A: By paid-up capital

S.no.	Paid-up capital ranges	No. of PEs	Paid-up capital	Percentage share
1.	Below 2 crores	14	10.35	1.07
2.	2 - 4.99 crores	10	31.99	4.85
3.	5 - 9.99 crores	9	59.33	9.00
4.	10 - 19.99 crores	3	39.71	6.02
5.	20 - 49.99 crores	4	142.50	21.61
6.	50 - 99.99 crores	1	61.48	9.33 ⎫
7.	100 crores and above	2	313.95	47.62 ⎬ 56.95
	Totals	43	659.31	100.00

PEs with paid-up capital of more than 50 crores: Singareni Galleries 130.74; APSRTC 183.21; APTDC 61.48.

Source: Extracted from <u>State Public Enterprises Performance</u>, 1986-7, Government of Andhra Pradesh.

B. By ownership

(Rs in Lakhs)

Type of ownership	Tax-paying No. of PEs	Tax-paying Amount	Non tax-paying	Total No.	Total Amount
1. State government (100%)	2	179.46	16	18	179.46
2. State government (75% to 99.9%)					
i) With central government			2	2	
ii) With others	1	12.79	6	7	12.79
3. State government (50% to 74.9%)					
i) With central government	1	8.20	6	7	8.20
ii) With others			3	3	
4. State government (below 50%)					
i) With central government					
ii) With others	2	94.40	4	6	94.40
All	6	294.85	37	43	294.85

PEs Paying Tax: APSFC, APSTC, Civil Supplies, Seeds Development, Warehousing and ESSCOM.

Source: Extracted from State Public Enterprises Performance, 1986-7, Government of Andhra Pradesh.

REFERENCES

Bagchi, Amiya K. (1987) 'The role of Public Enterprises in India'. Asian Development Review, 5 (2), Manila.

Commerce Year Book of Public Sector 1984-85 (1985) Commerce Publications.

Dutt, R.C. (1988) 'Public sector: soft option of privatisation', Mainstream, 27 Feb. 1988.

Government of Andhra Pradesh: Public Enterprises Management Board, Performance, 1986-87.

Government of India (1985) Seventh Five Year Plan, vol. 1.

Government of India: Bureau of Public Enterprises, Public Enterprises Survey, 1986-87.

Jha, Premshankar (1988) 'Need for privatisation', Hindustan Times, 21 March, 1988.

Raj, K.N. (1986) New Economic Policy, Delhi: Oxford University Press.

Raja, Chelliah (1988) 'Public sector reassessed', Business Standard, March 18 and 19, 1988.

Report of the Committee to Review Policy for Public Enterprises (1986) IPE Journal Hyderabad, July-Sept. IX (3).

Sankar, T.L. and Venugopal Reddy, Y. (1988) Privatisation of Public Enterprises India, A Case Study, (mimeo) April 4-6, Asia Kuala Lumpur, Malaysia: Asia and Pacific Development Centre.

Venugopal Reddy, Y. (1988) Stalemate in State and Market: Need for New Agenda for State Action (mimeo), IPE/CBS Seminar 22, 23 Jan., Hyderabad: IPE.

Venugopal Reddy, Y. Privatisation of Public Enterprises, Scope, need and limits (mimeo), IPE/CBS Seminar, 22,23 Jan. 1988, Hyderbad: IPE.

9

Privatisation in Sri Lanka

A.S. Jayawardena*

THE PUBLIC ENTERPRISE SITUATION

Two reviews of public-sector policy in the early 1950s, one by a government commission (Commission on Government Commercial Undertakings, 1953) and one by the World Bank (World Bank, 1952), suggested a policy of caution in extending public-sector activity; and a law was enacted (Government Sponsored Corporations Act, 1955) to privatise public corporations (particularly the industrial ones) in stages. This Act was superseded by another (State Industrial Corporations Act, 1957), passed by a new government with a strong commitment to centralised planning and public-sector activity. Not only were 'commanding heights' of industry reserved for the state and expanded (following India's example), they were called 'basic industries'. Many other activities, such as public-road passenger transport, insurance, petroleum distribution, port cargo handling, leading local banks, and several trading activities were also nationalised.

In the 1970s, the government's role was further expanded by land reforms (which vested more than one half of the largely export-oriented and partly foreign-owned agricultural plantations in state control) and ceilings on housing property (which vested excess houses in state control). Several omnibus legislative enactments such as the State Trading Corporations Law and the Agricultural Corporations Law permitted the quick setting up of public enterprises by mere ministerial notification in the

* Senior Deputy Governor of the Central Bank of Sri Lanka and Director General of Economic Affairs at the Ministry of Finance and Planning.

Government Gazette. (Earlier, only industrial corporations could be established in this manner.) A Business Acquisition Law of 1971 permitted the government to nationalise any private business, if judged by the co-operative sector (built on the early British model) was rapidly expanded islandwide, especially in trading and the supply of 'essential goods'. Whereas the village level multi-purpose co-operatives were strengthened, a central wholesale organisation of the co-operative movement, called the Co-operative Wholesale Establishment (CWE) was made to open retail outlets islandwide. In sun, the public sector's presence became an overwhelming one.

By the mid-1970s, however, some disenchantment with the working of a rapidly grown and widespread public economy activity was emerging. This was also a period of acute terms of trade deterioration for Sri Lanka, and recurring balance of payments deficits compelled the government to intensify trade and exchange controls. In a regime of increasing controls, public firms were often accorded monopoly rights in imports and distribution; and in a market of growing shortages of essential commodities and widespread rationing, public enterprises came to face the wrath of hard-pressed consumers.

Thus, in 20 years , the issue had gone through a full-cycle. A new government came to power in 1977. Reflecting the mass opinion, the governement opted for an 'open economy', when trade was liberalised, the controls were relaxed, the state monopolies were disbanded, income tax was reduced, and the private sector and foreign private investment were openly and conspicuously encouraged. The government categorically declared that it would not under-take any activity which the private sector could undertake.

THE PRIVATISATION PHASE

The critics of the pre-1977 economic regime have often described it as a 'command economy' or a 'siege economy'. In the period preceding 1977, there was a long period of a 'state of emergency', following an abortive attempt to overthrow the government in 1971, and the government was committed to a socialist policy. Although a considerable portion of the economy in the pre-1977 period still remained in the hands of the private sector, such as rice farming, gem mining, international trade, small and medium industries, and the like, most of those activities were closely regulated by government. There were over 6,000 items under price control and the private sector had to survive in a growing black market. Under such circumstances, ownership data can give a misleading picture of the extent of private and public enterprise. It would be fair to say that an overwhelming proportion of Sri Lanka's economic activity could be deemed to have been either owned, controlled or regulated by the State in the years immediately prior to 1977. There are over 214 public enterprises, by and large, in various fields, ranging from agriculture and manufacturing to education and culture. This number does not include certain economic activities operated directly in the manner of government departments, such as the railways and food trading activities of the Government Food Commissioner.

The post-1977 regime, too, declared itself to be committed to 'democratic socialism'. But it was clearly not interested in a command type of economy. Hence, it soon set about dismantling the elaborate control system that has been built up in Sri Lanka for over 20 years. The prevailing multiple exchange rate system was unified, after a substantial devaluation, and the exchange rate was thereafter allowed to float. This crucial decision permitted subsequent dismantling of controls. the quota-based trading system was converted to a tariff-based one, and most trade controls were eliminated. The monopoly powers granted to the government and public enterprises were systematically repealed. Among the more conspicuous acts of liberalisation were the following:

(1)   The nationalised public road passenger transport was thrown open to private competition in 1978, and a large number of private bus-owners entered the field.

(2)   The private sector was permitted to compete with state trading corporations in external and internal trade, by largely eliminating the import licensing system and by the non-enforcement of restraints on free trading. For instance, the Pharmaceutical Corporation lost its monopoly of medicinal drug imports. The monopoly of sugar and flour imports of the Food Commissioner was ended. The export monopoly of the State Gem Corporation was ended by the simple expedient of permitting free private exports, after registration with the Corporation. Most import monopolies granted to manufacturing corporations were abolished.

201

(3)   The exclusive monopoly rights of manufacturing, implicitly granted to public enterprises by the non-approval of private-sector entry, were lifted. For instance, private firms were permitted in the cement, fertiliser, packaging materials, and alcoholic liquor industries.

(4)   Many state enterprises (e.g. textiles, cement, hardware and plywoods) are now open to stronger import competition. Also, certain preferred tariffs extended to public enterprises to protect non-viable activities were withdrawn.

(5)   The private sector was once again permitted to engage in paddy milling and rice trading, so that very soon a more efficient private sector reduced the once mighty Paddy Marketing Board to a marginal role.

(6)   The government announced that it would not use the powers under the Business Acquisitions Act, other than as a measure of voluntary (at the firm's request) rescuing of a firm in difficulty.

(7)   The public enterprises were instructed by the Treasury that they should not seek the tax-payers' money to subsidise their inefficiencies. If the enterprises were non-viable under reasonable competitive conditions, they were closed down. For instance, the giant urea-manufacturing complex of the Fertiliser Manufacturing Corporation was 'moth-balled', despite a massive investment, because it was cheaper to import fertiliser and export the raw material - naptha - than manufacture urea locally. Similarly, the uneconomic units of the State Hardware Corporation were closed down.

(8)   Some public enterprises were deemed to be non-viable because of deficiencies in management and technology. For instance, the Tyre Corporation went into partnership with a reputed international manufacturer. The management and technology at the five textile mills operated by the Textile Corporation were found to be deficient. Hence, the textile mills were handed over on management contracts to international firms.

(9)   Many public enterprises were found to be saddled with large excess staff, which affected their viability. Hence, the government introduced retrenchment schemes, with compensation for redundant workers (e.g. in the textile mills - which were given out on contract - and in the Fisheries Corporation).

(10) The pre-1977 regime had vested state-owned lands in three large public enterprises, the State Plantations Corporation (SPC), the Janatha Estate Development Corporation (JANAWASAMA) and the Up-country Estate Development Board (USAWASAMA). The new government disbanded the last-mentioned. The other two were so large that management was perceived to be difficult under monolithic organisations. Hence, they were re-structured into eleven Regional Corporations, with two central boards which were later elevated to ministry level.

(11) The pre-1977 regimes had nationalised the Bank of Ceylon, the leading commercial bank. Also, a new bank - the People's Bank - had been established with part ownership by the government and the co-operatives. These two state banks were accorded special privileges by making the public sector bank exclusively with them, and later by prohibiting the private sector from opening new accounts in private banks. The post-1977 regime not only lifted these regulations, but also encouraged the entry of new foreign banks and permitted the registration of new indigenous banks. The state banks were relieved of their obligation to maintain economic branches.

(12) In instances where the public-corporation or government-department form was considered to be inhibiting commercial freedom, public enterprises were permitted to set up subsidiaries or re-organise themselves, under company law, as public limited liability companies. For instance, the former national airline, Air Ceylon, was closed down and a new Airline - Air Lanka Limited, was set up under company law. Several public enterprises, such as the Cement Corporation, the co-operative Wholesale Establishment and the Gem Corporation set up subsidiaries under company law. The Highways Department converted itself into a 'Road Development Authority'.

(13) The government monopoly of insurance, vested in the Insurance Corporation of Sri Lanka was whittled down, when the government created two competing state organisations, the National Insurance Corporation (NIC) and the Sri Lanka Export Credit Insurance Corporation (SLECIC). Recently, the government permitted the re-entry of private companies to the insurance field.

(14) The private sector was encouraged to take over public

enterprise service functions on an 'agency basis', by paying royalties or franchise fees. For instance, the Postal Department permitted 'agency post offices' and the Telecommunications Department franchised its telex and facsimile services to the private sector.

It is noteworthy, however, that this transformation in economic-policy was accompanied by a remarkable expansion of the role of government in the economy in terms of public expenditure and investment. Public expenditure as a ratio of Gross Domestic Expenditure (GDE) which hovered around 20 per cent during the preceding years, rose dramatically above 30 per cent in the decade since 1977, peaking at near 40 per cent 1978 and staying at near 35 per cent in 1987. Government investment, which amounted to around 5 per cent to 6 per cent of GDE prior to 1977, almost doubled to around 12 per cent during subsequent years.

Most of this investment was undertaken through public enterprises, some newly created for specific investments, some by expanding the activities of existing ones. Thus, capital transfers to public enterprises, which averaged about a third of total capital expenditure of the government in the pre-1977 period, increased sharply to nearly two-thirds in 1982 and declined thereafter to around 38 per cent in 1987. Inclusive of current transfers, total transfers to public corporations rose from about 10-12 per cent of government expenditure prior to 1977, to 35 per cent in 1982, declining thereafter to 18 per cent by 1987 (See Appendix on p. 215).

This phenomenal growth of the public enterprise sector in financial terms was directly the result of a massive public investment programme, through public enterprises, in irrigation, power, housing and construction, to provide what was perceived to be the necessary infrastructure for a dynamic private sector. Noteworthy among them were: the Mahaweli Development Authority (MDA), which undertook the gigantic task of developing the hydro-power and irrigation potential of Sri Lanka's largest river; the Urban Development Authority (UDA), which undertook the construction of a new administrative capital and a parliament, and, along with other construction organisations, a programme for the construction of one million houses; and the Greater Colombo Economic Commission (GCEC), which undertook the creation of the infrastructure for a Free Industrial Zone for foreign investors. No infrastructure for a Free Industrial Zone for foreign investors. No contradiction of policies was perceived in this situation, for public infrastructure had been neglected during a long period of balance-of-payments difficulties and regulation. Most of this massive public investment was financed by highly concessional foreign aid, which is generally available on a government-to-government basis, and not to the private sector. Moreover, the 'aid climate' for Sri Lanka was dramatically improved since 1977, when the change in economic policies from a controlled economy to a market-oriented economy was perceived by major donor countries as a welcome and positive change. At the same time, the world's capital markets were buoyant (after the re-cycling of petrodollars) and international lending was on the rise. Hence, the authorities, who were faced with adverse terms of trade, found a convenient environment to mobilise foreign savings for domestic investment in the public sector.

However, there was some overheating of the economy. Furthermore, the absorption of large-scale foreign resources required matching by domestic resources and there was the risk of crowding out the private sector, the very sector which the authorities wished to develop and foster. Inflation rose dramatically to near 30 per cent in 1981. The excess demand generated weakened the balance of payments, fiscal deficits rose alarmingly, largely owing to higher foreign-aid absorption, and rising interest rates tended to dampen private investment. Hence the government was compelled to continuously phase out its investment targets - in order to safeguard the balance of payments, contain inflationary pressure, and encourage private sector activity. This was not easy, however, because the government's commitments on large-scale projects could not be easily deferred, in view of contractual obligations. Hence, other desirable investments had to be phased out, to relieve the pressure on the economy.

The strategy was to scale down the public sector once the major lead projects were completed. With this end in view, the government announced a 'medium-term-policy framework' for the period 1987-1989, which envisaged a progressive reduction in government expenditure. However, this could not be implemented because of a dramatic increase in outlays on national security, arising from a need to contain a separatist movement which had resorted to terrorist activity. Since some progress was made in mid-

1987 towards achieving a negotiated peace settlement for the internal strife, the government perceived an opportunity to save on military outlays; and, in the budget speech of 1987, it once again adopted a path of fiscal moderation, with the explicit intention of reducing the size of the public sector, and encouraging the private sector. Included in this strategy was a strong move towards privatisation.

STRATEGIES AND PROBLEMS IN PRIVATISATION

Following the presentation of the budget speech in 1987, the government explicitly adopted a policy of moderating the role of the public sector and fostering the private sector (including progressive privatisation) in a medium-term policy framework for 1988-90. This policy is best enunciated in the Finance Minister's words in the budget speech itself:

> I contemplate a sweeping reform of our public enterprises. Sri Lanka has been saddled with a large number of public enterprises, whose justification to remain under public ownership today is highly questionable... Now that we have an active private sector, which is willing and able to run certain industries better than the State, there seems to be no particular reason for continuing these industries in the public sector... We do not propose to sell off all public enterprises without any consideration of the consequences. We do not think that privatisation is a panacea for all ills... We do not contemplate transferring these enterprises to our friends, relatives and our cronies - which is what happened in some countries in the name of 'privatisation'. We will offer the shares to the people of Sri Lanka by systematic public issues of shares after proper valuation and proper advertising. We will give special incentives to employees to buy shares in their own firms. We hope to cast the net wide and sell shares to as many people as possible. We will evolve special mechanisms ... to prevent the creation of new monopolies or 'crony capitalism' in our land. We will thus be emancipating the public enterprises from the clutches of inefficient bureaucrats and returning and people's assets to their rightful owners - the people themselves. Any employees who wish to leave of their own accord will be

compensated fully and adequately. They will not suffer under any circumstances.

(Minister of Finance and Planning,
Budget Speech, 1987: 43-44)

In keeping with this broad strategy, the President appointed three ministry secretaries from the public sector and three leading senior executives from the private sector to form a 'Privatisation Commission' in 1987. This body was expected to study the prospects of privatising public corporations, publicly owned companies, and other economic activities conducted directly by the government, with a view to ultimate privatisation. Prior to this, the government had been taking ad hoc measures - such as the disposal of a few small factories an the commissioning of an evaluation of the prospects of privatising the country's telecommunication network (as a result of an initiative by a foreign company).

Meanwhile, the government has announced publicly that it intends to privatise the ownership of the Telecommunications Department, the State Distilleries Corporation, the Ceylon Oxygen Company Limited, and United Motors Limited. The Telecommunications Department had a monopoly of internal and external telephone, telex, and facsimile systems. Some moves towards privatisation had already been made by franchising out telex and facsimile services to private operators. However, the technology was backward and the authorities felt that collaboration with a reputed international firm would generate the needed new investment have been under consideration for nearly three years now, and the delay has been due to the complex nature of the activity. Meanwhile, the Union of Posts and Telecommunication Officers (UPTO), the powerful trade union of the industry, has been vehemently opposed to the privatisation proposals. Their arguments are mainly based on the risks to national security and the fear of increasing tariffs, that a privatisation might cause (Jayasekera, 1988).

The State Distilleries Corporation is also a highly profitable public enterprise. It faces a fair amount of private sector competition, but at the higher end of the price scale. The Corporation is unable to expand production rapidly, on account of a shortage of coconut syrup and the practice of the government in arrogating profits to government revenue.

United Motors Limited and Ceylon Oxygen Limited were erstwhile private firms taken over by the previous

207

government under the Busines Acquisition Law, in the 'national interest'. They were small and profitable enterprises managed as 'government-owned business undertakings' (GOBU), under the management of a 'competent authority'. The government introduced a law which permitted their transformation to public limited liability companies, with the ultimate aim of divesting the shares. At the same time, the government announced the longer-term intention of divesting the remaining GOBUs.

Although the government after 1977 was committed to granting a greater role to the private sector, progress towards achieving this objective has been slow, owing to circumstances of the domestic situation. First and foremost, the Sri Lanka economy by 1977 had developed a most intricate and pervasive system of controls and regulations, which were extremely difficult to dismantle, and officials have been found reluctant to surrender their erstwhile powers. Even after import permits were done away with, other institutions (such as banks) would look for permits before opening letters of credit. Institutions that lost their relevance after liberalisation continued to function, with no effective tasks, sometimes arrogating to themselves some new tasks of dubious significance. For instance, the government's Department of Commodity Purchase, which purchased sheet rubber for export to China under a bilateral trade agreement, still continues to function, allegedly informing the public of daily cocoa prices, whereas sales to China under agreement ceased a decade ago when trade was liberalised. It would appear that public enterprises and regulation neither die nor fade away easily.

Public enterprises also tend to build up strong pressure groups, workers in particular, in support of their continued survival. The problem is that in Sri Lanka, where about one half of the workforce is employed in government or some public enterprise (largely on account of the inclusion of the plantation workers since the land reforms), working in the public sector carries some prestige and recognition, quite out of proportion to income. In fact, real wages in the public sector (as measured by minimum wages) appear to have declined during the post-1977 decade, but it appears that many workers supplemented their declining real wages by working 'overtime' or by moonlighting. Whatever the circumstance, there was strong pressure to preserve the levels of public-sector employment. This pressure was further encouraged by the propensity of those in power and authority to treat the public sector as a convenient means of employment creation and patronage. For instance, the government created a 'job bank' with lists of unemployed seeking public sector employment. The job bank's task was to pressurise public institutions to take on its registrants. Thus, despite a freeze on government employment (including the filling of vacancies) for a major part of the decade, employment in the public enterprise sector showed a noticeable increase.

It requires a strong political commitment to undertake a programme of privatisation. In Sri Lanka, such a commitment was evident among authorities responsible for broad macro-economic policy, but a similar enthusiasm was not evident among those responsible for sectoral or micro-economic policy. In fact, after the dramatic liberalisation measures of 1978-9, the process slowed down, and the liberalisation of the coconut industry (on the agenda since 1977) was only finally carried out in 1987.

The major concern relating to privatisation in Sri Lanka has been the fear of creating unemployment. This is understandable in a country where unemployment, at around 24 per cent of the labour force in the mid 1970s, is the major economic problem. However, that was a static view of the problem and no account was taken of the prospect of labour absorption by a more dynamic private sector, which could develop if the heavy hand of government regulation was removed and the fiscal overhang of a large public sector was moderated.

This raises the important issue of selling privatisation to the public. In Sri Lanka, the public sector is generally viewed as a benevolent form of economic organisation, compared with the private sector which is purely profit-oriented and hence likely to raise prices to the consumer. This myth is largely prevalent in regulated economies, where public enterprises are widely used to subsidise consumers and where price controls are widely used to contain private sector prices. Several factors are often ignored in this simplistic proposition, such as the need to increase taxation to provide for subsidisation of the public sector, the failure of price controls, and the resultant emergence of black markets. Hence, popular support for privatisation can be developed only if its apparent benefits are clearly explained to the people. In Sri Lanka, this was conspicuously lacking until the Budget Speech of November 1987.

Ideological opposition to privatisation was also evident in Sri Lanka. The Communist Party often characterised privatisation proposals as attempts to sell off 'people's assets' to 'mudalalis' (or merchant-capitalists) and supporters of the government, at give-away prices. In the case of privatisation of bus transport and insurance, the opposition parties threatened eventual re-nationalisation, if they came to power. In both instances, the government did not appear to give a convincing reply or response.

Fears of 'sell-outs' to cronies and retaliatory nationalisations or expropriation by later governments are some of the greatest impediments to successful privatisation, at least in parliamentary democracies. An important concomitant of spreading share-ownership would be an efficient capital market. Sri Lanka had a rudimentary share market until the 1972 land reforms. Since then, and under increasing regulation, the share market has been in a state of hibernation. In the 1980s, the share market became somewhat active again, but continue to be a small one, relatively unknown and operating with minimum supervision. In 1987, the government took several steps to set up an orderly stock exchange, and also established a Securities Council, to supervise its operations.

In public discussions on privatisation, government bureaucrats often described the delays as due to the need to carefully evaluate the assets of public enterprises before privatisation. An item-by-item evaluation of each asset of an enterprise would undoubtedly take much time, but it should be considered whether such a minute evaluation is actually necessary. After all, a public enterprise is likely to have much non-performing and redundant assets, which no private entrepreneur would be interested in. Hence, any attempts to transfer assets at 'official values' would hardly help privatisation. Interested private entrepreneurs are likely to assess the value of an enterprise as an investment yielding a desired rate of return.

Perhaps the most difficult aspect of privatisation in Sri Lanka has been the determination of guidelines to select individual public enterprises for transfer. In the absence of such accepted guidelines these decisions tend to be arbitrary, and the consequences can be damaging. For example, choosing the telecommunications industry for privatisation appeared to be dictated by the offer of a joint-venture partnership by a multi-national firm. The background to choosing the State Distilleries Corporation for

privatisation reads like a fairy tale. The Minister of
Finance, the most articulate advocate of privatisation, was
pressing a somewhat recalcitrant Industries Minister to part
with some public-sector industries; and the Industries
Minister, while 'offering' two small enterprises (United
Motors Limited and Ceylon Oxygen Limited) challenged the
Finance Minister to make his own 'contribution' to the
cause. The state distilleries corporation operated under the
Finance Minister! Besides, the decision to transform
twenty-three GOBUs engaged in diverse activities to public
companies, with the intention of eventual privatisation, was
probably dictated by their small size and relative
unimportance.

Many problems could arise unless the government's
choice of enterprises for privatisation are made on solid
economic criteria. For instance, telecommunications
industries the world over are generally owned by the State
or tightly regulated, on account of strong external dis-
economies of competition and the characteristic of the
industry to verge on 'natural monopoly'. Hence, privatisation
will have to be accompanied by some regulation to
safeguard consumer and national interest. It is not
surprising, therefore, that the review and restructuring of
the telecommunications system in Sri Lanka, pending
privatisation, has taken over two years so far.

Similar problems arose out of the decision to open
public-road passenger transport - another natural monopoly
- to private competition. History has been allowed to repeat
itself in Sri Lanka, as the following background details show.
In the early 1930s, such transport was privately owned but
came under regulation in the late 1930s; the failure of the
service eventually led to its nationalisation in 1958. After
deregulation in 1978, it soon became necessary to bring back
regulation, and already one hears of complaints regarding
the quality of service. The public sector operation is now
saddled with uneconomic routes, which have to be subsidised
by the tax-payer.

Apparently, the government's strategy is to privatise
profitable public enterprises at the outset, so that
privatisation could be demonstrated as a 'success'. It
believes that profitability of a public enterprise is a signal
that it no longer needs to remain under public ownership.
This curious argument is based on a philosophy that only
'loss-making' activities need to remain in the public sector.
That would exclude the most promising candidates for

privatisation - namely, those which are potentially viable but which are making losses now, because of weak management, bureaucratisation, over-staffing, etc.

An examination of the long list of 'public enterprises' in Sri Lanka indicates that there are a large number that do not need to be privatised. First, there are the institutions which perform research, promotional, cultural, and welfare functions, which could have been provided with funds directly by the government out of tax revenues but have been set up as autonomous bodies to facilitate operational flexibility (there are also well-known economies of collective operation in fields such as research). Second, it may be desirable to assign a lower priority in privatisation to activities displaying characteristics of 'natural monopoly'. These are activities which, by their strong externalities, non-excludability relative to pricing, and the continuously decreasing nature of their marginal costs, do not facilitate free competition. Even under private ownership, they will require government regulation to safeguard national and consumer interests.

The rest of public-sector activity could be deemed to qualify for a change in ownership, if that change is likely t improve performance and service. Here, priority should be given to those that are non-viable at present, but are potentially viable, after restructuring, to relieve the burden of past mistakes.

CONCLUSIONS

After the early attempts (1952-5) at privatisation were aborted, Sri Lanka entered a long period of nationalisations and conscious expansion of public-sector activity. By 1977, the State had expanded into all forms of economic activity, by regulation and by ownership. However, as the economy slowed down, supplies became scarce and unemployment rose to nearly a quarter of the labour force; the 'command economy' was abandoned and liberalisation was subsequently adopted. Privatisation, in the narrower sense of a change in ownership, would have been an inevitable aspect of the liberalisation of the economy, but the prevailing conditions of the economy did not permit such privatisation. The liberalisation of the economy, by reducing regulation and opening up the economy to internal and international competition, may be deemed as the first, or preliminary, phase.

The second, or intermediate, phase is the promotion of competition between public and private sector operators. In reality, this phase may co-exist with the first, as has happened in Sri Lanka. This phase may also be characterised by the creation of the necessary conditions of 'the rules of the game' for the smooth working of a competitive market, such as the development of capital markets and the restructuring of public enterprises.

The third phase may be described as the one where publicly owned assets are divested to private ownership, which is the narrower concept of privatisation. Sri Lanka could now be deemed as having reached this stage, after a period of over 10 years of overt commitment to private enterprise. The problems in the third phase are many. the government may find it difficult to reach a consensus on a vigorous privatisation programme immediately, because 1989 is a year of General elections. The privatisation Commission does not yet appear to have determined broad guidelines for policy. The receptivity and the capacity of the private sector to take on public sector activity is not yet known. Despite the pledge to offer share ownership to workers, the trades unions have yet to be convinced of the benefits of privatisation.

Hence, it is most likely that Sri Lanka's efforts at privatisation, in the narrower sense of divestiture of ownership, will proceed at a snail's pace. However, this will not rule out further strong initiatives in promoting competition in the economy, which could yield even greater benefits than conspicuous acts of divesting public enterprises.

REFERENCES

Business Undertakings (Acquisition) Act (1971) 35.

Central Bank of Sri Lanka, Annual Reports, Review of the Economy (annual).

Commission on Government Commercial Undertakings, (1953) Report of the Commission, Sessional Paper 19.

Committee of Public Enterprises; Reports 1 - 9.

Finance Act (1971) No. 38.

Friedrich-Ebert-Stiftung (1988) Aspects of Privatisation in Sri Lanka, Colombo.

Government of Sri Lanka (1987) Statement of Industrial Policy, Colombo.

Government Sponsored Corporations Act (1955) 19.

International Bank for Reconstruction and Development (1952) Economic Development of Ceylon, Colombo.

International Bank for Reconstruction and Development, various country economic memoranda, latest being 'Sri Lanka: a break with the past, the 1987-90 program of economic reforms and adjustment', Washington DC, May 1988 (unpublished).

Jayasekera, Upali S. (1988) 'The threat of privatisation of the telecommunications service in Sri Lanka', in Friedrich-Ebert-Stiftung, Aspects of Privatisation in Sri Lanka, pp. 121-6, Colombo.

Jayawardena, A.S. (1965) 'Economic problems and organisation of public enterprise in Ceylon. 1931-1963', unpublished thesis, London School of Economics.

—— (1970) 'Public sector industrial enterprises in Ceylon', in Industrial Development Board, Research and Industry, Colombo.

—— (1977) 'Public enterprise in Sri Lanka: investment, prices and performance', paper presented at Asian Center for Development Administration Seminar, Kuala Lumpur.

Minister of finance and Planning, Budget Speeches (annual).

Oliver, H.M. (1957) Economic Opinion and Policy in Ceylon, Durham, NC, USA: Duke University Press.

Parliamentary Series, Reports of the Auditor-General.

Snodgrass, D.R. (?date) Ceylon, an export economy in Transition, Yale University Press.

Sri Lanka State Trading Corporations Act (1970) 33.

State Industrial Corporations Act (1957) 49.

Union of Postal and Telecommunication Officers, Newsletters.

World Bank (1952) Economic Development of Ceylon, Colombo: World Bank.

APPENDIX: Government transfers to public enterprises

Year	Transfers to public corporations			Interest and dividends received from public corporations and companies
(1)	Current (2)	Capital (3)	Total (4)	(5)
				(millions of ruppes)
1973	166	384	550	108
1974	164	378	542	106
1975	134	770	904	137
1976	129	965	1,094	217
1977	146	868	1,014	363
1978	1,081	20,070	3,151	141
1979	920	3,112	4,032	205
1980	1,583	6,086	7,669	211
1981	1,350	7,174	8,524	199
1982	1,697	10,653	12,350	295
1983	1,920	10,422	12,342	318
1984	1,865	13,334	15,199	615
1985	1,370	12,762	14,132	1,269
1986	2,261	13,998	16,259	1,068
1987	2,488	9,581	12,069	297

Source: Central Bank of Ceylon, Review of the Economy 1980, 1986.

10

Privatisation in Malaysia

Ministry of Public Enterprises

THE PUBLIC ENTERPRISE SITUATION

The totality of public enterprises (PEs)

Statistics from the Central Collection Unit (CICU) of the National Equity Corporation (PNB) indicate that, as at December 1986, there are 736 PEs in Malaysia (380 federal and 356 state enterprises). They operate across a broad range of activities with concentrations in the following areas: manufacturing (23 per cent); services (28 per cent); construction (14 per cent) and agriculture (11 per cent): Table 10.1 shows how public enterprises can be broken down into sectors.

Table 10.1: Breakdown of PEs by sectors

Sector	Level State	Level Federal	Total No.	Total %
Agriculture, fishing, forestry etc.	64	19	83	11
Mining	8	12	20	3
Manufacturing	80	89	169	23
Transport and communications	10	38	48	7
Commerce and trading	34	24	58	8
Banking and finance	8	38	46	6
Construction	62	43	105	14
Others (services)	90	117	207	28
Total	356	380	736	100

Source: CICU (PNB)

At present, there is no information on the current share of Malaysian PEs in either GNP or total production of goods and services.

Size structure of PEs

The size of the government investment in PEs is quite staggering. In 1981, the value of investments undertaken by the public sector agencies amounted to M$2.527 billion or 27 per cent of the total public-sector investments i.e. Malaysian dollars. In 1982, federal-government equity in government-owned companies amounted to M$1.28 billion, whilst loans advanced were M$7.2 billion and investments in federal statutory bodies were M$13.5 billion. The size of the government investment as at September 15 1987, amounted to M$5.739 billion or 78 per cent of the total paid-up capital of these agencies. (Ministry of Finance, Economic Report, 1986-7) The size of the government investment is estimated to be 48 per cent during the Fourth Plan Period (1986-1990). However, after 1986, the investments of the PEs have been drastically reduced to reflect the cutback in development expenditure due to resource constraints. Table 10.2 shows the equity ownership of PEs in Malaysia in 1986.

Table 10.2: Public equity ownership of PEs in Malaysia in (1986) (in percentages)

Public Equity Ownership	Number of PEs
100	219
50 - 99	240
25 - 49	147
< 25	130
Total	736

Source: CICU (PNB)

The detailed breakdown of the public equity ownership by subsidiaries of some of the PEs monitored by CICU is given in Appendix 1 on pp. 232-3.

Supervision and monitoring of PEs

PEs are supervised by the central agencies and their respective ministries at federal level, and the state government through its parallel instruments at state level. Central agencies, like the Public Services Department, control the recruitment of key personnel in PEs, other than companies. The federal treasury plays a pivotal role in matters of equity participation, loans, and loan guarantees, and its role encompasses the whole gamut of public enterprises, irrespective of their form. The Prime Minister's Department, namely the Implementation and Coordination Unit, monitors the performance in return-to-investment-criteria appraisals. the twenty-three federal ministries undoubtedly play their ordained role in supervising public enterprises that fall under their respective jurisdiction. PEs involved in industrial and commercial undertakings are generally supervised by the Ministry of Public Enterprises and the Trade and Industry Ministry.

The supervision and feedback mechanism currently practised in the Malaysian public enterprises sector takes the following forms:

(a) Central agencies and federal ministries have represen-
     tatives on the boards of management to act as
     'watchdogs' and to ensure that their interests are well
     taken care of.
(b) Periodic feedbacks in the form of completed computer
     formats are sent to the various ministers and central
     agencies by PEs either quarterly, half-yearly, or
     annually, according to their respective needs.
(c) PEs are regularly visited by ministers and senior
     government officials, where on-the-spot briefings and
     ministerial directions are given; and
(d) Standing councils and committees of the Prime
     Minister's Department (e.g. the National Action Council
     chaired by the Prime Minister himself) regularly judge
     the performance of key public enterprises, in confor-
     mity with the spirit of the New Economic Policy (NEP).

As the public sector investments in PEs are large, it has been necessary for the government to strengthen its controls over these investments, and the Central Information Collection Unit was consequently established to collect information and monitor government companies and agencies. In addition, CICU also analyses, in detail, selected major agencies which are facing difficulties. A unit has also been set up by the Ministry of finance to undertake the study of sick companies and to provide proposals to the government on the appropriate action to be taken with respect to the future of these companies. PEs that are successful are normally transferred to the National Equity Corporation (PNB). This corporation currently operates a unit-trust scheme, whereby 'bumiputeras' ('sons of the soil') can buy shares in specific units and earn bonus issues and dividends through it. However, PEs that are continually 'in the red' are hived off to joint-venture partners or other interested parties, or closed down.

Performance of PEs

Table 10.3 gives the percentage return on capital employed (as at 1986) of some of the PEs monitored by CICU, and Table 10.4 shows the profitability structure (as at 1986) of PEs in Malaysia.

Table 10.3: Return of capital (ROC) employed for PEs in Malaysia, 1986

Percentage return on capital employed (%)	Public enterprises No.	%
> 20	126	17.2
15 - 19	40	5.4
10 - 14	59	8.0
5 - 9	70	9.5
0 - 4	255	34.6
Negative	186	25.3
Total	736	100.0

Source: CICU.

Table 10.4: Profitability structure of PEs in Malaysia, 1986

Accumulated profit/loss (as % of capital outlay)	Enterprises No.	%
> 100	68	9.3
50 - 99	41	5.6
25 - 49	43	5.8
0 - 24	307	41.7
Negative	277	37.6
Total	736	100

Source: CICU.

The overall poor financial health of PEs in Malaysia is partly due to the government's policy of transferring the more successful and profitable PEs to the National Equity Corporation, with subsequent listing on the Kuala Lumpur Stock Exchange, (e.g. MAS and MISC). This poor performance is also due to poor planning and management by the PEs themselves, further aggravated by the world-wide recession and a drop in commodity prices. However, in terms of their contribution to NEP objectives and stimulating economic growth, most PEs have assisted tremendously in alleviating the lot of the indigenous community of Malaysia by way of job opportunities, increased equity holding in the corporate sectors, entrepreneurial training and exposure, and a share of the economic pie of the country. Since privatisation is part and parcel of the NEP it is vital that PEs step up their performance so that the target of 30 per cent Malaysian ownership of the share capital of the corporate sector will be a reality by 1990.

THE THINKING ON PRIVATISATION

Privatisation in Malaysia is a relatively recent phenomenon. The key objectives on privatisation are:

(i) reducing the financial and administrative burden of the government.
(ii) reducing the size and presence of the public sector;
(iii) promoting competition, raising efficiency and productivity;
(iv) accelerating growth through increased opportunities for private sector involvement; and
(v) achieving the objectives of the New Economic Policy (NEP).

Concepts of privatisation

As privatisation in Malaysia is relatively new, the government is cautious about implementation. First, the Cabinet has decided that the government should consider privatising selected government-owned services and enterprises, in order to relieve the government's financial and administrative burden and with a view to raising the quality of the services provided to the public. All ministries and agencies have been directed to examine their programme and activities, and to consider the feasibility of privatising all, or parts, of their services. The Cabinet has also appointed an Economic Planning Unit (EPU) - with assistance from the Implementation Co-ordination Unit (ICU), the Treasury, and the Public Services Department (PSD) - to co-ordinate the work involved in preparing proposals for privatisation. Arising from the Cabinet decisions, a Committee on Privatisation, under the chairmanship of the Director General of the EPU, has been established. This committee will have overall responsibility for expediting the privatisation programme. Second, a number of Technical Working Committees (responsible for different sectors) have also been established to provide the technical support to the main committee. Third, Guidelines on Privatisation have been prepared to inform both the government agencies and the private sector on the privatisation policy, and to guide them on the major aspects of privatisation (including the objectives and forms of privatisation, the identification and selection of privatisation projects, and the institutional machinery for privatisation).

Forms of privatisation

Privatisation, in essence, involves the divestment of the existing interest of the government in favour of the private

221

sector. The forms of privatisation currently being adopted in Malaysia are as follows:

(i) Partial privatisation: The government retains a portion of the ownership of the enterprise. Control may or may not be exercised by the government. Joint-ownership will cover cases where the ownership of the share capital is on a 50 : 50 (per cent) basis.

(ii) Selective privatisation: An agency responsible for certain services or interests may sell or lease a part of its services while still retaining the remaining services under public ownership, control, and management.

(iii) Management privatisation: The management expertise and know-how of the private sector is invited through a management agreement, while the government retains complete or almost complete ownership and control of the enterprise.

(iv) Contract privatisation: There is private-sector involvement in the provision of certain services or activities, but there is no change in the organisational set-up of the government agency responsible for the services. The contracting-out of certain services (e.g. construction work, infrastructure services, maintenance work, and stevedoring to the private sector).

(v) Leasing privatisation: For financial or other reasons, leasing should be considered by the parties involved but the agency responsible will have to evaluate the costs and benefits of leasing, and to indicate whether it will be a permanent feature or only a phase in its privatisation plan. Leasing is essentially the renting-out of specific facilities and assets in return for specified payments for the use of these facilities and assets.

ACTIONS IN PRIVATISATION

The activities and services that have been privatised and those in the process of being privatised are indicated below.

Health and medical sector

The government devised a system of allowing general practitioners and private doctors to serve about 4 hours per session for a stipulated period in the government hospitals. As a start, the system was introduced in a pilot project at the Kulim Hospital. If this system works successfully. it would be extended to other government hospitals in the country.

Transport, storage and communication sector

Rail service: The rail service was among the first services identified by the government to be privatised. The main reason is to improve the efficiency and quality of the services provided. From the commercial perspective, its revenue generation from the service was barely sufficient to meet its wage and benefits expenditure for its mammoth 10,000 personnel. The national railway has been a losing proposition (at least since 1960); in 1979, it lost M$5.6 million, thereby bringing its accumulated losses to a total of M$147.78 million. As the Malayan Railways provide social services, the government has to consider carefully the social and economic implications arising from this privatisation exercise.

Ports: The government decided in 1984 as a matter of policy that some ports in this country be privatised to attract private investments and expertise (Numerous ports were earmarked under such a plan: among them were Port Klang, the proposed M$350 million North Container Terminal at Butterworth, and the proposed M$35 million Lumut port project). The reasons are mainly to inject a more commercial approach and a professional attitude in the management of the facility.

The Lumut port project is at present awaiting approval from the federal government. At the same time, the Perak state government had already begun discussions on its privatisation with a local company and the work on the project is expected to being soon.

Airline. Malaysian Airlines System (MAS), the national carrier, was privatised primarily to secure additional capital to help finance its expansion plans and fleet modernisation. MAS needed some M$2 billion for its 5-year plans. Though a portion of the money could be raised from MAS's retained earnings and loans, it still needs about M$500 million. This amount will certainly' drain a big portion of the government's resources, particularly in the current economic slow-down and will probably be out with its capacity to provide, given its other priorities.

Thirty per cent of MAS's equity (worth M$105 million

shares) was offered for public subscription, of which M$52.5 million is for the general public, M$17.5 million for MAs employees, and M$35 million for public institutions, including National Equity Corporation and the Employees Provident Fund.

The other outstanding feature on the privatisation of MAS relates to government control over the company. In spite of partial privatisation in share ownership, the government still retains full control over the board and management of MAs through the issue of one special-rights, redeemable preference share of M$1, also known as the 'golden share'. This enabled the government to ensure that certain major decisions affecting the operations of MAs as a national airline are consistent with its policies and national needs.

The privatisation of MAs is remarkable because, firstly it is the first government agency to be privatised through public flotation shares and, secondly, such a move includes a new concept of government holding, or retaining, a golden share.

National Shipping Line. The privatisation of the national shipping line, Malaysian International Shipping Corporation (MISC), has been on the same basis as MAS. It is eventually listed on the Kuala Lumpur Stock Exchange with the government holding majority shares.

Telecommunication services: As early as February 1983, the government identified the Telecoms Department as the first of its organisations to be privatised. The move was to enable the telecommunication services to be operated efficiently and profitably. (The Telecoms Department had been criticised for its inefficiency - for example, over-billing and the long waiting list for telephone subscribers). In March 1984, the National Action Council formally approved the move to privatise the Department.

In the case of Telecoms, the organisation is still a government department employing more than 28,000 staff who are civil servants. The privatisation of the Telecoms Department is complex, and requires not only the conversion of the organisation into a commercial company but also the valuation of its assets and re-employment of the civil servants in the new company.

Due to the complexity of the exercise, Arab Malaysian Merchant Bank has been appointed as the adviser, and has submitted its recommendations to the government. As a start in the privatisation process, a company called Syarikat Telekom Malaysia (STM) was formed and wholly owned by the government to take over the operation of the Telecoms Department, and subsequently the government will sell its shares to the public.

Private Television Station: Among the earliest privatisation projects was the establishment of TV3. As far back as December 1982, the government hinted at the possibility of establishing a commercial TV station to be operated by the private sector. At that time there were few interested parties. However, in September 1983, the first private television licence was given to the Fleet Group, with the Ministry of Information and the Ministry of energy, Telecommunications and Posts both acting as overseers.

To establish a private TV station, the Fleet Group incorporated a subsidiary called Sistem Televisyen Malaysia Berhad (STMB) with an authorised capital of M$20 million and a paid-up capital of M$10 million. The main shareholders of this company are Fleet Group (holding 40 per cent of the shares), Utusan Melayu (holding 20 per cent) Syedkechik Foundation (holding 20 per cent), and Maika (holding 10 per cent); the remainder is held by other private individuals.

One of the objectives of establishing a private TV station is to provide competition to Radio Television Malaysia (RTM). With this privatisation, the government would be getting a royalty of between 3 per cent and 7 per cent of the gross revenue of STMB. Besides this, TV3 is also required to pay for every programme it borrows from Filem Negara Malaysia and RTM. There is no question that the decision to privatise TV3 has not only reduced pressure on government financial resources but has also introduced an element of competition which so far benefits the viewing public.

A positive step taken by the government is the preparation of the amendment to the Broadcasting Act, to pave the way for private-sector participation in the field of broadcasting. Initially, five areas have been earmarked for the setting up of regional stations to supplement the services provided by the government-owned stations.

Overhaul, repair and maintenance of aircrafts: AIROD is the earliest military establishment to be privatised under the 'first-come-first-served' approach. The project was awarded to those who initiated the proposals. The facility operated

Malaysia

by the Royal Malaysian Air Force's engineering division was privatised - with the government, MAS, and United Motor Works (UMW) incorporating a holding company called Aerospace Industries Malaysia Sdn. Bhd. (AIM). AIM formed a joint-venture company with Lockheed Aircraft Services International (LASI) to operate AIROD. The company is also called Airod Sdn, Bhd, which was incorporated in October 1984 with AIM holding 51 per cent of the equity and LASI holding 49 per cent. Airod now provides maintenance and repair services not only for Royal Malaysian Air Force aircrafts but also for commercial airlines and military aircrafts from other countries.

Construction Sector:

Highways. The first news of a privatised highway in this country was made public in early 1984. Under this scheme the private firm would build the road, collect toll charges, and maintain it. Parliament passed the Federal Roads (Private Management) Act in 1984. The Act enables the government to privatise the running of the highway, bridges, and ferries.

The first privatised highway project was the North Klang Bypass where a new road, 15 km long, bypassing Klang and Port Klang town, was built by a private company. Other highway projects to be privatised in the same manner are the M$300 million four-lane flyovers at Simpang Tujuh at Klang, the widening of the federal high-way from four to six lanes from Subang Jaya, and the linking of Bukit Raja to Klang Expressway. In 1988, the north-south highway linking Bukit Kayu Hitam in the north and Johor Baru in the south was privatised in favour of a private firm, United Engineers Malaysia (UEM), at a cost of M$3.5 billion. This is by far the largest project in terms of monetary value ever privatised by the government.

Land or township development: With regard to the privatisation of land or township development, the government has two options, either to sell land outright to the private sector or to jointly develop the land with them. The only state that has actively privatised the building of a township is Selangor, by virtue of the demand for houses in the state. In privatising the above activity, the government has taken the second option (i.e. to jointly develop the land) with the modification that new townships are built on state land by developers of proven capability on 'build-now-pay-

226

later' basis. Under this concept, the developer need not pay the government the assessment value of the land immediately. Instead, the government would collect the payment owing in the form of cash, or in completed buildings, or both, according to the repayment schedule. A further variation of this is the form of profit sharing. The privatisation exercise has been applied to the development of some townships (e.g. Port Klang).

Agriculture sector:

In this sector there has been substantial achievement in privatisation, covering the poultry processing plant of the Federal Agricultural Market Authority (FAMA) and the Federal Land Development Authority (FELDA). With regard to FELDA, the government has agreed in principle to privatise it through share ownership, in an effort to reduce government participation. The scheme of ownership will be opened to the present FELDA settlers.

Public utilities sector:

The government is planning to privatise water supply in Selangor and in federal territory. Under this proposal, a local joint-venture company would be appointed to manage, plan, design, and construct the water supply system for both rural and urban requirements. The company is required to pay a certain sum of money for a period of time for the use of this facility. However, the Water Department will continue to provide the distribution services while the private company will sell the treated water to the government. This scheme, however, is still in the planning stages.

Wire and cable laying works are also being privatised. In the past, the laying of wires and cables for the Telecoms Department had been undertaken in-house. Due to delays, the government has now sub-contracted such works to the private sector. At the same time, the government is looking into the possibility of getting the sector to construct a long-range transmission system using microwaves, on the same basis as with the highways.

Other services or areas:

The government or its agencies are also involved in

divesting their interests in a number of activities that were previously considered as government activities, for example:

(a) Kulitkraf Sdn. Bhd., a Mara-owned subsidiary, is being divested to a level of 50 per cent of the shares to other organisations.
(b) Sports Toto Sdn. Bhd., where the Minister of Finance (Incorporated) has agreed to sell 70 per cent of its shares amounting to M$28 million to two private companies.
(c) The Tourist Development Corporation is in the process of privatising its hotels and motels throughout the country.
(d) The Majilis Perbandaran Petaling Jaya has privatised the collection of payment of car-parking payments.
(e) Inspection of private and commercial vehicles is presently under consideration to be undertaken by the private sector.

Although there are vast opportunities for privatisation, as there are approximately 900 profitable and losing companies, the progress in Malaysia has been slow in view of the complexity of the exercise, involving legal, social, and economic constraints.

CONCLUSIONS

Although Malaysian experience in privatisation is relatively new - it was formally introduced in 1983 - it is significant in its contribution towards the restructuring objective of the NEP. The National Equity Corporation (PNB) will continue to be the main force in achieving the restructuring objective of the NEP. As per the Fifth Malaysia Plan (FMP), by December 1985 PNB had an interest in 159 companies of which 103 were quoted companies worth a total value of M$6,163 million. The National Unit Trust (ASN) scheme was successful in transferring the potential wealth of Bumiputeras (which was held in trust by the government through trust agencies) to a wide section of the Bumiputera community. Up to December 1987, ASN (which is managed by PNB) has succeeded in mobilising Bumiputera funds worth M$4.3 billion from 2.4 million investors.

In spite of its success, this model of privatisation, with a view to achieving a socio-economic goal, needs further refinement. Of late, there has been some reluctance among some government agencies to transfer their companies to PNB. This partly explains why no company has been transferred to PNB since 1987. Certain quarters misconstrued PNB as the beneficiary of trust companies. An in-depth understanding of the share-transfer policy needs to be debated among the Bumiputeras, the real beneficiaries of the scheme.

However, the share of Bumiputeras in the corporate ownership will not reach 30 per cent by 1990 as envisaged in the NEP. Estimates from the Fifth Malaysia Plan show that the Bumiputera share, having grown from 4.3 per cent 1971 to 17.8 per cent 1985, will only reach 22.2 per cent by 1990, still short of the target. To achieve the target, a refinement of the policy is more likely than its abandonment. So far, the PNB model is the most effective way of increasing Bumiputera participation in the Malaysian economy.

To further achieve the NEP target, the government has adopted the holistic approach to achieve higher growth in the economy. The emphasis is to encourage the private sector, both Bumiputera and non-bumiputera, to exploit the vast opportunities made available under this last stage of privatisation and to increase their involvement in the economic development of the country.

Under this last stage of privatisation, the government has stimulated economic growth by liberalising market forces. In other words, in the best interests of the country the government has de-emphasised its intervening and instructive role and, instead, allows free market forces to dictate the best way to produce, consume, and invest. This is clearly reflected in the various approaches adopted by the govenment in its efforts towards privatisation. First, the government allowed the private sector to enter into those activities and services which are traditionally run by the public sector, such as treatment of water supply, rail services, electricity boards, government medical stores, etc. Second, to stimulate further private investments, the government has introduced the 'first-come-first-served' approach, to reward private-sector groups or individuals who generate innovative ideas for the implementation of privatisation projects. Under this approach, the govern-ment's interests in targeted activities would be divested to the first private-sector groups or individuals who initiated or proposed the project or agency to be privatised. If negotiations with them fail, the projects will be open to others. This is a governmental strategy to reward 'entrepreneurship and innovative ideas' generated by private-sector groups and individuals, and has been adopted in the following cases: Port Klang Container Terminal; the Metro-link Service for urban communities in Kuala Lumpur; the Tourist Development Corporation Complexes; commercial vehicle testing of the Road Transport Corporation Department; the north-south highway; and the garbage disposal services of city hall in Kuala Lumpur. This trend of encouraging and stimulating private-sector involvement in the economic growth and development of the country is certainly a healthy sign of the privatisation climate currently prevailing in Malaysia, and privatisation appears to be the appropriate policy to restructure the relative roles of the public and private sectors in the management of the country's resources.

The progress of privatisation so far, however, has been relatively slow, because of the various constraints and problems encountered as a result of the ad hoc implementation of the privatisation programmes - the most obvious being the lack of clear and precise information and understanding, within and outside the policy circles, on the concepts, modalities, roles, and implementation procedures. In view of this, the government has embarked on the formulation of the Privatisation Master Plan (PMP) which aims to overcome some of the problems encountered. It also hopes to smooth and accelerate the pace of privatisation so that the country can achieve the growth objective of privatisation and, subsequently, further the restructuring objective of the NEP, at the same time reducing the financial and administrative burden of the government.

REFERENCES

Affandi, R.M. (1979) Public Enterprises in Malaysia: Role, Structure and Problems, Kuala Lumpur: Government Printer.
Al-Haj, T.S.R.S. and Yusof, Z.A. (1985) Privatisation in Developing Countries: The Experience of Malaysia, Asian Development Bank Conference on Privatisation Policies, Methods and Procedures.
Clad, J. (1985) 'The omnipresent state sector in Malaysia', Far Eastern Economic Review, 25 July.
Government of Malaysia, Second Malaysia Plan, 1971-5;

Third Malaysia Plan, 1976-80; Fourth Malaysia Plan, 1981-5; Fifth Malaysia Plan, 1986-90, Kuala Lumpur: Government Printer.

────── Economic Planning Planning Unit of the Prime Minister's Department, (1985) Guidelines on Privatisation for Use of Developing Countries, Kuala Lumpur: Government Printer.

────── Ministry of Finance, Economic Reports 1986/7 and 1987/8, Kuala Lumpur: Government Printer.

Lean, L.A. and Lim, C.P. (1984) The Malaysian Economy at the Crossroads: Policy Adjustment of Structural Transformation, Kuala Lumpur: Malysian Economic Association and Organisation Resources Sdn. Bhd.

Ragunathan, A. (1987) 'Participation in the privatisation exercise'.

Salleh, I. M. and Salim, A.R. (1987) 'Privatisation in Malaysia: some guiding principles and strategies toward the formulation of a master plan', 26-27 October.

Sulaiman, D.R.A.R. 'Inaugural address at the Meeting on Privatisation of Public Enterprise'.

Tiew, H.S. (1986) 'Privatisation in Malaysia: from concept to practical fact' (unpublished thesis), Kuala Lumpur: Universiti Malaya.

Wahab, D.H.Y.A. (1987) 'Address at the Malaysia-Arab Trade and Investment Conference', Kuala Lumpur, Hotel Hilton, 10-14 November.

APPENDIX 1: Holding companies and subsidiaries

Holding companies	Number of subsidiaries (Equity in percentages)			
	100	50-99	25-49	25
1. Amanah Saham Pahang	11	1	2	3
2. Bank Islam Malaysia Berhad	-	3	1	-
3. Bank Nasional	-	3	1	-
4. Bank Pembanguanan Sabah Bhd	2	-	-	-
5. Bank Pertanian	-	-	-	1
6. Bank Pembangunan Malaysia Bhd	-	7	10	14
7. DARA	3	3	2	-
8. FELDA	2	14	1	2
9. FIMA	8	8	4	-
10. HICOM	3	5	5	1
11. JENGKA	7	14	11	-
12. KEDA	2	2	2	-
13. KEJORA	7	2	-	-
14. KTM	-	5	4	-
15. KESEDAR	6	-	-	-
16. KETENGAH	-	-	1	-
17. Koperasi Tenaga Sabah	-	-	-	2
18. Kumpulan Perangsang Sell Bhd	11	5	-	-
19. Lembaga Kemajuan Tanah Negeri Sabah	-	-	-	8
20. Lembaga Letrik Negara	-	1	-	-
21. Lembaga Urusan Tabung Haji	4	-	1	4
22. MADA	1	-	1	-
23. Majilis Amanah Rakyat	25	19	3	6
24. MARDEC	1	17	1	-
25. MAS	-	5	1	1
26. MIDF	-	4	2	1
27. Minister of Finance Inc.	1	2	1	-
28. MISC	-	7	2	2
29. MSE	1	1	1	-
30. MTIB	1	1	1	-

cont.

Holding companies	Number of subsidiaries (Equity in percentages)			
	100	50–99	25–49	25
31. Perbadanan Ekonomi Islam Johor	–	–	–	3
32. Perbadanan Kemajuan Bukit Fraser	–	–	1	–
33. Perindustrian Perhutanan Sabah	4	1	2	1
34. PERNAS	–	27	17	7
35. PETRONAS	–	18	–	1
36. PNB	6	28	28	18
37. RISDA	5	–	–	–
38. Sabah Gas Industries Sdn. Bhd	1	–	–	–
39. Sabah Shipyard Sdn. Bhd	8	–	–	–
40. STIDC	–	–	1	16
41. STMB	1	1	–	–
42. Syarikat Permodalan Perusahaan Pahang	5	1	–	–
43. TDC	4	1	–	–
44. SADCs	10	6	1	2
45. SEDCs	67	30	38	25
46. UDA	3	1	–	–
47. Yayasan Bumi Sabah	3	3	–	–
48. Yayasan Pahang	–	–	–	2
49. Yayasan Negeri Sembilan	–	–	–	8
50. Yayasan Negeri Sabah	1	–	–	8
Total	214	245	147	130

APPENDIX 2: The PNB model

The Bumiputera Investment Foundation was launched by the Government in 1978. Its main objective was to enhance the achievement of the NEP without having to nationalise the private-sector companies. The National Equity corporation (PNB) was incorporated as a wholly-owned subsidiary of the Foundation with an authorised capital of M$200 million. The main function of the corporation is to evaluate, select and purchase shares of both private and public limited Malaysian companies with good growth potential, to be held in trust for subsequent sale to a unit-trust scheme known as the National Unit Trust (ASN), and ultimately to the Bumiputera community.

The uniqueness of PNB is that it is totally commercial in character but is monitored by and answerable to the government through the Bumiputera Investment Foundation. The government chooses the management team, comprising a board of seven directors who are known for their record of independent judgement, experience in financial, industrial, commercial, and public affairs, and whose integrity and public standing are impeccable and widely respected. PNB operates within a policy framework on investments agreed upon by the government. Some of the main guidelines include the following:

(a) The investments of the Corporation should be confined to the share capital of companies operating in Malaysia, whether or not they are incorporated in Malaysia.

(b) The Corporation is eligible to be allotted shares of those companies which are willing to issue shares to the Bumiputera community in accordance with the NEP.

(c) The Corporation should be given the opportunity to evaluate the shares offered to it and should have the right to reject any offer made, should it consider it justifiable to do so.

(d) When it considers it justifiable to do so on the grounds of yield and capital appreciation, the Corporation should be 'the last-resort buyer' of shares alloted to the Bumiputera community.

(e) The Corporation is not restricted in its investment decisions provided its management applies rigorous standards of evaluation as to security, yield, liquidity and growth potential on the selection of its investments.

(f) The Corporation should not speculate or stand to risk substantial capital depreciation of its portfolio in view of the intention to re-sell shares in the portfolio to its own unit trusts.

(g) The Corporation must minimise risks and maintain a high average yield on its investments relative to other sources of investments to attract savings from the Bumiputera community.

(h) The Corporation should not be involved in direct management of the companies whose shares it has acquired but it could seek representation on the boards of those companies where its investment is substantial.

Chapter 11

Privatisation in Jordan

Rima M. Khalaf*

INTRODUCTION

Jordan is basically a free-enterprise and market-oriented economy. Direct ownership by the public sector of the means of production is limited. Nevertheless, the government, driven by a concern for equity, and by a perceived role as the provider of public services, has actually increased its direct and indirect intervention, over time, in economic activities in the country. This intervention, still limited, took the form of direct production of some goods and services, equity participation in a number of shareholding companies, and regulation of some private economic activities.

This paper will first look at the role of the public sector in Jordan in general and in each of the economic sectors. It will then elaborate on the current economic conditions which have triggered the privatisation drive. Finally, acts of privatisation will be mentioned along with the problems facing them. A brief evaluation will conclude this paper.

THE PUBLIC SECTOR IN JORDAN

Definitions

(1) <u>Pure public-sector departments</u>: These are the departments of the central government that undertake commercial activities. They form an integral part of the government budget and are run by civil servants.

* Director, Planning and Research Department, Ministry of Planning

(2) <u>Autonomous public institutions</u>: These are enter-prises wholly owned by the government, enjoying financial and administrative autonomy. Legally they are considered as independent entities. They can maintain a payment scale different from that of the central government. They have evolved either gradually by the transformation of govern-ment departments or administrative units, or by decree to serve a public purpose or need.

Despite their legal independence, autonomous public institutions are subject to the administrative and financial supervision of the central government. They are linked to a minister or the Prime Minister, and they are usually governed by a board of directors appointed by the cabinet. Examples of such enterprises include the Public Transport Corporation, the Water Authority, the Electricity Authority, and the Royal Jordanian Airlines.

(3) <u>Mixed enterprises</u>: These usually take the form of shareholding companies in which the central government or a public autonomous institution has equity participation between less than one per cent and almost 100 per cent. The government is usually represented on the board of directors of such companies. The extent of representation and the leverage that the government has, depend on its share in the company's paid-up capital.

The rationale for the government's participation in shareholding companies was, in most cases, the need to execute some capital-intensive project which were perceived to be essential for the development of the economy, but which were too big or too risky for private entrepreneurs to venture into (e.g. the Arab Potash Company which is the largest company in Jordan, and the resource-based Jordan Phosphate Mines Co.). The total share of the public sector in those companies reached 53 per cent and 69 per cent of paid-up capital respectively. Another reason for government participation was to provide additional revenues and support for the budget. This is particularly true in the case of the investments of autonomous financial public institutions such as the Pension Fund, the Social Security Corporation, and the Postal Savings Fund.

(4) <u>Pure private-sector enterprises</u>: These are small, medium-scale or large enterprises wholly owned and run by the private sector. Such companies, however, may operate under regulations set by the government which could limit the degree of freedom that they have.

Size of the public sector: macro level

The total value-added generated by the pure public sector (the central government) averaged 21 per cent of gross domestic product over the past 18 years. Such a figure, however, includes all kinds of services rendered by the government such as defence, public administration, education, health, etc.

Public investment, on the other hand, has averaged 46 per cent of total, gross, fixed-capital formation in Jordan since 1970. This share, however, has fluctuated over the years, reflecting the general economic activity in the country. It reached its highest level of 55 per cent during the past 2 years, and reflected the decline in private investment as a result of the general economic slow-down in the country since 1982. It should be mentioned at this stage, however, that the share of public investment is not a very good indicator of public domination of economic activity, and a differentiation should be made between the expenditure for the production of a service, and the actual production of it. The bulk of government investment went to the provision of infrastructural services such as roads, school buildings, ports, etc. But the actual production of those services was mainly done by the private sector through contracts by the government. Accordingly, this high figure of public expenditure on investment embodies increased private-sector activity in the production of assets demanded by the public sector.

Size of the public sector: the sectoral level

(1) Agriculture: Agriculture is predominantly a private-sector domain when it comes to investment and production. The public-sector role is limited to providing the infrastructure for this sector. Direct production of agricultural products by public enterprises is negligible with the exception of a few pilot projects which, if successful, are ultimately sold to private investors. Agriculture, however, is extensively regulated by the government. Retail prices of basic fruits and vegetables are fixed by the government for the benefit of consumers. In addition, grains are procured by the government at promotional prices to encourage their production. Such promotional prices are in some cases set at three times the world price, as in the case of wheat purchases.

The government also interferes in the types and quantities of agricultural output. This is done through the application of a 'cropping pattern' whereby the government regulates, through cropping licences, the production of vegetables on irrigated land. Such an intervention was triggered by the success in stimulating agricultural production which was not accompanied by a parallel improvement in marketing capabilities. This created domestic surpluses of certain products while the country continued to import heavily other agricultural products. Government intervention in the agricultural sector extends to the pricing of certain inputs. Water is priced at 3 fils per cubic metre, which is considerably below the distribution cost (estimated at 14 fils per cubic metre), let alone the capital costs. Animal feeds are also provided at subsidised prices to promote red-meat production.

(2) Mining: The mining sector is another in which there is no pure public-sector production. In this sector, however, there exists a significant amount of public participation in the form of equity shareholding in mixed companies. The mining sector is composed of three major activities: quarrying; phosphate mining; and potash mining. Whereas the central government has no interests in quarrying, it has a 38.4 per cent and 53 per cent equity in the Phosphate Mines Company and the Arab Potash Company respectively, both of which are mixed shareholding companies.

In addition, other public autonomous institutions, such as the Pension Fund and the Social Security Corporation, account for 30.6 per cent of the capital of the Phosphate Mines Company, As a result of its significant share, the public sector has a sizeable representation on the board of directors of those two companies, and can appoint general managers and affect the operations.

(3) Manufacturing: In manufacturing, there is also no pure public-sector ownership. However, the central government's total equity participation in the capital of manufacturing shareholding companies reaches 12 per cent. It actually ranges between 0.02 per cent in companies such as the Arab Aluminium Industry and 49.7 per cent in companies such as the Jordan Glass Industries.

(4) Water: The water sector is purely the domain of an autonomous public institution, 'The Water Authority', which controls all the phases from tapping resources to purification, transportation, and distribution.

(5) <u>Electricity</u>: Electricity generation and distribution is predominantly a public-sector activity. The Electricity Authority accounts for 88 per cent of the electricity generated in Jordan. Only around 11 per cent of electricity is generated by industrial companies such as the Petroleum Refinery, the Cement Company, the Phosphate Mines Company, and fertilizer companies. Companies in Jordan are allowed to generate electricity for their own use but are prohibited from selling the generated electricity to other parties.

As for the distribution of electricity, concessions were granted to two shareholding companies - the Jordan Electricity Company and Irbid Electricity Company - each covering a different area of the Kingdom. Those two companies are granted protection from competition and are regulated by the central government by virtue of the concession agreement. The government fixes electricity rates and supervises the companies technically and financially. The two companies account for 60 per cent of the distribution of the electricity generated by the Electricity Authority. The Electricity Authority distributes the balance directly to domestic consumers or for exports.

The government has significant equity participation in the electricity distribution companies (e.g. 55 per cent of the capital of Irbid Electricity Company), and, if the share of municipalities (local government) is added, the share of the public sector in this company exceeds 81 per cent of its paid-up capital. As for the Jordan Electricity Company, the share of the government is 13.6 per cent and that of municipalities 9 per cent, which increases the total share of the public sector in the capital of this company to over 24 per cent.

(6) <u>Telecommunication</u>: Telecommunication services in the Kingdom (for civilian purposes) are monopolized by the public sector. The Telecommunication Corporation is still operating as an integral department of the central government.

(7) <u>Transportation</u>: Transportation is a mixed sector. Air transport is monopolised by the national airlines Royal Jordanian, which is autonomous public institution. Rail transport is an oligopoly with two public institutions operating in the field: the Aqaba Railway and the Hijazi Railway. Ports are run by an autonomous public institution, the Port Authority. It is in land transport that the public sector operates in competition with private enterprises. On

the whole, the public sector accounts for two-thirds of the value-added in the transport sector in Jordan.

(8) <u>Financial and Business Services</u>: There are three important public financial institutions which undertake the investment functions of the public sector: the Pension Fund with extensive investments in shareholding companies in manufacturing and mining; the Social Security Corporation; and the Postal Savings Fund. The public sector runs three specialised credit institutions - the Cities and Villages Development Bank, Agricultural Credit Corporation, Jordan Co-operative Organisation - and has equity participation in the Housing Bank and the Industrial Development Bank. The government also extends credit to the public through the Housing Corporation. Overall, the role of the public sector in financial services is limited.

Autonomous Public Institutions

There are currently thirty-eight autonomous public institutions in Jordan. Not all of them, however, are involved in the production of goods and services sold to the public. Some are regional planning institutions such as the Aqaba Regional Planning Authority or the Jordan Valley Authority, some are universities and public training institutes, and others are institutions for social services. The Central Bank of Jordan is also considered to be one of those thirty-eight institutions.

The number of autonomous institutions that are relevant to a discussion on privatisation is eight. Those cover the production of goods and services in five economic sectors: electricity; water; trade; transport; and communication. The institutions representing these sectors are, respectively: the Jordan Electricity Authority; the Water Authority; the Civil Consumers Establishment; Royal Jordanian (RJ) Airlines, Hijazi Railway, Aqaba Railway, Public Transport Corporation (PTC); and the Telecommunications Corporation (TCC).

Some of those institutions enjoy a monopoly condition: for example, the Jordan Electricity Authority, the Telecommunication Corporation, Royal Jordanian Airlines, and the Water Authority. Others contribute only a small part of their output. The total investment by these institutions represented 25 per cent of total investment in the country in 1986.

Two of them can be considered as profitable enterprises. Return on equity stands at 7.5 per cent for the Jordan Electricity Authority and 18.5 per cent for the Telecommunications Corporation. The Aqaba Railway registered a surplus of its operations in 1986, which could cover only 80 per cent of its capital expenditures in that year. As for the Water Authority, its revenues from the sales of its product covered only 60 per cent of its current expenditure; the remainder being covered by transfers from central government. The Hijazi Railway barely broke even in 1986. Royal Jordanian suffered a loss (in 3 out of the 12 years 1975-86) amounting to JD1.8 million. Some of the losses reflect planned losses, as is the case of the Water Authority, since water for agriculture is priced at less than 25 per cent of its operating cost.

THE THINKING ON PRIVATISATION

The private sector has played a very important role in the development of the country, especially in industry and agriculture, and in services such as trade, and business and financial services. None the less, the public sector still monopolises the production of certain goods and services such as telecommunications, air transport, water, and electricity.

Such an arrangement worked very well until the mid-1980s. Gross domestic product grew at a real rate of over 8 per cent annually during the period 1973-83. Huge public investments on infrastructure, and public capital outlays on equity participation in shareholding companies, faced no serious financial constraints in the 1970s and early 1980s. Even the operating losses of some public enterprises were perceived to be sustainable in the medium term, or until they passed the infancy stage. This was possible, despite the chronic deficit in the government budget, because of the significant budget support that Jordan received from neighbouring Arab countries. Such support reached JD197 million in 1983 and was equivalent to 28 per cent of the total government (recurrent and capital) expenditures.

In the mid-1980s the Jordanian economy started to witness new trends. The rate of growth in the economy dropped from over 8 per cent annually during the period 1973-83 to around 3 per cent annually for the period 1984-7, mainly because of the slowdown in the economies of Arab oil-producing countries. This affected the Jordanian economy through a drop in the demand of Gulf countries for Jordanian manufactured and agricultural products, the decline in their absorption of Jordanian labourers and hence the levelling off of their remittances home, and a noticeable drop in official transfers from those countries to the Jordanian government. (The number of Jordanians working in Gulf countries is equivalent to more than half the numbers working in Jordan and their remittances exceed the foreign exchange earnings from total merchandise exports.) Unemployment increased from 3 per cent in 1980 to the present rate of around 8 per cent; and private investment suffered as profitable opportunities were diminishing, due to the slow-down in domestic economic activity and in that of neighbouring countries. Gross fixed capital formation by the private sector has actually dropped by over 20 per cent annually during 1985-87. Further, the government's budget situation became less sustainable with the decline in Arab budget support.

It is within such a context that the government's privatisation policies were initiated. In 1986 the first step towards formulating a strategy was taken by the cabinet through the establishment of a ministerial committee which was entrusted with the task of increasing the role of the private sector in the economy. Part of its mandate was to evaluate proposals for privatising public enterprises. This included commercialisation of public enterprises through introducing private-management policies and techniques on the one hand, and the actual sale of assets of such enterprises to the private sector on the other hand.

PRIVATISATION STRATEGY

Given the current economic conditions in Jordan, the privatisation strategy has two major interrelated components. The first is to promote private investment in the traditional domain of the private sector, and the second is to expand the domain of the private sector by privatising a number of public functions.

Promotion of autonomous private investment

The slow-down in private investments is partly due to the general economic slow-down and partly to the government's indirect intervention in the form of regulation.

In agriculture, the government applied a cropping pattern to deal with the excess supply of certain products. However, this led to a less efficient utilisation of resources. Furthermore, price controls suppressed additional investments in the sector, and worked as a disincentive for farmers to improve the quality of their product, which limited access to foreign markets and further aggravated the domestic excess-supply problem. The privatisation strategy for this sector started to emphasise the free-market incentives and a move away from supply control and price regulation. Current public investment policy is emphasising the provision of support services such as market information systems.

A similar deregulation strategy is currently being worked out for the manufacturing sector, rather than selling out the shares of the public sector. Today, all manufacturing projects need to be licensed by the Ministry of Industry and Trade. Some projects which are in line with the development strategy of the country can receive generous incentives in the form of tax exemptions and exemptions from customs duties, albeit through a lengthy appraisal process by government officials.

Certain industries which are granted protection from foreign competition through import prohibitions have the prices of their products set by the government. Other industries receive protection from the government whereby no similar project is awarded a licence for a specified number of years. Extensive studies have been initiated on the investment environment, the licensing system, procedures for establishing businesses in Jordan, studies on important export procedures, and the tariff system. Specific recommendations are awaited.

In general, the government is keen to minimise distortions in factor markets and product markets. Efforts are also directed towards developing its legal environment, to further protect property rights including patents and to upgrade the commercial law. In this direction a new company/law (commercial law) has been drafted, and is currently being discussed among the concerned parties.

In the formulation of the current 5-year plan, prominent private entrepreneurs participated in all sectoral committees, which worked out detailed plans for the investment projects, policies, and required organisational measures.

An economic consultation council was formed, chaired by the Prime Minister, and including the three ministers in the cabinet concerned with economic affairs, the governor of the central bank, and six representatives of the private sector representing the various interest groups. The council co-ordinates financial, economic, and monetary policies, and advises the cabinet on economic matters.

Privatisation of public institutions

The second components of the privatisation strategy in Jordan is the actual transfer of control to the private sector of assets held by the public sector in commercial activities. Some of the public autonomous enterprises which produce saleable goods and services have been incurring losses, due to their adherence to the rigid rules, regulations, and salary structures of the civil service. They have excess personnel and at the same time are unable to recruit qualified professionals. Freeing them from such rules is expected to improve their operations and efficiency. Privatisation of public enterprises is also perceived to reduce the burden on the government budget. Accountability to shareholders is expected to improve the quality of product and performance in general.

A number of institutions were initially considered for privatisation and actions were taken concerning three of them: Royal Jordanian Airlines, the Public Transport Corporation, and the Telecommunication Corporation.

Royal Jordanian Airlines (RJ)

Royal Jordanian, the national airline, is widely recognised as a well-managed enterprise. It was started in 1964 and has grown rapidly in terms of operations, revenues, and profits until the year 1983. In 1983, it suffered for the first time from a drop in revenues and incurred a slight loss. RJ was identified as a target for privatisation in an initial survey conducted in 1986. It was believed that the competitive pressures in the international aviation arena necessitate that RJ be given the additional operating flexibility that could be derived from privatising it. Among the goals to be achieved through privatisation cited by the government officials or by management are:

245

the availability of capital from private sources, without the need for guarantees from the central government; increasing the productivity of employees through providing profit incentives through stock ownership; reducing costs through freeing the enterprise from government requirements such as the requirement to purchase fuel at a regulated price or the obligation to provide 25 per cent discount for government employees, 50 per cent for ambassadors and retired army personnel and families (apart from the frequent free tickets); and improving the quality of products (and of employees) as a result of accountability to shareholders.

Another detailed study, conducted in 1987, to assess the viability of RJ as a private company, concluded that privatisation was feasible from the standpoint of airline operations. Different strategies are currently being studied. One option which seems to receive acceptance by most concerned parties is to reduce government ownership to 30 per cent over time, and to achieve this (at least in part) through sale of new stock rather than a portion of the present government equity-holding. This is expected to significantly increase total equity. The study also recommended the restructuring of the company's debt through the sale and lease-back of aircraft. This was later actually implemented by the airline.

The study also recommended naming a new board of directors, consisting of private-sector businessmen, with perhaps one government representative after full privatisation, and allowing the management and board to begin to act independently in accordance with a publicly stated profit mandate. The board and the management are also to pursue the implementation of the privatisation objective.

Public Transport Corporation (PTC)

Unlike Royal Jordanian, the PTC has always been an unprofitable enterprise. It has a book value of JD 7 million, and has so far cost the government over JD 5 million in capital funding. Moreover, it is currently losing on its operations over half a million JD a year. It is considered to be inefficient in more than one respect: it has a high turnover of operators as its workforce is poorly paid and without incentive; it has a low passenger attraction; and it carries only 20 per cent of public-transport passengers in the Greater Amman area, and it faces severe competition from small buses and shared taxis.

A study on the privatisation of the PTC was conducted in 1986 and enumerated a number of reasons for the PTC being the only loss-maker in a profitable field. These included uncoordinated action by at least four agencies which interfere in its operations, and the lack of an overall public transport policy. Although the original objective of the study was to identify the best means of privatising the PTC, it was apparent that there was little hope of the government disengaging itself successfully from its losses and poor services unless other changes were made. The study drew attention to the fact that the whole public transport situation required an assessment to improve the provision, operation and control of all transport modes. The privatisation of the PTC in the absence of a comprehensive sector reform was perceived to be a futile effort. Therefore the study recommended the establishment of a Public Transport Authority which would identify an effective public transport network, and franchise the identified routes of this network to groups of operators including a privatised PTC. Accordingly, work started on examining all forms of public transport in Greater Amman and articulating proposals for its improvement and modernisation. A comprehensive new route network for all modes of transport was also drawn up and finalised in March 1987.

The government announced, in July 1987, its decision to privatise the PTC. An inter-departmental committee was formed and charged with the task of establishing the market value of the PTC in preparation for privatisation. A working agenda for legislative changes, training, and further studies was established and agreed upon by all concerned parties. It is only a matter of time before the full reform of the sector including privatisation of the PTC is achieved, with the PTC working as a commercial company operating under an independent board of directors and with normal equity capital which in due course will be publicly purchasable.

The Telecommunication Corporation (TCC)

The Telecommunication Corporation is one of the first public enterprises to be targeted for privatisation. Although it was a well-managed and profitable organisation, it suffered from serious administrative and financial constraints as a result of adhering to Civil-Service regulations and payment scales. A comprehensive study on privatising the TCC was conducted and, as a result, the government decided to change the status of the company from an autonomous public institution to a shareholding company owned by the government. This was perceived to be a first step towards selling shares to the public.

Officials at the TCC are aware of the fact that there has to be a transitional period before complete privatisation of the corporation. Intensive preparatory efforts towards restructuring and 'commercialising' the TCC have been made in accounting, finance, legal affairs, administration, computerisation, and modernisation. The TCC is preparing the necessary legal amendments for transferring the public-owned corporation to a shareholding company.

Problems encountered in privatisation

Although the privatisation experience in Jordan is still limited in years and in coverage, a number of problems, some general and some enterprise-specific, have already been identified.

Among the more serious general problems is the current depressed state of the economy which has caused a number of profitable enterprises to incur losses, or has aggravated an already poor financial performance for others. The prospects for making a successful public offering of shares are, therefore, slim for many enterprises. Most candidates for privatisation have to undergo extensive restructuring before such a move is contemplated. The slow-down in the economy, culminating in a drop in national savings, has also affected the availability of capital in the country and the willingness of private investors to subscribe to the shares of privatised firms.

The second serious problem is embedded in the general perception of the Middle East by foreign investors as an area of civil and military disruptions. Despite the fact that Jordan is a very stable country, socially and politically, many foreign visitors are reluctant to invest in the shares of Jordanian companies because of the situation in the area in general.

The third problem relates to the poor state of development of the domestic financial markets, despite the fact that considerable attention is being paid to their possible improvement. Another factor is that the support of middle management for privatisation schemes in many enterprises is not always very strong, despite the fact that the privatisation programme has the full support of government officials and the top management of those enterprises. As efficiency and cost savings are seen as the primary benefits, middle management tends to perceive their sectional activities as adequately profitable, mainly because they ignore sunk costs and those elements of costs shouldered by the government, such as the interest and amortisation of loans contracted by the government on behalf of those institutions.

As a result of the afore-mentioned problems, the government has decided against an early sale of shares in any of the three companies under consideration for privatisation. It was perceived that an offering which is not significantly over-subscribed could lead to a depressed market price and jeopardise the privatisation effort, not only for the concerned companies but for all the others as well.

CONCLUSION

Privatisation in Jordan is perceived basically to consist of a change in the investment environment in order to enhance the role of the private sector in the social and economic development of the country. Devolving control of public enterprises is only one way to achieve this goal. Even privatisation in this sense does not solely imply the change in the legal status of an enterprise (i.e. from being owned by the public sector to the status of a shareholding company owned by private entrepreneurs); it includes a thorough assessment of the industry or the sector in which the enterprise operates. Priority is therefore to be given to the reform of the sectors as a whole, in order to make privatisation schemes possible and to ensure that the expected increase in efficiency will eventually materialise. So far, no public offering of government shares in an autonomous institution has been made. Nevertheless, the government is very serious in its privatisation plans, and is currently undertaking all the preparatory steps towards achieving this end.

12

Privatisation in China

Hua Sheng*

It is well known that China has carried out its economic reform for nearly 10 years. During this period, the Chinese economy has been transformed from a highly centralised planning system (that is, a system where the government dictates all important economic activities, sets prices and comprehensive physical quotas, collects and re-distributes all the profits, and even a large part of the enterprises' depreciation fund) to a model called 'The State Regulates Market and Market Guides Enterprises'. This historic transition is far from complete now. Nevertheless, the new trend of reform and openness has changed the landscape of Chinese economy a great deal. The purpose of this paper is not to deal with the reform as a whole, but to give a brief survey of the latest Chinese attempt to remove the bureaucracy from public enterprise, which is quite relevant to the issues raised and heatedly discussed under the topic of privatisation.

PUBLIC ENTERPRISE IN CHINA

Economic structure in terms of ownership

Public ownership plays a dominant part in the Chinese economy. Except in the agricultural sector it consists of two categories: mainly state-run enterprises and a considerable number of 'collective' enterprises. The latter are usually on a small-scale basis and thus belong to the authorities at a lower level and enjoy somewhat lower but usually unified

* Professor, Institute of Economics, Chinese Academy of Social Sciences

wage and welfare structures. In all other aspects they are similar to (or the same as) state enterprises. Table 12.1 shows the ownership classification of different categories of enterprises.

Table 12.1: Ownership classification in terms of enterprise numbers (in percentages)

	1985	1986
State-owned	20.2	19.4
Collective enterprises	79.4	80.1
Township enterprises	49.9	49.3
Others	0.4	0.5

The state-owned industrial enterprises account for only a fifth of the total number of industrial enterprises, but they are usually much larger in scale. This is revealed by the distribution of employees (as shown in Table 12.2).

Table 12.2: Distribution of employees in industrial enterprises, 1986 (in millions)

State-owned enterprises	39.546
Collective enterprises in cities	17.509
Others	0.456

We can obtain a much clearer picture of ownership structure from the detailed data of 353 cities (as shown in Table 12.3).

Thus far, the emphasis has been on industry, but if we look at the national economy as a whole, a different story emerges in terms of economic performance.

Table 12.3: Industrial enterprises in 353 cities (1986) in China

	State-owned	Collectives	Others (including private)	
Output (billion yuan)	563.5	227.9	15.8	3.8
% in the country's Industry	90.9	86.4	98.1	
Profit and tax (billion yuan)	121.5	17.3	4.5	n.a
% in the country's Industry	90.6	90.1	71.4	n.a.
Fixed assets (billion yuan)	570.6	94.0	n.a.	n.a.
% in whole country's industry	84.6	84.4	n.a.	n.a.

Table 12.4: Economic performance of different ownerships

	State-owned	Collective	Others
Output/fixed assets (%)	109	223.8	217
Fixed assets/per capita * (thousand yuan)	18.118	4.692	12.171
Productivity (thousand Yuan)	15.451	8.6	28.238
Capital return (profit and tax) (%)	20.4	19.4	23.2

* Data of 353 cities

The 'others' column, which includes private enterprises/ partnerships and different forms of joint-ventures, shows better results. This is one reason why the Chinese government now encourages some development of the private sector and foreign investment. Nevertheless, because these developments are too small to exert a significant impact on the economy as a whole, any serious attempt to improve economic efficiency has to tackle the problems within the public sector itself.

Characteristics of public enterprises

Public enterprises have the following characteristics, which have changed little in essence in the course of the economic reform.

Subsidiary of the government

The leadership of every enterprise was appointed by the authority it is subject to. Efficient managers or party secretaries (they actually pursued the same target although secretaries were usually of lower status) were usually promoted to higher posts in government, and those who were incompetent were transferred to either another similar post, or a lower-grade position. Just as in politics, sometimes the personal loyalties and relations rather than the imper- sonalised performance of task (leaving aside the fact that the task itself may have been rather ambiguous) played a decisive role here. Although all the decisions about price, profit, wages and welfare were made above the enterprise, the administrative departments in an enterprise were as many as in the government, and at least half of these had little to do with production. Moreover, the over-staffing in these non-production departments (such as propaganda, political education, family planning, military training, and so on) scandalised and discouraged the people who worked on the production front.

Mini-society

The enterprises depending on their specific situation, especially their geographical location, usually undertook an extensive social obligation. For instance, they were responsible for their employees' accommodation, dining hall, medical service, nursery, and sometimes the primary and secondary schools, or even a worker university. Large enterprises, which owned their own shops, hotels, and even farms, developed a self-reliance system.

Separation and immovability of assets

Although theoretically one of the main superiorities of public ownership is to allocate and re-allocate resources rationally, owing to the bureaucratic apparatus assets were actually immovable once they had been put in an enterprise. The differences between various enterprise administrations has predisposed towards insularity in these enterprises. That is why in China a so-called enterprise looks like a factory or workshop divided geographically rather than a company organised economically. Obviously, this separate structure of assets is at the root of the repeated duplications and non-economies of scale.

Inseparability of enterprises and workers

The government is supposed to guarantee full employment in urban areas. Subject to the formidable pressure of latent unemployment in the countryside, the government strictly controlled the increases in employment and carefully allocated a quota of new employment to each enterprise. Workers obtain wages, accommodation, medical subsidies (extending to their families), and pensions from the enterprise. A worker loses all financial resource and cannot survive, let along sustain his or her family, when he or she leaves an enterprise. Transfer from one working place to another is extremely difficult, if at all possible; for, apart from finding a new place to accept him, a worker must also persuade his old place of work to let him go with all his political and financial certificates.

Early steps of reform: Decentralisation and Expansion of enterprise autonomy

Many measures have been taken since the beginning of economic reform in order to improve the efficiency of public enterprises:

(a) Enterprise retained funds are used for investments, bonuses, and welfare, subject to specific instruction. The links between performance (mainly profit) and reward were further strengthened. The bonuses have been as much as 40 per cent or 50 per cent of fixed wages in recent years.

(b) Depreciation funds are left to enterprises, which could be combined with retained profit for investment.

(c) With the development of plan and price reform, enterprises are accorded more decision-making power to choose the suppliers of materials, to develop horizontal business relations and even to negotiate directly with overseas trade partners subject to certain regulations. Since the 'dual-track system was introduced in 1985, enterprises have been allowed to buy and sell products in the market so long as they have fulfilled the planning quota. Nearly 50 per cent of producer goods are trading in the market or quasi-market now.

(d) the administrative relations between ministries and enterprises are substantially reduced or even severed. Consequently, the economic functions of the city administrative apparatus is strengthened.

(e) More investment is being gradually diverted from government budget to the banks' loans.

Admittedly, thanks to these efforts, the power of the enterprises has expanded substantially, with the profit intention of enterprises remarkably improved. But the basic constraints mentioned above still exist.

THEORETICAL MODELS OF ENTERPRISE REFORM

Most Chinese economists agree that in the transition from central planning to the model of 'The State Regulates Market and Market Guides Enterprises', a reconstruction of the economic foundation is inevitable. This means divorcing ownership from management, or even changing the forms of public ownership and diluting exclusive state ownership, while still maintaining the ownership of majority assets in the public sector rather than in the hands of private individuals. However, on the question of how to reconstruct the micro-economic foundation, the ideas are far from crystallised. Basically, there are two different approaches, which do not diametrically conflict with each other, but they do have different emphasis and assumption on certain key points.

Public shares economy

The suggestion of organising a public shares company was first put forward by the World Bank in 1984. It proposed that the assets of state-run enterprises should be allocated among the different government departments which are already their actual supervisors. It was argued that in this way the responsibilities could be specified and the allocation of assets could be improved. However, the suggestion did not appeal to many people, partly because they suspected that this approach would legalise the existing bureaucratic intervention and change nothing else. This topic became the burning question again early in 1985. Two Chinese economists suggested mixed shares economy: that is, to divide the single state-run enterprise into three sectors - the state, the enterprise, and individual mixed ownership - with each party holding a certain amount of shares. Many researchers argued that the post-tax profit and its re-investment should belong to the enterprises themselves. They further claimed that, if this were not done, the enterprise would have no incentive to invest and would never have long-term prospects.

People in business circles were ready to accept the new explanation, for they found that it gave them justification to amplify their provincial interests. Many enterprises offered their staff free shares with high fixed interest, plus extra dividend. Some tried to divide a larger part of the state assets into enterprises; others issued a certain amount of shares to solve their financial problems. But all these experiments were at the cost of the state, because they ignored the property rights of predominantly public assets, assuming that the state had obtained everything by tax. This kind of 'reform' was rightly prohibited early in 1987.

Nevertheless, this was not the end of the public shares economy debate. On the contrary more and more people in China are convinced that we can learn something from the western shares economy, especially the forms of organ-isation and management of property in joint stock companies. The dispute is concentrated on the following points.

First, what is the function of the individual share-holder? Some believe that the staff buying shares can enhance their master's consciousness. Critics argue that workers do not necessarily buy the shares of the company they work in, quite apart from the fact that people have different financial resources and different tastes. As far as a worker's incentive is concerned, the floating bonuses have much more weight.

Second, what is meant by the enterprise owning its own shares? Advocates claim that enterprise shares are the corner-stone of a socialist shares economy, for too many state shares would lead to bureaucracy and too many individual shares would lead to polarisation. An enterprise owning a significant part of its own shares keeps the balance between efficiency and equality, and guarantees the rationality of the enterprise's behaviour. Critics argue that collective enterprises with unidentified property rights have never been successful in a big economy, and were a misunderstanding of the shares economy, since a company cannot consistently possess a significant part of its own shares. It would create confusion about property rights. On the other hand, if all new accumulations of the company belong to the enterprise's shares, no one would like to invest in this kind of a company. They suspect that to set up a public shares economy largely based on enterprises owning their own shares is a blind alley on the shares economy.

Third, what is the role of the state's shares? If the government owns the majority of shares in most enterprises, what is the difference from the traditional bureaucratic model?

The debate on public shares economy is still going on in China and has been depending the discussion of reconstruction of the micro-economic foundation. Due to the first wave of turmoil, however, the experiment is now confined to a limited area, mainly in some small collective enterprises; and its prospect looks promising.

Assets Responsibility System (ARS)

ARS was put forward by my colleagues and myself late in 1985. A basic hypothesis of ARS is that enterprise reform should be phased in China for several reasons.

First, China's enterprises are still a political, social and economic mixture. No economic method would succeed without the separation of enterprises from politics. A new form of institutional change would mean nothing so long as feudal subordination predominates in the economic field.

Second, it is necessary to set up an independent social assurance system; otherwise the enforcement of firing workers and bankruptcy of the enterprise would be a social disaster.

Third, a combination of capital and labour markets is indispensable in organising a commodity economy, which not only increases the choice for the ordinary person but also hardens the constraint of the actors who are on the scene. The establishment of these markets further requires an effective legal system. Obviously all these elements need time and systematic implementation. So the suggestion is that enterprise reform should be in two stages. The first stage is to liberate human capital, especially the most wanted entrepreneurial talents, to tap the potential of present assets and achieve productivity efficiency. The second stage is to gain allocative efficiency by establishing an assets operating system and introducing certain forms of shares companies as well as financial markets.

The assumptions as regards the first stage are as follows:

(i)   The entrepreneurial stratum is the backbone of the management of modern economy; and its creation is the crux of improving economic performance and a necessary preparation for setting up self-balance within the enterprise. But both the scale of modern economic activity and China's political background have not allowed us to repeat the same road in history of entrepreneurs usually originating from the owners of the factories.

(ii) Amateurism of party organisation of the enterprise is a necessary condition for the independence of management.

(iii) The essence of the traditional hierachial pattern is its leadership structure. It predetermines that managers can never become entrepreneurs but remain subordinate to their bureaucratic superiors. This, on the one hand, brews the feudal network of loyalty and protection and, on the other, blocks millions of latent talents or even genius from getting a fair crack of the whip. Therefore, whether to abandon the bureaucratic appointment system at enterprise level or not, is the touchstone of any real reform.

(iv) This, however, does not imply that the managers should be elected by workers. Because the staff are not exclusive owners of the enterprise, their decisions do not always coincide with the interests of the owners of the enterprise, who are either individuals or society as

258

a whole (in the case of a public enterprise. However, a manager is not a politician and ability should play a larger part than popularity.

(v) In order to pursue the rationality of enterprise behaviour in the long run, it is not sufficient to be confined to the concept of annual profit. The concept of assets is necessary in selecting managers and assessing their contribution. When there is no capital market, it is possible to imitate the market value of assets by socially expected capital return (a trend of expected profit in coming years). So far as the creation of the entrepreneurial stratum and improvement of production efficiency are concerned, one can make do with the latent concept of assets as the first step to harden constraints on property rights.

The model in the second stage is as follows:

(i) The bureaucratic appointment system should be abolished and a socially competitive system should be introduced instead. The selection of top managers may take the form of openly invited bidding. Anyone could be a tenderer provided he or she puts forward a competitive profits forecast for the coming years (usually 5 years) and a corresponding set of convincing measures. An examining and appraising committee, which consists of the experts and the representatives whose interests are concerned, will choose the winning bid through debate. The person who wins the bid naturally becomes the general executive who organises a team to run the enterprise, and shoulders the responsibility for the contract he or she has signed.

(ii) It is necessary to distinguish the top manager group from the ordinary staff and workers. Their income should be connected with profit to streamline the internal organisation and refuse any interference beyond the contract. The government will only control the aggregate wage fund, and managers will have the discretion to pay according to the staff's different performances. This can accord managers sufficient power to run the enterprise without being able to fire a worker at will for the time being. The manager group will be punished when it fails to fulfil the contract and will be rewarded materially and spiritually if it does well.

(iii) In order to prevent any short-sighted behaviour of the incumbents, a new round of bidding is demanded whenever the term of a contract expires. The disparity between the previous winning bid and the new bid roughly indicates the variation of the assets (including tangible and intangible assets); so it could be regarded as an important indicator by which to assess the real contribution the managers have made. This should ensure that anyone who operates an enterprise ineptly cannot get away with it.

The establishment of managers in a central position with prior selection through competition is the target to be achieved in the first stage of ARS.

The second stage refers to pursuing allocative efficiency and organising an operating system of public assets. It is at this stage that an independent assets management system, which is exclusively responsible for state-owned assets has to be established. Capital return is the only criterion by which this system operates. Financial expert groups can bid for the managerial power of state-owned assets; so state-owned assets will be automatically divided into many pieces and operated by a number of financial companies. These financial companies compete and interact with one another. Inter-investment will soon make it inevitable for assets to assume the form of shares. Assurance companies and pension funds can also join in buying and selling equity in order to diversify ownership and heighten competition. All these financial organisations are profit-oriented and play a two-fold role; the first is to assign representatives to participate on a board of directors in enterprises where they have a stake. The second is to deal in the equity market, acting as legal owners of the assets they operate. The board of directors of an ordinary enterprise is composed of representatives of shareholders, workers, and managers. By making use of the diverse interests of the three sides and mutual restrictions, the rationality and self-balance of an enterprise can be reached and maintained, and public enterprises would be completely non-governmentalised. In a broad sense people can argue that this is a special form of privatisation, for the enterprise previously belonged to private rather than governmental sectors and operated acccording to the principles dominating the private economy. The point is, however, that the majority assets are ultimately owned by the public and run by agents of the public, whose capital return is used for the public interests.

The ARS has drawn a lot of attention. The main economic policy-makers have been involved in detailed discussion. The first-stage project of ARS was implemented experimentally in 1986 in some 100 enterprises, was spread over five provinces, had the consent of policy-makers, and gained momentum later on. Needless to say, ARS did not pass without question or criticism. Some people within the administrative apparatus poured scorn on the idea of public bidding as 'an intellectual's whim'. Some suspected that the stimulation of the management stratum could offend workers. Other people questioned the necessity of a two-stage strategy and argued that a shares economy would solve the problems of enterprises altogether. There have been so many people in both academic and practical circles joining the debate that the model of ARS has been revised time and time again and is therefore very much a collective effort.

THE REALITY: CONTRACT RESPONSIBILITY SYSTEM

Practice

Practice is never a simple duplication of theory. It develops according to its own logic through theoretical thinking and can sometimes influence the way it will develop. Until the autumn of 1986, at least, policy-makers felt it imminent to bring about a fundamental change at the enterprise level. The first successful experiments of leasing practice in small collective enterprises and the assets responsibility system in larger state-owned enterprises further convinced policy-makers that the key point of enterprise reform is to accentuate the role of managers, to link the manager's personal interests with the performances of enterprise, and to steady and legalise the relationship between the state and enterprises by notarised contract. Immediately afterwards, the ministries concerned hastily laid out a new plan which embodied this fresh thinking so as to organise the experiment on a large scale. During the process they claimed that ARS was too complicated and it should be simplified. it seemed to them that the only meaningful thing in this new thinking was to increase the responsibility and material rewards of managers and to draw new lines of profit distribution between the state and enterprises. Partly because profit redistribution usually implies that enterprises can get further financial concessions from the state, partly because this new projected arrangement would hurt no one who is in power and has vested interests, the new plan (called 'Contract Responsibility System') aroused tremendous response. It soon grew out of the experimental stage in a few cities and became a nationwide movement within several months.

Fortunately, it was not long before the main policy-makers realised how essential competition and public-bidding mechanisms were for changing the internal operating mechanisms of the enterprise and for creating an entrepreneurial group in China. Since the middle of 1987, the government has stressed competition in selecting managers. Consequently, on 27 February 1988, declared a formal regulation of the contract responsibility system. Its main items included the following:

1. The term of contract should be no less than 3 years.
2. In principle, a public bidding should be invited, and managers appointed through competition. Profit distribution between the state and the enterprise should be based on the average performance of the enterprise in the last 3 years. A fixed rule will be set to allot increased profits between them.
3. A certain linkage between workers' income and the performance of an enterprise will be built up. Top managers' incomes should have much closer connection with the peformance of the enterprise and could be as much as three times (or occasionally even more) as those of ordinary staff (before that the difference was only 20-50 per cent). However, it they fail to fulfil the target set in the contract they could only retain half of their basic wage.
4. A managerial market should be phased in such a manner that all the people who have entre-preneurial potential can collect the necessary information about enterprises and have a fair chance of competition.

It takes some time for the government to bring these items from paper into practice, but up to the beginning of 1988, 80 per cent of the state-owned enterprises have been operating under some form of contract responsibility system.

The first outcome of contract responsibility system has been impressive, if not remarkable. In 1987 the profit of the state-owned industry increased to nearly 10 per cent more than in the previous year, and productivity went up 7.6 per cent. In the first quarter of 1988 profit further jumped to 15.8 per cent over the same time as in the previous year. Profit even went up 30 per cent in fifteen provinces where the new system was implemented in a relatively better way. The most encouraging scenes were witnessed in the areas where real public bidding was introduced. For example, in Han Dan area they implemented the Assets Responsibility System at the beginning of 1987. In the past, the negotiation of the production plan, especially the profit target, was usually an exhaustive bargaining between government and enterprises. Because of the rachet effect, enterprises have an instinctive tendency to conceal their real capacities. The implementation of competition forced up bids for the target profit in signed contracts several times, and sometimes dozens of times, higher than the actual performance. In many cases younger and more educated people defeated the previous managers or party secretaries in public bidding with more competitive targets and convincing measures. What is most promising is that, even when the former managers regained their posts in the same of other enterprises through competition, they usually took a completely new stance in coping with much more demanding requirements and hardened budget constraints, at least from the viewpoint of their personal interests. Further competition offers an equal chance to everyone, which brings fresh air into the bureaucratic environment. No wonder, when General Secretary Zhao Zhi Yang briefed foreign leaders about Chinese enterprise reform he put it this way:

> We implemented the contract system in state-owned enterprises. That is to say, the property right still belonging to the state, operating power handed over to managers, managers being selected by public bidding and introducing competition into the contract system.

He predicted that all these would bring a revolution to the personnel system in business circles and would gradually spill over into non-business and government sectors.

Problems

The Contract Responsibility system has only just been put into operation. Obviously its many possible problems have not yet surfaced. The problems we have encountered can be categorised under three heads:

(a) <u>Lack of Competition</u>. It seems that the lack of competition is due to the government not stressing the need for it in the first place, and once the system was in motion it became tough to change the title due to inertia. Closer observation, however, shows that there are more profound reasons. Replacement of bureaucratic appointment with public bidding and competition are the essence of the new approach which breaks the foundation of the feudal network. So it unavoidably meets the most vehement resistance from vested interests. Not surprisingly, some managers and their patrons in government even directed disguised 'public bidding' when they were cornered. More often than not they sought every possible excuse in order to avoid the trial at all. For all the aforementioned reasons, there still has not been genuine competition in the majority of enterprises and hence the managers are not entrepreneurs but officers who pay more attention to their seniority than to markets. First, managers have little incentive and no pressure on them to change the enterprise's internal mechanism, to reshuffle labour make-up, to get rid of excess counter-productive departments and to reward or punish staff according to their performance; for all these measures may cause offence to the people who have enjoyed vested interests. Moreover, managers themselves are the products of hierarchical networks. Second, open-ended bargaining develops because of one-to-one negotiation, which softens the budget constraints of the enterprise. What is worse, it diverts people's attention from a fundamental change of operating mechanisms to profit distribution. Ordinary staff are obviously not pleased at the enhancement of both the power and income of managers without fair competition. This accumulates the pressure for wage increases and inflation.

(b) <u>Short-sighted behaviour</u>. Exploitation of agents is a common problem in any leasing contract practice. The way to reduce it is to lengthen the term of the contract and increase supervision. However, the former is constrained by certain outside circumstances and the latter is very costly, or even counter-productive (especially when the principal is the government). The Assets Responsibility System designed a mechanism for the second public bidding to prolong managers' vision and try to prevent them from abusing their power without being punished. However, ARS has only been attempted in some thousand enterprises; whether the design works unexceptionally is still to be verified. The urgent problem now is that most enterprises have single-term constraints only. Under the single-term contract too few indicators (e.g. over-emphasising profit and overlooking other factors could virtually encourage managers to chase short-term profit at the cost of long-term development of the enterprise, while too many indicators (e.g. observing profit as well as investment, invention, innovation, products, quality, and so on) could severely restrict manoeuvrability for managers, and could strengthen bureaucratic intervention. This is avery awkward dilemma. Unfortunately, in some cases the situation is a distorted mixture of both extremes.

(c) <u>Instability of external conditions</u>. The Chinese economy is in a transitional period from direct control to indirect regulation. A considerable investment fund is still controlled by bureaucratic apparatus. The opportunity and significance of obtaining this sort of fund often distract enterprises from market-orientated operation. The government also controls quite a large part of raw material and some key products as well as their pricing. Price adjustment by the government will also affect and sometimes dramatically change the macro-environment in which enterprises operate. All these influence the stability and continuity of the contracts between the state and enterprises. Another fundamental challenge is the validity of the government directly as principal (i.e. on one side of the contract) because it is in a monopolistic position. One way out would be to set up many financial intermediaries, but whether these fund-agents can work properly further depends upon the soundness of a market's mechanism. Obviously these handicaps and loopholes amplify friction and error in the present enterprise reform.

CONCLUSIONS

Strictly speaking, the Chinese experience up to now is not sufficient for me to draw any firm conclusions. So what is summarised below may be regarded as hypotheses which are still to be tested.

(a) Privatisation in the sense of denationalisation is not the only way to improve economic efficiency. This is not only because privatisation usually tends to further polarisation, especially in developing countries, and thus increases social conflicts and economic cost to society, but also because, in general, modern companies are not directly controlled or run by their ultimate owners. Therefore, it is possible to demarcate and protect public property rights by institutional arrangements based on constraint of interests.

(b) However, debureaucratising public enterprises from government intervention and protection (in other words non-govermentalisation) is an inevitable step in pursuing economic efficiency. Only when public enterprises are completely independent of government and economically subject only to their owners can efficiency be achieved.

(c) The creation of the entrepreneurial stratum as well as its ethos is vitally important. This is particularly true in an undeveloped economy, for the latter usually implies fledgling markets, poor communication, inflexibility, low capital accumulation, personal networks, feudal legacy, and so on. All these hindrances can only be overcome in the course of development. Exploitation of human capital and entrepreneurial resources above all could (first and foremost) prove to be very expedient.

(d) Whether public enterprises can survive and compete rigorously in a market environment after obtaining independence from the government will decide the fate of the market-orientated reforms in China as well as in other socialist countries. This further depends upon whether people can find a self-balancing mechanism to rationalise public enterprise behaviour, if such a mechanism exists at all.

REFERENCES

Chinese Statistical Yearbook 1987. All the data in this chapter come from this.
People's Daily (1988) 24th and 27th February; 5th March, and 22nd August. Sheng, Hua et al. (1985) 'Dual price

mechanism', Economic Research, 2.
—— (1986) 'Assets responsibility system', Economic Research, 2.
Zuo, Jing Li, and Xiang, Wu Jia (1985) 'The transformation of government's function, World Economic Herald, 17th March.

13

Privatisation in Kenya

R. W. Karanja*

INTRODUCTION

Nearly all post-independence state corporations in Kenya were established in realisation of commitments made in the ruling party's (KANU) manifesto and reiterated thereafter in the Sessional Paper No. 10 of 1965 on African Socialism and its application to planning in Kenya. These commitments included the elimination of hunger, disease, ignorance, and poverty, and called for the decolonisation of the economy, the promotion of development and regional balance, an increase in citizen participation in the economy, and greater public control of the economy.

An effective mobilisation of all available local resources was necessary. The government, therefore, found it imperative to participate in directly productive sectors of the economy by setting up a series of state and quasi-state organisations for the execution of national and regional development policies. These organisations were in addition to the public enterprises established during the pre-independence era.

THE PUBLIC ENTERPRISE SITUATION

The economy of Kenya is controlled jointly, albeit in differing proportions, by the following sectors: the co-operative movement; the public sector; the private enterprise; and the informal sector. The principal differences among them are in the areas of mobilisation and application of funds. Thus the co-operative movement mobilises

* Inspector of State Corporations, Kenya

resources from people and applies the same to mass-owned investments administered jointly with the government; the public sector draws on funds mainly from the government and applies them to state and quasi-state investments; the private sector is financed from both publicly and privately mobilised resources and applies them to private joint-stock investments; and the informal sector procures resources from personal savings, private or public-sector savings and applies them to mainly informal single proprietorships.

The public sector, has since independence, assumed an increasingly significant role in national development. By 1984, the sector comprised 43 per cent of the wage employment with a wage bill of 22 per cent of the overall national figure. In the same period, the government had committed a cumulative total of £1.3 billion which was 35.9 per cent of the total gross domestic product. Government participation has been by way of equity finance, loans, grants, subsidies, and guarantees. Thus, by 1984, total cumulative loans amounted to £571.6 million of 43.08 per cent of total state participation, guaranteed funds were £635.5 million or 47.89 per cent while over £119.8 million or 9.03 per cent of the cumulative commitments were in equity funds.

Over the period 1979/80 - 1983/4 cumulative government investment in state corporations in equity and loans was 27.9 per cent of total cumulative development expenditures. This was exclusive of companies in which the government has direct or indirect minority shareholding and of indirect commitments by way of fiscal concessions and subventions.

The sheer size and extent of government financial commitment, as observed above, is a clear indication of the importance of the public sector in the implementation and administration of national development policies.

Over the last two decades, state corporations made a tremendous contribution to the country's economic growth. (The term state corporations was defined in the State Corporations Act 1986.) This was at a time when the government was at pains to attract foreign investments and harness the little domestic enterprise then available. Agricultural marketing boards handled a substantial proportion of domestic production. Since more than 70 per cent of the Kenyan population depends on agriculture and related activities, the efficiency and effectiveness of state corporations led to marked reductions in marketing

Table 13.1: Some data on state corporations

Corporation (1)	Total assets (Shs) (2)
1. Kenya Cashewnuts	93,722,299
2. Pyrethrum Board of Kenya	352,939,380
3. Catering Levy Trustees	134,687,474
4. Coffee Research Foundation	20,955,080
5. Kenya Wine Agencies (Ltd)	96,142,620
6. Industrial Development Board	1,254,645,179
7. National Irrigation Board	357,967,867
8. East African Fine Spinners	133,250,000
9. Agricultural Development Corporation	562,765,000
10. Kenya Ports Authority	2,971,500,000
11. Kenya Ports and Telecommunications Corporation	6,642,931,540
12. Kenya Railways	2,512,082,013
13. Kenya Re-Insurance	1,134,995,798
14. Jomo Kenyatta Foundation	57,385,873
15. Salt Manufacturers	44,934,062
16. Kenya Post Office Savings Bank	1,175,000,000
17. Cereals and Sugar Finance	5,952,530,712
18. National Cereals and Produce Board	3,932,179,105
19. Kenya Seed Company	119,164,908
20. Industrial and Commercial Development Corporation	1,121,865,090
21. Kenya National Capital Corporation	867,777,217
22. Kenya Fluorspar Company	122,614,359
23. Kenya Meat Commission	34,784,900
24. Kenya Pipeline Company	1,134,207,000
25. National Bank of Kenya	2,999,533,980
Total	33,830,553,056

Net profits (Shs) (3)	Total number employed (4)
21,751,085	1,700
6,045,420	760
7,615,490	90
12,403,260	775
29,686,140	185
10,219,376	-
(20,139,410)	939
10,405,000	571
15,616,120	12,400
213,700,000	11,368
457,301,960	19,993
(127,050,000)	22,971
41,894,562	352
7,178,934	84
806,278	225
(27,898,367)	800
218,464,665	12
(712,647,778)	3,461
39,982,056	300
23,888,320	352
(4,397,056)	25
14,348,876	585
(57,305,020)	1,650
142,031,000	500
1,616,310	900
352,517,221	80,421

overheads. State corporations also handle about half of the country's visible trade and require substantial amounts of foreign exchange for their importation of equipment and machinery. The policies pursued by the corporations and their affiliates therefore have a major impact on the standards of living of both the rural and urban populations.

State corporations have made enormous investments which have yielded direct contributions to the gross domestic product or value-added in the form of wages and salaries paid to their employees, and the operating surpluses. A random sample of some twenty-five state corporations (as shown in Table 13.1) revealed an investment of Shs 33,830,553,056 in total assets. This investment has yielded a toal surplus of Shs 325,517,221 and created employment totalling 79,521 employees. The surplus may appear trivial in relation to the total investment. However, we must not lose sight of the fact that, along with the objective of profitability, state corporations have had an important social function to perform.

During the five-year period to 1984, the government received dividends from state corporations amounting to £138.75 million comprising an average annual return of 6.52 per cent on an investment of £483.81 million. Although small in relation to the investment, the dividend return has enabled the government to extend development activities to wider spheres thereby complementing the efforts of the state corporations.

For instance, the Agricultural Finance Corporation (AFC) disbursed some £24.79 billion between 1973 and 1982 by way of land development loans; and the peasantry, who comprise the bulk of the small-scale farmers, co-operative societies and other farmers received the largest share of the total credit. In order to fulfil the objective of making capital available at reasonable cost, AFC has consistently charged rates that are relatively low.

There are, in addition, corporations which cater for each sub-sector within the agricultural sector. Thus the Horticultural Crops Development Authority caters for horticultural farmers while the Pyrethrum Board of Kenya caters for pyrethrum farmers. The same may be said of cashewnut farmers (Kenya Cashewnuts Limited), not to mention other crops such as coffee and tea (Coffee Board of Kenya, Coffee Research Foundation, and the Tea Board of Kenya, and the Kenya Tea Development Authority).

The Industrial and Commercial Development Corporation (ICDC) and the Kenya Industrial Estates Limited, among others, have been active in assimilating the indigenous entrepreneur into the main-stream of economic activity. By June, 1985, ICDC had invested a cumulative total of Shs. 1.1097 billion in subsidiary and other companies by way of equity, loans, and advances. The ICDC has also assisted some sixty-eight companies since independence. The transport sector also has felt the impact of state involvement, particularly the railways and the ports.

During the five year period 1979/80-1983/84 a number of corporations repaid both the principal and interest of monies lent to them by the government (as shown in Table 13.2). The payments have no doubt been low, but the corporations have had an impact on development.

Table 13.2: Loan and interest re-payments by some state corporations to the Kenyan government

Year (1)	Total loan outstanding £M (2)	Interest paid £M (3)	% (4)	Principal paid £M (5)	% (6)
1979/80	192.27	7.04	3.6	2.55	1.33
1980/81	256.30	8.76	3.4	3.23	1.25
1981/82	285.1	7.70	2.7	3.13	1.1
1982/83	326.9	10.99	3.4	6.18	1.89
1983/84	397.0	8.32	2.1	4.99	1.26

State corporations have also made contribution in the following areas: gross capital formation (in 1984 the gross fixed capital formation by state corporations amounted to £32.92 million rising to £37.96 million in 1985, compared to £11.41 million and £10.70 million for the rest of the public sector for the same period); marketed production; and mobilisation of investable funds (this is evident from the large sums of funds that statutory finance houses have been able to collect in deposits and disburse for various development functions). Other economic contributions which are less direct and not easily measurable are: the value of national income and foreign exchange channelled through the various state corporations; the influence of development effort undertaken by marketing boards on the growth of production and employment outside the public sector; the effect of marketing efficiency and market regulations upon the level of incomes and the alleviation of poverty; and the general multiplier effects.

Government investment and public institutions span a wide spectrum covering banks, financial and insurance institutions, development authorities and corporations, processing and trading organisations, research and educational organisations, regulatory/advisory organisations, and miscellaneous, consultative, professional, and advisory organisation. Table 13.3 shows how many organisations are in government ownership and the proportion of government participation interest. Among the organisations in Table 13.3 are a number of holding state corporations having several subsidiaries and/or associated companies under them. These are shown in Table 13.4

Table 13.3: Government ownership and participation in public enterprises

Public ownership (%) (1)	No. of public enterprises (2)
100	155
50-100	53
25-50	34
Below 25	50
Other	33
	325

It has been noted over the years that the performance of public enterprises has been poorest in the manufacturing sector, perhaps owing to stiff competition from the private sector. Thus, the following corporations in which the government has a controlling interest either directly or indirectly have not made profit since inception and a number of them have been carrying out a negative net worth: Yuken Textile Industry Limited, Ceramic Industries

Table 13.4: 'Holding' complexes in state corporations

State corporation (1)	Subsidiaries/associated companies (2)			
	100%	50-100%	25-50%	Below 25%
1. Industrial and Commercial Development Corporation	10	11	23	16
2. Industrial Development Bank	0	-	4	23
3. Agricultural Development Bank	2	4	-	-
4. Kenya Commercial Bank	2	-	-	-
5. National Bank of Kenya	-	1	-	-
6. Kenya National Assurance Company	1	-	1	-
7. Kenya Re-Insurance	2	-	-	-
8. Kenya National Trading Corporation	1	1	-	-
9. Kenya Tourist Development Corporation	2	13	8	2
10. Kenya Tea Development Corporation	9	8	1	21
11. Cotton Lint and Seed Marketing Board	5	-	-	-
12. Kenya Airways	2	-	-	-

(E.A.) Limited, Pan Vegetable Processors, Kenya Drilling Limited, Synthetic Fibres (K) Limited, Kenya Engineering Industries Limited, Mepal Plastics Limited, Kenya Fibre Corporation, E.A. Publishing House, Kenya Meat Commission, Uplands Bacon Factory, South Nyanza Sugar Company, Nzoia Sugar Company, E.A. Sugar Industries, and National Construction Corporation. Several Corporations have been undergoing extensive rehabilitation programmes; and some are in the process of being wound up or under partial divestiture. It is perhaps in this sector, therefore, that any de-nationalisation or privatisation would be expected to take place if ony to curtail rapid erosion of public resources.

In the recent past, steps have been taken towards divestiture from the following public Corporations: the Uplands Bacon Factory is in the process of being wound up; the Kenya Meat Commission has been re-organised to give 60 per cent equity-holding to the ADC and 40 per cent to co-operatives in what appears to be partial divestiture; and the National Construction Corporation is in the process of being wound up. The Government is also considering seriously the future of corporations which have been considered as non-starters.

THE THINKING ON PRIVATISATION

In July, 1982, a detailed report on government expenditure was prepared by a working party appointed by the government. The report observed that the commercial investments of the government have spread into virtually every area of private-sector activity. It noted that the government presently own shares, directly or indirectly, in textiles, shoes, sugar, tyres, alcohol, pharmaceuticals, canning, mining, salt, drilling, paper, hotels, cement, batteries, vehicles, radios, fishing, engineering, beverages and food processing, and even retail shops! Most of the investments are not of a strategic nature and, in most cases, management control in particular lies in the hands of foreigners, with Kenyans holding only token shares and very few management positions. This form of government involvement was considered to be neither effective Kenyanisation nor an effective means of regulation. It is, for the most part, a means of underwriting with public funds risks which should otherwise be borne by private investors. It was noted that few pay dividends to the exchequer and many seek additional finance from the government whenever they encounter difficulties in the market place. The recommendation of the report which was subsequently accepted by the government was that government participation in commercial enterprise has been carried well beyond original conceptions and has reached the point where such participation is inhibiting rather than promoting development by Kenyans themselves. It was therefore considered a matter of high priority for the government to reverse the trend by working out a viable programme of divesting itself of some of its investments to Kenyan investors who are prepared to take the risks of enterprise in the pursuit of profits.

It was accordingly recommended that a careful review of all state corporations be carried out with a view to determining the following: those whose retention as government agencies is essential to accelerated and equitable national development and the regulation of the private sector; those whose objectives have been achieved and which should be discontinued; those whose functions could be absorbed by parent ministries; and those whose functions would be more efficiently performed by the private sector.

To this end the Task force on Divestiture of Government Investments was established in 1983 under the auspices of the State Corporations Advisory Committee. Its principal object was to ascertain the extent and modalities of such divestiture. it is now the desire of the government that state corporations which will be allowed to exist should be self-sustaining. Those whose activities are not revenue-generating should produce tangible results as required in their enabling instruments.

The success of the recommendations would involve devising an effective strategy and appropriate mechanisms for the divestiture of shares or assets for enterprises the following types of enterprises: those which are currently profitable and whose shares can easily be disposed of; which are currently unprofitable but which can be made profitable before disposal of shares; and those currently unprofitable and without promise, and should be wound up through the sale of assets and dissolution. The Task Force on Divestiture of Government Investments is in the final stages of compiling its report and recommendations. It is clear, however, that since the thinking on public investments veered in the direction of divestitute, the government has taken deliberate steps to influence public opinion in favour of sustainable commercial viability in the public sector.

As is inevitable, political forces have come in to play. Although the government is in full support of maintaining only those corporations which can stand on their own, there are those who would want to consider the problem from a political angle. This then brings into the picture the geographical and regional distribution of state corporations and their impact on the respective social environments, considerations which inevitably give rise to political sensitivities.

Notwithstanding these factors, cautious but steady progress towards divestiture in one form or another appears to be in the offing. The government has approached the issue from diversified angles including the following: the sale of a proportion of the state corporations' shares to the public; the sale of a proportion of state corporations' shares to the co-operatives; and the disposal of investment through receivership and winding up.

ACTIONS IN PRIVATISATION

Privatisation or contemplated divestiture of public investments is a recent phenomenon in Kenya. The following trends or contemplated actions point towards divestiture or a certain degree of privatisation. It has already been agreed that the wholly state-owned banks - the Kenya Commercial Bank Limited and the National Bank of Kenya Limited - will sell out to the public some 30 per cent of their shares, to be effective from June 1988. The Kenya Meat Commission is having its ownership structure redefined to provide for a 40 per cent ownership by co-operatives and 60 per cent by the Agricultural Development Corporation, Uplands Bacon Factory, which has been in receivership for sometime, is in the process of being wound up. The National Construction Corporation is in the process of being wound up. Kenatco Transport Corporation is in the process of being wound up. Kenatco Transport Company was liquidated not so long ago to give way to a new smaller company, Kenatco Taxis Company Limited. Kenya Fishing Industries, Kenya Fibre Corporation, and East African Publishing House are all in receivership. The mere fact that the receiverships have been permitted without any intervention whatsoever is perhaps an indication of the seriousness with which the government views the situation of deteriorating performance in the public sector. It should be noted also that some of these actions have not been prompted by poor performance or inadequacy of any sort. The Kenya Commercial Bank Limited has been a profitable venture with its net surpluses growing steadily in recent years. Although the National Bank of Kenya Limited has not performed as well as the other bank, it cannot altogether be said to be an unprofitable venture. It was intended that the banks release some 30 per cent shares for controlled sale to the investing public starting June 1988 thereby turning the two banks into public corporations whose shares will be quoted in the Nairobi Stock Exchange.

The Kenya Meat Commission has been retained as a Government agency because of its strategic nature as a buyer of last resort. This point was underscored most vividly during the nationwide drought of 1984 when small beef farmers had only the Commission to fall back to, as private butchers would not look at their stocks. This is not an issue which can be ignored easily as it often assumes political dimensions.

Others have had their own peculiar problems. Thus, while the Uplands Bacon Factory was plagued by poor management and obsolete technology and machineries, the National Construction Corporation appears to have 'eaten' itself up following the non-performance of the very indigenous construction entrepreneur it was created to promote. Yet others have suffered in different ways (for example, from lack of raw materials at competitive prices, or due to import restrictions, or have been strangled out of business through price competition or dumping of cheap imported equivalents or substitutes. Any planned de-nationalisation or privatisation in Kenya would be a straight-forward exercise, since the private-sector framework is already ingrained in public enterprise formation and operations. The majority of the corporations' accounts are in parlance with private sector financial statements. Moreover, most of the state corporations have been able to borrow directly and competitively from the money market locally or abroad with only the necessary clearances from the government, particularly where the latter's guarantees are required.

As has been observed elsewhere, the only official body that has been set up to deal with the question of divestiture has been the Task Force on Divestiture of Government Investments. It was set up not to identify corporations for auction or determine prices for such disposals but to make recommendations on the likely areas of divestiture and the modalities of such divestiture for consideration by the government.

It seems that the need to pull out of unprofitable ventures had been recognised as early as 1979 at the formation of the then Parastatals Advisory Committee.

Among its terms of reference was, 'To consider and advise the government on the desirability of amalgamating or winding up some parastatals'. Such amalgamation has been seen in the case of the Kenya Posts and Telecommunications Corporations when it was merged with the Kenya External Telecommunications Company Limited; and, more recently, there was a merger between the Kenya Cargo Handling Services Limited and the Kenya Ports Authority. There have been isolated requests, even in the National Assembly, for the establishment of a privatisation commission to study particularly loss-making State Corporations in particular, and to make recommendations on how they may be disposed of to the public. Such requests have to date elicited only very minimal support, particularly from the law-makers.

PROBLEMS ENCOUNTERED

A blanket decision to completely privatise public enterprises by way of whole or partial divestiture has never been expressly made by the government. Any problems regarding the issue of divestiture can only be anticipated. These problems will involve determination of the following issues:

(a) The type and mode of government participation or involvement that is desirable for Kenya;

(b) Whether divesting will be a total solution to the problem or a mere transfer or postponement of the problem;

(c) State corporations have acted as a deliberate training ground for most of the country's manpower requirements. It is not clear whether the disposal of these corporations will also mean the death of this crucial facility;

(d) Doubts have been expressed as to who would eventually acquire the State corporations. It has been the intention of the government that any divestiture of public investment should be carried out in such a way that the investments do not end up in the control of foreigners. Moreover, the issue of indigenisation which has been fairly close to the heart of Kenyans cannot be ignored. It is therefore necessary to tread carefully, as haphazard privatisation would almost frustrate any indigenisation programme;

(e) The regional distribution of state corporations is also another issue at stake. At times, divestiture may mean withdrawal in a region of the only economic investment (one in which the people have been able to have a say through their represen- tatives). It is therefore likely to be viewed as a move that will destabilise the regional balance in the country, as, in quite a few regions, have not been able companies (other than state corpor- ations) have not been able to attract investment other than state corporations.

Perhaps, owing to the above reasons, the issue of privatisation seems to have received little support in practice from the political fora. Politicians and trade unions have often expressed fears on the consequences of divestiture relating to the fate of the employees (excessively employed in many corporations) and other economic benefits to particular regions. The concept has, however, enjoyed support from the intellectual community and a large portion of the civil service. This is perhaps because the latter have been able to look beyond the narrow ethnic values into the wider benefits deriving from the multiplier effects inherent in private ownership.

CONCLUSION

The divestiture of public investments is a fairly recent phenomenon. Kenya attained independence only twenty-five years ago, and several of the existing state corporations were created after independence. The time lapse between the actual formation and the determination of performance of the public sector has been a bit too short. Aside from the corporations referred to in the divestiture report and others in the manufacturing sector which are already under rehabilitation, it will perhaps take a little longer to determine the propriety or otherwise of retaining various other organisations as government or public agencies. The decision to tie Kenya's development strategies to parastatal organisations is historical. During the pre-independence period, only economically viable areas were opened by and continued to thrive. Several regions which are disadvantaged owing to geographical location or lack of natural resource endowment were largely ignored. It is particularly in these latter areas that the public sector has had the biggest impact and there would be the most resistance if divestiture were contemplated. It is probably a little too early, taking into consideration all social, political and economic issues, for Kenya to divorce herself on an across-the board basis from state participation as this would be likely to have undesirable social repercussions. The present on-going piecemeal strategy of the disposal of a few shares in profitable corporations while, at the same time, winding up those worst hit, may, in the long run, prove much more socially and politically acceptable.

REFERENCES

Detailed Review and Investigation of Statutory Boards and other Parastatals, December, 1979.
The Exchequer and Audit Act (Cap. 412).
The KANU Manifesto.
Report and Recommendations of the Working Party on Government Expenditure, 1982.
Review of Statutory Boards Report, 1979.
The State Corporations Act, 1986.

14

Privatisation in Nigeria

John Edozien* and S.O. Adeoye**

THE PUBLIC ENTERPRISE SITUATION

Public enterprise in Nigeria dates back to the days before independence in 1960. In the years following independence the Government of Nigeria established several public enterprises as part of its attempt to provide services and to promote economic development. (The state governments also set up several public enterprises including investment companies.) The government wanted to ensure that the commanding heights of the economy were controlled by it in the overall interest of the citizens. In a few isolated cases, its equity holdings in certain private companies were a result of statutory forfeiture by former public officers found wanting by various Assets Investigation Panels. Also, in pursuance of the policy of indigenisation in the 1970s, the federal and state governments acquired substantial shares in financial institutions, such as commercial banks and insurance companies, in order to influence the direction of their policies.

The totality of public enterprise

It is known that there are over 100 public enterprises at federal-government level. At the state level, each state government (individually or jointly with others has several enterprises which it either owns completely or holds controlling interests in. Almost all the state governments

*Permanent Secretary, Ministry of Planning, Nigeria
** Principal Secretary, Cabinet Office, Nigeria

have holding outfits which are usually known as investment corporations or development companies. They are also joint owners of the bigger holding companies. Presently there is no holding company at federal level since The Ministry of Finance Incorporated (MOFI), which oversees, is neither enpowered nor organised to play that role. There is now a proposal to set up a National Investment Corporation which will act as portfolio manager for the federal government in partly-privatised enterprises as well as in all commercialised enterprises. It will also be responsible for undertaking the capital restructuring of commercialised enterprises and engaging in new areas of commercial investments on behalf of the government, either from its own resources or in partnership with others.

Data on public enterprises

While data on the numbers of public enterprises can be easily obtained, the same cannot be said of information on their capital outlays. Table 14.1 presents the available data: the main numbers in column (2) are in respect of enterprises in which all the equity now held by the federal government may be sold (full privatisation). The numbers in parentheses relate to those enterprises in which government participation will only be partially privatised.

Actual divestitures

The main exercise of divestiture is expected to commence as soon as the legal and institutional framework is put in place. However, something in the nature of early denationalisation has already taken place, as is shown in Table 14.3.

THE THINKING ON PRIVATISATION

The thinking on privatisation, as a policy option, whether in the narrow or broad sense, dates back to 1981 in Nigeria. In that year, the federal government set up a presidential commission on Parastatals under the chairmanship of Mr G.O. Onosode, in response to agitation by public enterprises to be taken out of the 'Udoji' unified grading system, for purposes of remuneration, fringe benefits, and other conditions of service.

284

Table 14.1: Federal public enterprises

Sector (1)	Public enterprises (2)	(3)a
Agriculture, fishing forestry, etc	29	N221,471,049b
Mining		
Manufacturing	10(22)	N1,613,621,000c
Transport and communications	2(2)	N541,381,066
Commerce	(3)d	
Banking and insurance etc.	11(4)e	N732,196,078f
Others (including hotels etc)	9	N118,057,211

a   See the Report of the Sub-Committee on Commercialisation of the Federal Government Parastatals/Companies, 16th October, 1986.
b   Only sixteen of the twenty-nine enterprises are included here.
c   Figures in respect of some companies were not available.
d   The three listed are the three oil marketing companies to be partially privatised.
e   The eleven listed companies are all insurance companies, while the four banks in parentheses are either development banks or savings banks.
f   These figures do not include capital outlay in Niger Insurance Company.

Table 14.2: The ownership pattern

Public equity ownership (1)	No. of public enterprises (2)
100%	28
50 - 100%	30
25 - 50%	9
25%	5

Source: Report of the Sub-committee on Commercialisation, Annexes A-C

Table 14.3: Public-sector companies which have divested ownership from the state

	Nature of divestiture
Commerce	
Nigerian National Supply Co.	Full
Transport	
National Freight Co.	Partial
Agriculture	
Nigerian Dairies Co. Ltd	Full
Madara Dairy Co. Ltd	Partial
Nigerian Ranches Co. Ltd	Full
Nigerian Livestock Production Co. Ltd	Full
Kano Abbatoir Company	Full
Nigerian Rubber Board	Full
Nigerian Grains Board	Full
Nigerian Palm Produce Board	Full
Nigerian Cotton Board	Full
Nigerian Cocoa Board	Full
Nigerian Groundnut Board	Full

Having examined the management of parastatals and made appropriate recommendations, the Commission in its report addressed a number of what it regarded as special issues. Under the title 'privatisation' the Commission compared the levels of efficiency and effectiveness in the private and public sectors and the operational freedom and flexibility available to both. Thereafter it advocated that 'in those cases where service delivery to the nation is a more paramount consideration than that of security or other sensitive aspects of public policy, an increased role by the private sector must be considered as an alternative.

The Commission thereupon advocated the injection of private-sector participation in the equity of Nigeria Airways to the extent of 40 per cent, and the licensing of indigenous airlines to operate scheduled services, which will bring relief to the Nigerian public while giving Nigeria Airways an opportunity to improve its image. The Commission similarly suggested that private-sector involvement should be injected in the energy sector by getting NEPA to farm out, as it were, parts of its distribution system to private operations for maintenance and general management. The Commission also condemned what it observed as a proliferation of parastatals and underlined the desirability for the federal government, in the interests of economy and efficiency, to hold, if not roll back, the frontiers of government. While applauding the then federal government's action 'in being content merely with selecting manufacturers which are to establish five light commercial vehicle assembly plants ... without government itself having to participate financially in any of them. The Commission urged the government to recognise 'the need for privatisation as a deliberate policy for inducing efficiency'.

The problem of the efficient and profitable management of parastatals and state-owned companies persisted even after the Onosode Commission. By 1984, the public outcry, discontent, and frustration over performance of parastatals, as reflected in the popular Press, had reached such a level that the then federal military government, in September of that year, appointed a 'Study Group on Statutory corporations and State-owned Companies' to undertake the following tasks:

(a) to examine in all their ramifications the factors responsible for the inefficiency of parastatals and state-owned companies;

(b) to undertake an in-depth study of the desirability or otherwise of privatisation of parastatals and state-owned companies, to identify those which could be privatised and recommend the methodology of achieving such a programme in the public interest;

(c) to appraise the management structure of parastatals and state-owned companies and to make appropriate recommendations; and

(d) to examine the issue of subsidies and cost recovery as they relate to parastatals and state-owned companies, etc.

In the White Paper issued on the Report of the Study in 1985, the federal military government accepted some of the recommendations of the Study Group.[1] A recommendation which is particularly relevant to our topic is that the 'performance targets and measures for assessing management performance must be built into the functions of these organisations', and that sanctions should be prescribed for failure to meet these targets. The Study Group did not make a general recommendation on the privatisation/commercialisation of the public enterprises. Its approach was to make a specific recommendation on each of the parastatals after detailed consideration of its functions, management structure, relationship with the government and capital structure. While it advocated further study, to determine the feasibility or other wise of privatising the Nigerian Electric Power Authority (NEPA), it considered the Nigerian Ports Authority to be ripe for some form of privatisation and recommended that the government should arrange to sell part of its equity interests after a new capital structure had been determined for the organisation. Furthermore, the Study Group recommended that the Nigeria Airports Authority should be allowed to operate on strictly commercial lines and that the External Telecommunication Limited (NET) and Nigeria Airways should be partially privatised with the federal-government equity holding limited to 30 per cent in each case, while the rest should be distributed among Nigerian citizens (60 per cent) and the staff of the parastatal or company (10 per cent). With the coming into power of new military administration in 1985,[2] the level of subsidies to parastatals and government companies as part of the overall public expenditure policy assumed a new dimension. In his broadcast to the nation on the occasion of the Silver Jubilee Independence Anniversary in October 1985, President Babangida made an important policy pronouncement on the future of parastatals and government companies when he announced that, as part of the process of mopping up liquidity in the Nigerian financial system, the government would divest 'equity holdings in several potentially viable parastatals and state-owned companies' (such as hotels, breweries, and distilleries). In addition, the President declared that parastatals would be generally encouraged to subject themselves to the discipline of the capital market.[3] A few months later, the federal government's statement of intent (as highlighted above) crystallised into a coherent and clear-cut policy which was announced in the 1986 Budget Speech. On that occasion, the President said:

Government has now decided that, as from 1986, the volume of non-statutory transfers to all economic and quasi-economic parastatals would constitute no more than 50 per cent of their present levels. They are to find the balance from increases in their price charges, tariffs and rates.

Continuing, President Babangida stated that:

in respect of existing public holdings in commercially-orientated enterprises, government has also decided to divest its holdings in agricultural production, hotels, food, beverages, breweries, distilleries, distribution, electrical and electronic appliances, and non-strategic industries. It will also reduce its holdings in banks, insurance companies and other financial enterprises without losing control.[4]

A detailed articulation of the Government's policy on privatisation emerged in the Structural Adjustment Programme,[5] which was embarked upon in July 1986, as a comprehensive attempt to tackle the economic crisis from its roots. Two of its main features are:

(a) adoption of appropriate pricing, especially for petroleum products and public enterprises; and
(b) encouragement of rationalisation and privatisation of public sector enterprises.

The programme document, in stating the objectives and strategy, highlighted the need to 'lessen the dominance of unproductive investments in the public sector, improve the sector's efficiency and intensify the growth potential of the private sector'. In enunciating the case for reform, the document disclosed that government investment in the public enterprise sector was over N23 billion but that the returns had been less than N500 million annually, and concluded that the government was 'clearly not receiving a fair return on its investment outlay while it continued to pay interest charges and principal on the huge loans'. It also revealed that as much as 40 per cent of the federal government's non-salary recurrent expenditure and 30 per cent of its capital investment budget had gone to support public enterprises, and went on to declare that the state of affairs would no longer be allowed to continue.[6]

Furthermore, all the affected public enterprises were classified into five broad categories, on the basis of which they would either be (a) fully privatised, (b) partially privatised, (c) fully commercialised, (d) partially commercialised, or (e) remain as public institutions. Those to be fully privatised, according to the SAP Document, are the public enterprises which function in a fully commercial manner. Full privatisation would imply that government ownership and control will be removed to permit such public enterprises to operate like their private-sector counterparts. In the enterprise to be partially privatised, part of the government's equity holding will be sold out and, following that, they would be expected to operate as private companies. These two groups of enterprises would not longer receive any operating subvention and their future financial needs would have to be met from the capital markets.

The group of enterprises to be partially or fully commercialised will continue to be owned by the government but will have a financial structure that will enable them to raise capital. The fully commercialised ones will be expected to operate without government operating subventions and without Treasury support for future capital development. The partially commercialised ones will necessarily have to generate 'a fair proportion' of the financial requirements for their operations but might continue to need some government support towards the operating costs of future capital programmes.

Public institutions comprise parastatals such as educational and cultural institutions, research institutes, universities, teaching hospitals, and other specialist hospitals and allied bodies. They are to continue to be funded largely from Treasury sources while at the same time trying to raise some revenue through user charges.

In the period between mid-1986 and now, privatisation and commercialisation has been widely debated in the country. Apart from well-informed comments and articles in the popular Press, several symposia, seminars, etc. have been held to discuss the concepts, forms and detailed steps that should be followed in privatising or commercialising, partially or fully, the public enterprises at federal and state-government levels. In discussing the concept of privatisation that could be generally upheld in Nigeria, the point of departure should be the Structural Adjustment Programme (SAP), of which privatisation or reform of public enterprises is an important aspect. The SAP also stresses (a) stimulation of domestic production with a view to broadening the supply base on the economy, (b) movement towards trade liberalisation, and (c) reduction of administrative controls and their replacement with greater reliance on market forces, particularly in the allocation of scarce resources.

Since privatisation can be conceived of in more than one sense, it is to be expected that, in the Third World countries, the process would assume more than one meaning, for reasons such as: (i) the requisite awareness threshold for privatisation has not been reached; and (ii) political power structures are volatile and engender instability. With particular reference to Nigeria, what in the Third world is loosely termed 'denationalisation', or divestiture, may be expected to become predominant. It must be recognised, however, that as it is a country with one federal and twenty-one state governments, privatisation will be conceived, perceived, and carried out in more than one sense. Indeed, methods and procedures for privatisation will depend on several factors, such as the objectives of the various governments, the current state of affairs of a particular public enterprise, its performance so far, and the availability of audited statements of account covering the previous 5 years (which is one of the requirements of the Securities and Exchange Commission when evaluating shares prices). Other factors will comprise the attractiveness of the sector to which the parastatals belong, the assessment of private investors, and even the timing of placement in the marketing of each enterprise. In Nigeria, at federal-government level, the objectives of privatisation and commercialisation policy have been identified as follows: (i) reduction of the burden imposed by parastatals on the resources of the government; (ii) enhancement of the efficiency of government enterprises; (iii) improvement of the generally poor returns on overall government investment in parastatals: and (iv) withdrawals of government from activities that are best suited for the private sector.

Privatisation in Nigeria will, several years hence, be regarded as a success if, as defined by a Nigerian economist, it turns out to be 'not just denationalisation of nationalised businesses, but a process by which the size of an inefficient and ineffective public sector is reduced by transferring some of its functions to a relatively more efficient private sector'.[7]

ACTIONS ON PRIVATISATION

Because of the absence of readily available data it is difficult to provide a picture of the actions on privatisation already taken by different states in Nigeria. Suffice it to say, however, that the country has been experiencing creeping privatisation in the last 3 years.

Recent denationalisations

From time to time, governments at federal and state levels, as part of the process of restructuring the economy as a whole, had reached decisions to liquidate some of the public sector enterprises.

Thus at federal level, the Nigerian National Supply Company (which was established in the 1970s to bulk purchase scarce food items from abroad and distribute all over the country) has been liquidated and all its outstanding loans to the government paid back. Other enterprises which are in the process of liquidation include National Freight Company Limited and National Fish Company Limited. Some of their assets have been sold while others were leased out. The process of liquidation of the National Livestock Production Company has also been recently completed. Some of its assets were reported to have been distributed to certain government organisations.

Government investments in two dairy companies under the supervision of the Federal Ministry of Agriculture have either been sold to private companies or to state governments' investment companies. In one of the companies, the federal government's share was reduced from 80 per cent to 25 per cent which will now be held on behalf of the government by the Nigerian Agricultural and Co-operative Bank, another public enterprise that may be subjected to its own dose of privatisation at a later stage. A lease option is being examined in respect of two cattle ranches and three poultry production units located in different parts of the country. Although figures in respect of prices paid for the enterprises already disposed of are available, it is not quite clear from the available records how the valuations were arrived at. Federal Government's shares in eight companies engaged in beverage production, root crops production, grains, palm-oil production and integrated livestock production are in the process of being sold. A consultative committee comprising officials of the

Federal Ministry of Agriculture, Water Resources and Rural Development, Ministry of Finance Incorporated, and the Securities and Exchange Commission (SEC) is said to be monitoring the activities of the eight companies. The inclusion of a representative of the SEC, which is responsible for valuation of all shares, stocks, etc before they are advertised for public subscription, would seem to imply that the shares of the eight enterprises might have been evaluated on the basis of the usual SEC criteria.

In 1977, the federal government carried out a reform of the agricultural produce trade and set up seven commodity boards which served not only as buyers of last resort but also enjoyed monopoly rights of selling outside the country products such as cocoa, rubber, palm produce, etc. Operational funds to the commodity boards were obtained in the form of loans from the Central Bank and guaranteed by the Treasury. Persistently poor trading results by all but one of the boards led to an investigation of the commodity-board marketing system as a whole. The investigation revealed that at the end of 1985, five of the boards owned the Central Bank over N900 million in the form of outstanding loans an accumulated interest. All the boards have since been abolished with effect from December, 1986, and received managers appointed to wind up their affairs. Assets disposal committees were later set up to sell their assets and to pay all certified creditors.

Preference for joint venture: injection of private capital

Measures recently announced by the government point in the direction of full commercialisation and partial privatisation of the petroleum sector in Nigeria.

The commencement of operations of the Nigeria National Petroleum Corporation (NNPC) on commercial lines was confirmed by President Babangida in his policy statement on the industry in which he stated that the Corporation would be financially autonomous in its operations and procedures to ensure efficiency and profitability. The NNPC is now free to raise loans in the capital market to finance its projects. To complement the new status the Corporation was given the freedom to fix prices of petroleum products without consultation or approval by the federal government but subject to the consent of the Productivity, Prices, and Incomes Board.

Furthermore, the Corporation was empowered to

acquire equity interest in downstream activities in the area of refining and product marketing. Under the commercialisation programme, all customers of NNPC must henceforth make prompt payment for services rendered. NNPC has recently been re-organised and divided into eleven companies in order to become a commercially integrated international oil company.

In recognition of the inability of the government to continue to finance the high-cost projects of the petroleum sector and the need to inject a dose of privatisation into it, President Babangida invited financial participation of the private sector in phase II of the Petrochemical Project when he announced that, although phase I was financed by the federal government, the second phase would be financed mostly through direct investment by local, industrial, and institutional investors, as well as joint-venture participation by foreign interests.[8]

The government of Onodo State seems to be blazing the trail in another form of privatisation (i.e. 'non-sale' privatisation or privatisation of management such as management contracts). In 1986, the state government entered into a management contract of four years' duration with a firm of indigenous consultants to 'oversee the day-to-day running of twenty-three companies in which the holding company was full or part ownership'.[9] The management consultants actually took over twenty-eight companies but five were allowed to die 'because they never made profit and where they did it was never enough to sustain them'. The novelty of this type of management of state-government enterprise did attract some criticism; however, the management contract is said to have been a success, as noticeable improvements were recorded in the activities of the subsidiaries of the holding company in the areas of turnover, harvesting, and regularity of payment of staff salaries, respectively, within a few months of the management contract. One of the cocoa-products subsidiaries was reported to have turned a loss of N1.8 million to a net profit of N10. 1 million within one year of the management contract. As a result of improved management of its affairs it was able to pay back outstanding loans totalling N4.3 million to the state government and the Nigerian Industrial Development Bank - all within one year, in 1987.

In his assessment of the factors responsible for the hitherto poor performance of the public enterprises, the managing consultant described the main problems as lack of effective control over those running the enterprises, lack of a systematic staff development plan, bad deployment of staff, and poor arrangement for replacement of worn-out equipment. In spite of the success of the scheme, however, a decision has been taken to privatise those companies which are wholly owned by the holding company and to sell a substantial part of their shares to the public in future.

The oldest surviving indigenous commercial bank - National Bank of Nigeria, owned by one Odu's Investment Company - is to sell 49 per cent of its shares to individual and private enterprises. In preparation towards that, the Bank has been carrying out a programme of reorganisation and restructuring which has already resulted in the closing down of several branches, and dismissal, retrenchment, or retirement of staff, including the acting chief executive. The state government of Lagos will be winding up its burnt-bricks factory and will limit itself to 30 per cent shares in the five companies in which it is presently involved.

The Ogun State Hotel, Abeokuta, wholly-owned previously by the state government appears to have been recently privatised, going by a newspaper report. There have been cases of sales of shares by some other state governments (e.g. in the Nigerian Cement Company, Nkalagu, Golden Guinea Breweries, Cross River Breweries Limited, and West African Glass Industries Limited). The governments of Imo, Bendel and Anambra states are reported to be leading the way in the privatisation of their enterprises.[10]

While the state governments are known to be inclined towards privatisation, it is expected that the process will atttain the necessary momentum only after it has started at federal level. One noteworthy peculiarity of the process of privatisation, in so far as it has taken place in Nigeria at federal level, is that some of the public-sector enterprises or their assets have been bought or taken over by the state governments or their companies, rather than by private-sector interests. The military governor of one of the new states recently budgeted a sum of N7 million to be used in purchasing shares of the federal enterprises to be privatised. perhaps there is a need to re-examine the desirability of this trend in the interest of the objectives to be served by privatisation.

Nigeria

Public agencies for setting prices for the sale of enterprises

Compared with many of its African neighbours, Nigeria has a fairly well developed capital market which started business in 1961 as the Lagos Stock Exchange (LSE). In 1977 the LSE was transformed into the Nigeria Stock Exchange with branches in Lagos, Kaduna, and Port Harcourt. Several stockbrokers are licensed to deal on the three floors of the three branches of the stock exchange. Nigerian stockbrokers are experienced in capital market operations, having taken part in the spate of public issues which accompanies the implementation of the Nigerian Enterprises Promotion Scheme (i.e. indigenisation scheme) between 1972 and 1979. The shares of a few of the companies in which the equity held by the federal government is to be sold are already listed and being traded on the stock exchange. However, poor accounting records may yet prevent many public enterprises from getting on the market. Some of them will only manage to get a listing on the second-tier securities market of the stock exchange if they cannot meet the stringent criteria of the main market.

Initially, the valuation of stocks and shares, etc. to be sold on the stock market was undertaken by a public agency known as the Capital Issues Commission. After evaluating the experiences gained in the 1970s, particularly in connection with the indigenisation programme, a new body called the Securities and Exchange Commission was set up in 1979. Its responsibilities include: (a) price determination, timing, and amount of sale of securities; (b) allotment of securities; and (c) surveillance over and development of the market.

The Securities and Exchange Commission is well aware that controversial issues which attended the indigenisation exercise - such as the so-called underpricing of shares, the spread of stock among investors from different geographic zones, and extensive diffusion of share-holding (to the extent that there might be no effective participation in the management of the enterprises) - will need to be better addressed this time.

Others expected to take part in the privatisation operations of one kind or another will include merchant banks, management consultants, accounting and auditing consultants, etc. Nigeria can boast of having many firms in these categories who are staffed by experienced experts, both local and expatriate. As part of their preparation for the privatisation exercise, many of these firms have issued brochures enumerating the services which they (in alliance with overseas partners with experience of privatisation elsewhere) can offer to the government.

Finally, the government intends to set up an agency to be called the Technical Committee on Privatisation (TCP) which will be responsibile for the implementation of the policy on privatisation. The committee's function has a bearing on the pricing of the shares to be sold and, in this regard, will not only advise, but submit proposals to the government, with a view to ensuring a fair price and an even spread of ownership of shares to be sold.

PROBLEMS ENCOUNTERED:

Very little is known about the problems encountered outside the government agencies that have privatised their parastatals. Considerable preliminary work has been undertaken on reforming public-sector enterprises. Initially, an Implementation Committee on Privatisation/Commercialisation of government parastatals (comprising the Secretary to the Federal Military Government, Permanent Secretaries, and Head of Extra-Ministerial Departments) was set up. This committee later appointed two sub-committees (namely, the Sub-committee on Privatisation and the Sub-Committee on Commercialisation). The sub-committees, among other things, spelt out what the objectives of the reform should be in respect of enterprises to be privatised or commercialised. The Sub-Committee on Privatisation drew up general principles to guide the exercise. Its recommendations included the following:

(a) companies to be privatised should first be incorporated into public limited liability companies, while those that are financially weak and could be difficult to sell through the capital market should be wound up before the sale of the their assets;

(b) the shares of the enterprises must be properly valued by the Securities and Exchange Commission; and

(c) the exercise should be properly phased in order to avoid over loading the absorptive capacity of the capital market.

In order to prepare a realistic time-table for privatisation, other issues which were addressed included the following: the need to ensure an even spread of ownership of shares, so as to guarantee geographical and inter-personal equity; an institutional framework to be put in place for the implementation of privatisation; audited accounts to be prepared; and the affairs of the enterprises to be put in good order prior to privatisation.

Political support for privatisation

Political support for privatisation policy is an issue which no government can afford to ignore. The Sub-Committee on Privatisation in Nigeria, as far back as 1986, had drawn attention to the fact that an effective publicity and enlightment campaign would play an important role if the objectives of the reform were to be achieved. Most of the support so far enjoyed by the Nigerian government in pursuing privatisation policy is from business groups. This is not surprising as it is that segment of society which has in the past clamoured for the government's withdrawal from running public enterprises, particularly those operating in the area, where, in their assessment, the private sector could perform better. It must not be forgotten that this is the sector which is most likely to benefit from the privatisation exercise. Also, if the privatised enterprises show improved performance, it is the business sector that will be saved the additional costs it now has to bear (for example, due to inefficient service from some of the parastatals, the business sector has to provide its own water, power supply, etc, in order to be able to do business).

Opposition to privatisation should never be under-estimated; rather it should be acknowledged, and addressed with a view to removing it through sustained education, and publicity of the positive role it could potentially play in generating faster growth and development.

Civil service reaction

It is difficult to assess accurately the reaction of the Civil Service to the privatisation policies and their several modalities. As has been observed in other countries, it may be worse off under privatisation in view of the expected loss of influence, etc. However, the Nigerian government sets up the Technical Committee on Privatisation, doubtless the

Civil Service will co-operate and assist the Committee to achieve the government's objectives.

Public reaction

It may be too early to assess public reaction to privatisation measures, as such measures have been few. What is not in doubt, however, is the stand of some groups to the policy as a whole. The organised representatives of the Nigerian workers - Nigerian Labour Congress - has left no one in doubt as to its opposition to the policy. It has used every possible opportunity to demonstrate that the policy will not only lead to unemployment but will also set workers behind, in terms of gains made over the public sector. The position, however, is privatisation and deregulation (which are related) have the effect of changing the mix of employment opportunities in society without necessarily leading to a net loss in total employment. We do, however, recognise that there will be a short-term period in the transition to privatisation which will entail retrenchment and severance of employment. Workers must be educated to see privatisation, deregulation, and job creation in a holistic way, so that they begin to understand that the reform measures being undertaken are not altogether against the interests of workers.

Active consumer groups hardly exist in Nigeria. The Nigerian Consumers Association is a rather weak one and is almost moribund. Because the privatisation measures that have taken place have not been generally announced, the citizens at large may not be aware that the process has started, albeit in a creeping fashion.

Issues in the sale of enterprises

The Sub-Committee for Privatisation sent questionnaires to the enterprises which had been tentatively scheduled for privatisation. Having analysed the information gathered from the exercise, the Committee recommended, as a prelude to privatisation, the appointment of consultants to bring the accounts of the enterprises up to date, and investigate the structure of their debts. It is pertinent to add that the government has since directed that federal ministries should submit proposals for restructuring the capital base of the parastatals for which they are currently responsible. The National Council of Ministers has also directed the annual audited accounts of each parastatal should be published within 6 months of the end of each year, in at least two national newspapers, and that failure to do so should disqualify such a parastatal or company from any type of government funding.[11] This measure was introduced by the government as part of the efforts to encourage financial discipline. One other relevant step in preparing the public enterprises for privatisation is their conversion to limited liability companies. A clause covering the transformation of the enterprises into public limited liability companies has been included in the draft law on privatisation now awaiting promulgation.

The fixing of the price for the enterprises to be sold, whether partially or fully, has been always one of the sensitive issues of the whole exercise, be it in the developed world or in developing countries. In respect of the enterprises still to be privatised, the Technical Committee on Privatisation and commercialisation will be given the responsibility to approach 'the Securities and Exchange Commission for a fair price for each issue'. In cases a particular enterprise does not lend itself to the approach of the SEC, the Technical Committee will submit to the government for approval, proposals that will ensure 'a fair price'.

Obviously, the sales techniques to be applied will be those that are determined by the objectives defined by the government and by the peculiarities of the enterprises concerned. Among those already found to be useful are: outright sale to the private sector; and liquidation accompanied by disposal of assets. With regard to future sales, the Technical Committee will be well advised to ensure that shares in those companies in which all the existing equity of the government is to be privatised are disposed of through the capital market and by public offering of shares. Where private sales will have to be resorted to, it will be advisable to advertise for open bids, which could later be narrowed down to a few bids before final selection is made. This will ensure that the public is kept informed of developments before the sales are concluded and will thus reduce the room for suspicion and criticism of the scheme as a whole.

Who is the buyer?

The buyers of public enterprises or their assets so far sold or wound up, respectively, include individuals and corporate bodies. Beneficiaries of enterprises that were 'transferred' have been either state governments or their agencies (companies). When the privatisation exercise finally takes off in a more-co-ordinated manner, other buyers will include the general public (who will be able to buy shares in the companies) and institutional investors (such as pension funds, trades-union and co-operative organisation, and state-government investment companies, etc.). The issue of allotment of privatised shares, with a view to ensuring geo-political and inter-personal equity, is not only important but could be crucial to the success of privatisation, at least in the short term. The current thinking is that carefully determined proportions of the total shares on offer should be allotted to associations and interest groups - such as state-government investment companies, trade unions, market-women organisation, universities, friendly societies, and local and community associations - in cases of both under - and over subscription. The idea is to ensure that all the important sections of society are well served. Participation by non-Nigerians has been accepted in principle, so long as such participation does not infringe the provisions of the Nigerian Enterprises Promotion Act, 1977.[12]

CONCLUSION

It is dangerous to assume that privatisation will be an easy exercise. One area to which enough attention does not seem to have been paid is the relationship between government and the privatised commercialised enterprises. There will be a need to draw up clear-cut guidelines which will clarify the roles and responsibilities of each side; this will be particularly necessary in the case of commercialised enterprises.

A properly implemented privatisation programme has the potential to promote productivity and profitability through the exposure of public enterprises to the commercial discipline of the market. The private sector in Nigeria has developed sufficient know-how to be able to take over the investments that will result from divestitures. The financial and capital markets are also sufficiently developed to be able to play the role expected of them. Opposition to privatisation on grounds other than economic should, however, not be under-estimated. Conscious enlightenment campaigns may be required to broaden the base of support if privatisation is to succeed to the extent envisaged.

NOTES

1. Views and comments of the Federal Military Government on the (1985) Report of the Study Group on Statutory Corporations and State-owned Companies, Lagos: Federal Government Press.
2. Broadcast to the Nation by Major-General I.B. Babangida on 1st October, 1985, pp. 6-7.
3. Ibid.
4. Address by Major-General I.B. Babangida on the 1986 Budget, pp. 11-12.
5. See the SAP document, Structural Adjustment Programme for Nigeria, July 1986-June 1988, Lagos: Government Printer.
6. Ibid., p.13.
7. See Ibie, C.C. (1986) 'Restructuring the Nigerian economy: the place of privatisation', Bullion (Central Bank of Nigeria Publication), 10 (2), April/June.
8. Address by General I.B. Babangida on the occasion of the commissioning of the Linear Alkyl Benzene (LAB) Plant in Kaunda on Monday 21st March, 1988.
9. See supplement on Onodo State Investment Holding Company, The Punch, May 10 1988.
10. See Ahmed, M. (1986) 'The role of capital market operations in the privatisation process', Bullion, 10 (2), p. 23.
11. The Draft privatisation/Commercialisation Decree has already been discussed by the National Council of Ministers (NCM). However, it will not become law until it is approved by the Armed Forces Ruling Council (AFRC) which is the council with power to pass draft decrees into laws.
12. The provisions of the Act are being reviewed with a view to attuning it to the present-day economic conditions and facilitating the attraction of foreign investment.

15

Privatisation in Ghana

William Adda*

THE PUBLIC ENTERPRISE SITUATION

The preponderence of state-owned enterprises (SOEs) in the Ghanaian economy has its roots in the very strong expansion of the role of the state immediately after achieving political independence (particularly in the early 1960s). The development philosophy at the period was based upon a combination of nationalism, pan-Africanism, and African socialism, and, supported by the economic development theories of the era, pointed towards the creation of a great number of public enterprises (PEs) or state-owned enterprises, covering most areas of economic activity. It was during this time (1961-6) that many of today's SOEs were established.

Between 1966 and 1972 the role of the state in the economy was de-emphasised. The private sector was encouraged more and some state enterprises were privatised. However, even in this period, when less importance was attached to non-commercial objectives, a few new SOEs were created: for example, the Ghana Tobacco Company, the Electricity Corporation of Ghana (ECG), and the Food Distribution Corporation.

In 1972, the new government of the National Redemption Council (NRC) signalled a return to the development strategies of the 1961-6 period. The government accordingly took majority interest in all companies engaged in the extractive and timber industries, which, next to cocoa, were, and remain, the principal source of Ghana's export earnings. As a sequel to this policy thrust, an Investment Policy Decree was promulgated which required

* Chairman, State Enterprises Commission

all private foreign enterprises to form partnerships with either private Ghanaian enterprises or with the state.[1]

Lastly, during the Armed Forces Revolutionary Council (AFRC) era (in 1979), a large number of private enterprises were confiscated to the state because their owners were found guilty of financial or economic malpractices. However, with the exception of Achimota Brewery, the enterprises involved were relatively small groups of companies, such as the George Amuah and Associates (GEA) Group of Companies, Ghamot Group of Companies, and the National Industrial Company (NICOM) Group of Companies.[2]

The rationale

The main reasons for creating more SOEs were as follows: to ensure the government's controlling interest in the national economy; to promote public entrepreneurship in areas where private capital was unavailable or too risky for private investment; to offer competition to private enterprise and thereby ensure the stabilisation of prices; to create employment opportunities for the unproductive workforce; and to ensure equitable distribution within the geographical entities of the country.

The SOEs were intended to operate as commercial entities and to generate revenue for the development of social services. The state expects them to provide reasonable financial returns on investment; provide goods and services to the population at reasonable prices; ensure regular income to the workers; and generally act as a focus for the development process by creating the necessary revenues to support the national budget.

In Ghana, almost all the fully state-owned enterprises (excluding the confiscated ones) were incorporated under the Statutory Corporations' Act or under a Legislative/ Executive Instrument. Against this background, SOEs were established in virtually all sectors of the economy (electricity, water, power generation, transport, mining, agriculture, manufacturing, forestry, trade, oil refining and distribution, construction and tourism) and continue to play a major role in the economy of the country. The term SOE is used here to refer to an enterprise controlled to some extent by government, in the sense that it owns all the shares or at least the majority of such shares.[3]

The totality

In one form or another, the government owns shares in at least 235 enterprises. In 181 of these, its holding represents a majority of the share capital, and thus a controlling interest. The government has a minority interest in the rest, the control of which is in the hands of the private sector.

In about half of the SOEs (ninety-three), the government itself is the sole shareholder, and in a further five it has joint control with one or more other state-controlled shareholders. The government exercises indirect control over another eighty-three enterprises, which are in the hands of financial and some non-financial SOEs, Most prominent among the financial institutions which have established subsidiaries and/or hold shares are the National Investment Bank, the Agricultural Development Bank, and the Bank for Housing and Construction. Even the Bank of Ghana has investments in six enterprises, three of them wholly-owned.

Holding companies

The principal non-financial SOE which holds shares in other enterprises is Ghana Industrial Holding Corporation (GIHOC), which has twenty-four subsidiaries, majority holdings in twenty-two companies, and minority interest in two others. Other non-financial SOEs which have investments in companies include the National Industrial Company (NICOM) group, the State Gold Mining Corporation, and the Ghana Cocoa Board. Formally, the shares held by the National Trust Holding Company Ltd (NTHC) should also be considered as indirect state participation, but as the NTHC is little more than a depository of government-owned shares, they are here included among those being held directly by the government.

Joint ventures

The government has entered into a number of joint ventures with private partners, both domestic and foreign. Among the twenty-three ventures with foreign partners, the government has a controlling interest, directly or indirectly, in fifteen.

Ghana

The general structure of SOEs

This is broadly outlined in Table 15.1.

Table 15.1: The general structure of SOEs

Public equity holding	
Public equity (%) (1)	No. of enterprises (2)
100	93
50-100	43
25-50	39
Less than 25	15

Cashflow between the SOEs and the public budget

The state-owned enterprises sector constitutes a major part of the civil machinery of government. No wonder, therefore, that the malfunctioning of enterprises within the sector will constitute a threat to the national economy.

Over the last 8 years, support for SOEs increased from ₵1.1 billion in 1982 (10 per cent of government expenditure) to ₵7.35 billion in 1986 (8 per cent of government expenditure).[4] The sector has been a significant burden on government in terms of indirect support through tax and loan arrears, absence of dividends and, in some cases, inability to repay government-guaranteed foreign loans. SOE tax arrears doubled from ₵1.27 billion in 1984 to ₵2.5 billion in 1985. In addition, outstanding government loans to SOEs increased from ₵500 million in ₵1.9 billion in 1985. Virtually no interest or principal repayment is being made on these loans. Over the 5-year period 1979-84, SOEs repaid only ₵45 million in principal and ₵7.3 million in interest on their outstanding loans, at an effective interest rate of less than 1 per cent.[5]

Given that the government was generally not able to finance directly substantial capital investment by SOEs through loans and equity, some SOEs have financed their expansions from foreign loans guaranteed by the government. The level of outstanding loan guaranteed by the government. The level of outstanding loan guarantees is

306

difficult to estimate, as data are incomplete. However, figures as at 30 June 1986 conclusively show that government-guaranteed loans from external and internal sources for only eighteen SOEs amounted to about ¢15.681 billion.[6] In 1982, the SOEs received a total of about 13 per cent of government expenditure in the form of subsidies, equity contributions and capital grants. But by the end of 1984 this shot up to about 25 per cent.

Official records on loans provided by the government for the SOEs indicate that in 1984 the sector owed it about ¢1.882 billion. However, there are serious discrepancies in the calculations. Interest charged on loans granted to SOEs in 1985 ranged from 2 per cent to 6 per cent, while the bank rate was 19 per cent.

Foreign exchange adjustments increase the figure of the loans, particularly since the SOEs have not been revaluing their assets, or even charging depreciation and depositing the amount in depreciation account as demanded by law. It is pitiful that by the middle of 1985 the Bank of Ghana held for 14 SOEs only ¢3 million in depreciation account.[7] With respect to dividends, most SOEs which make profits often retain them rather than pay out dividends. Thus, returns on investment to the government are low, because only a few SOEs are profit-making, only a small share of profits is declared as dividends, and the dividends are often not paid out but retained by the SOEs. In April, 1985 it was estimated that thirty-nine of the SOEs owed the government the colossal amount of ¢900 million in the form of company taxes, of which ¢300 million were for 1985 alone.[8]

As operating losses increased sharply in the early 1980s illiquidity has been a serious problem for many SOEs, building up arrears to the government, other creditors, and suppliers. For example a cross-debts study on eighteeen SOEs (about 8 per cent of all SOEs) undertaken in early 1987, reported cross-debts between SOEs totalling ¢5.2 billion,[9] and showed their indebtedness to the government to be ¢40.2 billion (taxes ¢6.0 billion; unpaid dividends ¢85.0 million; and domestic and foreign loans ¢2.7 billion and ¢31.4 billion, respectively).

Attempts at divestiture

As already indicated, the government that came to power after the overthrow of the First Republic decided to divest

307

the state from the burden of financing and managing the numerous SOEs created by the former government, and to place them under the supervision of the Industrial Development Corporation (IDC) and the Agricultural Development Corporation (ADC).

In this attempt two options were adopted: (i) outright sale, and (ii) private participation in the form of joint ventures. The government was able to sell four companies; the State Furniture and Joinery Corporation; the State Bakery Corporation; the State Laundries Corporation; and the State Tyre Retreading Corporation. Three others - Bonsaso Rubber/Tyre Factory, the State Match Factory, and the Tema Cement Works (now Ghacem) - became joint-venture companies with foreign private participation. The State Timber products company became a part of the Timber Marketing Board, now the Timber Export Development Board (TEDB); The State Hotels Corporation, the Film Industry Corporation, the State Publishing Company, and the State Farms Corporation have, to date, remained individual SOEs.

At that first attempt at divestiture, the issues involved were not clearly analysed and/or co-ordinated. As a result, the programme became very controversial and unsuccessful. The expected impact was not felt and the programme had to be abandoned.

The companies for which joint-venture arrangements could not be concluded at the time were later (1978) incorporated into the first holding corporation, Ghana Industrial Holding Corporation (GIHOC), which today constitutes the largest manufacturing unit in Ghana.

THE THINKING OF PRIVATISATION

The idea of the state maintaining a hold on a wide sector of the economy, notwithstanding economic unjustifiability, still persists. This partly explains the reason why, irrespective of the hopeless state of some of the SOEs, governments in the past rarely agreed to their privatisation, preferring to sustain such moribund enterprises indefinitely with fiscal or other subsidies - a practice that has contributed in no small way to the stagnation of the sector.

However, to enable industry and commerce make their optimum contribution to the realisation of the objectives of the government's economic recovery programme, it is imperative that the public and private sectors demonstrate a far higher level of management and implementation capacity than has so far been the case. This is particularly required of the state-enterprise sector because it is the larger of the two in terms of investment and employment levels.

The abysmal performance of the SOEs was due, specifically, to:

(a) constraints attributable to inadequacies, inconsistencies, and the unclarity of government policies in the SOE sector;

(b) the sheer oversize of the sector, in relation to available management capacity;

(c) too frequent changes in top management personnel, resulting, among other things, in instability and deviations in the pursuit of enterprise objectives;

(d) lack of adequate managerial skills;

(e) excessive political interference in the day-to-day operations of the enterprises;

(f) lack of adequate incentives to stimulate higher performance and productivity;

(g) ineffective monitoring and evaluation of enterprise performance;

(h) inadequate capitalisation and working capital;

(i) lack of adequate inputs as well as disruptions in input delivery;

(j) stifling of entrepreneurship arising from excessive governmental regulation or controls, as well as protectionism in the form of subsidies, government guarantees for loans, etc.; and

(k) the adoption of outmoded accounting and financial management systems.

In brief, therefore the SOE sector has failed to achieve the objectives for which it was created.

Since April 1983, there has been a marked improvement in both policies and economic management. There has also been an impressive recovery of the economy, with considerable progress in the realization of the government's stabilisation and adjustment objectives. The government recognises that to sustain these initial gains will require substantial further adjustment over the remaining years of this decade, if not longer.

In pursuance of this goal, a task force was put in place

Ghana

to crystalize the government's thinking on privatisation, among other issues. It prepared a draft policy statement on the government's thinking on privatisation. It was subjected to vigorous debates at various public fora and seminars which were attended by accredited representatives of organised labour, revolutionary organs of the government, government officials (including secretaries of state), and the public at large. The consensus emerged that there was a need for privatisation but that the programme must proceed cautiously.

In the policy statement, rationalisation was defined to involve:

> the process of modifying the ownership and/or management structures of enterprises with a view to ensuring adequate capitalisation and adequate working capital, as well as the enhancement of management capacity, thereby equipping the enterprises to achieve optimum performance within a given policy, legal and institutional environment.[10]

With this understanding, the following types of ownership were identified and incorporated in the policy statement: (i) public shareholding; (ii) related company shareholding; (iii) institutional shareholding; (iv) community shareholding; (v) workers' shareholding; (vi) joint ventureship; and (vii) outright sale.

SOEs have therefore been categorised on the criteria of: (a) strategic importance; (b) profitability; (c) net foreign exchange earning and/or saving capability; and (d) economic/financial performance; and the candidates for divestiture and those that will remain fully state-owned were indicated. The application of these criteria resulted in the identification of the following ownership structures and other arrangements: (i) fully government-owned SOEs; (ii) fully government-owned enterprises whose management is contracted out to local and/or external agencies; (iii) joint ventures with local or foreign participation; (iv) outright sale; (v) liquidation or closure; and (vi) amalgamations and mergers.

The necessity for privatisation

The central government's commitment to privatisation is rooted in the following statement:

310

Given the generally negative performance of Ghana's SOEs, a re-examination of the extent of state involvement in enterprises is not only urgent but also unavoidable. Many enterprises that are potentially viable are on the verge of bankruptcy through mismanagement of the originally invested resources and the government alone is not able to undertake the massive capitalisation needed by most of them. As a result, the government had acknowledged the necessity of reappraising the management and ownership structure of the enterprises.[11]

There are five basic reasons why the central government pursues its privatisation initiatives:

1. The changing economic environment: For many SOEs the original objectives behind their creation are no longer valid. In addition, the government has other options than ownership - taxation, spending, regulation - available to meet public policy needs.

2. Effectiveness: There is abundant evidence to suggest that many SOEs are not as effective in serving their clients as the private sector. Privatisation, by putting SOEs under the test of the market place, can improve efficiency.

3. Public funds: Public ownership of the SOEs places enormous demands on government resources to manage and financially support various enterprises. Many ministries have responsibilities for multi-billion cedi SOEs as well as many other responsibilities. On a day-to-day basis, accountability is not always as focused as it should be.

4. Management styles: The public institutions use taxpayers' money to operate. There is slow decision-making and unwillingness on the part of management to take risks; whereas in a commercial milieu, adaptability to rapid changes in markets and technologies is essential.

5. Fairness and equity: Many SOEs compete directly with the private sector. In effect, some businesses see their own tax monies being used to compete against themselves. This is hardly fair, or conducive to the enterprise system our development programmes are geared to establish.

One can suggest that the Ghanaian government's approach to privatisation is based on specific objectives designed to ensure the appropriateness of the SOEs, while encouraging a vibrant private sector.

ACTIONS IN PRIVATISATION

Present attempts at privatisation

The present attempts at privatisation are based on the Government's strategy to reform the whole SOE sector through a Public Enterprise Project (PEP). Implementation of this policy requires a combination of macro-economic and sectoral policy-based operations to support the broad policy measures, sectoral rehabilitation measures to strengthen many of the core SOEs through new capital investment and institutional strengthening, and assistance in developing and implementing sector-wide SOE reforms.

Essentially, the programme is intended to provide critical technical assistance needed to implement the agreed reforms and also to lay the groundwork for longer-term reforms by strengthening the key institutions and assessing and developing further SOE reforms and restructuring measures. The PEP was therefore processed separately from the Structural Adjustment Loan (SAL) to allow the government to adequately restructure the State Enterprise Commission (SEC) to enable it to manage the SOE reform programme, including the divestiture programme.

Several guiding principles define the general orientation of the reform programme: first, to scale down the number of SOEs to a level which is commensurate with the budgetary and administrative resources of the government; second, to strengthen the SOE management and government's ability to monitor and evaluate managerial performance; and third, to create a divestiture programme.

The divestiture programme

To initiate the divestiture process, the government undertook a preliminary categorisation of its SOEs into those to be retained, divested (partially or totally) and liquidated. It was recognised that the programme would have to be phased to reflect the Government's administrative capacity as well as resource availability. The government was initially reluctant to divest profitable SOEs; however, it was recognised that this could have benefits both for the SOEs (in terms of increased equity investment, new management, and technology) and for the government (in terms of revenue from divestiture, increased taxes from higher profitability; and elimination of future demands for financial support). Accordingly, the government decided to: (i) include some profitable SOEs in the first phase of the divestiture programme; and (ii) be flexible in its future selection of SOEs for divestiture.

Categories of SOEs to be divested

The government has approved a list of thirty SOEs for the first phase of the divestiture programme. These include: (i) several smaller industrial SOEs that are likely to be sold on a private-placement basis to existing management, or to Ghanaian private investors; (ii) five inactive SOEs to be liquidated; (iii) a major loss-making SOE - State Fishing Corporation; (vi) five major agricultural SOEs; and (v) some profitable (or potentially profitable) SOEs which may be attractive to investors and thereby provide some momentum to the programme. The initial thirty SOEs have a total employment of roughly 12,000 out of a total of 480,000 in the SOE sector.[12]

Under the SAL, the government is committed to initiate divestiture action on ten SOEs - the first five for liquidation and the other five for total or partial sale, by December 31 1987. Due to initial difficulties, this time-frame has suffered serious delay and new time-frames are being negotiated. The initial focus will be upon five of the preliminary list of thirty SOEs for liquidation. The dossiers prepared on all the companies for divestiture contain, inter alia, viability assessments, preliminary valuations, recommended divestiture modality, satisfactory analysis of any legal issues, and proposed financing strategy (including handling of possible liabilities).

Government's approach to the programme

The following broad programme guidelines and policies are to be adopted:

(a) valuation should reflect earnings potential rather than book value if the SOE is to be sold as a going concern;

(b) no undue advantage or protection will be offered to investors;

(c) all legal issues should be resolved before putting an SOE up for sale;

313

     (d) in SOEs to be converted into joint ventures, the private sector partner(s) having majority shares should have management control to avoid undue interference from the government;

     (e) where an SOE is not viable and cannot be sold as a going concern, the government will wind up the SOE and sell the remaining assets;

     (f) there will be agreed procedures for evaluating bids and negotiating with potential investors to ensure propriety in the divestiture process; and

     (g) non-strategic SOEs which are inactive or clearly have no potential for commercial viability, or for whom it has not been possible to attract investors, will be liquidated.

The divestiture implementation committee (DIC)

To implement the divestiture programme, the government established a Divestiture Implementation Committee (DIC) reporting to the Committee of Secretaries. The Committee is chaired by the SEC Chairman (a member of the Committee of Secretaries) and includes senior officials from the Ghana Investment Centre (Chief Executive), the Bank of Ghana, Ministry of Finance and Economic Planning, the National Trust Holding Company, the Attorney-General's Office, and sector ministries (Agriculture, Industry, and others, on a rotating basis as required). There are also representatives from the Committee for the Defence of the Revolution (CDR) and the Trades Union Congress (TUC). The DIC is being supported by a technical sub-committee which undertakes the tasks required to prepare the SOEs for divestiture (viability analysis, valuation, modalities, etc.). A core group of SEC staff is also included in the sub-committee to develop in-house expertise in divestiture. The secretariat of the DIC is located within the SEC.

Terms of reference of DIC

The DIC was given the following terms of reference as its guiding principles:[13]

(1) To manage the execution of a programme of divestiture of the state's interest in such statutory boards and corporations or companies as the Provisional National Defence Council shall from time to time determine;

314

(2) To ensure that the divestiture process is implemented in a co-ordinated, business-like and timely manner;
(3) To ensure consistency in procedures to be followed in proceeding with the divestiture, especially with respect to analysis required, valuation procedures, inviting bids, negotiating the sale of shares and settlement of claims;
(4) To address, where necessary, issues that may require some uniformity across various divestiture options (e.g. redeployment/compensation);
(5) To ensure that appropriate consultations are carried out and that the government's objectives in the divestiture process are communicated effectively to the public;
(6) To ensure the application of lessons from previous divestitures to new initiatives; and
(7) Any other responsibilities assigned to the Committee.

Divestiture fund

The divestiture programme could involve potential financial net liabilities to the government on such matters as severance pay, debt settlement, and pension liabilities. A Divestiture Fund has been established to handle all the proceeds and claims relating on the sale of assets. In cases where the proceeds exceed the liabilities, the surplus could be used to cover other SOEs where there are net liabilities. While the final liabilities will have to be worked out on a case-by-case basis, for fiscal planning purposes; the government will estimate the net liabilities for the divestiture programme for the following year and include an appropriate amount in its annual budget, if required. Payment of the liabilities could be phased over a period to ease the possible fiscal burden.

Memorandum for action in the divestiture programme

On the basis of the provisions in the divestiture programme, the Chairman of the DIC, a PNDC Secretary, and the Executive Chairman of the SEC have already submitted a memorandum on the divestiture programme, including the following, to the Committee of Secretaries for approval:-

(i) Dossiers on the first five companies for liquidation;
(ii) A request for the appointment of liquidator(s) to undertake the winding-up process;

315

(iii) Guidelines for the liquidation process; and
–(iv) The recommended mode of communication with interested investors.

The DIC has already offered for sale the government's shares in five existing joint ventures to the private partners. Consequently, in the above-mentioned memorandum, the DIC requested the approval/ratification for its action from the Committee of Secretaries. The DIC memorandum has been approved by the Committee of Secretaries and the PNDC has already endorsed it for implementation.

The next batch of five dossiers, including the State Fishing Corporation, has been completed for various divestiture options, which will be submitted to the Committee of Secretaries for approval. With these actions, the timely take-off of the divestiture programme is assured. The divestiture programme has not been offically announced and a public education programme is under way.

PROBLEMS ENCOUNTERED

In the early attempts at privatisation there existed conceptual unclarity because the purpose of privatisation was not clearly defined and the benefits not stated. The Ghanaian public was not well educated on the subject and negotiations for the sale of enterprises were not open. It is small wonder, then, that members of the committee supervising the privatisation process were later openly accused of having sold the SOEs to their cronies or agents.

The PNDC, on the other hand, has learnt a lesson from the past and started the programme with a thorough analysis of the impact of the SOE sector on the economy and finances of the state. The establishment of the DIC was not done on an institutional basis as it appears at first sight. Members of the DIC are people of integrity. The DIC is therefore a committee of men of integrity rather than people representing individual institutions. However, the fact that some sector heads and secretaries are represented by officers (who may not be the most senior officers) makes the character of the DIC a shade contentious as regards its being a committee of men of integrity. However, as the need arises, the composition of the committee will be reviewed to maintain the high calibre and integrity expected.

One school of thought holds the view that only 'dead' SOEs, or those not performing well, should be privatised. However, the government has decided that, in order to make the programme attractive, some SOEs recording fairly good results should also be privatised, so that their operational results can be improved upon. The flexibility which the government intends to adopt in the privatisation process and the adaptability of the programme make it unique. It is open and subject to change without causing any serious ripples in the economic set-up.

The fear of loss of jobs by workers in enterprises to be divested from is another problem. To resolve this, the government has already initiated redeployment, training, and retraining programmes, while assuring all workers that all contractual obligations (under their collective bargaining agreements and conditions of service) will be honoured in full.

It has been mentioned that the programme has not yet taken off fully. Several difficulties can be envisaged when there is a fully-fledged take-off: for example, (i) organisational and logistical problems; (ii) selection of possible SOEs for divestiture; (iii) legal implications; (iv) financial problems (especially settling the debts of the divested SOEs, capital markets, etc.); and (v) the origin of the buyers of the assets.

The politically sensitive problems cannot be treated here. This part will therefore be limited to the following areas:

(1) <u>Questions on the eligibility of an SOE to be put on the divestiture list</u>: The issue that inefficiency of the SOEs is a basic reason for the implementation of the process is sometimes contended by workers, most of whom assert that the SOEs have not been totally inefficient. The government has had reason to come out with the explanation that inefficiency and non-viability alone cannot be the criteria for privatisation. The government's concern, among others, is to maintain a sectoral balance in the economy. It is therefore important to mention here that the thirty SOEs earmarked for initial divestiture were selected sectorally (i.e. from manufacturing, agriculture, the cocoa sub-sector, tourism, transport, construction, and commerce).

(2) <u>Organisation and logistic difficulties</u>: A basic problem in the implementation of the divestiture programme was the delay in organising the logistics necessary for a smooth, business-like take-off (e.g. vehicles,

office machinery, etc.). The DIC was inaugurated in August 1987 and started attending to the logistics in February 1988. Also the SEC (which is to supervise the programme) is housed in rented accommodation where there is inadequate space for consultants. It is forseen that the Commission will therefore build suitable permanent offices.

(3) <u>Updating company accounts</u>: The divestiture programme contains certain actions which have to be completed so that other related actions can commence. One such is the preparation of dossiers on the companies for divestiture. Difficulties being encountered in this area stem from the fact that the accounts of some SOEs are in arrears, due to the inability of the SOE accountants to prepare the accounts for auditors. The DIC has therefore initiated action to have the accounts of all SOEs audited up to date.

(4) <u>Valuation of company assets</u>: Another difficulty arises from the writing of valuation reports. The Land Valuation Board has organisational and logistical bottlenecks and, at times cannot, cope with the volume of work, thereby hampering the work of the TSC. However, attempts are being made to use the services of private valuers where necessary, but resorting to the use of private valuers on a large scale can make the programme very expensive because of the scale of fees demanded by these valuers.

(5) <u>Plantations for divestiture</u>: Another area where difficulties of a political, organisational, economic, legal, and even social nature are encountered refers to the cocoa and coffee plantations of the Ghana Cocoa Board (GCB).

The GCB was the first to announce the sale of its plantations to both local and foreign private investors. However, further action by the TSC on this programme shows that there are many difficulties to be surmounted. Issues awaiting attention include the following:

(a) land acquisition;
(b) payment of compensation;
(c) legal title to the lands;
(d) problems associated with valuation of the farms by LVB;
(e) incentives to the investors (foreign);
(f) production and sale of cocoa and coffee beans by the private foreign investor; and
(g) the reaction of local cocoa farmers and traditional councils on farms for sale. Reconciling acreages declared by the GCB as acquired and cultivated

with what can be seen on the plantations is yet another problem. Due to the sensitive nature of the difficulties encountered here and the need for political will and solution, the GCB has not been able to present even one of the fifty-two plantations for the initial stages of divestiture. However, the DIC, the TSC, and the GCB are trying to resolve these difficulties.

(6) Legal issues: Some other difficulties arise in the case of the confiscated companies, because confiscation is not backed by law. Often the DIC has to intervene and cause the appropriate legislation to be enacted.

(7) Identification of assets of confiscated companies: Also in the smaller confiscated private limited liability companies, which are in groups of companies, it is very difficult to identify some of the assets, since most of them were even not covered by proper documents by their former owners due to perhaps the illegal nature of their acquisition. All these tend to constrain the timely preparation of dossiers for the divestiture process.

(8) The origin of buyers of assets: The economic experience of the negative practices of transnational corporations (TNCs) in the developing countries invariably lingers in the minds of very many Ghanaians who may view the purchase by foreigners of the assets of some of the SOEs as being neocolonialistic or another way of entering Ghana by the back door.

This seemingly volatile situation is, however, taken care of in the guidelines for divestiture, in which it is stated that foreign participation would be entertained in areas where foreign currency and technological know-how are needed. There is, therefore, an in-built security valve to check any inordinate domination of the economy by cantankerous foreign investors. This situation allays any suspicions or fears that may be encountered.

A related problem is that of a suitable climate for the foreign investor. Investors may ask how safe their investments will be without the fears of future national-isations. The Government is endeavouring to remove this 'investor fear' by designing legal documents for the transfer of shares and assets, amongst other measures, to protect the investor. Other investor fears concern transfers of dividends and repatriation of loan repayments as and when due. Our Investment Code provides adequately for them. In addition, the Government is reviewing the Code and other regulations to meet such fears of investors.

The programme forsees the liquidation of non-viable SOEs. This would raise many other problems. Of particular importance is the question whether Ghana may not end up liquidating a large number of SOEs, since in their present situation most of them may not be attractive to foreign investors, or due to liquidity problems they may not be purchased by private Ghanaians. In this connection the question to be answered is whether we are not paving the way, whereby the most attractive SOEs would be purchased by foreigners, whilst the moribund ones go to private Ghanaians or are liquidated and their assets sold cheaply. The socio-political and economic problems that may arise can just be imagined!

Another issue concerns whether the Government should finance a rehabilitation of the SOEs before placing them for sale. Can the State provide the funds needed? And if so, can these funds not be used otherwise? Will the divestiture programme have been purposeful and needed at all in the face of all these formidable odds? Until the reforms introduced to restructure the financial sector of the economy have taken firm roots and restored sanity in the operations of the banking system, one of the problems to be expected will be the inability of the private sector to finance the purchase of the assets offered for sale, especially in the absence of a capital market (stock exchange). This problem needs greater consideration in view of the heavy outlay of capital required to purchase the assets and the inability of the banking system to regulate the problems of liquidity in the financial sector.

(9) <u>Redeployment</u>: The greatest problem besetting the divestiture programme in Ghana is the twin issue of redeployment and severance/terminal benefit payment. The amount needed to pay the labour force is colossal. It is not a question of retirement benefits, but of redeployment - which means retraining the displaced workers and finding them suitable jobs or incorporating them into the informal small-scale sector. The magnitude of this problem can be illustrated with a small example. The government will have to make ready about ₵5 billion to settle the retirement benefits and liabilities of workers of only ten SOEs (out of the 30 scheduled for divestiture). This sum will be deployed as follows:

(a)	Terminal benefits for approximately 2,000 workers	¢1.7 billion
(b)	Long term liabilities to ten SOEs	¢1.5 billion
(c)	Liabilities on account of divestiture	¢1.8 billion
		¢5.0 billion

It is important to note that five of these SOEs are for liquidation and the other five are for other divestiture modalities.

It is simplistic to argue that these SOEs would attract some proceeds and so the programme is worth following. Other considerations may negate the argument. If the government is ready to come up with the colossal amount needed to pay retirement benefits and redeploy the displaced workers in the labour market, why should the same amount not be used to rehabilitate the SOEs and keep them? Privatisation is a double edged sword. It has to be handled with care.

NOTES

1. NRC Decree (NRCD) 392, Accra, 1975.
2. AFRC Decree 64, 1979.
3. See: Mary M. Shirley, Managing SOEs, World Bank Staff Working Papers, no. 577, and Praxy Fernandes, Managing Relations between Government and Public Enterprises, Management Development Series no. 26, 1986.
4. Data from SEC/Ministry of Finance and Economic Planning (MFEP).
5. Data from SEC.
6. See SEC Cross-debts Studies.
7. Data from the Bank of Ghana.
8. Data from the SOEs.
9. SEC Cross-debts Study.
10. Government policy statement on the SOEs.
11. ibid.
12. This includes more than half of the recorded employment in public enterprises (commercial and non-commercial) employing more than ten people. See BMB Report, Quarterly Digest of Statistics, June 1987.

16

Privatisation in Africa

Myrna Alexander*

This chapter explores the experiences of the World Bank's support for public enterprise (PE) reform, with a specific look at Africa. It provides a preliminary assessment of the evolution of the Bank's assistance for PE reform, starting in the late 1970s, highlighting some of the lessons learned that may be applicable to the further development of PE reform programmes. It also raises some unresolved issues in carrying out these reforms and provides a broad basis for approaches to reforming PE sectors, whether they are development projects for selected enterprises or are part of larger PE reform programmes. Admittedly, at this point it is too early to judge whether or not these reforms tackle the problems correctly and whether or not they can be sustained. It is certainly premature to claim success until more experience has been gained. However, the initial impressions have been very encouraging and give reason to hope that reforms of this nature will improve economic performance significantly. The contents of this chapter are the author's sole responsibility and should not be attributed to the World Bank.

INTRODUCTION

Reeling from severe drought, decline in export commodity prices, and worsening terms of trade, many countries in sub-Saharan Africa now find themselves in the position of having to confront the basic fiscal imbalances and deficiencies of their economies. The process of adjustment, often with the

* Chief, Public Sector Management Division, Technical Department, Africa Region, World Bank

assistance of the international community, entails a fundamental reassessment of the capabilities and effectiveness of the various governments' policy formulations and the various administrative mechanisms set up to implement those policies. On many counts this assessment shows that both the policies and their implementation have been lacking.

One of the most striking features of economies of Africa, in contrast to many Asian economies for example, is the dependence of governments on parastatal organisations to execute development plans as well as to provide goods and services for the general populace. The proliferation of public enterprises in the industrial and service sectors as well as the basic public services - water, electricity, telecommunication, transport, etc. - has resulted in governments being overextended financially and managerially.

Lacking incentives for good performance, bound by bureaucratic procedures and controls, and subject to patronage and government interference, public enterprises have on the whole shown poor results. (Examples of many African countries can be cited.) In addition to poor investment decisions, there are many reasons why public enterprises (PEs) do not function up to expectations. Some of these reasons are institutional while others are technical and financial: a full discussion of the performance of PEs can be found in other papers and articles.[1]

Need for comprehensive reform

Whatever the specific reasons for the poor performance of public enterprises, the fundamental issues affecting overall PE performance cannot be addressed without a comprehensive approach. This approach has been pursued by the World Bank in its adjustment efforts in Africa for several years, and consists of six main themes, as follows:

(1) Enhancing the policy environment to encourage greater competition, more market oriented policies, and less government intervention in PE operations;
(2) Rationalizing the size and scope of the existing PE sector through divestiture programmes;
(3) Re-establishing financial discipline in the sector to ensure that government/enterprise financial transactions are done on a commercial, transparent basis;

323

(4) Streamlining existing legal frameworks - and instituting improved structures, capabilities, and systems - for planning, controlling, and monitoring the sector's performance;

(5) Restructuring the financial position of PEs through debt rescheduling, settlement of interlocking debts, and recapitalisation; and

(6) Technical, managerial, and organisational rehabilitation of elected enterprises and key subsectors.

The following sections of this chapter trace the evolution of the growing number of PE reform programmes, with a particular focus on those programmes in Africa. Without exhaustively reviewing the nature and root causes of the problems of PEs, this papers looks more at the proposed remedies, experiences, and insights gained thus far on those programmes.

THE EVOLUTION OF PUBLIC ENTERPRISE
REFORM PROJECTS

The World Bank has long provided direct support to public enterprises; most of the Bank's projects in water supply, power, transport (excluding highways), industry, and telecommunications sectors are executed by publicly-owned or mixed public/private corporations. In the agricultural sector, major components of Bank-financed agricultural programme depend on the operations of rural development agencies, marketing boards, and similar public agencies, while assistance for urban development includes publicly-owned mortgage banks and housing construction bodies. The Bank has also expanded its provision of long-term credit to the industrial sector through publicly-owned development financial institutions and similar intermediaries.

Assistance to improve the operations of public enterprises is therefore not new. Increasing attention in recent years, especially since the early 1980s, to institution building has further more heightened the need for management and technical reforms for PEs. What has changed more recently is the perception and understanding of the problems facing public enterprises and the nature of the support to overcome those problems. These are being examined comprehensively and governments encouraged to adopt a global approach to PE reform as part of more profound economic adjustments. Direct support for the reform of public enterprises has now become a part of the Bank operations, in addition to the support that continues to be channelled to individual enterprises.

Their genesis

The genesis of the Bank's support for PE reform in Africa was Senegal. The first technical assistance (TA) project for the parapublic sector (Cr. 764-SE), approved in 1978, arose out of an earlier Bank report on the para-public sector. The reasons for focusing attention on the para-public sector in Senegal were principally: (1) the ever increasing drain on public finances through subsidies, loans, equity contributions, and various forms of non-budgetary support to PEs; and (2) the growing frustration in dealing with the enterprises selected (and sometimes created especially) as executing agencies for Bank- and other donor-financed projects. This led to a more general awareness that PEs constituted an important dimension to a country's economic and development policy and thus had to be dealt with explicitly.

Concomitant with the TA project in Senegal, the importance of PE sectors and their profound economic and social implications was reflected in the Bank's initial efforts at structural adjustment lending (SAL). Specifically in West Africa, the use of SALs to promote PE reform started in Senegal, followed by the Ivory Coast and Togo. As noted in an internal Bank report (Institutional Reform: Some Lessons from Structural Adjustment Lending), SALs have in almost all cases included some reform of the state-enterprise sector, As at end 1985, SALs in Bolivia, Turkey, Pakistan, Korea, Jamaica, Malawi, Thailand, Mauritius, Panama, Kenya, Ivory coast, Togo, and Senegal all included reform of government-enterprise regulatory/institutional/policy framework, or reform of particular enterprises, or both. Since then, the number of SAL programs with PE components amounted to about fifty as at end December 1987. In addition, there are some forty-nine sector-adjustment operations. Simply put, this means that PE reform has been an element of almost every adjustment operation supported by the Bank.[2]

The need for capital and institutional support

While great strides can be achieved by improving the policy framework for PEs under SALs, more support for PEs can be justified as the basis for two needs: (1) to pursue long-term institutional reforms in the sector; and (2) for physical as well as organisational rehabilitation of individual enterprises. The perception that concerted action on PE institutional issues was necessary arose from the early experience with SALs as highlighted in the following: 'the reform process has proved to be longer and more complicated than was originally anticipated ... SALs are most useful for initiating such processes but are unlikely to see them through'.[3] On the other hand, the second perception - that physical rehabilitation, in addition to institutional change, is needed for PE reform - has evolved mainly from the Bank's experience in free-standing technical assistance loans (TALs) for PE reform. A review of some seventeen such operations indicated that: 'some staff feel that technical assistance by itself does not supply enough support for the sort of sweeping changes the TALs envision.' There is a strong feeling that the commitment of governments and enterprises to undertake major policy reforms is enhanced if physical rehabilitation as well as institutional support is financed.

In addition to adding to the appeal by recipient governments, there are technical reasons for adding capital support to PE reform programmes. Substantive change in the performance of individual public enterprises is often predicated by the availability of tools, spare parts, and well-functioning equipment, especially in cases where enterprises have neglected maintenance and eroded their capital stock. Moreover, poorly designed investments could be in need of redesign/modification, or replacement, in order to make them function properly. Relatively minor complementary investments could also be required in order to improve overall operations.

Need for financial restructuring

More recently, PE reform projects have begun to include financial restructuring of PE sectors, as is the case of the sector-adjustment operations currently being prepared for Mali and for Niger. The financial needs of the reform programmes are often well beyond the capabilities of governments and enterprises. Typically, the debt burden of the public sector is so excessive that any move to reform it must come to grips with the debts between enterprises, with government, the banking system, private suppliers, and foreign creditors. In particular, divestiture of non-strategic enterprises and the liquidation of unviable PEs would be blocked, unless resources were available to settle their outstanding liabilities. The need for programme financing (i.e. funds not tied to specific physical investments which can be used more liberally by governments to settle arrears, refinance outstanding debts, and recapitalize enterprises) has proven to be very large, and now constitutes one of the major thrusts in reforming PE sectors in Africa.

Links with macro-economic policies

The pervasive nature of the public sector's problems, and the relative importance of PEs in many economies, elevates the resolution of these problems to a high policy - and decision-making level in government. The reforms necessary to restructure PE sectors, even selected enterprises, are thus often incorporated as features of broader macro-economic adjustment programmes supported by the Bank (and, on occasion, by the IMF) as part of stabilization programmes. Moreover, increasing competition, a sine qua non for improved performance, has to be a key part of the adjustment process affecting both private and public enterprises. Depending on the particular issue at hand, the nature of the policy dialogue with governments, and the timing of various actions, the result is that PE reform questions may be as readily dealt with under a structural adjustment programme as a separate PE reform project, or under both types of operation. The options for the right vehicle to use, in order to put the reforms into effect, are therefore wide and, in many respects, interchangeable.

THE FIRST PUBLIC ENTERPRISE PROGRAMMES

The evolution of the Bank's understanding of the nature and scope of the problems facing PE sectors, as accumulated through past country economic and sector work, public expenditure reviews, technical assistance projects, and adjustment programmes, has led to its direct support for the PE reform programme in about seventeen countries in

Africa, with several programmes being prepared, and the problems of the public sector being studied in others. In total, the Bank is currently active in assisting governments overcome the problems of PEs in over thirty countries in sub-Saharan Africa. These efforts provide the vehicle for addressing PE policy issues in a broad sense and include components aimed at specific enterprise rehabilitation and financial restructuring. They also combine technical assistance for institutional development, policy reforms, and funds to support the financial restructuring and physical rehabilitation of selected enterprises. The following section briefly describes some of these PE reform programmes and other related activities.

Second para-public technical assistance project in Senegal

As a follow up to the Bank's first para-public project in Senegal, approved in 1978, the second para-public project (US$11 million) was approved in 1982, and provides mainly technical assistance and limited capital support for enterprise rehabilitation (US$1.5 million for emergency spare parts, stocks, etc.). The technical assistance (TA) programmes is aimed at strengthening the government's capabilities in preparing and monitoring 'contract plans', generally managing the PE sector, preparing enterprise rehabilitation plans, improving enterprise accounting, and auditing and providing management training to both the government and the enterprises. Major efforts have focused on redefining government PE relations and reorganizing the structure of key sectors (e.g. post and telecommunications). It also includes assistance to launch a privatisation programme in Senegal in collaboration with USAID.

In contrast to the first PE project, which focused principally on strengthening the government's overseeing agencies, this second project includes assistance directly to enterprises, and anticipates additional assistance to selected enterprises for specific rehabilitation programmes. The focus of this part of the project is on the basic public services -water, electricity, port, post/telecommunications, urban transport, railway, and urban housing. It should be noted that most of these enterprises (electricity, rail, urban housing, water supply, telecommunications, port) have already benefited from Bank assistance through direct support, and that future operations are planned for the power, water, and telecommunications sectors. The rehabilitation programmes designed under the PE project could thus constitute the basis for these planned projects.

More recently, two structural adjustment operations were approved for Senegal. These broad-based adjustment programmes include specific actions on PE reform, building upon activities initiated under the para-public projects. These projects thus mutually reinforce the reform process, deepening and extending it over time.

Public enterprise rehabilitation project in Mauritania

The PE project in Mauritania consists of a general-sector reform component, essentially providing TA for developing appropriate PE policies, information systems, staff development, and carrying out enterprise diagnostic studies, audits, and separate components for support to three major enterprises - SONELEC (water and electricity), EMN (port), and OPT (post and telecommunications). In the case of SONELEC and EMN, key financial, technical, and organisational problems are being addressed through TA and physical rehabilitation (spares, replacement equipment, tools, etc., plus repairs to physical works). OPT will receive only limited TA for improvements to financial and information processing systems. None of these enterprises had previously received direct Bank assistance and the PE project provided an opportunity to initiate Bank involvement in these key sectors.

Having got the rehabilitation programme under way for the three priority enterprises, a second set of PEs have been studied. These include companies in pharmaceutics, urban transport, low-cost housing, and petroleum distribution. These enterprises are to undergo financial and management audits as the basis for designing specific reforms. In the meantime, work is under way to improve the legal framework for PEs and to set up a PE Monitoring system, as well as to propose a new salary policy and PE training programme.

The recent appraisal of a structural adjustment programme in Mauritania, following stand-by arrangements with the International Monetary Fund, also focuses on PE issues. Again, the SAL operation will provide a vehicle for extending and deepening the reforms initiated under the PE project. The SAL concentrates mainly on enterprises in the energy sector, addressing major financial restructuring issues in SONELEC and the role and operations of the government-owned petroleum import and distribution company.

Technical assistance project in Guinea

A key component of the Bank-financed technical assistance project in Guinea (totalling US$9.5 million and approved in 1985) is the divestiture of the numerous PEs that existed under Guinea's First Republic. Reflecting a shift in policy away from direct public ownership, which had formerly dominated the economy, the government is now divesting its commercial and distribution companies - enterprises that were not profitable and whose activities can best be carried out by the private sector. The programme of divestiture also focuses on the industrial sector and the banking system, which have totally been restructured. Assistance under the TA project is focused on helping the government to implement its divestiture programme, with assistance also aimed at general institutional reforms. Follow-up work is expected to broaden the reform progress and include more general policy questions. These efforts have been supported by two SALs, that at the same time address general questions of liberalisation and macro-economic policy.

Public enterprise project in Mali

The recently negotiated PE-sector adjustment operation in Mali combines policy adjustment with direct support to the government to implement the agreed PE reform programme and institutional strengthening for PE management. This particular project arose because of the need to support the macro-economic policy reforms in the absence of a SAL. It also complements plans for rehabilitation of OPT (telecommunications) and EDM (water and electricity). The operation has an important element to settle outstanding debts of PEs that are being restructured, liquidated or privatised, and to restructure BDM (development bank).

Structural adjustment programmes

All the African Region's structural adjustment programmes already, or are planned to, incorporate features to address PE questions. These programmes, which can be preceded by separate PE projects as a way of initiating the reforms in a key sector, or in parallel to or followed by PE projects to deepen and institutionalise the specific reforms, frequently entail the following: the closure and/or divestiture of specific PEs; a curb on future investments in new PEs; limits on investment by existing PEs; liberalisation of price controls (for public as well as private enterprises); deregulation of monopolistic practices by PEs; cuts in PE labour forces; changes in personnel practices; settlement of government and PE debts; adequate budget provisions for government consumption of PE goods and services; prompt payment by government to PEs; and so on.

Other related efforts

Much of the Bank's sector work, economic reviews, technical assistance, and general policy discussions with the countries in Africa include a PE dimension. Examples include technical assistance to review the situation of PEs in Guinea Bissau, an internal study of PEs in Tanzania, general support for PE reform in Liberia, technical assistance to governments in the Central Africa Republic (CAR) and the Congo, and Bank staff seconded to advise the Government of Malawi on monitoring PE performance. In some of these cases, the studies and investigation of enterprises under the technical assistance programmes laid the basis for more intensive work on PEs, either under SALs or separate PE projects. More generally, technical assistance can start the process of reform by compiling an inquiry of PEs, collecting and analysing PE financial performance, carrying out audits and feasibility studies of selected enterprises, preparing rehabilitation plans of key enterprises, and reviewing the legal and legislative framework for managing PEs. With this basic knowledge of the sector, a reform programme can quickly be developed.

MAJOR THEMES AND ISSUES

It has become apparent in the Bank's work thus far that there are several predominant themes in PE reform programmes. While differences between countries exist, and are pronounced between English-speaking and French-speaking countries in terms of the institutional framework for PE control by governments and the involvement of local banking systems to finance PE deficits, these themes tend to re-occur in all countries. Without discussing particular countries and elaborating on these differences, the following section briefly sets out the main themes that have so far emerged in the PE reforms being prepared and under implementation in Africa.

The nature of the problem

The persistent difficulties now confronting the PE sectors of most African countries reflect the profound over-extension of governments beyond their available means. Many governments are financially, technically and managerially unable to sustain public enterprises on the scale that currently exists. More specifically, the economic cost of continuing to operate certain enterprises - those that perhaps should never have been created in the first place - lays too heavy a burden on African economies, outweighing any perceived economic benefits by way of increased employment, import substitution, or regional development offered by these enterprises. The inefficiencies of key public services have furthermore created bottlenecks in the functioning of essential parts of the economy - notably electricity, water, telecommunication and transport services - that are vital for economic development. Conceivably one of the most important problems faced by the public sector is the widespread misuse of funds, due to the lack of proper internal management and control; this is aggravated by the public's perception that the services these enterprises offer are a right and the political system's perception that enterprises afford ideal opportunities for personal gain. Needless to say, the penury of skilled technicians and managers in government and enterprises is another fundamental problem facing all but the most elite of public enterprises.

Potential remedies

The remedies sought under the PE reform programme must tackle constraints at both the macro-economic level and the enterprise level. Attention is typically focused on the following:

(1) Enhancing the policy environment by undertaking macro-economic reforms to encourage more market-driven policies and ensuring the application of these reforms to the PE sector, particularly as they concern

(i) public finances (direct subsidies, loans, guarantees, tax concessions and so on); (ii) price controls and other market/trade restrictions (licensing, import quotas, monopolies); (iii) employment and incomes policies (guaranteed employment, salary scales); and (iv) credit and monetary policies (foreign exchange allocations, preferential interest rates, access to credit);

(2) Rationalizing the size and scope of the existing PE sector to reduce its effective burden on the economy through closures, liquidations, rationalization of service levels and products, and divestiture;

(3) Re-establishing financial discipline within the sector in terms of (i) government as a consumer of PE services, tax collector, guarantor and source of financing, and owner; (ii) PEs as consumers and suppliers of each other's services; (iii) the banking system, especially if government owned.

(4) Instituting improved structures, human resources capabilities and systems for the planning control and monitoring of the sector's overall performance, in order to increase the effectiveness of resource allocation to PEs, and the efficient use of those resources by enterprises;

(5) Establishing sound financial bases from which to operate and eliminating the debt overhang, particularly for enterprises to be divested; and

(6) Strengthening the physical, financial, and human means available within enterprises to carry out their operations more efficiently, concomitant with the appropriate degree of enterprise autonomy and corresponding accountability, including the development of a management cadre and performance incentives.

The time dimension

Sobering assessments of the future economic prospects of African nations lessen the likelihood that PE sectors will re-emerge as the central agents of economic development because of the weakened public resource base of most governments. Notwithstanding future shifts towards more state intervention, it is anticipated that the reduction in investment funds in the 1980s, as compared to those of the 1960s and 1970s, will have encouraged greater selectivity among investment proposals, thereby eliminating many 'white elephants'. It is also hoped that the lessons learned from past failures will inhibit a recurrence of failures in the future, as fiscal restraints impose self-discipline on the political system.

The problems of many PE sectors can thus be considered to have two time dimensions - one being the past and what to do with the accumulation of past problems (that is, the existing stock of public enterprises), the second dimension being the future operation of those enterprises to remain with the sector, and decisions about the future investment and creation of new PEs. The first dimension leads to actions to rationalise the sector - that is, to weed out the non-viable enterprises and to reduce the size of the sector to within more manageable proportions. Such actions, typically involving liquidations, privatisation, and other forms of divestiture, are largely one-time affairs with relatively short time-horizons. Similarly, efforts to straighten out the web of financial transactions (e.g. interlocking debts) between enterprises, and restructuring the finance bases of enterprises, are attempts to deal with 'stock' questions.

The other dimension of the problem - the future creation and operation of PEs - is more long-term in nature, requiring extensive investment in human capital, staff development and training, plus profound changes in personnel motivation, incentives, and attitudes, on the part of consumers, government officials, politicians, and enterprise management and staff. Without such changes, efforts under PE reform programmes to improve the policy environment, technical capabilities, and physical assets of enterprises will not be sustained in the long run. Viewed in this light, the long-term institutional objectives of PE reform programmes must be assessed realistically and cautiously, while recognising the systemic and pervasive nature of the difficulties to be overcome.

Classification of enterprises

One of the first steps in PE reform programmes has typically been to assess the existing stock of enterprises. As a result, preparation of PE reforms has, in most instances, been initiated with an inventory of existing PEs followed by an assessment of each enterprise's problems and overall prospects. This exercise then leads to a ranking, or classification, of enterprises, typically into categories such as: (1) those 'strategic' enterprises to be retained and rehabilitated; (2) those enterprises to be closed and liquidated which are obviously chronic losers and have no economic or strategic importance; and (3) those enterprises that a government can leave to private interests with some chance of successful operation. Practically speaking, this classification exercise can be done quickly, especially if a government has a clear picture of its objectives and what it expects from its PE sector. Without this sense of overall strategy for the sector, however, the exercise can degenerate into a very time-consuming and costly experience.

The secondary purpose of the classification exercise is to determine enterprise viability once the overall strategy for each enterprise is set out. It is important to stress the concept that a comprehensive reform programme must first address the reasons why an enterprise should exist (i.e. what purpose/function it is to service), and then address the question of whether or not this function can be financially and economically viable, whether changes are needed to make it so, and, if not, to decide its ultimate fate. Viability in its own right is a necessary but not a sufficient condition for a government to retain the particular enterprise. The argument of whether to privatise or retain an enterprise is thus not based on profitability but on a government's objectives.

Some of the issues that have arisen in recent work are the questions of when governments are ready to undertake a comprehensive classification exercise, and how to go about this process. There have been views that the process can be costly, confrontational, and superficial, especially considering that many PEs have a relatively minor impact on the overall economy. Clearly there is no ready answer: the timing of such an exercise depends on each government's ability to reach internal consensus and articulate a comprehensive strategy. In some instances, it may be better to concentrate on the few important enterprises for rehabilitation and on obvious cases for closure or privatization, and leave the less important enterprises for a second-round discussion, once a government has clarified its objectives. Furthermore, where there is reasonable doubt about an enterprise's prospects, the decision can be deferred by allowing a government to pursue privatisation on a best-efforts basis (that is, to attempt privatization of enterprises before concluding that there may not be buyers, or that the economic cost of attracting private ownership through concessions may be too high).

Questions of ideology and nationalism

Many African countries follow pragmatic economic policies, so that the question of state versus private ownership, while a factor, is not typically the determining force. Nationalism is, however, a very strong force, with most countries placing considerable weight on the nationality of owners. It has often been the case, for example, that governments nationalised foreign-owned enterprises or created new enterprises because of the fear that the indigenous private sector did not have sufficient funds or entrepreneurial skills to invest and manage ventures needed to further economic development. The continuing dearth of venture capital and management talent in most African countries is thus likely to constitute a very real and continuing constraint on the execution of PE reform programmes. Politically, no doubt, it will be even more difficult for countries to sell a large portion of their holdings in PEs to foreign interests unless those interests being scarce capital and technology, and are therefore perceived to be making an economic contribution. In the long term, accompanying measures to promote indigenous entrepreneurship are crucial.

Is regulation an alternative?

Irrespective of ideology, there is a commonly held perception that certain functions are best owned and managed by governments - especially basic services for electricity, water supply, ports, telecommunications, railways, airlines, transport services, and agricultural marketing - because of their social importance, economies of scale, existence of natural monopolies, and the need to capture externalities. However, even these public enterprises can be privately owned. Notable examples of this can be seen in the United States (airlines, railways, telecommunications, electricity, and water services); in Canada, where there is typically a mix of ownership - some companies private and some government-owned (e.g. rail, airline, telecommunications); and in the United Kingdom (in many areas after the recent privatisations). Africa has its examples - Ivory in water supply and Nigeria in airlines and agriculture produce marketing.

Public ownership need not thus be seen as the only way of controlling the operations of enterprises in vital areas, if appropriate regulation is in force to prevent abuse on the part of the natural monopolies and to ensure the capturing of social costs and the effect of other externalities. However, many African governments are ill-equipped to enforce various regulations and are for some time likely to lack the administrative capacity to develop and apply effective regulations. As it stands now, regulation of private monopolies can be easily subject to abuse, as many of the present flaws in the system of control for PEs would be transferred to the private owners who may be even more effective at circumventing regulations.

Will the private sector respond?

As a corollary to the immediate objective to reduce the size and of scope of existing PE sectors, through divestiture, a longer term view is that governments will no longer feel as compelled to create PEs as vehicles for economic development and that they will have other options, including the private sector, to fulfil their development objectives. This implies that the private sectors in these countries can and will effectively substitute, at least in part, for PEs. Yet constraints to the private sector exist and, unless measures to promote private-enterprise development are included, the programmes risk failure in the long run. While it is obvious that, by reducing the size of the PE sectors, these programmes will create opportunities for private sector development in the short run, there are more important considerations to attract private sector interest - such as the need to eliminate monopolies, relax price controls and streamline government regulations concerning taxes, customs, etc., in order to improve the general business environment for private enterprise. Further actions are warranted, particularly regarding credit (if PEs have preferred access to credit), investment incentives (stream-lining application and approval procedures), reorientation of vocational technical training, and generally creating a more conducive economic climate. While the initial round of privatisations can probably still go forward without these specific accompanying measures, sustaining the private sector interest requires more creative efforts at private enterprise development.

Debt settlement and the need for financial restructuring

One of the major impediments to carrying out a PE reform programme is the outstanding debt burden of most PEs. The years of accumulated PE losses, the build-up of arrears in payment by government for services rendered by PEs, the over-extension of credit by domestic banks, and the heavy debt-load of external ongoing loans or loans guaranteed by governments, have left PEs with a tremendously large debt burden which they are unlikely to be able to service. Many enterprises are technically bankrupt and, if not viable, will eventually be liquidated, with governments often legally obliged to honour the enterprises' debts and to make due compensation to the workforce upon dismissal. Other enterprises, even with rehabilitation, will need debt relief, rescheduling, and conversion to equity, to attain an appropriate financial position. Again, governments may have to intervene, either to provide new equity funds or to restructure existing debts. In certain cases, governments may have to continue to service existing debts for many PEs for a long period.

The arrears of governments to PEs can be another critical area: governments tend not to settle their debts to PEs, especially for consumption of telecommunication and postal services, electricity and water services and, to lesser extent, transport and airline travel, because of chronic underestimation in governments' budgets of the actual use, and because of general laxity. Efforts to settle these debts necessitate strict measures by governments to increase budgetary allocations (difficult in times of fiscal restraint), reduce unnecessary consumption (number of direct telephone lines, for example), and allow enterprises to take appropriate measures to recover amounts due (cut service to the military, high-ranking officials, diplomats, etc.).

An essential prerequisite to the settlement of these interlocking debts between government and PEs is to collect the relevant data on PE debts and to construct an interlocking or cross-debt matrix. This facilitates the netting out of the off-setting amounts between parties, and the identification of the chain of payments from one party to another as part of the settlement process. Subsequent to that, a detailed case-by-case analysis of debt service capabilities must be done to determine the appropriate financial restructuring for each enterprise. Experience thus far in this process indicates that the amount of interlocking debts can be exceedingly large, and require direct contribution by governments as well as indirect support by the banking system, via rescheduling and debt write-offs.

Impact on the banking system

While some local banking systems, notably in the anglophone countries of Africa, have managed to limit their exposure to PEs, other banking systems, in particular banks that are government owned, have been prompted (at the urging of government) to extend loans that subsequently cannot be serviced. Eventually, this process leads to severe liquidity problems in these banks, impairing their profitability and financial position. Liquidation of the non-viable PEs and privatization of others (which can involve financial restructuring), can further damage the financial health of the banking system, with the whole process having an important impact on the banking system. Ultimately, there is the need for banking reforms, particularly changes to credit approval procedures and banking regulations, as parallel adjustments.

Increasing public awareness and public accountability

In contrast to nations where public accountability is relatively high, thanks to a free Press, public interest groups, and organised political opposition, many African countries lack independent means to being questions of PE accountability to the public's knowledge and subsequently to exert a countervailing influence in cases where collusion limits the extent to which one party can offset the interests of the other. Interesting experiences in other regions (for example, Korea's PE performance evaluation system, which publicly prints annual results, and Thailand where the water company manager was able to use the Press to curb corruption and to facilitate sanctioning of employees) indicate that public opinion, if mobilised, can be a powerful tool to change PE performance.

So far, PE reform programmes have not explicitly involved the general public, although members of the private sector have participated in PE enquiries or commissions (e.g. Nigeria). Efforts have instead focused on altering the power of selected civil servants and individual politicians in making key decisions in isolation, by raising the level at which such decisions are taken (e.g. from minister to prime minister or president), increasing the number of concerned parties (instead of one minister, several ministers as part of a PE committee), and making decisions more transparent by reinforcing legal requirements. In these ways, it is anticipated that an enlarged view of the public's interest will be taken rather than just the parochial and personal interests of one or a few persons.

More could be done, nevertheless, to increase public knowledge. Additional information could be made available through the publication of enterprise financial results, contracts awarded, promotions and staff appointments, bad debts and arrears problems, and so on. The Press can also be a more effective tool, as part of a government's programme to increase enterprise/government accountability through the increased transparency of enterprise operations. At the grass roots level, other possibilities exist (for example, reporting staff delinquency, theft, negligence, faults in service, etc.) via the formation of local consumer and user groups and existing self-help groups or co-operatives, in order to pressure enterprises for improved levels of service.

Appropriate institutional set-up

The institutional set-up within governments to manage PE sectors must recognize the inherent conflicts of interest within the government structure in the role of owner, regulator, policy-maker, and protector of the public interests. In addition, the structure within governments must take into account the potential conflict of interest of the concerned individuals who are responsible for taking investment decisions, appointing managers and senior staff, fixing tariffs, approving budgets, and awarding contract. Furthermore, there must be a focal point for making high-level decisions regarding the creation of new enterprises, or the restructuring and/or elimination of old ones, when vested interests may bias the decisions in a certain way. At present, most governments have attempted to counter these effects by complex systems of a priori controls to ensure that expenditures by PEs are correctly made. However, the effectiveness of these controls is usually limited, since there is rarely sufficient expertise and information to evaluate expenditures properly. Controls, moreover, do not intervene at an appropriate point and they are often too late in the expenditure cycle to have an impact. If anything, their impact is futile, and undermines the authority in PE management.

An alternative system must therefore be put in place, one which establishes clearly the accountability of PE management to achieve results, and yet awards PEs sufficient autonomy to be able to operate effectively. Thus far, the concept of acountability versus autonomy has focused on developing systems of corporate planning, objective setting and performance monitoring (i.e. 'contract-plans'), combined with appropriate ex post controls and external audits. The idea is to establish the objectives of the PE, as mutually agreed by the government and the PE, monitor achievement of those objectives over time, and finally evaluate and reward performance for actual results. Performance can be measured against targets or historical trends or even against other PEs in a relative sense. The evaluation should ultimately be linked to a system of performance incentives and rewards for PE personnel. Finally, this new approach needs to be reflected in the PE legal framework, the structure and operations of PE boards, and the various regulations that govern PE operations.

A question of serious concern in applying this concept is what is the most appropriate structure for the focal point responsible for carrying out these functions within government? There is a need to transcend the vested interests of various ministries. There is also a need to have the results of the objective-setting exercise and subsequent performance evaluation reflect broad political and economic consensus. These constraints point to placing the unit within (i) a quasi-independent ministry, such as planning; (ii) the Ministry of Finance, because of the serious financial implications; (iii) the presidency or prime minister's office; or (iv) an independent body reporting to parliament or the national assembly.

Physical rehabilitation

There appears to be considerable justification to include physical rehabilitation as well as organizational and management reforms directly for selected enterprises under PE reform programs. Technical assistance alone is very likely to be insufficient to bring enterprises to the point where their operations can improve significantly; capital investment is critical to achieve improved operating procedures, maintenance practice, and stock management, and it is vital for improvements to enterprise technical performance and capacity utilization. Without adequate means to carry out operations efficiently, it may be futile to speak of improved financial results and management capabilities. There still remains, however, the question of the extent of the physical rehabilitation and possible expansion of enterprise facilities under PE reform programme. The approach used thus far limits capital support to replacement and rehabilitation of existing plant and equipment, and excludes large-scale capital investment.

The reasons for this restrained approach to physical investment are basically the following: (1) enterprises have very often over-invested, leaving them with excess capacity that is not presently used effectively; (2) without broader reforms taking hold, enterprises may not have the financial base upon which to undertake major investments, nor do governments have the funds needed for capital investment; (3) technical and management skills are usually scarce and may be stretched even further if operations are expanded; and (4) the extensive organizational and management changes implicit in carrying out a reform programme may sufficiently distract from the day-to-day operations so that a period of restraint is necessary while these changes take hold. Moreover, if enterprises do not have a proven track record of performance, it may not be prudent to finance new investments, especially when capital is scarce. In general, since capital support should reinforce organizational change, it should be relatively quick to have an impact and generally match the period over which technical assistance is being provided. Investments with long gestation and/or construction period that require considerable external engineering services should thus be avoided under PE reform programme, and proceed as separate investments once reforms are in place.

Selection of enterprises for specific reform

The enterprises targeted so far for major restructuring are generally those strategic enterprises that are determined to be retained under government ownership, principally those that provide basic public services (mainly water, electricity, port, post and telecommunication services) plus others that have special strategic significance in the economy (for example, major exporting companies). Public utilities and these other key enterprises in particular are most often given priority on the basis of the following: (1) their effective operation is critical to the country's economic recovery; (2) they will be likely to remain in the public sector, even after a sector restructuring programme, and governments will therefore have a continuing interest in them; (3) because of their socio-economic objectives, they often constitute the most challenging cases of conflicting objectives, government interference, misallocation of resources, subsidies, and distorted pricing/tariff policies; and (4) reflecting their importance in the sector, these enterprises frequently employ the most unskilled labour, receive the most public subsidies, and involve major capital investments. Addressing these enterprises' operations therefore is critical to the sector as a whole.

The remaining enterprises typically found in the portfolio of publicly owned enterprises are usually industrial (cement, sugar, petroleum refining, textiles, breweries), commercial (wholesale and retail outlets, import/export companies) and services (trucking, transit, banking, construction, insurance, hotels, etc.). Their economic impact often varies considerably, with some enterprises having very limited operations, while others constituting major forces in the economy. On the whole, enterprises in these sectors tend to be those targeted for privatisation and/or liquidation on the grounds that they are either not economically justified (i.e. many import substitution industries) or can be attractive to private investors (e.g. breweries, hotels, trucking, commerce). Since it is debatable that government-sponsored rehabilitation[5] of the latter type of enterprises will enhance their appeal to the private sector, they have generally not been included in PE reform programme as candidates for rehabilitation. Instead, they are usually included as part of the restructuring programme aimed at divestiture. There will nevertheless be cases where these enterprises play a critical strategic role, so that their direct rehabilitation could be justified on a case-by-case basis. Ideally, rehabilitation should be coupled with effects to privatise or commercialise management and to stimulate competition through deregulation, breaking-up of monopolies, relaxation of price controls, and other policy changes.

PRELIMINARY CONCLUSIONS

While it is obviously premature to claim that ongoing PE reforms have been successful in improving the performance of PE sectors in Africa, there are several encouraging signs to indicate that these programmes are on the right track. The soon-to-be-published results of a study financed by UNDP and executed by the World Bank, on data collection related to development programmes and aid flows in Africa (RAF/86/058), approved in September 1987, coroborate these tentative conclusions. That study has revealed that early trends suggest an improvement in the financial performance of some PEs, and a general slowing of growth in the sector in Africa. Nevertheless, the deep-seated problems facing African economies in general, and PEs in particular, point to a continuation and intensification of PE reform efforts.

The continuation of the PE reforms should reflect the experience of the past. A few preliminary conclusions of that experience are highlighted below:

* Country commitment is a critical factor for the success of PE reform programs: they require the fullest support and endorsement of the highest levels of government. Indeed, there has been considerable commitment from African countries, as demonstrated in their own past efforts at PE reform.

* Quick gains can be made on improving financial performance of PE sectors by closing down losing operations, undertaking cost-cutting measures, reducing staff and increasing tariffs/prices. However, structural deficits are harder to eliminate and will likely persist even after major adjustments, notably in postal operations, railways, and transport, where social policies inhibit either closing them down or making them fully self-sufficient financially.

* Rationalisation of the sector through privatisation and liquidations on the margin is quick and relatively easy: most obviously not salvageable and probably have not operated for a while, in fact, they can easily identify such cases. Similarly, there are usually certain obvious candidates for sale to the private sector; these may be enterprises that are performing very well. However, more extensive privatisation programmes run the risk of surpassing the private sector's interest, once the

more attractive enterprises have been sold and those at distress prices have been picked up. There may also be more resistance as governments become more experienced and sophisticated in their approach to valuating enterprises and negotiation deals. Since most privatisation programmes are still at an early stage, the threshold on the extent to which privatisation is feasible may not yet have been reached.

* <u>Privatisation is not a panacea</u> to Africa's economic ills; finding appropriate buyers takes time, the political ramifications are important and, once privatised, these private enterprises can be as economically inefficient as public enterprises unless the overall policy environment is changed. Moreover, in light of the paucity of resources, small domestic markets, and natural protection isolated, landlocked countries in sub-Saharan Africa, it is often difficult to stimulate sufficient competition, especially if commercial and industrial investment is concentrated with a few, privately-owned 'quasi-monopolies'. The general economic environment must therefore be improved and market distortions eliminated to ensure the overall improvement.

* <u>Remaining enterprises, even after privatisation and other forms of divestiture, are still likely to account for a substantial portion of the economy</u> and a large share of government investment and financing. It is probable that, given the constraints to privatisation combined with the inherent nature of most PEs, a sizeable number of enterprises will remain in government hands. The long-term efforts at PE reform must therefore concentrate on improving the efficiency of those enterprises.

* <u>The need for donor co-ordination is high</u> in PE reform, especially to carry out specific enterprise rehabilitation programmes. Not only do public investment programmes have to be strictly assessed, requiring a critical look at all externally funded projects, there must be a concomitant shift in the approach by donors, in order not to over-extend existing PEs and to avoid creating new ones. It is vital to avoid the proliferation of parastatal organisations, often set up especially to execute a donor's project, and to insure that parastatals are not crowding out private interests.

Furthermore, cost-recovery and user-charge policies must be explicitly built into projects if the enterprises are going to be able to sustain their operations.

* Institutional development is at the crux of sustained PE reform. Even though considerable improvement is evident at the early stages of implementation of these programmes, through immediate measures to reduce the financial burden of PEs on government, the long-term nature of the problems facing those enterprises remaining in the public sector mitigates against 'quick fixes'. There will always be some form of direct-government participation in the economy and the key public services and major developmental activities will require continued development and assistance to optimise their performance. Certainly, the critical issues of government PE relations, enterprise autonomy, performance monitoring and evaluation and performance incentives, among others, will take time.

* Applicability to different borrowers will vary. The need and scope for PE reforms varies considerably among borrowers and a varied menu of instruments to encourage PE reform is needed. In some countries, it is practicable to start out only with institutional strengthening, while, in others, rehabilitation of enterprises combined with a general reform programme is justified. The differences lie in (1) the degree of institutional development existing within the country to manage a reform programme; (2) the strength of each government's commitment to undertake reform; (3) the receptivity of enterprise management to participate in sector-wide reforms as well as internal reforms; and (4) the extent and nature of enterprise rehabilitation needs.

In addition to these general observations and conclusions, concomitant efforts are needed to assess more concretely and systematically the impact of ongoing programmes, so that the experiences of the past held to shape future programmes. Given that PE reform programmes have been in place in some countries for several years, there is now an opportunity to evaluate those reforms and to incorporate lessons learned into the design of the second generation of PE reform programmes, and the adjustment necessary for ongoing programmes. This is the next stage in the continuing process of adjustment.

COMMENTS ON PRIVATISATION IN FRANCOPHONE WEST AFRICA

Range of programmes

Among francophone (French-speaking) countries in Africa, the World Bank is currently working with about eighteen countries, of which about half have active programmes of public enterprise (PE) reform underway and about five under preparation. All of these programmes include privatisation as one of the instruments used as part of the reform programme. In almost all cases, PE reform programmes are part of the broader, acro-economic recovery/structural adjustment programmes that the World Bank is supporting.

Some of these programmes have been going on for many years: Senegal started in 1978; Cote d' Ivoire in 1980-1; Mali in 1982; Mauritania in 1982-3; and Guinea in 1983-4. Among countries with the most advanced programmes are Guinea (which underwent a very profound change in economic policy in 1984 with the change in government), Togo, and Niger; while programmes are currently being prepared in Cameroon, Gabon, and Chad.

Typical experiences

There are numerous interesting experiences in privatisation that can be cited (e.g. in Togo, with the privatisation of the steel mill). This has been a controversial case because of the tariff protection and quantitative restrictions on competing imports granted to the new owner, an American business-man. Nevertheless, production is well up, capacity has been expanded, and Togolese investors have been included in the expanded company. The textile company is another example. This company was sold to Korean investors, among others, in order to acquire access to US markets that would be closed to more Korean imports. Production is booming and exports via Togo to the USA are high. In the case of Togo, this apparent success is privatising PEs along with liberalising the economy, has stimulated substantive private sector interest in undertaking new investments in Togo - as much as CFAF 15-20 billion (US$50-70 million) is planned for the next 2-3 years.

In Guinea, the changes have been very dramatic; almost all industrial enterprises (about ten to fifteen) have been already sold, mainly to French investors but with an average of 51 per cent local participation. The banking sector has been totally restructured and/or privatised.

In Mauritania, an interesting approach to privatisation has been used in the case of the pharmaceutical company which had a monopoly on the import and distribution of all such products. The first step by government was to abolish the monopoly which permitted the private sector to establish at the retail level and then to import, leaving the PE with mainly the public-sector market (hospitals, etc.). Dissatisfaction with its performance, in the face of competition from the new private pharmaceutical company eventually led the government to sell the company completely to the former employees.

In the Central African Republic (CAR) there have been several privatisations, with one case in particular showing how a privately owned establishment may have greater flexibility to adapt than a public enterprise. The government-owned slaughter house had faced numerous technical problems due to the constraints imposed on it as a public institution (e.g. more efficient ways of killing the animals could not be used for fear of offending conservative religious interests). However, as the private owners are not bound by these same social concerns, they have been able to increase the efficiency of the existing operation.

Some conclusions

These diverse experiences have shown that privatisation is possible, albeit still not easy. The general conclusions that can be drawn include:

- There are many alternatives (direct negotiations, tendering, private placement, employee buy-out, etc.) for privatisation.
- Privatisation is easiest/most successful in the service and manufacturing sectors (typically, enterprises in activities such as textiles, beverages, hotels, building materials, etc., that do not offer major challenges in terms of technology or capital requirements and can

therefore appeal to local investors).

- The large, capital-intensive PEs (such as the public utilities) are less amenable to privatisation and are most likely to stay within the public sector, albeit subject to restructuring/commercialisation programmes to increase efficiency.
- Market constraints in the typical African economy (due to the small size, narrow resource base, and low income levels/purchasing power) imply that competition is hard to stimulate. Privatisation measures must be accompanied by other steps to liberalise the economy, lower protection, reduce barriers to entry, and deregulate government controls.
- The inadequate legal base in many African countries means that privatisation may need to be accompanied by revision to the legal system, especially to bankruptcy procedures, and to improve general company laws.
- The costs of privatisation and other PE restructuring can be very high, to pay off debts and to make severance allowances to redundant employees.
- Foreign investors have played a big part in privatisation thus far; a suitable policy towards foreign investment must also be worked out as part of the privatisation process, if not already existing.
- No matter what the political system, considerable efforts at developing consensus are needed even in one party and/or in military states. Besides the general public, consensus is needed between the technical level in government, the political decision-making levels, the enterprises themselves, the employee representatives, and party structures.

English and French differences

In discussing the experiences in francophone Africa, it may also be interesting to highlight some of the possible differences in the approach and the apparently greater use of privatisation as a means of improving PE performance in the francophone countries, as compared to the anglophone countries. At the very least, the efforts started in francophone countries earlier, have gone past the discussion stage into actual implementation, and are widely spread among a large number of francophone countries. The difference has been the legal structure, which in francophone countries is highly structured, making large distinctions between PEs and private enterprises. The conversion to commercial corporations therefore requires effort. Moreover, bankruptcy and general commercial laws are deficient and need improvement. The banking sectors, whether privately or publicly owned, were often drawn into the financing of PEs. The problems of PEs in servicing these loans therefore spread to the rest of the economy, severely hampering the domestic credit system and the solvency and liquidity of the domestic banks. The final difference is the apparent acceptance of foreign investment and the interest of foreign investors, especially of French origin, in purchasing shares of PEs. Most of the privatisations thus far have included a significant portion of foreign shareholding.

Role of the World Bank

Over the past 10 or so years, the World Bank has been active in supporting the preparation and implementation of numerous reform programmes in sub-Saharan Africa. This support can come in three forms. First, the Bank provides assistance for macro-economic adjustment and the reform of the policy environment for PEs, mainly through structural adjustment programmes (SALs). The second form is to provide advice and technical assistance for these programmes (mainly audits, diagnostics, rehabilitation programmes, training, etc.). The third form is direct assistance towards rehabilitating specific enterprises, mainly the public utilities, which are to be retained in the public sector. Assistance can also extend to financing the costs of reform, (especially to recapitalise PEs), repay debts and arrears, and make severance payments to redundant employees.

NOTES

1.   An excellent overview of the PE sectors in sub-Saharan Africa can be found in a paper by John Nellis (1985) 'Public enterprises in sub-Saharan Africa'.
2.   Since many countries have several adjustment operations over time, the total number of countries with PE adjustment programmes is much less.
3.   Institutional Reform: Some lessons from Structural Adjustment Lending, PPD, October 5, 1984.

4.   A Review of Bank Lending for Reform in State-owned Enterprises, PPD, August 1984.

5.   The argument that rehabilitating these enterprises will <u>not</u> enhance their saleability is based on the following:

(a)   government involvement in their rehabilitation may only strengthen forces within government to retain ownership by creating more vested interests;

(b)   external assistance to rehabilitate these enterprises while encouraging government to divest itself of the same type of enterprise may produce conflicting signals to government; and

(c)   prospective private investors will likely discount the value of government rehabilitation efforts and therefore not fully compensate government for its investment, which could lead government to retain the enterprise on the ground that it cannot get 'fair' value.

Moreover, governments by their past mistakes have proven to be poor investors and their choices are often wrong. A private buyer, by putting up his own funds, will be more preoccupied with returns and will make better investment choices.

17

Privatisation in Ethiopia, Malawi and Uganda

Roger C. Sullivan*

INTRODUCTION

This chapter discusses the status of privatisation discussions in Ethiopia, Malawi, and Uganda. These countries are basically agricultural with a relatively small industrial base. They have a relatively large number of public enterprise and they are looking for ways to improve their efficiency and return on capital. In Malawi and Uganda, privatisation is one of the options being considered, within certain constraints. In Ethiopia, the socialist government does not include privatisation as one of the strategies; therefore it is concerned with improving efficiency within the framework of public-controlled assets.

The chapter is divided into five parts: (1) a discussion of the problems; (2) a statement of objectives to be achieved through privatisation or improved efficiency in the use of assets; (3) the strategy being pursued by each of the three countries to achieve its objectives; (4) the approach being pursued to carry out the strategy; and (5) how the World Bank has assisted in the above process.

PROBLEMS

The problems facing the public enterprises (PEs) in Ethiopia, Malawi, and Uganda are similar to those in most African countries. The PEs were loss-producing entities, requiring huge operating cash transfers from the treasury. On

---

* Senior Financial Analyst, Public Sector Management Division, Technical Department, Africa Region, World Bank.

average, the transfers to the PEs from 1980-5 came to more than 15 per cent of public revenue.

The PEs in many cases were expected to increase the country's foreign exchange earnings. In all three countries, one of the largest PEs was the agricultural marketing board, responsible for the largest exports in these countries (coffee in Uganda and Ethiopia; tobacco, maize, and tea in Malawi). However, the governments found that foreign exchange earnings from these companies were falling, in part because of their inefficient operations but also because of the government's producer-price policy which discouraged production. A final problem stemmed from employment practices. Many PEs, with government concurrence, had acted as employers of last resort. Employment in many cases was two or three times that required to operate the PE.

OBJECTIVES

Faced with the above problems, the governments of the three countries subscribed to several common financial objectives. Each sought to increase the growth rate of GDP, and it was felt that the PEs had a key role to play. Though agriculture would remain, in the short term, the main engine of growth, in the long run these countries needed to deepen their capital base and expand their non-agricultural sectors. A second common financial objective was to increase the efficiency of employment. Often this involved reforming public-sector policies and therefore presented difficult political problems. However, without some type of programme to remove redundant employees, there was a strong feeling that PEs could never be put on a commercial footing. A third objective was to improve the country's self-sufficiency through enhanced production. This meant increasing the production of industrial light goods and manufactured items, which most PEs had been created to produce.

Most PEs were set up on an import-substitution basis rather than export-orientated, but they had failed to meet production targets, despite often benefiting from high tariff barriers. In achieving self-sufficiency, the intention was to do it at a smaller cost to the economy, hence with lower tariff barriers in order that foreign competition could act as a competitive stimulus to more efficient, lower-cost

353

domestic production.

The three countries did not share the same <u>social</u> objectives. Ethiopia had gone through a socialist revolution in 1974 and still followed a centrally planned economic model. Ethopia's agenda specified that improvements in financial/economic performance had to be accomplished through a means where state control predominated. Both Malawi and Uganda were open to a mixed economic model, where the private sector had an acknowledged role, but with constraints. Both were concerned about foreign private participation, particularly if it were concentrated in certain racial groups which had at previous times been residential and exercised control over selected sectors.

STRATEGY

The governments, faced with mounting losses and the need to improve efficiency in the PEs, have adopted strategies which, in general, have led to a similar approach to analysing the problems and developing solutions. This approach will be described in the next section. The important thing to note is that the governments concerned limited the breadth of the approach based on their social objectives. Rather than having the freedom to examine all possible means of improving efficiency, returns on assets, foreign exchange earnings, etc., the governments conducted the examination in the following ways:

Ethiopia

The option of privatising, or permitting private-sector minority participation in PEs, was not a possible option, as this meant local private-sector involvement as well as foreign. The Ethiopian government's strategy was to improve efficiency, in this case commercialisation, within the framework of state control.

Malawi

Malawi had no problem with privatisation as an option; in fact the country already had a dynamic private sector, most of which (i.e. the largest industrial enterprises - sugar factories, textile mills, etc.) was owned by multi-national corporations. The PEs were predominantly in the agricultural sector, the largest being the Agricultural Marketing Corporation. In permitting privatisation, the government wanted control to remain within Malawi, and not see an increase in the share controlled by foreign interests.

Uganda

During a prolonged period of civil unrest, Uganda had nationalised many private industrial and manufacturing PEs. When the present government came to power in 1986, it sought to rationalise its PE portfolio. However, it faced two problems when it came to opening up ownership to private sources. First, it faced numerous claims from previous owners who had not received adequate (if any) compensation. Second, it did not want to return control to certain minority ethnic groups (originally non-African) who had controlled much of the trading and legal manufacturing sectors.

The approach

The three governments have to a certain extent been following the same approach. It generally has three distinct phases. The first phase is an attempt by the government to exert some control over PE operations. Usually this has meant creating a strong central body, in all cases reporting directly to the President or Council of Ministers. This body is then able to begin to stabilise the situation by requiring accounts and audits to be brought up to date. In all three countries such bodies have been created. In Malawi, the parastatals report directly to the Parastatal Commission and no longer to the technical ministries. The Parastatal Commission in turn reports to the Office of President and the Cabinet. The Parastatal Commission has begun to establish a common set of audits and reports, and requires standardised requests for capital and recurrent financing. In Uganda, a Public Enterprise Commission has been created, but at present it does not have executive authority over the PEs. Most report to their respective sectoral ministries, with the Ministry of Industry controlling directly or indirectly (through the Uganda Development Corporation) over 50 per cent of the 120 PEs, in order to establish balance sheets which can be used to determine the ultimate disposition of the PEs. In Ethiopia, the Department of Public

Enterprise Administration has been created within the Ministry of Finance to monitor the financial requirements of the PEs. This department intends to require updated accounts as a precondition for considering budgetary requests.

The second phase of the approach consists of studying the PEs in some detail to determine their financial status and prospects. These studies are undertaken with the help of foreign consultants, usually from large multinational management-consultancy firms. The studies are intended to evaluate the structural soundness of the PEs, to evaluate their balance sheets, to assess their business plans and prospects, and to recommend a future strategy for the PE. Generally, the strategy calls for the PE to follow a particular course of action; this could be liquidation (where the operations are suspended and the assets sold off); or commercialisation (where a decision is taken that the PE should continue operating). The issue of privatisation is certainly associated with liquidation. The premise is that an operation which is liquidated will be bought by the private sector, which can redeploy the assets for other purposes (buildings, equipment, machinery, vehicles, etc.) or can use them to continue running the business. However, the sale price is set at the value of the assets and does not include anything for goodwill -- because the financial analysis has shown that the business is not a financially viable proportion. The government in these cases takes responsibility for settling employee claims arising from shutting down the operation - these claims do not pass to the purchaser in the liquidation sale.

PEs which are considered for commercialisation may or may not be commercialised. A decision may be taken to commercialise initially, in order to maximise the government's value in the enterprise, and then privatise. In the case of Ethiopia, commercialisation is as far as the government is prepared to go, not privatisation.

Once a study or studies of PEs have been completed (which may easily take several years) a plan is drawn up. (It is worth noting that, in larger economies with thousands or even 500 or more PEs, it would be necessary to undertake the PE studies in phases, perhaps by sector or some other common denominator). This plan establishes priorities for liquidation and commercialisation activities based on financing required by the government either to pay off debts or to improve the PEs operating capability, managerial availability (i.e. the need to identify local or expatriate management for the PEs), and market absorptive capacity for liquidated assets. the latter case is important, because the local capital markets may need some development prior to significant liquidation operations. A further issue is whether the government will permit foreign interests to acquire liquidated assets. Certainly if foreign capital is allowed to come in, this will quicken the pace at which liquidation can be carried out, as the pool of available capital will likely be larger. So far, in the three countries being discussed, action plans have got to be developed.

Role of the World Bank

The World Bank has been involved in all stages of the last phase (i.e. the approach). It works with the strategy developed by the government, unless it has a strong technical reason to question it. For example, in the case of the domestic building construction industry in Ethiopia, which the government had nationalised and now wanted to commercialise, the Bank felt strongly that these activities were most efficiently and economically carried out by a competitive private sector. Thus, where the bank disagrees with a particular country's strategy in whole or in part, it will discuss these issues and try to reach a consensus. If one is not forthcoming, the Bank may choose not to continue with a programme to assist the sector concerned. The Bank may have chosen to assist with the commercialisation of the domestic building construction industry, if it felt that the entities used, in effect, compete, but the Ethiopian government was not prepared to accept this approach. The world Bank assistance is normally in the form of programme technical-assistance credits, public-sector management programmes, and operations-supporting studies defining programmes of PE reform. The Bank also provides assistance to carry out agreed programmes - funds for management contracts, for employee redeployment, and support to the local banking system. The Bank can also help with capital-market development and regulatory reform where this is appropriate.

Chapter 18

Privatisation in Peru

Felipe Ortiz de Zevallos M.*

THE PUBLIC ENTERPRISE SITUATION

According to Law Decree 216 (June 1981), there are four
modes of participation of the government of Peru in the
property of enterprises:

(1) Enterprises under public law to develop activities
    pertaining to the state, which has direct and exclusive
    ownership of enterprise capital. Their liquid assets are
    considered public funds and their management is
    subject to the general budget regulations. Their fixed
    assets can be bought or sold only through public bid.
(2) State enterprises under private law - owned entirely by
    the state, either directly or through holdings.
(3) Mixed enterprises - private corporations in which the
    state participates. The state must have, directly or
    indirectly, a 51 per cent share or, alternatively, must
    own more than 20 per cent of the stock besides having
    veto power over all major decisions of the shareholder's
    board.
(4) Enterprises with state shareholdings - private
    corporations in which the state has an indirect minor
    participation, and the rights and obligations of any
    other stockholder.

As of December 1987, there were 235 enterprises, each one
falling into one of the above four categories. Of these, 135
are under the control of the ministries of the different
productive sectors, or of other public institutions, and 100

*Chairman and President, Apoyo S.A. and former Chairman,
CONADI

under the Ministry of Economy and Finance. The government owns more than 50 per cent of the stock in 174 of these corporations and less than half in the remaining 61. Unlike in other countries in Latin America, the expansion of state-owned enterprises (SOEs) in Peru was a phenomenon of the 1970s under a nationalistic left-wing military government. From 1968 to 1975, the Peruvian state, as measured by total public expenditures, practically doubled in size. Although the number of SOEs is not extremely large by Latin American standards, the very recent development and wide diversity of the Peruvian parastatal sector is rather atypical in the region. Table 18.1 shows the various types of government involvement in SOEs.

The significance of SOEs to the economy

SOEs currently play a major role in the Peruvian economy. They are responsible for an estimated 20 to 25 per cent of GDP. The state is the sole owner of the four largest production complexes in Peru: PETROPERU (oil); CENTROMIN (mining); SIDERPERU (steel); and Paramonga (paper). SOEs account for over half of all public investment and give employment to about 150,000 persons: 15 per cent of them in Banco de la Nacion; 11 per cent in CONADE; 17 per cent in mining; 19 per cent in transport and communications; 8 per cent in electricity, 5 per cent in fishing; and 25 per cent in the rest.

Enterprises with state participation dominate certain sectors of the economy. They control all production of electric power, gas, water, fertilisers, iron, railway transport, and telecommunications, and dominate the steel and fish-processing industries, as well as the production of paper and, to a lesser extent, cement. PETROPERU purchases all oil produced locally by foreign companies and controls domestic sales and exports. State-owned mines produce 25 per cent of the copper output, and 40 to 50 per cent of zinc, silver, and lead.

SOEs also control much of Peru's trade. Until recently, mineral exports were a monopoly of MINPECO, and similar trading enterprises import, or purchase domestically and sell, such basic foodstuffs as rice, wheat, corn, sugar, coffee, vegetable oil, and milk products. A study made in 1980 showed that about 70 per cent of all exports and 35 per cent of consumer and raw material imports passed through the hands of SOEs. Total sales of the fifteen largest SOEs add up to approximately 15 per cent of gross national sales.

Similarly, even before a recent nationalisation law, still to be fully enforced, state banks dominated Peru's financial sector. They were responsible for three-quarters of all loans and two-thirds of all sight and savings deposits. State financial institutions have done virtually all medium and long-term lending in Peru.

Administrative structure

There is no coherent system for administering the shares in SOEs. Many are held directly by a ministry, which means that the minister appoints the state representatives to the shareholders' board and instructs them to appoint the corresponding members of the board of directors. The remaining shares are held indirectly by other enterprises, whose shares may also be owned by others or, at the end of the chain, by the ministries. More than one public entity may hold the shares of a given company. With few exceptions, the enterprises run directly by a ministry have had far less decision-making capacity than those run indirectly. However, there is also little managerial experience regarding the network of links between an enterprise and its parent holding company.

Assessment of SOE performance

A 1981 multi-sectorial commission, concluded from the data available for ninety-seven SOEs for 1980 that, as a whole, these companies earned a profit amounting to a 4 per cent return on equity. A mission of the World Bank made an in-depth assessment of a smaller sample (twenty firms), all but one of which were entirely state-owned, chosen to represent some of the most important enterprises with state participation (Alvarez, 1985). The sample included thirteen companies producing cement, paper, steel, petroleum, copper and other minerals, fish products, tractors, and seven service enterprises providing electricity, port services, telecommunications, air and water transport, water and sewerage, and marketing services. These firms fall into two categories: (a) companies, often nationalised ones, that have been allowed to operate with considerable autonomy under private law and have enjoyed continuity of management; and (b) companies, often state-created ones, that have been subject to extensive government interference in their

Table 18.1: Peruvian SOEs

Type of ownership	Enterprises under public law	State enterprises under private law	Mixed enterprises	Enterprises with state shareholdings	Total
Direct	10	18	5	1	34
Indirect	10	60	73	58	201
Total	20	78	78	59	235

Source: Lineres Gallo J. (1987) La Actividad Empresarial del Estado, United Nations.

Table 18.2: Net profit by economic sectors of the Peruvian SOEs (US$ millions)

Company	1980	1981	1982	1983	1984	1985	1986	1987
Hydrocarbons	24	2	6	32	9	39	(217)	(235)
Mining	50	(2)	(212)	(45)	(57)	(60)	(130)	(138)
Industry	(20)	(76)	(169)	(220)	(96)	(75)	(24)	(67)
Electricity	0	4	11	(75)	(73)	(34)	(58)	0
Commerce	8	6	(67)	(43)	26	(19)	(43)	(80)
Transport	10	13	(27)	(46)	(67)	(77)	8	10
Communications	26	26	1	1	13	1	0	(50)
Services	5	9	5	13	25	22	(1)	1
Water	0	(1)	1	(9)	(2)	(9)	(6)	2
Housing	0	(1)	0	2		0	(1)	(33)
Totals	103	(20)	(451)	(390)	(222)	(212)	(472)	(590)

Source: CONADE's unpublished information.

structure and daily operations and that have had a high turnover of managers.

The performance of the twenty SOEs in the sample was below that of the average Peruvian private firm. The 1980 return on assets of the sample, for instance, was 0.4 per cent, compared to 10.1 per cent for a sample of private manufacturing companies. Measures like subsidised prices and costly government intervention sacrificed profits. In addition, the monopoly position of most of these firms, plus a lack of incentive to maximise profits, contributed to a lower operating efficiency compared to that of private companies. In general the more autonomous firms earned higher profits - 6 per cent return on assets in 1980 - and had a lower debt and greater liquidity than the others. At the same time, their production was expanding more slowly, probably reflecting the fact that their investment decisions were more attuned to market and financial constraints. Their debt/equity and liquidity ratios were also more in line with those of private firms in Peru.

Legal framework

In spite of Law Decree 216, the legal framework for SOEs remains very confusing. Many state enterprises under private law have their own legislation, which in some cases strictly limits their autonomy. The powers of the directors and shareholders' boards may also vary from company to company.

Although general budget regulations should be restricted in principle to enterprises under public law, they normally refer indiscriminately to all SOEs. There is a constant conflict in the government between those supporting entrepreneurial autonomy and those who prefer to treat SOEs like appendages to the central government, and they are therefore subject to all budget regulations. Little progress has been made regarding the elimination of legal duplication and the appropriate simplification of the structural framework of SOEs. A new bill is currently being discussed in congress with the purpose of simplifying their functioning.

Some basic data

According to unofficial documentation, the total net worth in books of SOEs may add up to about US$2 billion in a country with a GDP of about US$20 billion. Company-specific figures should be taken with great care since there are significant variations due to exchange rates, accumulated losses due to subsidies and new capitalisations. (For instance, figures for 1986 are overvalued because of an unreal official exchange rate.) There is a 75 per cent concentration of net worth in the largest ten productive SOEs and an 82 per cent concentration in the five holding SOEs in the finance sector. The biggest three SOEs are Electroperu, Senape, and Petroperu.

Table 18.2 shows the profits or losses of Peruvian SOEs, by sector. A general conclusion is that, in aggregate values, SOEs have lost money almost permanently. Capital formation has been basically funded with external financing. Table 18.3 shows the profitability composition of SOEs and Table 18.4 the accumulated losses.

Divestiture

The general trend of nationalisations reached a peak in 1974 with the take-over by the state of the media enterprises. Prior to that, there was only one case of attempted rationalisation through divestiture. In the first semester of 1974, PESCAPERU received specific authorisation to transfer the assets and reassign the equipment of the fishing companies nationalised in mid-1972. The company was to keep proceeds from the sales and capitalise them.

A Multisectorial Commission - which included representatives of the private sector - was appointed in November 1976 with the objective of proposing norms for improving the efficiency of SOEs and drafting a regulatory law for them. This Commission recommended that some SOEs be divested to the private sector.

This, as well as the other recommendations, however, was not implemented by the second phase of the military government (1975-80), which was more concerned about how to solve the short-term financial crisis. By 1978, a harsh IMF-supported programme, which very significantly reduced domestic expenditure, was implemented. In the area of public divestiture, the government modified the by-laws of the Stock Exchange Regulatory Commission in order to offer potential national buyers some shares of the stock it owned. Some months later, this was followed by a law permitting ministers to propose 'the suppression, merger, or restricting' of any decentralised agency, including SOEs, as

Table 18.3: Profitability of SOEs (1986)

Profitability (%)	No. of companies	Net worth (US$ millions)	Proportion of total net worth
0	26	3,954	79.6
0.5	10	444	8.9
5.10	6	158	3.2
10.15	3	33	0.7
15.20	2	112	2.3
20	9	141	2.8
n.a.	10	128	2.6
Totals	66	4,970	100.0

Table 18.4: Accumulated losses in SOEs (expressed as the reduction of net worth between years)

Net worth	Number of SOEs			
	1985/86	1984/86	1983/86	1983/86
	(Productive sectors)			(Finance sector)
100	1	3	4	-
50 -100	2	5	5	-
25 - 50	4	4	5	-
0 - 25	7	5	6	5
SOEs with accumulated losses	14	17	20	9

Source: CONADE'S unpublished documents and the Superintendency of Banking and Insurance.

well as 'the total or partial sale of shares of public enterprises, or of those in which the government has a holding', as long as the activities did not correspond to tax-related or reserved activities.

Several companies and shares were proposed for sale in the 90 days allotted to the ministers under the law, but no interested buyers appeared, partly because of the depressed conditions of the economy, and partly because the terms of the offer called for the establishment of new commissions to value the firms and set up the mechanisms for the divestitures of shares. Also, the income generated by the sale of stock held by a holding SOE was to be transferred to the Treasury and matched by a corresponding transfer of 10-year government bonds paying only 10 per cent interest with a 2-year no-interest grace period. With inflation running at over 70 per cent a year, this mechanism was very unattractive to SOE managers and boards, who were eager to defend the asset values of their companies' portfolios.

However, an agreement was reached with the former national owners of cement plants, who had refused to accept any payments from the government and were fighting the expropriation through the judiciary. An amiable compromise emerged in the form of 20-year concessions for mixed enterprises, in which the former owners would eventually regain control, but in which the state would retain possession of 49 per cent of the stock.

In 1980, a new civilian government was democratically elected. It decided, on its very inauguration day, to re-privatise media enterprises, allowing the former owners to reduce the number of administrative personnel and compensating them for the effects of the expropriation.

During the 1980-5 period, however, very little was achieved regarding privatisation beyond the liquidation of a few SOEs. The current government, elected in 1985, is definitely in favour of greater state intervention. Along with the nationalisation of the banking and insurance business, it has partially 'privatised' two industrial companies (Motores Diesel Andinos S.A. - MODASA) and Cemento Norle Pacasrnayo S.A.). In the first case, Volvo and Perkins have capitalised their debt, gaining control of the enterprise, and the state has allowed COFIDE to divest its remaining stock through the Bourse. In the case of Pacasmayo, a cement plant where the state had 49 per cent of the stock, divestment is currently being done, again through the Bourse.

By the end of 1987, the government also announced that in the coming 2 years CONADE, the main holding company, was planning to divest up to thirty small enterprises, with a net value of about 10 per cent of its net worth.

THE THINKING ON PRIVATISATION

The second phase of the military government called for a Constitutional Assembly in 1979, for the drafting of a new constitution. In its approved text, it calls for a mixed social-market economy in which private initiative, as well as free trade and freedom of the Press, are supposed to be guaranteed. Several of its articles deal with the responsibility of the state as planner and entrepreneur. Article 113, for instance, assigns state entrepreneurial activities 'the goals of promoting the nation's economy, providing public services, and achieving development objectives'. The law may also reserve for the state, according to Article 114, certain productions or services for 'social' or 'national security' interests.

The positions of the major political parties regarding SOEs during their confrontation before the 1980 elections, the first to be held in 17 years, were very general. It is important to remark that the lack of civilian liberties during the military government did not allow for a coherent understanding of the intervention of the state in entrepreneurial activities.

According to Accion Popular (the party of Fernando Belaunde Terry) which finally won the elections:

It [was] necessary to define and specify, within the context of current realities and limitations, that the state has over-expanded and that it is necessary to define a set of priorities for its areas of intervention. Our government plan proposes the divestment of some enterprises to the private sector, especially through a diffused shareholding. The ministries' lack of orientation toward regulatory functions, which should be the essence of government, has caused those functions to be replaced by an increasing orientation toward the direct production of goods and services.

The more conservative Popular Christian Party (which was to become an ally of the government during 1980-84) affirmed that 'public enterprises have grown in a disorderly and accelerated way. [It is necessary] to affirm the subsidiary role of the state as director and promoter and to review its entrepreneurial activity in the context of its real possibilities'.

The left-of-centre populist APRA Party - an opposition force during 1980-85 and currently in charge of the government - expressed back in 1980 that:

> state entrepreneurial activities demand new legislation oriented toward the reduction of the current number of enterprises to those strictly needed, the submission of their performance to criteria of efficiency and results, and the simplification of their wide diversity of operational frameworks.

In a survey made before the elections by the Universidad del Pacifico, Accion Popular was presented with a sample list of SOEs and asked to propose an ownership structure for each of them. From a list of twenty-four, Accion Popular's explicit position was to keep thirteen wholly owned by the state and partially divest the remaining eleven to local investors, thereby establishing mixed enterprises with variable levels of state participation (see Table 18.5). Nothing of this was achieved through its 5-year government.

Some of Mr Belaunde's ministers - like Pedro Pablo Kuczynski, who as minister of Energy and Mines was in charge of the largest SOEs - did believe in the need of forcing SOEs to operate very much as private firms. The general mood in the government was stated in an article in the Budget Law for 1981 which read: 'Public enterprises should self-finance their operating expenses. Otherwise, the executive should fuse them with other enterprises or liquidate them to maintain a balanced budget.' In fact, however, only a few were fused or liquidated. Time was lost with the new Multisectoral Commission for the Evaluation and Reorganisation of Public Enterprises, which faced serious difficulties in fulfilling its duties: their members had a lack of familiarity with state entrepreneurial activities; many government officials directly involved with public firms were resistant to surrender the power residing in SOEs supervision; and President Belaunde was not firmly committed to the purpose of privatisation.

Table 18.5: Accion Popular's response to a survey, 1980

	Should remain state-owned	Should become a mixed enterprise with local private partners	Percentage of proposed state participation
AEROPERU	X	X	40
Banco Continental	X		
Banco International	X		
Banco Popular	X		
Centromin	X		
CPV	X		
COFIDE	X		
ELECTROPERU		X	40
EMADI	X		
ENAFEr	X		
ENCI (EPSA)		X	40
ENTEL		X	49
EPPA PERU		X	40
EPSEP			
ESAL			
MIERRO PERU		X	40
INDUPERU		X	50
MINERO PERU		X	50
MINPECO		X	50
PARAMONGA		X	50
PESCAPERU		X	30
PETROPERU	X		
SIDERPERU	X		
SIMA	X		

Source: <u>Peru 1980: Elecciones y Planes de Gobierno CIUP,</u>
Limo: Universided del Pacifico.

Only in June 1981, in compliance with the extraordinary powers given by Congress for the reorganisation of public entities, the Executive issued a set of new laws, including Law Decrees 206 (Law of the System for Financial Support and Promotion of Entrepreneurial Development) and 216 (Law of the Entrepreneurial Activity of the State). Law Decree 206 created CONADE (Corporation Nacional de Desarrollo), ah enterprise under public law, to direct and orient state intervention in entrepreneurial activities. Law Decree 216 was the first coherent legal effort to discriminate among the different modalities of SOE enterprises under public law, state enterprises under private law, mixed enterprises, and shareholdings of the state. It was also the first attempt to regulate organisation, function, economic and financial status, labour laws, methods of evaluation, and relations with the various levels of the central government. However, it did not specify which the specific areas for appropriate state intervention should be, whether exclusive or not. It thereby granted wide latitude for the sale or retention of current state holdings. During those days, the fate of SOEs began to be discussed in an increasingly emotional climate, and the topic became a highly sensitive political issue.

In January 1982, the former Prime Minister, Manuel Ulloa, called for a national consensus on the role of the state and a public debate that should result in a law authorising the executive to carry out a rationalisation process, including privatisation. During the senate discussion of the divestment bill, the APRA party proposed a different wording for the classification of enterprises subject to state intervention - natural resources, defence, essential public services, basic infrastructure, large transportation and communication systems, and finance and insurance - and opposed the divestment of some enterprises suggested by the government as suitable for such a process. The Aprista proposal also asked for congressional authorisation each time an enterprise was to be divested or liquidated.

When Pedro Pablo Kuczynski resigned as Minister of Energy and Mines, in July 1982, he included a section about SOEs in his final report:

> It is not only the divestiture of SOEs that should be discussed, which for the larger ones is not only an impossible objective, in view of scarce private national savings, but an undesirable one, taking into

consideration power and wealth distribution. What is currently missing is an all-inclusive definition of policy regarding the operation of SOEs.

Belaunde's government achieved little in the way of clarity of concept towards this end. During the first two years it was set on a liberal macro-economic policy in all but the fiscal area. The World Bank endorsed a 5-year programme of public investment for well over US$11,000 million. The action units of several of these projects would have been SOEs. Unfortunately, in 1983, Peru suffered under the onslaught of a series of natural disasters - the GDP fell by 12 per cent - and its short-term financing made adjustment programmes necessary, for which it counted on IMF support.

In contrast with the more neutral World Bank attitude, the IMF staff appeared to be strongly in favour of privatisation. The government was split in two. One group convinced itself that abruptly selling state shareholdings might quickly and magically raise cash to fulfil the short-sighted and, at times, impossible, IMF goals. Others, more worried about the political implications or the actual feasibility of raising immediate cash in a weakened domestic capital market, began to believe that the entire liberalisation of the economy had been a failure.

During the 1985 election campaign, while Accion Popular and the Popular Christian Party maintained their stand concerning the re-scaling of SOEs, and Izquierda Unida (a group of Marxist parties) advanced the notion of the convenience of nationalising the Banco de Credito (the largest private bank) and Southern Peru (the largest foreign mining company). APRA proposed:

> making them stronger and more efficient through giving priority to the state's entrepreneurial activity in order to ensure their orientation towards activities strategic for economic development; through the consolidation and re-launching of those strategic enterprises, and the assessment of the convenience in maintaining those of less priority, thus establishing forms of transfer to the sector of social co-operation ownership, to preclude the de-nationalisation and hurried selling which would be against the interests of the country; through the promotion of new enterprises needed by the country, and the application of a wide-ranging consultancy

programme to improve their management and regulation.

President Alan Garcia's government has been, up to the present, increasingly interventionist in economic matters. It has applied a policy of strict control of production, and of the external and financing sectors, which during its first 2 years in office permitted a significant expansion of production - an accumulated 15 per cent at the risk of fostering economic disequilibrium that could result in hyper-inflation. In July last year, when the official interest rate was well below the monthly inflation rate, the government decided to propose the nationalisation of the banking system as a way of facing those 'powerful groups directing the process of capital accumulation'.

The strange thing was that instead of the 80 per cent support expected by the government, public opinion split fifty-fifty regarding this measure. Mario Vargas Llosa, the famous novelist, led massive demonstrations in the main cities of the country. Debate in congress held back the passing of the law and when it was finally passed, it was most tactlessly applied by the government: a small tank was used, for instance, to break down the door of the main bank to be expropriated, in spite of the fact that the owners were protected by a court decision. Public opinion turned two to one against the government, and the nationalisation process -to all practical effects - has resulted in failure. It has even managed to set up Mario Vargas Llosa as a potential strong candidate for the presidency of the republic.

The political history of Peru has been characterised throughout by intense ideological discussion. At the moment, Peru is the only country in Latin America where a Marxist - Dr Alfonso Barrantes - happens to be the candidate with the highest option to win the next election. Concerning the role of the state, public opinion maintains an ambiguous position; on the one hand, there is a massive feeling that there ought to be 'more state' meaning more water, electricity and transport infrastructure; on the other hand, the suggestions concerning the divestiture of specific enterprises which do not provide basic services are also supported by the majority, and there is a general consensus that the state is a bad administrator.

What are the reasons or circumstances that have prompted the thinking in favour of privatisation? The first, obviously, is the inefficiency of the state, especially at a time when it has no foreign credit. The surge of state capitalism was totally a making of the first phase of the military government under General Juan Velasco. Loans were raised to pay expropriations and to fund large investment projects. There was even a new architectural style for SOE's headquarters. When General Velasco was replaced by General Francisco Morales Bermudez, an economic crisis was already in the making. General Morales Bermudez had been General Velasco's prime minister; so corrections of economic desequilibrium had to be done in a way that might consolidate the 'structural reforms' of the Velasco revolution. General Morales Bermudes has paid, politically, the financial bills of General Velasco's policies, but after returning power to the civilians, he has not been able to develop a political base as he intended to do. However, General Velasco, who led Peru in the wrong course, is remembered as one of the most popular Peruvian presidents in history although, curiously enough, his followers have not been able to cash in on this political capital.

When Mr Belaunde, Mr Ulloa, and Mr Kuczynski returned to power in 1980, they had been in exile for quite a while and were not fully aware of the new size of the Peruvian state. They had very little staff and the military dictatorship had not allowed the emergence of new civilian figures. Mr Belaunde, an architect by profession, has always been fond of public projects and has cared little for administrative and financial matters. During his government there were some radicals in his party who proclaimed the need for an urgent and total dismantling of the state apparatus, but they had little political support. Also, the opposition started criticising the possibility of covert operations with private illegal interests. The fact that foreign consultants, funded by the World Bank and USAID, began working very openly on the subject matter may have also been detrimental to the privatisation process. There was no powerful member of the government party willing to address the subject in a coherent and consistent way. Mr Ulloa played his liberal policies on trade and financial policies against Mr Belaunde's expenditure demands for public projects. The result was very messy and, after the ecological disasters in 1983, everybody was left with the taste that the overall economic management - with World Bank and IMF support - had been a complete failure. In the 1985 elections, AP received only 5 per cent of the votes.

For the coming elections in 1990, the role of the state will probably be the main topic, basically because the nationalisation of the banking system was the event that marked Mr Vargas Llosa's appearance in the political arena. A strong admirer of Mrs Thatcher's policies, Mr Vargas Llosa will probably run an aggressive campaign on this subject. Public opinion is increasingly changing against state intervention and bureaucratic control; furthermore, inflation is reaching levels never suffered before in the country.

A World Bank team has recently proposed a programme for re-establishing Peru's elegibility for receiving further disbursements from that institution. It is obvious that, in the current situation, privatisation need not be on the short term agenda, but could be incorporated later in a medium-term programme. A gross estimate of the sale value of shares and enterprises, the divestiture of which could easily be accepted by public opinion, may be US$200 million -about 1 per cent of GDP.

The thinking regarding privatisation has become more rational in recent years. Although Izuierda Unida (IU), a conglomerate of all Marxist and socialist parties, still believes that all basic productive activities should be developed by the state, its 1985 platform called for the nationalisation of only two enterprises, one of which has already suffered a change in property. The current government has turned out to be more radical in this matter by expropriating an American oil company and the entire financial and insurance sectors. It is possible that for the 1990 elections IU might be split in two, with Mr Barrantes - the front runner - leading a more moderate group hardly suggesting any further nationalisation.

Mr Vargas Llosa's commitment to privatisation will probably force all other candidates to a clear stand on this subject, which could be very useful for establishing the next government's agenda in this matter. Until now, the topic has been normally discussed in terms of ownership, with little analysis regarding changes in the organisational structure, or effective introduction of market criteria in the areas of investment, capital procurement, pricing, surplus generation, employment, etc., or possibilities like leasing out certain assets of SOEs.

ACTIONS IN PRIVATISATION

As described before, a minor denationalisation occurred in 1974 when Pescaperu was allowed to sell some of the assets that had been acquired through the nationalisation of all the private fishing companies. In 1972, the fishing industry suffered a severe crisis due to the depletion of anchovies in the Peruvian coast. Instead of allowing private firms to adjust to this new and difficult reality, the government nationalised the entire fishing industry in Peru. What happened in 1974 was little more than a garage sale of unneeded assets.

The case of the media was obviously marked by political considerations. The experiment of transferring the newspapers to social organised groups was a complete failure. Divestiture was a response to the political demand for Press freedom. Nobody really considered it as a precedent for further privatisations. A more illustrative case was that of the cement plants. Of the five existing in the country, the private sector had invested in three (i.e. the larger and more efficient ones) while the State had developed the remaining two, which were oriented towards the satisfaction of regional demands in the southern part of the country. Private industrialists, who have been affected in their interests by state intervention, preferred a future joint-venture with the state rather than recovering completely the property of their firms under the premise that this could be, from a political point of view, a more stable long-term arrangement.

During the 1980-5 period, very much against the government ideal, the size of the Peruvian state sector was partially increased by the bailing out of failing private banks. On the positive side, some minor firms and assets were liquidated but, as explained before, the government let its time go by without a clear political definition, and when by its mid-term a formal proposal was spelled out, no consensus was reached because of its lack of priority in the political agenda.

The two cases of partial privatisation under the current government correspond to joint ventures in which the state has reduced its participation: in one case - Motores Diesel Andinoa (MODASA) - because of its inability to match capital increases with its partners; and in the other - Cemento Nort Pacasmayo - to raise cash urgently needed by its holding company in order to attend to the demands of other public ventures.

The wide range of approaches to privatisation is not yet fully understood. Obviously, privatisation being a long term process, it can only work properly in a political environment which favours competition and the dynamism of market forces. At present, Peru has a government which could be more willing to divest stock in its SOEs than to surrender its macro-interventionalist policies. It is possible that in a few years' time the conditions will be set for establishing a coherent and long-term privatisation programme.

PROBLEMS ENCOUNTERED

The main problem in Peru in past years has been the lack of conceptual clarity on the matter of privatisation. After the poor political results of the banks' nationalisation last year, there may be a stronger support for privatisation if it could be explained in a more rational way and administered by people with a minimum of credibility. (Profiting from concessions given by government has been a national pastime in Peru, just like in any other country with a colonial past. Salaries in the civil service have fallen in real terms to levels that have induced bribery and corruption throughout the state administration. A very easy way to stop future privatisations in a country like Peru could be to accuse this process of being nothing but a set of immoral deals.)

The very few cases of privatisation in Peru and their exceptional characteristics do not allow the identification of issues that could be relevant for future processes. In the case of the media, the overwhelming political support made it simple not only to fix compensation for the legitimate owners but to allow them to reduce personnel in a country where the Constitution establishes job stability as a right. In the cement plants, the deals were private and with the previous owners; in the recent case of MODASA, it has fallen to the foreign partners in the joint ventures to capitalise their debts. This last case, however, is interesting in the sense that the majority holding has passed from the government to foreign companies, with no adverse reaction from any party concerned with the deal.

CONCLUSIONS

The significant participation of the Peruvian State in entrepreneurial activities is a rather recent political process. Privatisation has been put to public debate since 1975, but little has been achieved in the last 13 years.

It is likely that privatisation will become an important issue in the next elections (1990). The debate will reopen at a very difficult time for Peruvian society. The country is on the verge of total collapse, with terrrorist insurgents calling for a Maoist revolution and inflation reaching four-digit annual figures. However, there are very few options - aside from state totalitarianism on the one hand, and a rational privatisation with a minimum democratic consensus, on the other. One thing the Peruvian state, five years from now, will be very different from what it is at present.

REFERENCES

Alvarez Rodrich, A. (1985) Los Objetivos de las Empresas Publicas, Lima: Fundacion Ebert.

Caravedo, Baltazar (1986) Automonia y Eficiencia en las Empresas Publicas de Servicio. El caso de SEDAPAL, Lima: Fundacion Ebert.

Departamento de Investigacion de ESAN (1984) Algunos indiacadores e Interrogantes sobre las Empresas Publicas Peruanas.

Gallegos, Armando, Lozano, Ampuero, and Pacheco, John (1985) Mapa Economico financiero de la Actividad Empresarial del Estado Peruano. ESAN.

Linares Gallo, Jose (1987) La Actividad Empresarial del Estado, Lima, Peru: Naciones Unidas, Proyecto PER/87/014/PNED.

Ortiz de Zevallos, M., Felipe (1986) 'Peru: an insider's view', in William P. Glade State Shrinking: A Comparative Inquiry into Privatisation, Austin, Texas: Institute of Latin American Studies.

——— (1982) 'The entrepreneurial role of the Peruvian State', Intercampus, February.

Saulniers, Alfredo (1983) Public Enterprises in Latin America: The New Look? Brasilia: Institute of Latin American Studies, University of Texas at Austin.

——— (1985) Cuatro Mitos sobre las Empresas Publicas en America Latina, Lima, Peru: Fundacion Ebert.

Saulniers, A. and Revilla, J. (1983) The Economic Role of
  the Peruvian State 1821-1919, Mexico City.
Stephan, Alfred (1978) The State and Society, Peru in
  Comparative Perspective, Princeton, New Jersey.
World Bank (1982) Peru, The Management and Sale of State-
  Owned Enterprises, Report No. 4088, Document of the
  World Bank/IFC, August 27.

19

Privatisation in Jamaica, Trinidad and Tobago

G.E. Mills*

INTRODUCTION

Jamaica, Trinidad and Tobago are members of a group of countries which together constitute a distinct region with a sense of commonality reinforced by the trend towards regionalism reflected, for example, in the creation of the Caribbean Community (CARICOM) and the Caribbean Development Bank (CDB). Jamaica, the largest island of the group, both in area and population size, with 2.3 million people (90 per cent of African origin) is twice as large as Trinidad and Tobago (with a population almost 50 per cent 'East Indian' and over 40 per cent 'African'). Trinidad and Tobago had an oil bonanza in the 1970s and is consequently wealthier, with a GDP of US$5,550 per head) than Jamaica (with a GDP of US$1,030). Perhaps the most significant difference, relevant to public enterprise and privatisation, rests in the contrast in the development of their political parties. In Jamaica, party rivalry is the most intense in the region; the two major parties, the People's National Party (PNP) and the Jamaica Labour Party (JLP) continuously alternating in office since party government was introduced in 1944. By contrast, opposition parties have tended to be weak in Trinidad and Tobago; one party, the People's National Movement (PNM) remaining in office for 30 years continuously until losing to a coalition of parties by a landslide defeat in December 1986.

In addition, the evolutionary pattern of trade unionism and of the party systems is quite different. In Jamaica (as in Antigua, Barbados and St Kitts) the major trade unions form

* Professor of Public Administration, University of the West Indies, Jamaica

the base of the main political parties, or are closely aligned with them; not so in Trinidad. 'Public enterprise' in Trinidad is treated as:

> an organization which is owned and/or controlled by a public authority, established to serve a set of public purposes, is subject to public accountability, is engaged in activities of a business character which involve investment and return and the marketing of outputs'.

For the purpose of this chapter, privatisation means, first and foremost, denationalisation; and, second, the public issue of a proportion of the shares of a publicly-owned undertaking. In addition, the term will be used to include the leasing of such an enterprise to a private-sector interest, and similarly, the contracting out of the operation of a service which is normally regarded as a public responsibility and previously so operated.

THE PUBLIC ENTERPRISE SITUATION IN JAMAICA

The previous PNP government

During the decade of the 1970s, with the accession to power, in 1972, of a democratic socialist (PNP) government in Jamaica, there was an increasing trend towards the development of public enterprise. In a declaration of its ideological approach, the government indicated:

> the government must supervise the running of the economy through a combination of direct ownership, control by participation, regulatory machinery... (and proceeded to delineate the) areas which require public sector involvement (to include) basic nutrition, infrastructure and public utilities, mineral resources, salvage operations, trail-blazing.

Based on these principles, a centralised agency, Jamaica Nutrition Holdings (JNH) Limited, was created as a state company designed to search for cheap supply sources and to import, in bulk, nutrient-rich foods (e.g. grains, soya, milk solids). Later, an umbrella-type institution, the State Trading Corporation (STC) was established (with JNH Limited as one of its subsidiaries) 'to take over control of all

379

imports deemed essential for national development and in the public interest'. The STC - in the face of strong private-sector criticism and opposition - was seen by the government, as a 'bulwark in cushioning the consumer from massive price increases for basic food items which would have resulted from devaluation (of the Jamaican currency) and international price inflation'.

In the area of 'salvage operations' - that is, 'to acquire ownership of any industry which produces an important commodity or provides employment for a considerable work force, but which private enterprise is not prepared to continue to operate' - a textile plant was purchased, and a number of large hotels, sugar estates, and factories were acquired during a period of decline in the tourist and sugar industries.

However, despite the PNP's socialist orientation and the declaration by its founder and first leader, the late N.W. Manley, that 'every socialist, of course, believes that an overwhelming case can be made out for public ownership of essential public utilities', these undertakings remained in private ownership (foreign) throughout the period of the first government of that party (1955-62). It was the 'free-enterprise' JLP which initiated the moves towards nationalisation of these utilities, beginning with the electricity generating and telephone companies. The new PNP government completed these moves by nationalising the urban transportation system by the mid-1970s. But these actions were impelled primarily by the problems encountered in effectively regulating these hitherto foreign-owned/controlled undertakings.

Earlier, shortly after the country became independent, the government of the time (JLP) established a national airline, Air Jamaica Limited, primarily as a support to the tourist industry: a 'decision dictated by hard economic necessity, not by prestigious or status considerations - but as an adjunct to an important economic activity. Later, the cement manufacturing plant was nationalised, as was the old, foreign-owned, Barclay's Bank. The share ownership in the external communications enterprise was increased to 51 per cent (a joint venture with Cable and Wireless) and equity was purchased in three North American bauxite/alumina firms - in one case, Kaiser, a 51 per cent majority holding/

By October 1980, then - the end of the PNP's regime - public ownership had extended to areas of transportation (air and inland, including railway and bus), communications (radio/TV broadcasting, telephone and telegraph - internal and external) and other public utilities - agricultural development, export marketing and internal distribution; mineral exploitation and processing; banking; tourism; sugar; housing; land development; food importation and trading. These developments had taken place in an economy in which bauxite/alumina, tourism, and sugar have been the dominant industries. The government also owned (through holding companies) eight of the country's twelve sugar factories producing 75 per cent to 80 per cent of total sugar output; and fourteen hotels (including some of Jamaica's largest) with an aggregate room capacity of almost 50 per cent of the hotel industry as a whole.

As mentioned earlier, these acquisitions had taken place during a period of dramatically declining GDP and foreign exchange earnings and of currency devaluation. As a consequence, stringent policy measures of licensing and regulation of the economy were introduced. However, the movement towards public ownership of the utilities (electricity generation, telephones, and bus transportation) was accompanied by discontinuation of the operations of the regulatory mechanisms such as the Public Utilities Commission and Rates Boards, while an Advisory and Monitoring Unit was simultaneously developed in the Ministry of Public Utilities and Transport.

The current JLP government

The elections of October 1980 brought a new government (JLP) to power in a landslide victory - a government committed to divestment as indicated in its manifesto and early policy pronouncements. However, it retained not only most of the public utilities (and indeed considerably increased the investment in them) but also the much criticised and opposed State Trading Corporation (STC), merely changing its name to the Jamaica Commodity Trading Company. The new JLP Minister of Industry and Commerce (in his capacity as President of the Jamaica Manufacturers Association) had described the STC when it was first established three years before, as 'a blood-sucking economic vampire... the beginning of Jamaica's economic enslavement'.

Further, the JLP government took even more significant steps; first, in the acquisition of the Esso oil refinery; next (and more recently) in increasing from 6 per cent to 50 per cent the equity ownership held by the previous government in the bauxite/alumina company, JAMALCO - a joint venture with Alcoa Minerals. Both actions were taken 'in the national interest'; the first in order to protect the consumer against higher prices for petroleum products (e.g. gasolene and kerosene); the other, in order to 'give Jamaica equal voice in determining the operation of the plant ... ensuring that the plant will operate at whatever production level we require - and saving the highly-skilled jobs of workers.

Currently, then, the most significant state-enterprise holding in Jamaica, in terms of their impact on the economy, have remained substantially in the same broad areas as under the socialist PNP government, with the addition of oil refining and distribution. This empirical experience seems to validate the hypothesis that, in developing countries, a degree of public enterprise is imperative, irrespective of the ideological orientation of the governing party. However, in keeping with its policy, the JLP government has undertaken a number of divestment exercises, which will be described later.

On the basis of the information available to the author, twenty-one of the most significant of these enterprises involved capital investment of approximately J$$1.1 billion during the year ended March 1988. (Note that 1 US dollar equals 5.5 Jamaican dollars). This does not include investments in the bauxite/alumina industry in which the government holds 50 to 51 per cent ownership in two companies and a small minority interest in another (the recent acquisition of an equal share in JAMALCO involved expenditure of J$145 million).

The twenty-one undertakings mentioned above, taken together, earned surpluses on operations amounting to J$754 million during 1987/8 - showing a considerable improvement over the gross deficit of J$37.7 million in 1980/1. This position has been achieved partly through the implementation of stricter central financial controls and improvement in management efficiency, and partly by substantial increases in rates imposed by the monopoly public utilities of water, electricity generation and distribution, and the telephone system. These last three enterprises contributed $33^{1}/3$ per cent of the gross surpluses. Four entities incurred deficits, the most significant being the national radio/TV broadcasting and airlines companies.

The operations of all these enterprises should be seen

within the context of (a) a government budget of J$2.32 billion capital; (b) J$4.19 billion recurrent actual expenditure in 1987/88; and (c) a GNP of J$1.170 billion. Aggregate employment in public enterprises is approximately 50,000 - sugar industry representing more than 50 per cent - in a labour force of 821,000. A more detailed set of statements is attached as Appendices.

Actual divestitures

Shortly after the JLP's accession to power, attempts at divestment were initiated, especially in the areas of hotels, sugar factories (and estates) and agro-industry processing enterprises, but such early efforts proved unsuccessful. Of fourteen hotels placed on the market, only one has been sold, and twelve have been leased on long-term arrangements; the bus transportation system for the metropolitan Kingston area was de-nationalised in December 1983, franchises being granted to a number of private mini-bus operators. Of the eight public-sector sugar factories, three have gone out of operation entirely.

More recently, there have been significantly successful divestiture exercises, beginning with the public sale, in December 1986, of 51 per cent (J$91 million) of the equity in the National Commercial Bank (NCB), the country's largest commercial bank - an offering which was over-subscribed by 170 per cent attracting more than 30,000 individual applications, including 98 per cent of the Bank's employees.

Six months later, 71 per cent (J$160 million) of the Cement Company's shareholding was publicly sold; and a small percentage of the holdings in Jamaica International Telecommunications Limited - a joint venture company covering internal and external communications - was re-sold to Cable and Wireless, a multi-national enterprise, increasing their holding to 39 per cent. In addition, responsibility for street cleaning and garbage collection (hitherto provided by local government services) has been contracted out to private companies, and an airlines catering service has been divested.

In the agricultural sector (excluding sugar factories) the public sector holdings in the banana industry have been privatised, acres of sugar-cane land have been sold for other uses, and the non-marketing activities of some of the traditional crop marketing boards have been disposed of,

383

either to growers' associations or to individual private-sector interests.

THE PUBLIC ENTERPRISE SITUATION IN TRINIDAD AND TOBAGO

In Trinidad and Tobago, as in Jamaica (and Guyana), public enterprise burgeoned during the 1970s. The trend began from the 1960s in the fields of public utilities (electricity telecommunications, bus transportation, and water), electronic broadcasting, manufacturing industry, and the national airlines (regional). In this oil-rich country, the state spent its newly acquired wealth lavishly, venturing into highly expensive undertakings in areas such as petroleum, gas, petrochemicals, energy-based industries (menthol, urea, and ammonia), and iron and steel manufacture. In addition, considerable investments were made in sugar production and other agro-industries, and in finance, banking, and insurance.

It should be emphasised, however, that these trends were motivated, not, as in Guyana and Jamaica, by socialist ideological considerations, but through considerations 'of the national interest' and to accelerate transformation of the economy; in cases such as acquisition of the telephone system and the airlines, this 'interest' included not only an emphasis on local ownership, but also 'rescue operations' (i.e. to save the jobs of workers who are faced with retrenchment).

Developing the theme of the national interest, the former and long-serving Prime Minister, the late Dr Eric Williams had declared in 1970 (after 14 years continuously in office) the policy of 'enlarging the national decision-making over the national economy'. According to him, 'in this respect, we (Trinidad) have already gone further than any other Caribbean territory, except Cuba.' Part of these objectives was the intention 'to accelerate the transfer of foreign-owned firms to local hands'.

Extent and impact of government participation

At the end of November 1985, the Government owned or held participatory interest in sixty-six enterprises, with net assets of T$11 billion (note that 1 US dollar is equal to 3.6 Trinidad and Tobago dollars) and the nominal value of its shareholding amounting to approximately TT$2.5 billion. Of these, the government owned 100 per cent of the shares in thirty-seven enterprises (its shareholding being a nominal value of TT$1.9 billion); it held a majority of shares in eleven enterprises, (owning holdings of TT$200 billion); a 50 per cent holding nominally valued at TT$8 million in one undertaking; and a minority equity interest in seventeen enterprises (its holdings nominally amounting to TT$62 million). The major shareholdings were in the petroleum and related sectors (including gas-based industries and iron/steel) with shareholding valued (nominally) at TT$1,590 million; and in agriculture and related sectors, valued at TT$227 million.

The Trinidad and Tobago government also hold interests in two joint ventures with the Barbados government - in cement manufacture and air cargo shipping - and five regional (Caribbean) government-owned enterprises; the total Trinidad shareholding in these seven valued nominally at TT$73. Tables 19.1 and 19.2 set out the distribution of government shareholding by sectors and size.

In summary, the data set out in Table 19.3 discloses that, during 1985, the contributions made by the major state enterprises (including the public utilities) were as follows: to GDP, 16 per cent to direct employment, 54,000 persons in an employed labour force of about 470,000; to capital investment, 26 per cent of the national total; and to gross exports, TT$3.9 billion. On the other hand, they 'were also responsible for TT$2.6 billion or 39 per cent of the country's external debt' obligations, which carry a government guarantee.

While the petroleum and related enterprises 'performed creditably', recording an operating surplus of almost TT$1 billion and savings above TT$200 million, the non-petroleum enterprises recorded negative savings of almost TT$700 million.

Divestiture

The former People's National Movement (PNM) government had declared in many public statements, as long as 1972 (before the current world-wide trends in privatisation), its intention to divest significant proportions of its share-holdings to the public as circumstances permit, since it was 'conscious of the fact that its shareholdings in these private undertakings are a trust held on behalf of the people of this country'. Six years later, in reiterating this policy intention, the Prime Minister observed that 'this course will be followed until appropriate institutions have been developed to facilitate planned and equitable divestment protecting the smaller shareholder against the encroachment of conglomerates and "big shots" '.

Accordingly, in a successful venture, six million shares involving 49 per cent holdings of the state-owned National Commercial Bank were sold to more than 25,000 persons, and part of the holdings in the primary hotel in Port-of-Spain was divested. However, other stated divestment intentions (in the national gas and sugar industries) were not pursued.

The new National Alliance for Reconstruction (NAR) government, assuming office in January 1987, has confirmed the selective divestment policy enunciated in its election manifesto. This will be elaborated in the next section.

THE JAMAICAN THINKING ON PRIVATISATION

During the PNP regime (1972-80) critical comment on the mushrooming of public ownership surfaced from time to time, expressed not only by the parliamentary opposition, but by private sector individuals and organisation, and the Press. The JLP Opposition adopted what appears with hindsight to be an ambivalent posture. While supporting the views and sentiments of the private sector, they nevertheless made full use, when they assumed power, of the state institution. The concern of the then Leader of the Opposition (as Chairman of the Public Accounts Committee) for stricter control of the considerable capital expenditure on the state enterprises ultimately led to the creation of a Commission of Public Accountability when his party assumed power in 1980.

The JLP election manifesto had stated the intention to 'create a market system of economics ... to shift unnecessary public enterprises to the private sector so as to remove the burden of finance from Government'. By March 1981 the government had set up a Divestment Committee and had laid down guidelines and procedures for the committee's actions. Two fundamental principles were emphasised:

(1) The policy of divestment of equity and control in commercial enterprises at prices based on commercial criteria after taking into account the

nation's interest. (These enterprises are to exclude the public utilities.)

(2) The intention to discontinue operating enterprises not commercially viable; but where appropriate, attempts would be made to establish viability via private sector participation, failing efforts at outright sale.

The principal objectives set were:

(i) To ensure that public funds were not mis-allocated to inefficient enterprises;

(ii) to reduce and eliminate the strain on the budget; and

(iii) to release government's resources from commercial enterprises for alternative uses.

Priorities and the determination of urgency would be based on: (a) the budgetary impact; (b) the economic impact; (c) employment and linkage; and (d) the social impact. As to the method of divestment, where practicable, opportunities should be provided for the widest possible public participation. This could be facilitated through the stock exchange. The Prime Minister emphasised, in an address to Parliament, that the JLP policy must be viewed from the perspective of the extensive losses incurred by public enterprises during the 1970s, which had to be subsidised out of tax revenues. Later in 1981, the government, in a Ministry Paper to Parliament' indicated that, as an essential ingredient in the economic recovery programme, the economy would be freed from the 'hamstrings' of regulation and control in order to perform with the minimum of restriction. Thus was born the government's policy of deregulation, aimed at freeing the economy by 'a progressive liberalisation of import restrictions leading eventually to the elimination of all licensing requirements'.

Two years later, the Prime Minister re-iterated in Parliament the JLP's ideological position conceptualises development in an economy in which the private sector is seen as the engine of growth. The appropriate role of the public sector would be to provide the infra-structural framework to facilitate the efficient operation of the private sector.

It should be observed that the government's policy was not formulated entirely independently of external influences. The parlous condition of the economy in the

387

1970s (buffeted by dramatic oil price increases and international inflationary forces) impelled the government to seek IMF and World Bank assistance to relieve the disastrous balance of payments situation, to provide relief in substantial inflows of foreign exchange, and to improve productivity and production. The ensuing Structural Adjustment Programme (1982-7) was associated with conditionalities prescribed by these multi-lateral agencies - including an emphasis on deregulation and privatisation. The accession of the Reagan Administration, within a few months of the JLP return to power, also fuelled and bolstered these policies via the mechanism of a USAID-sponsored conference held in Washington D.C.

Meanwhile, the government had created the National Investment Bank of Jamaica Limited (NIBJ) to serve as a catalyst for new investments and as a depository for vesting the assets of certain enterprises (e.g. the Cement Company). In a further statement on policy, the Prime Minister indicated in the House of Representatives (November 1985) that certain other commercial enterprises would be vested in the NIBJ in order to overcome the problem of divesting undertakings whose value was too substantial for 'straight divestment' (i.e. too large for local private capital). Thereafter, NIBJ would offer shares in these enterprises to the public on an annual basis.

The Prime Minister further stated that, in implementing its divestment policy, the government had avoided the sale of major national assets - which would be retained in the national interest. It was the government's policy to lease rather than sell certain types of assets (e.g. hotels and large tracts of commercial land - the latter a scarce commodity).

Recent developments

Shortly after attaining power, the government announced its intention to undertake a programme of partial divestment in the radio and television broadcasting media. In 1985 decisions were taken and announced whereby some services of the fully-owned Jamaica Broadcasting Corporation - both radio and TV - would be leased to private operators, and 50 per cent of the television ownership would be divested to the public. The 25 per cent holdings in Radio Jamaica and Rediffusion would be sold. These decisions, currently being implemented, have evoked considerable controversy.

Two recent ministerial statements are of special

interest. The first, by the Prime Minister in his capacity as Minister of Finance, winding up the 1988-9 Budget Debate, indicated that 'it would be necessary to use money from divestment proceeds to meet shortfalls in taxation revenues over the next six years'. He continued:

> A total of J$430 million is expected to come from divestment this year... J$300 million from hotel divestment, J$100 million from divestment of shares in Telecommunications of Jamaica, and J$30 million from the divestment of the electronic media. The other is a comment by the Minister of Public Utilities and Transport that while the previous government had owned, managed, and attempted to control the bus transportation system, the present government had divested its ownership and management and were involved in control only.

The private sector organisation of Jamaica has been expressing concern about the slow pace of the divestment process. Its document 'The Role of Government in the Jamaica Economy' (March 1988) has emphasized that:

> even where public sector companies are marginally profitable, divestment is recommended. This will allow for re-allocation of resources, and concentration on such resources in areas which are the proper concern of government (e.g. health, national security, etc.).

THE THINKING ON PRIVATISATION IN TRINIDAD

The scenario in 1979

In 1979 a committee was appointed under the chairmanship of the Central Bank's Governor (Bruce) and consisting of representatives from significant state enterprises, to 'consider and make recommendations on the question of divestment of shares in state enterprises'. (A parallel committee was set up at the same time, to consider the appropriate climate under which an efficient state enterprise could operate.)

The principal findings/recommendations of the 'Divestment Committee' were that:

(1) A programme of divestment could serve the purpose of improving income re-distribution and thus contribute towards the development of a money and capital market in Trinidad; the process could also assist in improving the viability and profitability of enterprises by the injection of expertise.

(2) Generally, divestment should take place when there was clear evidence of stability and growth (as indicated by financial viability and profitability) in a company.

(3) The divestment programme should be aggressive, well formulated, preceded by a planned education programme, and undertaken in phases.

(4) A proportion of the shares being divested should be allocated to employees of the issuing institutions.

(5) The enactment of securities legislation should be expedited to improve the conditions in which the process would take place and assist in safeguarding the investor's interest.

Interestingly, the Committee did not 'feel itself able to make a firm recommendation at this time' on the extent of divestment.

The changed context of 1984

Following the down-turn in oil prices and the decline in a hitherto buoyant economy, the government became increasingly concerned about the drain on foreign exchange reserves and on the national budget stemming from the operations of state enterprises. Moreover, concern also began to be expressed about the growth of conglomerates. Accordingly, the Cabinet appointed a committee 5 years after the Bruce Committee, with Bruce's successor as Governor of the Bank, as Chairman (and comprising the chief executives of several significant institutions) to review the policy of participation in industrial and commercial enterprises which had been enunciated and elaborated more than a decade before. This Committee considered that although the policy had fulfilled much of its promise and intentions, it needed to be re-assessed in the light of significant change in the circumstances which had prompted initiation of the policy.

390

Among the issues addressed by the new Committee, were:

(1) Should government continue to hold all or part of its existing portfolio of state enterprises?
(2) What criteria should guide divestment?

It concluded that some of the rationale for the objectives of state ownership originally enunciated were no longer valid. The objectives could be more appropriately achieved by private sector ownership/management, and via appropriate legislation and regulation.

In view of the government's initial commitment to divestment 'as circumstances permit' - enunciated in 1972 - and its current financial constraints, the Committee noted that 'divestment' must mean the gradual and progressive increase in shareholding of the public in those state enterprises which have been made sufficiently attractive on the capital market'. Hence:

(i) The portfolio should be rationalised partly by divesting gradually, 'those non-strategic enterprises which are or can be made viable and attractive to the investing public'.
(ii) Enterprises which are not commercially viable and 'do not perform a strategic developmental or social function' should be liquidated or sold off.
(iii) In the case of the 'apex industries' (e.g. petroleum, fertilizers, energy-intensive industries) and in areas such as finance, telecommunications and 'high technology', holding companies could be formed, and part of the government shareholdings divested. Such companies would ensure better management and control and enterprises within the group.

As far as I am aware, no action was taken on the recommendations of the Committees of 1979 and 1984.

The Post-PNM Period

In its manifesto for the December 1986 election, the NAR paid special attention to the problem of the state enterprises, especially in the context of a rapidly declining economy. The party's policy on state participation was subsequently adopted as a policy document by the new NAR Cabinet. Focus is directed on the dismal performance of some enterprises which remain a financial burden on the national treasury and the intention expressed to embark on a programme of divestment of state enterprises engaged in the supply of private goods. Shares in such undertakings are to be offered to workers and their affiliated trade unions and to local capital -- a 'tri-sector approach'.

The elements of the approach to divestment are also set out as follows:

'Enterprises which are essential for the public welfare, even though they may not be economically viable immediately, will be left under state ownership and control. Those that are not essential for the public welfare, but which can be viable if operated under different management, as well as those which are competitive with the private sector with no special benefit accruing to the citizens, will be divested'.

In addition, in areas such as Caroni Limited (sugar estate and processing) it is proposed to continue profit sharing and distribution of land equity to reduce further wage burdens.

The political orientation of the NAR coalition of parties is <u>not</u> fundamentally different from that of the PNM. Like the latter, the new government appointed (in May 1987) a team to review the performance, assess the viability and future prospects of the state enterprises, and make recommendations for their re-structuring. In its terms of reference the team was asked to give priority attention to five state companies operating in the service sector, including a national hospital management company and a solid waste management undertaking. This team soon recognised the importance of 'structuring the enterprises to equip them to face the capital market test and, as far as possible, be absorbed by local investors'.

In an interim report, the team has recommended:

(i)   the winding up of some service companies;
(ii) the sale of others - to their employees and the public;
(iii) the search for a foreign joint venture partner for two large enterprises in communications and manufacturing; and

(iv) the lease of another very significant manufacturing company in which government investment is considerable.

The most critical of these recommendations still await Cabinet decisions. The Press has occasionally - especially since 1987 - urged the need for divestment of the most capital intensive enterprises.

However, the Council of Progressive Trade Unions (not a significant group) in a 'May Day' resolution has recently urged the government to halt its policy of privatisation and to nationalise the oil industry and take other similar measures.

PROBLEMS ENCOUNTERED

Trinidad and Tobago

The experience here is much too limited for proper and meaningful evaluation, though on the whole it has been one of 'inaction'. An Austrian conglomerate was recently reported to be negotiating for the purchase of ISCOTT - the state and steel complex.

Jamaica

The Jamaican experience has been mixed: showing significant success in a few areas (e.g. National Commercial Banks (NCB) 51 per cent share divestment, the privatisation of a number of public hospitals, public sanitation, and local-government street-cleaning and garbage-disposal services). On the other hand, considerable difficulty has been encountered in fully divesting any of the twelve remaining state-owned hotels and a number of agro-processing companies which, like the hotels, were put up for sale not long after the government assumed power near the end of 1980. Mention should also be made of the abortive and more recent NCB attempt. In between is the case of the Cement Company, which the National Investment Bank of Jamaica Limited (NIBJ) attempted to divest fully in 1987, but succeeded in selling only 71 per cent of the equity. Special note should be made of the divestment (at the end of 1985) of bus transportation in the metropolitan area of Kingston, the capital. Ownership has certainly been 'democratised' in terms of the number of private minibus operators, but at great cost to the travelling public in terms of discomfort, poor schedules, and road fatalities. This points clearly to the necessity for effective regulatory mechanisms.

Partly contributing to the failure of the hotels offers is, perhaps, the stipulation that a significant part of the sale price should be paid in foreign exchange. Such a condition limits potential buyers to non-Jamaicans, and the government hopes for joint-venture arrangements on a foreign-exchange, part-payment basis. An associated constraint, too, is the unpredictability of tourism, even though the industry has been performing well over the past 3 years.

As for the Cement offering, it seems that its limited success reflected a failure to study the conditions of the market carefully enough and the setting of a price based on an unjustified estimate of earning prospects in the light of a not too strong record of performance. Yet, the arrangements were managed by the same local NIBJ team which had master-minded the NCB divestment exercise, though it is not clear whether they had the benefit of foreign expertise on this occasion.

The NCB Case

It appears that the overwhelming popularity and success of the first NCB exercise was mainly the result of a number of factors: a well-thought-out study of the potential market, the Bank's earning record, an attractive share price, an advance publicity and public education campaign, and the state of the market at the time. Indeed, there are those who contend that the price was set too low - in fact, some buyers, who bought for speculative purposes, sold immediately after, to great advantage. According to the Public Sector Organisation of Jamaica (PSOJ) President, NCB was profitable only because its top management was recruited from the private sector.

As stated earlier, strong external support was provided to the local NIBJ team by USAID and the World Bank, not only financially, but via the services of technical advisers. Technical, financial, and strategic advice was provided by merchant bankers N.M. Rothschild, whose two staff members on the team had been advisers to the Thatcher Government in respect of the British Telecom and British Gas privatisation projects. The team leader, a senior partner of Price Waterhouse (Jamaica) had served for a few years as

Executive Director of the Bureau of Management Support in Prime Minister Seaga's office.

This offer was twice as large as any previous public share sale in Jamaica's history and created a great deal of comment. Apart from this, a significant and perhaps ominous feature involved the reaction of the leader of the opposition PNP - the party which had nationalised the Bank. Mr Manley condemned the exercise as an act of 'ideological aggression' which would favour the 'oligarchs', and threatened to re-nationalise it on the PNP's return to power. (It should be noted that the PNP has for some time been ahead in the polls by a wide margin in an election year. Manley has also insisted that he is not against 'small people getting an opportunity of ownership'.)

In rebuttal, the Prime Minister has re-emphasised the limit of $7\frac{1}{2}$ per cent of total issued capital placed on ownership by a single individual or institution; and that the government no longer has an input in the Bank's decision-making process, having withdrawn its voting rights and its rights of appointing some of the directors. Even more significant, the Prime Minister has warned that:

> [in achieving its objective to] democratise the ownership by as wide a cross-section as possible ... [this] will make it virtually impossible for any government to renationalise ... [The Act] is irreversible... no power on earth can change it.

More recently, in March 1988, the government, through the NIBJ, offered more than 50 per cent of the remaining 49 per cent ownership in a private placement to a 'select group of institutions'. Shortly after, the offer was withdrawn when, according to the NIBJ Chairman, a 'cartel-like activity' was discovered among some applicants who were 'attempting to act in concert'.

The abortive issue had initially been condemned by the PNP as a 'demonstration of arrogance, insensitivity and an act of the betrayal'. The 150-year-old Jamaican national daily paper The Daily Gleaner, in an editorial strongly criticised the government for reneging on its undertaking to divest all the NCB shares to a wide cross-section of ownership. One of its columnists, however, was critical of divestment and argued that: 'state-ownership and state-intervention applied judiciously are necessary devices to be applied by governments in protection of the national interest'.

CONCLUSIONS

The experience of Jamaica and Trinidad and Tobago, each in its own way, validates the view that public enterprise must play a significant role in a developing country, irrespective of the ideological orientation of the party in power at a particular time.

Jamaica poses the problem of the inevitable return to power of the socialist party, bent on re-nationalisation, with its concomitant dislocations - especially in a small developing economy and society. Of obvious importance to the success of a divestment exercise is the state of the financial market; hence, critical decisions on pricing and timing are the essence of the exercise.

The NCB case, which seems to be regarded in some circles as a model for the Third World, has also demonstrated the importance of mounting a comprehensive country-wide publicity and public education campaign via the media (radio in particular) well in advance of a share offering. Such a public education exercise, set in simple lay person's terms, is essential in a developing country. This case also highlighted the important role played by a high-powered team of technical advisers, some from overseas. The abortive second NCB offering led to criticism of the appropriateness of relying on foreign technical know-how which was unfamiliar with the local situation.

Finally, in focusing on privatisation actions and strategies, governments - even those which emphasise de-regulation policies - need to take into consideration the issue of protecting the national and consumer interest, through proper regulatory mechanisms. This is particularly critical where public utility monopolies are being privatised.

REFERENCES

The Daily Gleaner (1985) 'The Government's media policy' (editorial), September 27.
—— (1985) 'Media policy' (editorial), September 29.
—— (1987) 'Media divestment' (editorial) August 7.
—— (1988) 'Public offer for RJR divestment' (article) January 23.
—— (1988) 'NCB shares going to select group' and 'What the PNP said' (articles) March 12.
The Economist (1987) 'Privatised grief' (article) November 7.

Fielding, Mary (1988) 'Divestment and the national interest', Financial Gleaner, April 22.

Jamaica Government (1965) 'Air Jamaica', Ministry Paper no. 98, December.

—— Guidelines and Procedure of Divestment Committee, March.

—— 'Prime Minister's Addresses to House of Representatives', Hansard, vol. 6, 1980-1, and November 1985.

—— (1984) 'Establishment of the National Investment Bank', Ministry paper no. 24, May 18.

—— (1985) 'Report on Programme of Divestment/Participation', Ministry Paper no. 19, July 19.

—— (1987) 'Divestment of electronic media', Ministry Paper no. 39, August.

—— (1988) 'Selected public enterprise sectors financing plan for 1988/9', Ministry Paper no. 12, April.

—— (1988) 'Selected public sector entities - estimates of revenue and expenditure year ended March 31, 1988', April.

Jamaica Labour Party (1979) Change Without Chaos, Election manifesto 1979-80.

Jones, Edwin S. (1981) 'Role of the State in public enterprises', Social Economic Studies, March, University of the West Indies.

Law, David (1987) 'Return state enterprises to the private sector', The Express, Trinidad and Tobago, January 25.

Mahfood, Sam (President of PSOJ) (1987) 'Divestment policy', Sunday Gleaner, April 7.

Mills, G.E. (1973) 'The environment of Commonwealth Caribbean bureaucracies', International Review of Administrative Sciences 1.

—— (1974) 'Public policy and private enterprise in the Commonwealth Caribbean', Social and Economic Studies, June, University of West Indies.

—— (1981) 'The administration of public enterprise: Jamaica and Trinidad-Tobago', Social and Economic Studies, March, University of the West Indies.

The Nation (1970) 'Perspectives from the new society' (article) Trinidad, August 25.

Nettleford, Rex (ed.) (1971) Norman Manley and the New Jamaica, Longman Caribbean.

People's National Party, Jamaica (1974) Democratic Socialism, the Jamaican Model, December.

PSOJ (1988) 'The role of government in the Jamaican economy', Daily Gleaner, Supplement, March 2.

Rampersad, F. (1985) 'Public sector participation in directly productive activities and economic transformation', Paper addressed to the Conference of the Trinidad and Tobago Economics Association, December.

Stone, Carl (1987) 'Public enterprise and divestment', The Daily Gleaner, March 18.

Swaby, Raphael A. (1981) 'The rationale for state ownership of public utilities in Jamaica', Social Economic Studies, March, University of the West Indies.

Trinidad and Tobago Government (1970) Third Five Year Plan, 1969-73, Port of Spain.

———— (1975) Public Sector Participation in Industry, White Paper no. 2, Trinidad: Government Printer.

———— (1979) Report of Committee to Consider Divestment of Shares in State Enterprises (Chairman: Victor Bruce) July.

———— (1987) A Note on the State Enterprise Sector, Report by Team, May 19 (Chairman: F. Rampersad).

———— (undated) Report of Committee to Evaluate the Strategy for Dealing with Five State Companies Operating in the Service Sector (Chairman: Mr Baksh)

Williams, Hon. R. Danny (Ministry of Industry and Commerce) (1977) 'Statement of State Trading Corporation', The Daily Gleaner, December 11.

APPENDIX 1: Trinidad and Tobago: government shareholding (nominal) in enterprises by sector, 1985 (excluding statutory authorities e.g. electricity, water)

Shareholding	Total No. of companies	Total investment	Petroleum and related industries	Agriculture and related industries	Manufacturing	Transport, communication, and broadcasting	Hotel and related activities	Finance, banking, and insurance	Other
Wholly owned	(37)	1944.5	1474.3 (9)	213.9 (7)	168.3 (9)	45.6 (4)	5.8 (1)	0.2 (1)	36.4 (6)
Majority owned	(11)	197.6	115.7 (2)	0.8 (1)	-	23.0 (2)	0.4 (1)	47.7 (5)	-
50/50	(1)	8.4	-	-	-	8.4 (1)	-	-	-
Minority owned	(17)	61.6	-	1.8	48.8 (8)	4.5 (2)	3.5 (2)	3.0 (3)	-
Totals	(66)	2212.1	1590 (11)	226.5 (10)	217.1 (17)	81.5 (9)	9.7 (4)	50.9 (9)	36.4 (6)

Source: Updated data from Central Bank

APPENDIX 2: Size of nominal shareholding and number of participations in Trinidad and Tobago government shareholdings, 1985

	All sizes	Over TT$100 million	TT$50-100 million	TT$25-50 million	TT$5-50 million	TT$1-25 million	Less than TT$1 million
Wholly owned	37	7	-	3	6	15	6
Majority owned	11	-	1	1	8	-	1
50/50	1	-	-	-	1	-	-
Minority owned	17	-	-	1	2	4	10
Totals	66	7	1	5	17	19	17

APPENDIX 3: Performance of state enterprises and utilities, 1985, in Trinidad and Tobago

	Non-petroleum enterprises	Petroleum and related enterprises	Utilities	Total
		(TT$million)		
1. Value added	674.2	2,037.4	231.8	2,943.5
2. Capital Investment	274.9	572.5	168.0	1,015.4
3. Employment (nos.)	25,000	9,700	19,000	53.700
4. Exports	261.0	3,611.2	-	3,872.2
5. External debt (1986)	895.0	772.9	907.9	2,575.8
6. Financial data				
a) Inflow				
i) Operating surplus	-404.5	938.6	-82.7	451.5
ii) Non-operating receipts	238.1	82.6	-	320.7
iii) Transfers	7.2	0.3	17.8	25.3
iv) Total	-159.2	1,021.5	-64.8	797.4
b) Outflow				
i) Taxes, dividends, interest, rent, and royalities	433.4	295.9	19.4	748.7
ii) Transfers and provisions	42.1	60.2	21.8	124.1
iii) Savings	-687.7	207.5	-106.0	-586.2
iv) Totals	-159.2	1,021.5	-64.8	797.4

Part III

Concluding Review

20

Concluding Review

V.V. Ramanadham

This review of the preceding chapters included in this volume is not intended to summarise them but aims at a concise critique of certain issues raised or suggested therein. It is far from being a photocopy of the Workshop discussions (for which one has to refer to the Report on the Workshop); nor is it strictly limited to what transpired in those discussions. There are inevitable overlaps but at several points this chapter goes into intensive analysis.

THE COUNTRY EXPERIENCES

First, I comment on the country experiences as revealed in the papers. They cover a wide spectrum: at one extreme lies China, centrally planned and public-enterprise-orientated, and, at the other, comes Jordan with its dominant private sector. In between these extremes are various other country experiences: Pakistan, where, like in Sri Lanka, the relative orientation to public enterprise has swung with political changes in government; India, where public enterprise continues to be a sacred cow; Malaysia, which claims that public enterprise as well as privatisation aim at endowing the 'sons of the soil' with capital ownership; Ghana, Nigeria, and Jamaica, which have felt the impacts of structural loan agreements with the IMF, but have had varying patterns of exposure to consequential privatisation; Kenya, with an apparently decisive pronouncement on, but without commensurate implementation of, privatisation measures; Peru, which faces a 'determinative' election in a state of economic chaos; and francophone Africa where divestitures, (essentially owing to French capital investment) have been proceeding at a relatively fast rate.

Concluding Review

While the experiences of these countries have been diverse, there are basic themes of commonalities as regards the underlying issues; it will be the purpose of the second part of this review to discuss some of them.

Pakistan

The chapter on Pakistan clearly illustrates certain conceptual aspects of privatisation. For example:

(a) the idea of privatisation in the macro sense i.e. private, rather than public, investments in industry increasing as the sixth and seventh plans proceed;

(b) the concept of comparative advantage underlying the rationale of privatisation; in fact, the chapter raises the interesting point that this is not easy to establish in the case of a profit-raising public enterprise; and

(c) the options approach; closures, management contracts, outright sale, partial divestiture, re-organisation only, and operational criteria of marketisation, have all been in evidence.

Moreover, the necessary condition of 'definiteness' in government policy or privatisation obtains in Pakistan. It appears that the plan strategy has undergone a change in favour of small and quick-yielding projects, which are precisely the more attractive investment choices for the private sector in a developing country.

There is, however, reason to infer that some in-built brakes on the pace of privatisation do exist. First, the undiminished role of financial intermediation by the public sector, including the nationalised banks, maintains the imperfections of the capital markets. Second, how liberal is liberalisation, when one considers the actual limitations on the availability of infra-structural facilities for an industrial unit, some of which depend on state-government disposition? Third, the recent mobilisation of resources, through the Water and Power Development Authority bonds, do not signify a surge in entrepreneurial and risk-taking faculty on the part of the private investor.

Two unique aspects of the financial processes of privatisation in Pakistan call for attention. The first is the involvement of the Pakistan Banking Council in formulating fairly extensive guidelines concerning the sale transaction. The other relates to the involvement of the Auditor General (AG) in the valuation of the shares or assets to be transferred. On the surface this protects the tax-payer's interest. In practice it may end up entangling an otherwise non-controversial, constitutional office in debatable and suspicion-prone details of valuation. Besides, what is the expertise that the AG commands in these matters, especially when it comes to estimating the future earning power of the enterprise on sale? It cannot be overlooked, either, that at least some transactions here and there are bound to be under political and bureaucratic pressures, which the AG ought to expose but may find it rather unrealistic to do.

India

The prominent message of the chapter on India is that the assumptions on which the country's development strategy is built greatly limits the scope for privatisation in the sense of ownership transfers to the private sector. However, this must not deflect the policy-makers from devising measures ranging between partial divestiture at one end and drastic marketisation of the operations at the other. The 'memorandum of understanding' being formulated nowadays between the government and individual public enterprises, represents a valuable device from this point of view, if experience in the next five years or so suggests that it is meant to work scrupulously.

If one takes it as axiomatic that the development strategy ordains the government's continued 'ownership' of several basic sectors ('core' sectors) heavy limits to privatisation automatically follow. 'Core' enterprises making profits produce the impression among policy makers that privatisation is unnecessary to consider in their case. In fact, their efficiency may be low, as alleged recently by a central minister in India with reference to the Oil and Natural Gas Commission.[1] Even if the ownership options are ruled out, non-ownership options of privatisation (in the sense of improved efficiency through marketisation) may be justified. Indian Airlines Corporation would be another example of monopoly profits with very poor consumer orientation; and it would be advisable to pursue several options of organisational disintegration within its public-ownership status.

In the same vein the point may be made that the

407

distributional effects claimed for public enterprises, and feared to be lost under privatisation, need rigorous testing. It can be shown that the distributional results of many public enterprises are not the most valid from the angle of a national-incomes policy for India. On the other hand, from the national income-distribution angle, there is a need to move from the level of generalisation to the level of specific enquiry into the comparative advantage of a given public enterprise.

An interesting paradox strikes us as we look at the Indian situation. Serious disenchantment has been expressed at the highest levels of the government itself at the performance of public enterprises; simultaneously, heavy doubts are expressed about the efficiency potential of the private sector as a cross-section. If the private sector is itself to be privatised first, the earlier the government privatises financial intermediation and practises effective deregulation, the better. How effective are the acts of deregulation so far undertaken?

While privatisations have been few, in so far as the central government enterprises are concerned, it should not be forgotten that, at state level, several options of privatisation, including liquidation, joint ventures and organisational innovations, are being undertaken, at least for the significant reason that the state governments are under more severe constraints than the central government in finding budgetary resources for several of their enterprises. As in Nigeria, the state governments are achieving more in India than central government at the moment. But it would make for an orderly development if central government, along with the state governments, resolved the broad outlines of an approach to privatisation, however restrictive they might wish it to be. Incidentally, India is perhaps the only country covered in this volume that has not so far had a high-powered committee to look at privatisation.

Sri Lanka

The chapter on Sri Lanka provides empirical support to the view that privatisation is a 'continuum' of options and illustrates the proposition that deregulation is the basic direction of marketisation policies, of which privatisation, in the extreme sense of denationalisation, is one. The encouragement given to banking in the private sector is especially noteworthy.

The point that, public investments grew phenomenally in Sri Lanka at the same time as some privatisations were taking effect, deserves notice in a wider context. In many a developing country - India is a typical example - the government may consider it essential for development to adopt investment rotation over time. As the sale of some enterprises, or some equity, brings in cash, the funds may be used for public investment in directions that call for governmental initiative on valid grounds. In this way, the approach tends to be pragmatic rather than doctrinaire.

The privatisation measure concerning road transport lends support to the fact that competition can sometimes be wasteful, especially in a developing country, and that it calls for public action to regulate it, such that its effects are beneficial. Apart from this, the need for maintaining certain non-viable operations does not disappear with privatisation. Contractual arrangements with the operating units will be necessary, under which the government (or some public agency) offers a payment or subsidy for the services concerned. In Sri Lanka, these are confined to one public enterprise, the Ceylon Transport Board, and, as time passes, the proportion of non-viable services rendered by it increases. Although this is an obvious point, it is often overlooked by those who assume that the losses sustained by a road transport corporation (say, in India, to take another example) can be avoided by privatisation. At best they can be minimised, but only if effective competition exists among the operators that bid for the provision of services in the unremunerative routes.

Malaysia

The chapter on Malaysia highlights a basic element of the National Economic Policy, enunciated in 1971 (i.e. the restructuring of society in favour of shifting at least 30 per cent of the country's corporate wealth to Bumiputera ownership). This has ben the major rationale of public enterprise; and it is now the driving force behind privatisation efforts.

While the three-tier mechanism of the Bumiputera Investment Foundation, its subsidiary, the National Equity Corporation (PNB), and PNB's subsidiary, the National Unit Trust, reflects the government's intention of transferring the shares to private hands, it is not clear whether or not it encourages the dynamic evolution of private entrepreneurship. Equally, it is not certain that this pyramidical ownership structure provides real marketisation of enterprise behaviour. The more important it becomes as a transitory depository of shares, the more government agencies exercise powers, even if clothed as 'guidelines', and that would be the antithesis of what must be achieved under privatisation. There is already a reluctance on the part of certain ministries to release shares to PNB.

An interesting aspect of the Malaysian approach to privatisation is that private sector interests can submit proposals for privatisation. Those who do so will have the privilege of negotiating with the government first; only when the negotiations do not bear fruit will the project be open to others. Although this technique can have some advantages, along with the merits of private placements, at the same time one cannot overlook the possibility of errors, innocent or wilful, which are bound to raise criticism by the public. The problem can be lessened to some extent if the issues of valuation and sale price are ultimately brought within the same public mechanism as applies to the generality of cases; otherwise there can be a public outcry against the way in which sales are conducted.

The Malaysian measures of privatisation range over many modalities and the administrative attention from the government seems to be fairly thorough. Apart from the Committee on Privatisation, supported by technical working committees, the government issued comprehensive guidelines in 1985 'for use by the private sector', which spell out the objectives, the modalities, the identification of candidates for privatisation, the opportunities for privatisation, and guidelines on specific issues. On the important issue of the valuation and pricing of assets, however, the guideline reads as no more than a statement of the need for proper valuation. The government has also embarked on the formulation of the Privatisation Master Plan. This should provide a system which will guard against privatisations taking place in an ad hoc piecemeal fashion.

Jordan

Jordan presents the case of a country where the government's emphasis has all along been on promoting private enterprise. Privatisation is limited to some eight enterprises. Even here, the recent slow-down in the economy and in savings seems to have induced the government to defer the actual sale of shares. Meanwhile, measures that provide for the marketisation of public enterprises are being pursued, including extensive deregulation.

An interesting point emerges from the context of the Public Transport Corporation (PTC). It is losing, no doubt; but its problems owe basically to the conditions of the transport sector as a whole. Privatisation is not a ready cure; a comprehensive reform of the sector is necessary, which at the minimum can help PTC to establish whatever comparative advantage it possesses as a unit of organisation in the public sector.

China

The recent changes in China's economic policies smack of debureaucratisation or de-governmentalisation to the greatest possible extent, in order that the enterprises move towards market-oriented behaviour. Privatisation, in the sense of ownership transfers, is hard to accept, except for some changes within the structure of public ownership itself (e.g. as some shareholding by local authorities or by 'enterprises themselves'). Large-scale ownership by individuals constituting the private sector is bound to be ruled out.

The concentration on developing the managerial stratum, independently of linking managerial efficiency with ownership, underlines that the crucial issue is not who owns but how the assets are managed. The management bids, which are implicit in what is termed the Assets Responsibility System (ARS), are an advanced and novel device by any standard. If enough care is taken to ensure the long-term prospects of enterprise performance within the immediate framework of short-term bids by potential managers, the system can render the enterprises fairly market-oriented.

Yet there is enough room for us to doubt whether the environment within which the ARS works will be sufficiently promotive of marketisation. Capital markets continue to be under the heavy influence of government actions, for the reason, among others, that a considerable investment fund is controlled by the bureaucracy. Nor is genuine competition in the managerial-bids system unexceptionally perceptible. Further, the range of price and other impacts from 'external' (i.e. government) agencies is unlikely to diminish, though there can be marginal improvements from time to time and from sector to sector. All these considerations limit the scope for entrepreneurial dynamism, act independently of governmental decisions.

It is not as if the point is not realised. In fact, slow but steady progress is being made, within the constraints of public reaction, in improving government-enterprise relations and in diverting the financing function to some extent from the government budget to banking institutions. Many developing countries have been making experiments in these directions in recent years; and it might be useful for China to avoid, even at the start, such arrangements as are good on paper but ineffective in practice, in degovernmentalising the enterprise operations.

Reverting to the ownership aspect, two modalities within the structure of public ownership call for comment. The first is the decentralisation of ownership to the level of local authorities and 'groups', analogous to investment trusts. While relieving the enterprise of the disadvantages of ownership decisions by the totality of government, it does not fully address the need for the emergence of entrepreneurship within the admittedly planned system of China. Nevertheless, it does help to create an identity for each unit of ownership, so that the spirit of managerial competition through enterprise performance can characterise the various units that operate in a sector or in allied sectors.

The other modality refers to the enterprise owning its own shares. Apart from its merits as a disaggregated unit of management, the question is raised as to 'who' owns the shares or what is the meaning of the enterprise owning its own shares? The proposition is not without precedent, in the substantive sense. For instance, who owns the Yugoslav enterprise? Not the employees, not the banks which are creditors only, and not any level of the government. Who owns the major port trusts of India or the nationalised industries of the UK, which have only loan capital? Once again, the real question concerns what criteria characterise the enterprise operations and managerial behaviour and how near to market disciplines they happen to be.

Kenya

In Kenya, privatisation was conceived as early as 1982 but relatively little has yet been done, except for a few belated receiverships of small enterprises. The government has not yet announced any decisions on the recommendations of the Task force on Divestiture.

The government has rightly been busy with the restructuring of major public enterprises, especially in the financial sphere. This, it may be expected, will enable them to vindicate their comparative advantage as enterprises in the public sector; and measures of divestiture can then follow, if found necessary, in particular cases.

The so-called privatisation of the Kenya Meat Commission (KMC) which has been characterised by severe losses for many years (mainly because of the dearth of working capital and the need to finance accumulated losses) raises certain interesting questions. For the Agricultural Development Corporation (ADC), a major public enterprise, in which 60 per cent of KMC's capital will be vested, this will be a peripheral activity, and the dictates of restructuring ADC itself so as to make it an effective body with a homogeneous package of (promotional) objectives raise doubts about this step. How 'marketised' will its managerial behaviour be? Besides, what will happen to the KMC's obligation of being the buyer of last resort? Can an ADC-owned-and-controlled KMC drop this obligation without creating political tensions? One may read into this a case of non-ownership option of privatisation, whose substantive merits are not conclusive.

Perhaps major developments may be expected in the shape of joint ventures for the subsidiaries of the holding complexes - most importantly the Industrial and Commercial Development Corporation - with the public sector proportion of equity sliding down substantially in the course of time.

Nigeria

The foremost inference prompted by the chapter on Nigeria is that here the concept of privatisation is appreciated precisely as a 'continuum', and that the essence of marketisation is explicitly sought through the implementation techniques. The classification of public enterprises, under the heads of full privatisation (meaning divestiture), partial privatisation, full commercialisation, and partial commercialisation, illustrates the multiplicity of options (emphasised in the first chapter), and confirms the integral relationship of privatisation policy decisions with the macro-economic strategies of development. Except for the first group, all these categories explicitly call for determining market-oriented performance objectives, organisational forms, and operational techniques.

While great care seems to have been taken in evolving a conducive administrative framework for privatisation, a few problems merit mention. In different states, governments are moving at varying speeds and faster than the federal government. While there is probably nothing fundamentally wrong with this state of affairs, it would be preferable (given the nature of privatisation with its potential social and equity implications) for the federal government to set the pace, in order to ensure that there will be at least a modicum of uniformity in the essential directions of implementation.

State governments buying federal shares and enterprises is not really privatisation. In future it will be an advantage to spell out what merits such a development has in any individual case. It is to be hoped that the proposed Technical Committee on Privatisation will give due guidance.

The critique part of the Nigeria chapter mildly opens up a fundamental dimension of privatisation. So far, the major source of support has been the business class, for it is 'likely to benefit most from the privatisation exercise'. How broad-based can the benefits be in practice, and how will they vary from sector to sector and even from enterprise to enterprise? This is an equity issue which cannot be pushed under the carpet, lest there should soon be an adverse reaction.

Equally thought-provoking is the brief mention of the need for proper guidelines on the relationships between the government and privatised or commercialised enterprises. In the case of fully privatised (i.e. denationalised) enterprises, a new interface is necessary in order to assuage the consequences of ownership-change in the short run and to ensure market-orientation in the long run. The problems are compounded in the case of 'commercialised' enterprises remaining in the public sector. Decades have passed by without clear rules of government interface having been set. Decisive commitment will alone make possible governmental adherence to ex ante formulations of substantive interface. This observation applies not only to Nigeria but to all countries, developed and developing.

Ghana

The chapter on Ghana brings out the enormity of the privatisation problem, since the size of the public enterprise sector in this country is extremely large and its performance suggests that it has 'failed to achieve the objectives with which it was created'.

The lapses in proper and up-to-date accounting can be a source of serious disadvantage in several ways. Bringing them to a reasonable state, in the context of successful privatisation, might entail errors, both genuine and wilful, in the valuation of assets and in the treatment of 'accruals', especially on the expenditure side. Any obvious error can arrest public attention, and cause suspicion and resentment at the sale that follows. Herein lies a practical problem.

A more serious one lies in the likely structure of privatisation sales. The desire or need for the foreign influx of capital and technology may, by and large, result in foreign ownership (in whatever proportion) of enterprises having a high viability potential, while enterprises with low or doubtful viability potential may end up in Ghanaian ownership. This could be a gradual source of both economic and social problems. Attempts to assuage the disadvantage likely to be sustained by the Ghanaian groups could take the shape of offering special inducements to the buyers through soft terms - again a source of social tensions on equity grounds.

A unique issue raised by the Ghana chapter concerns the extremely large payments necessary towards workers' benefits, including those for redundancy. Is there a way of capturing back a good proportion of these monies for investment purposes in the names of the workers themselves? If this cannot be done, there is a danger that large sums of money (which, strictly speaking, represent the capitalisation of the future incomes of the workers) may be frittered away (i.e. that a substantial proportion may be wasted in conspicuous consumption). The way in which the Divestiture Fund is expected to work confirms this fear, since the proceeds of asset sales could substantially end up as payments towards contractual benefits. Here is a macro-problem of investment-and-savings strategy for the country, which the government can ill afford to overlook.

There is in Ghana an administrative arrangement that merits appreciation. The State Enterprises Commission (SEC) has been set up as a focal point not only for public

415

enterprise matters but for the divestiture programme also. (For instance, the Chairman of the Divestiture Implementation Committee (DIC) is the Chairman of the SEC.) This permits automatic attention to all options of policy, for the SEC does not (or need not) have a vested interest, either in (a) perpetuating a public enterprise (even where it is worth privatising); or (b) forcing a privatisation in instances where some non-ownership options (as specified in Chapter 1) will do - or will, in fact, be preferable. It has to be noted, however, that within the policy unification at the apex (i.e. the SEC), adequate provision is made for functional expertise in privatisation through the DIC.

Ethiopia, Malawi, and Uganda

It is clear from the chapter covering these countries that commercialisation rather than privatisation (in the sense of a transfer to the private sector) is all that can be contemplated in socialist Ethiopia, whereas all options are open in Malawi and Uganda. A major problem, common to these last two countries, is the local resentment at letting ownership pass into the hands of non-indigenous groups. Uganda has the additional problem of the past owners persisting in their claims for compensation.

The fact that most of Malawi's large private units are owned by multinationals is perhaps of portentous significance in the context of attracting privatisation capital.

The recent creation of focal points in governments to deal with public enterprises (e.g. the Parastatal Commission in Malawi, the Public Enterprise Commission in Uganda, and the Department of Public Enterprise Administration in Ethiopia) is a step in the right direction up to a point. They can play the lead role in privatisation matters, but these bodies have the subtle danger of over-centralising the bureaucratic interface with the enterprises, weakening sectoral policy guidance and monitoring, and placing a premium on power being located near or within the Presidency, to the neglect of technical expertise as a component of the interface.

Francophone Africa

Privatisation has proceeded faster in the francophone countries of Africa than in the anglophone, beginning with Senegal in 1978. Guinea, Togo, and Niger have the most advanced programmes.

It has been relatively easy to privatise the service and manufacturing enterprises, whose requirements of capital and technology are relatively low. De-monopolisation of a public enterprise - through policies of liberalisation - has generally exposed its rather low comparative advantage in many cases, leading eventually to privatisation, as with the pharmaceutical unit in Mauritania.

A distinctive aspect of privatisations in francophone Africa has been the predominant role played by foreign capital, especially of French origin. It is believed that there has been an incidental impetus for the influx of investor interest, independent of the privatisation purchases.

Peru

The Peru paper amply brings out the ethical overtones, the political genesis of policies, and the critical absence of conceptual clarity with regard to privatisation, and also refers to the weight of external pressures - from the IMF, for example.

The issue of privatisation seems to be highly politicised in Peru, and this is highlighted by the fact that there is an imminent General Election (in 1989). The economy is so heavily public-enterprise dominated that privatisation is bound to be a very slow process, if in the sense of de-nationalisation. It could be more manageable as well as meaningful if other options towards marketisation were also adopted. This would be another way of saying that, since the non-financial as well as the financial sectors of the economy are so heavily governmentalised (through direct or indirect ownership), what is needed is a clear change in the strategy of national development and in the direct role of the government in materialising it.

Jamaica and Trinidad and Tobago

The chapter on Jamaica and Trinidad and Tobago, two 'small' economies with relatively large public-enterprise sectors, brings out some points of general interest in the context of privatisation. On the one hand, too little has been privatised in Trinidad and Tobago, despite repeated committee reports on the subject ever since 1979. The Jamaican experience, on the other hand, certifies to the inevitability of a considerable degree of public enterprise in a developing country; also, several options other than de-nationalisation (e.g. leasing and contracting-out) have been adopted.

The National Investment Bank of Jamaica Ltd (NIBJ) represents an interesting experiment, in some sense analogous to the PNB of Malaysia. By being an intermediary in the passing of shares to private hands it does not guarantee any substantive change in the sale scenario, except for some expertise in conducting the transactions. However, if NIBJ is obliged to hold the assets or shares for a long time, in its capacity as a catalyst, a new problem arises, viz. that the management culture of the enterprises concerned would be in a 'neither-here-nor-there' situation.

The Jamaican experience, with measures limiting 'single' ownership to a small percentage ($7\frac{1}{2}$ per cent) of the total equity in a privatised enterprise, suggests difficulties of ensuring the spirit of the stipulation in practice. There can be a 'cartel-like' subscription, as in the recent abortive offer of National Commercial Bank shares. More funda-mentally, the imperfections in the capital and managerial markets in developing countries tend, in effect, to encourage ownership concentrations (even if covert) to ensure the success of the enterprise, to start with. Ownership concentrations and linkages are quite charac-teristic of the private-sector corporate structures in many developing countries. Privatised enterprises will be no exception to such features as time goes on.

The holding company structures recommended in Trinidad and Tobago for the 'apex industries' in the public sector (i.e., the 'commanding heights') raise many questions about marketising the operations of the enterprises concerned, in a search for efficiency and exposure to the forces of competition, even if simulated. It appears that these recommendations have not yet been acted upon; hence there is hope that they will be reviewed from the angle cited here.

What the country studies reveal

On the whole, the country studies reveal diversities in implementing privatisation. These have resulted partly from political circumstances, including elections round the corner, but, more importantly, from country-specific attitudes to growth and equity, ethnic preferences and foreign capital. However, a two-fold undercurrent is traceable in all the experiences; viz., that the state of public enterprise in coverage, organisation and operations is creating serious concern from the angle of efficiency, savings and growth, and that some appropriate action in the direction of marketisation (in other words, privatisation in its wide connotation) is recognised as the need of the hour.

The country studies bring out the importance of regarding privatisation as a concept of 'continuum', in which organisational and operational options - going under the name of 'commercialisation' in some countries like Nigeria, Jordan, and Jamaica - are as important as, if not more immediately relevant than, ownership privatisation. Thus the problem in developing countries is more difficult than in developed countries like the UK, and calls for the play of shrewd skills in articulating the precise form of privatisation most purposeful in a given case; for an untimely or basically illogical denationalisation can boomerang in the course of time as a self-defeating exercise.

In all the countries covered by the studies, it is inevitable that privatisation, in the sense of a progressive increase in the proportion of private investments, is scheduled to materialise as time passes.

THE OBJECTIVES

The following are the objectives of privatisation which the country papers suggest explicitly or implicitly:

1. To relieve the budgetary strains on the government:
    (a) because of losses of public enterprises;
    (b) because of their investment requirements; and
    (c) so as to permit the release of government funds for 'other uses'.
2. To improve the efficiency of enterprise performance:
    (a) through market disciplines and competition; and
    (b) by eliminating governmental interventions.
3. To improve the allocational efficiency of investments:
    (a) by improving the rates of savings and growth; and
    (b) by developing money markets.
4. To withdraw from activities more suited to private enterprise, and where the original objectives of a public enterprise are fully achieved or are no longer

valid; to eliminate unfair competition with private enterprises.
5. To relieve the administrative burdens of the government.
6. To widen indigenous ownership:
   (a) by encouraging a share-holding democracy;
   (b) by making workers share-owners; and
   (c) by raising productivity through stock-owning incentives.

The objectives constitute a multiple range, in the same way as the objectives of public enterprises do; and some of them conflict with certain others - for example, 3 (a) and (b), and 6 (a).

Furthermore, the objectives are stated in overall terms, whereas there is need for an 'enterprise-wise' specification. This might minimise the element of inter-objective conflicts. Precision on the objectives in each case is essential, since the modality and techniques of privatisation substantially depend on the objectives aimed at.

A close look at the list of objectives suggests that some of them should really be considered as being of a secondary order and represent rather the techniques of privatisation arrangements (e.g. the offer of (some) shares to employees). The more refined the objectives of a given measure of privatisation, the more satisfactory the formulation of the consequential regulatory framework.

Some of the objectives seem to belong to the 'borrowed category', drawn from the experience of developed and market economies. It would be wise for each developing country to examine in depth how qualified, if not totally unrealistic, certain of the objectives can be in its own circumstance: for example, the one relating to the promotion of competition, the one seeking to eliminate the complexity and impact of governmental relationships with enterprises or the one directed towards the widest spread of share ownership. It would therefore be wise for developing countries to articulate the objectives of privatisation with a full understanding of the above considerations.

DISTRIBUTIONAL EQUITY

One of the complex issues raised by privatisation, in the sense of divestiture, concerns the distributional consequences. This is especially important in countries where distributional equity ranks high in the goals of development strategy. Many developing countries come within that description, and even regard public enterprise (rightly or wrongly) as a tool in implementing income redistributions of the desired kind.

The distributional implications of privatisation are under the impact of six factors:

(i)   the profit status of the public enterprise(s);
(ii) the scale of privatisation sales;
(iii) the pricing of the enterprise of the shares;
(iv) the pattern of ownership or the privatised enterprise;
(v)   the degree of monopoly enjoyed by the privatised enterprise; and
(vi) the distributional content of the enterprise operations while in the public sector.

The profit status

A public enterprise making profits has the distributional implication that it rewards the ultimate sources of the capital outlay (i.e. the lenders or holders of government bonds or enterprise bonds) at interest rates which are likely to be lower than the net revenue rates. Thus, the excess of net revenue rates over interest rates leads to an accrual of income benefit to the public exchequer or the tax payer. When privatisation takes place, the profits go fully into private hands as a reward to equity. Extra income benefits therefore accrue to erstwhile bond-holders at the expense of the exchequer and the tax payer. If the latter, on an average, belongs to a relatively low income bracket, the result is distributionally an unfavourable one.

The size of privatisation sales

The larger the aggregate of privatisation sales, the greater the distributional inequity mentioned above, as evidenced by the shaded portion in Figure 20.1. The X-axis represents the scale of privatisation in terms of capital involved and the Y-axis represents the corresponding net revenue and interest segments.

421

Figure 20.1: Privatisation and distributional equity

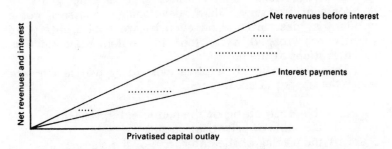

Thus, ownership changes in the case of profitable public enterprises entail elements of distributional inequity, and in two ways: first, because of the direct accrual of extra income benefits to the investor groups; and second, because of the needs of the exchequer to undertake additional tax efforts in order to meet the budget imbalances created by the divestitures - unless the cash incomings (on a privatisation) are reinvested in compensatorily revenue-yielding directions. Short of such a proviso, the impact on the tax-payer is most likely to be adverse.

Now let us look at the opposite circumstance - where the public enterprise under sale is a losing enterprise. It is likely that the interest payments made to the bond-holders are subsidised by the tax-payer. Privatisation can relieve him of the burden and thus contribute to distributional equity. It is generally argued that a major segment of the public-enterprise sector in most developing countries is making losses; hence privatisation agrees with the criteria of equity. The larger the losing proportion in that sector and the larger the bulk of losing enterprises in the privatisation basket, the stronger this argument.

Subject to one qualification, most relevant to developing countries. If the losses are the result of social policies implemented through public-enterprise operations, the reason for them continues even after privatisation, and the government has to formulate an appropriate measure of compensation or payment for the services imposed on the privatised enterprise. (The losses of the state electricity boards in India, which sold power to the agricultural sector at 19.885 paise per unit, as against a cost of 80.22 paise in 1986-7, illustrate the point).[2] If such an arrangement were not made, the services concerned would be discontinued; and the benefits implicit in their provision at relatively low prices would be lost.

Experience suggests, however, that in a majority of cases the losses are not justifiable on grounds of the distributional benefits that take place. In some cases the benefits are not invariably defensible on distributional grounds and in several others the losses result from sheer inefficiency, distributional motivations being a neutral event.[3] Hence, caution is needed before building up the argument in a given case that the losses are in the nature of 'planned losses'.

The pricing of the enterprise or the shares

Here, the reference is essentially to the propriety of the price at which an enterprise is privatised. Where the price is fixed at a relatively low level, whether to ensure a successful flotation or through a genuine mistake in price-determination, the buyer derives a benefit at the expense of the exchequer and the tax-payer. This is alleged to have occurred in the case of certain early privatisations in the UK.[4] Conceding that the pricing cannot be very accurate, one has to accept that the result represents a distributional shift, probably of an unfavourable kind, considering the skewness in share ownership in the economy.

Private placements are particularly prone to this consequence; for they could, though not necessarily, tend to be in favour of the buyer, price-wise. The basic assumption of such a transaction is that there is no competitive capital market ready to absorb the privatisation.

Patterns of ownership of the privatised enterprise

Two particular aspects of this question may be examined at this point. First, while 'block' share ownership reflects concentration and hence an adverse distributional situation, does a fairly wide spread of shares represent a better circumstance? Yes, in the sense that large numbers hold shares; yet, they may not account for a proportionately large quantum of share ownership. Apart from this, shareholders in developing countries belong to clearly higher income brackets than the general work force. Thus, income disparities through share ownership continue to exist, if not get intensified.

The other aspect is the allotment of some privatised

shares to the workers and pensioners concerned on concessional terms, including a certain number of 'free' shares, as has been done in the UK (see Part III of Chapter 1). This practice begs questions on the special merits of those groups for favourable treatment, since the damage implicit in the transaction is sustained by the exchequer and the tax-payer, and not by a private vendor of shares. On macro grounds, are they the people who deserve the benefit of low-priced, or free, share offers most?

The degree of monopoly enjoyed by the privatised enterprise

Where a privatised enterprise is constituted or permitted to operate as a monopoly, the distributional inequities associated with monopoly power unfold themselves. It is a sad commentary on several UK privatisations, publicised under the banner of promoting competitive efficiency, that they have ended up as near monopolies. However, opportunities of unequal competition are being promoted.

There is an asymmetry between private and public monopolies. Though the consumer might suffer equally badly under both systems, the resulting profits in the case of a public enterprise reach the exchequer for the benefit of the tax payer; whereas private monopoly profits reach the investors. Measures of privatisation that do not lead to effective competition in the sector concerned are exposed to this disadvantage from the distributional angle.

The distributional content of the enterprise operations while in the public sector

Some reference has already been made to the distributional implications, if not motivations, of public enterprise losses. Here the idea may be broadened to cover all enterprise policies that may not necessarily lead to losses. For instance, employee benefits, concessional purchase of ancillary industry inputs, price discriminations, regional price and output inequalities, may have been implemented on 'equity' considerations. These may be lost after privatisation, since the private owners will not be willing to carry those obligations (unless they are adequately compensated). Privatisations can thus imply the loss of certain distributional benefits. (We do not raise here the ethics and economics of the latter in the first place. Where these are unproven, there will be no real disadvantage.)

It can be concluded that the implications of privatisation for distributional equity are substantial, so far as developing countries are concerned. While this cannot be a conclusive bar to privatisation - for there may be a strong case for it on other grounds - it has to be borne in mind that the equity lost through privatisation will have to be re-introduced through budget policies. Where the budgetary resources for the purpose are scanty, privatisation can be disadvantageous on equity grounds. Once again the familiar question can arise: which has priority in a given case -equity or growth?

ENTERPRISE RESTRUCTURING

The question of 'restructuring' is of intrinsic importance in the case of many public enterprises; and there are additional dimensions to the problem in the context of privatisation. The country experiences contain implicit indications of the problem.

At the least, an enterprise which has accumulated losses is in need of a financial reconstruction. If these losses are less than the equity, a reduction in the latter so as to wipe them out is possible. Where the figure exceeds the equity, the government has to inject cash in order to pay off the creditors who have been financing the losses. It would be short-sighted to shy away from such a measure on the ground that the government has no financial resources for the purpose. The financial plight of the enterprise is a <u>fait accompli</u> - inaction will needlessly perpetuate the costs of financing past losses and, in any case, the claims of the creditors have to be met at some future date. The problem occurs in a peculiar way when the government decides to divest from the enterprise. The potential buyers do not wish to take over the loans; hence the government has to meet them, outside the sale transaction. However, if the buyer is required to assume the loans, the purchase consideration for the enterprise tends to be correspondingly reduced.

Up to this point, therefore, there is little room for any serious difference of opinion on the need for restructuring, in so far as it relates to financial restructuring. The question becomes complicated when the desirability of physical or technical restructuring is brought into the discussion. There is acute need for this in several cases, in the sense that the production planning, product mix

425

and technology call for thorough rationalisation - with the objective of cost minimisation, demand stimulation and, eventually, net revenue maximisation. (It is well known that many public enterprises in developing countries have, for various reasons - including helpless dependence on foreign collaboration - been saddled with uneconomical technologies, often with permanent disadvantages.)

Should such restructuring be undertaken before the government decides on divestiture, or before the government effects the sale after the decision to divest has been taken? There are two strong arguments in favour of such restructuring. First, it establishes the viability status of the enterprise which its run-down condition hardly reflects; and then would be the right time to apply the 'comparative advantage' criterion to the divestiture decision. (It is even possible that the enterprise so improves that the question of divestiture becomes irrelevant.) Second, it helps fetch the highest possible sales proceeds for the exchequer; and correspondingly minimises the damage to the taxpayer's interest and the 'equity' disadvantages discussed already.

A major hurdle can be that the government lacks the resources necessary for carrying out the restructuring. In this case the problem takes the familiar shape of an objective that is intrinsically justified but is not fully supported by financial resources. The government may meet the situation in any of the following ways:

(i) By raising funds from public borrowings, on the justification that the returns from the investment will exceed the debt-servicing costs;
(ii) By attracting private capital into the enterprise, while not divesting its own equity interests;
(iii) By undertaking partial divestiture and re-investing the sale proceeds in the self-same enterprise for the restructuring; and
(iv) By financing the restructuring from the proceeds of divestitures elsewhere in the public-enterprise sector.

(Incidentally, there are aspects of proper programming of the utilisation of privatisation processes - an issue which will be considered later).

It is also argued by some that the restructuring could be expensive, that is raises the worth of the enterprise (and, therefore, the price at which it is to be offered for sale), and that there might be fewer potential buyers. This line of thinking has practical value, but essentially reflects the assumption that the aim is privatisation per se rather than privatisation as a means to an end. An 'as is' sale can inflict serious disadvantage on the exchequer; for its bargaining strength would be so low that what it derives would be in the nature of a distress price. Where the potential buyers are wealthy groups or foreign investors, the transaction can get charged with emotional overtones besides.

There is one other aspect that merits notice at this point. If the decision to divest is firm, it may sometimes be a good idea to leave the restructuring to the buyer; for he will plan it in the way he considers most economical under his own strategy of operations. He will naturally consider it an advantage not to be conditioned by a prior pattern of restructuring.

Some balance may be aimed at, as is done in practice - for example, potential buyers may be taken into confidence and the patterns of restructuring most appropriate for the long-term interests of the enterprise negotiated with them. There is a caveat here: the government should not undertake a restructuring exercise just to maintain the status quo of the enterprise, but should explore the best possible response to market signals concerning the maximum viability of the enterprise in the future.

It seems relevant to refer to the Malaysian system, which provides for potential investors coming up with privatisation proposals. That system could adequately be availed of, in ensuring the right kind of restructuring suited to the enterprise and the potential buyers.

In concluding this section we may look at a special version of the problem, highlighted in Ghana, where the redundancy payments are excessively large. Should labour be retrenched in an enterprise which carries a surplus? The financial costs of the payments are themselves extremely high. Instead, can the resources useable for redundancy payments be employed for restructuring the enterprise if there are prospects of improving its degree of utilisation, raising productivity, or selling outputs for which markets exist, in many sectors? And there will be no retrenchment. The resources found for the purpose would be put to investment or modernisation purposes and the comparative advantage of the enterprise in terms of viability would improve. The arithmetic has to be worked out carefully; but there is some point in this line of thinking.

PRIVATISATION PROCEEDS

The country experiences, on the whole, have not looked at the question of a programmed utilisation of the cash incomings into the public exchequer as a result of privatisation (divestitures). The reason is perhaps that divestitures have so far been rather few in most developing countries. The question is nevertheless of conceptual as well as practical significance.

There are several options open to governments in the use of privatisation proceeds: for example,

(i)   for current expenditures;
(ii) for tax- reductions;
(iii) for 'social' capital expenditures;
(iv) for 'commercial' capital expenditure, including the restructuring of selected public enterprises;
(v)   for financing private investments; and
(vi) for public debt reductions (or non-increase in public borrowings).

It would be useful, first, to recognise that the sale proceeds are a capital receipt and should preferably not be utilised for current purposes such as (i) and (ii) above. The temptation for such utilisation would be great - governments being collusions of short-term interests; but the receipts are a one-time event while the commitments of tax-reduction and current-expenditure enhancements will have a recurring impact on the budget. It may be noted that, while the capital receipts dry up, the debt-servicing costs of the public borrowings that supported the assets since disposed of, continue to be met year after year.

The use of funds for capital expenditures of a 'social' rather than commercial character might be a development compulsion in many countries; in fact a proper programming of infra-structural projects can have a good effect in activating private investment. The continuing costs of such capital expenditures may be treated as a defensible public aid for development. It is possible that the exchequer derives compensatory tax revenues from expanded business activity.

The commercial investment of the proceeds does not necessarily conflict with the privatisation policies; for each privatisation, ideally, rests on the concept of comparative advantage, so that, while some enterprises losing it are chosen for divestiture, there might be others in which the comparative advantage of public sector organisation is high. In fact, many developing countries will be in need of some degree of investment rotation in the public sector. For empirical support, one may look at the experience of Jamaica and Sri Lanka. Even on the narrow ground of budget balance, this would be the optimal channel of fund utilisation; for the original public debt that accounted for the assets disposed of can be serviced with ease from the net revenues on the new investments, subject to gestation.

To finance private-investment activity (which is probably sluggish) out of the divestiture proceeds is a question-begging proposition. This intensifies financial intermediation in the public sector and can be the antithesis of privatisation, in the sense of marketisation and entrepreneurial autonomy on the part of the private investor. Several specific areas of this device are canvassed from time to time - for example, in favour of the workers subscribing for the shares. A recent illustration comes from the Indian Finance Minister's budget proposal in 1988 to introduce a scheme whereby 5 per cent of the capital issues under divestiture are reserved for the employees; and, in order to facilitate their purchase, banks would be asked to provide loans liberally to them!

The last channel of utilisation is, in a way, the best, for the debt obligations of the government get scaled down correspondingly with the sale of assets. Or, new borrowings would be under control, with a similar result. There is an incidental advantage. The funds withdrawn from the private sector in the course of divestiture will again go back to it through public debt retirements; or a new draft on it through public borrowings will not be there. And the quantum of investible funds on the part of the private sector will remain unaffected.

Let us consider the allied question relating to the public exchequer, namely, that divestiture connotes the selling of 'the family silver'. What takes place is the conversion of a future stream of profits into a capital sum. The effects on the budget from year to year depend on the arithmetic of the several variables which the transaction consists of: the viability of the divested enterprise, the magnitude of the divestiture proceeds, and the channel of utilisation of the proceeds.

Assume that the enterprise sold was a profitable one and that the exchequer was enjoying a net balance of revenue between the profits and the servicing costs of the related public debt. If the divestiture proceeds are used for corresponding reductions in public debt or if they help keep down fresh borrowings correspondingly, the budget will be at a disadvantage year after year to the extent of the net balance mentioned above. If the proceeds are used for any expenditure programme, revenue or capital, not accompanied by an inflow of net income, the budget will be at a disadvantage in continuing to meet the costs of debt servicing without any prospect of related revenue. It is only when the proceeds are invested in some project that brings in net returns in excess of the corresponding debt-servicing costs that the position of budget balance will not undergo a change for the worse.

There can be two alternative profiles in the use of the divestiture proceeds over the long term. The first is where the government, true to the philosophy of privatisation per se, does not undertake any fresh investments. The exchequer will be under a disadvantage, as argued above. The other is where the government undertakes investment rotation, but in such a way in practice that the projects are relatively low-and slow-yielding. Now the effect on the budget will be one of disadvantage in the short run, but not possibly in the long run unless the relatively profitable investments begin to be monopolised by the private sector and the government is constrained to go in for low-profit or developmental activities almost ad infinitum.

Let us, finally, assume that the divestiture relates to losing enterprises. The first impression is that the government budget will experience a change for the better since it is relieved of debt-servicing costs. This may be partially true, but the sale proceeds of losing enterprises are likely to fall below the figure of total investment (i.e. below the figure of the corresponding public debt). The costs of debt-servicing will not, therefore, be completely saved. Applying this logic, we can suggest that the sale of a profitable enterprise is likely to fetch proceeds that exceed the corresponding figure of public debt; and the arithmetical effects on the budget would be superior to what have been described in the foregoing paragraphs.

There are two significant qualifications to the above analysis - one is favourable and the other unfavourable to the budget. The first qualification (favourable) indicates that progressive privatisations bring in expanded tax revenues, if it is assumed that as private enterprises the operations concerned make higher profits than in the public sector <u>and</u> that there is no tax evasion. By giving an impetus to activity, they may in fact widen the tax base.

The unfavourable qualification, rather forceful in developing countries, is as follows. The divestiture programme entails large redundancy payments which would end up as a budget debit. Where funds are borrowed in order to meet them, continuing effects of debt-servicing will also be there. Further, the extent of real or perceived 'social obligations', which major privatised enterprises will be expected to assume on appropriate arrangements of governmental subsidy or compensation, will be quite considerable; and this will be a continuing burden on the budget. (In principle, the phenomenon is the same in developed economies, as well. For example, in the context of privatising sports services in the UK. It has been proposed that 'the admission charges and access for under-privileged groups would be safeguarded by councils' freedom to provide subsidies and dictate policy'.)[5]

Yet another burden arises from the fact that the transaction costs are bound to be severe; and the costs of underwriting and losses in purchase consideration in connection with private placements - especially with foreign capital - are likely to be high. Some countries like Ghana are under heavy 'external' pressure to materialise a specified number of divestitures in a time-bound manner; and these are linked with the structural adjustment programmes and loans from the World Bank. To meet the obligation, if for no other reason, the pace of privatisation costs are bound to be higher than would otherwise be the case.

Finally, while it is too early to make any empirical generalisation on the impacts of foreign-capital involvement in privatisation programmes, an analytical comment is possible. If it is accompanied by governmental guarantee of any kind, the budget will be under the impacts of possible exchange depreciation in the future.

NOTES

1. As reported in the <u>Hindu</u>, Hyderabad edition, July 1988.
2. <u>Deccan Chronicle</u>, Hyderabad, 19 July 1988.
3. For a full discussion of the problem, see V.V. Ramanadham (1988) <u>Public Enterprise and Income Distribution</u>, London: Routledge.
4. Ibid.
5. <u>The Independent</u>, London, 2 July 1988, p.4.

Index

accountability 33
accumulated losses 35-6,
    90-2
    Pakistan 108
allocative efficiency 126
Africa 322-51
    nationalism 336
    parastatals 323
    privatisation 322-51
    public enterprise 322-51:
    banking 339; capital
    and institutional
    support 326; classifi-
    cation of 334-5; debt
    settlement 338-9;
    financial restructuring
    326-7, 338-9; macro-
    economic policies 327;
    management 340-1;
    physical rehabilitation
    341; problems of 332;
    public accountability
    339; reform projects
    322-51; selection of
    enterprises for 342-3
    regulation 336-7
    structural adjustment
    programmes 330-1
    World Bank and 350
Africanisation of industrial
    employment 98
aggregate buying capacity
    42-3
Amersham International plc
    63, 64, 66, 68, 70, 71, 83,
    104
Aluminium Extrusion Ltd,
    Nigeria 93
anti-competitive action
    127-8, 129

Argentina 31
Associated British Ports
    Holdings plc 21, 63, 66,
    68, 71

Bangladesh, public
    enterprise 98
Berg Report 94
Bharat Heavy Electricals
    Ltd, India 7, 46
Bharat Tanneries, India 186
borrowings, government 12-
    13
Brazil 31
British Aerospace plc 21,
    27, 30, 63, 64, 66, 68, 70,
    71, 83, 104
British Airports Authority
    plc 21, 22, 23, 26, 31, 64,
    66, 68, 70, 71, 74-5, 76,
    83, 130, 131
British Airways plc 22, 25,
    26, 30, 64, 66, 68, 70, 71,
    76
    Helicopters 64, 65
British Ceylon Corporation
    92
British Ceylon Milling
    Corporation 92
British Gas plc 21, 22, 23,
    26, 27, 64, 66, 68, 70, 72,
    76, 83, 130, 131
    Wych Farm 63, 65
British Leyland Trucks 21,
    64, 65
British Petroleum Co. Ltd
    21, 23, 63, 66, 69, 72, 83,
    109, 110
British Rail 31
    Hotels 63, 65

British Shipbuilders 65
British Steel plc 7, 22, 81-2
British Technology Group
  Holdings 65
British Telecommunications
  plc 21, 23, 26, 63, 64, 66,
  69, 70, 72, 76, 83, 112-3,
  116, 130, 131
Britoil plc 21, 22, 63, 66, 69,
  72, 76, 77-80, 83
Brooke Marine Ltd 63, 65
budget balance 12
bus transport, UK 18, 26,
  129
Butler, Adam 19
buyers of privatised enterprises 42-9

Cable & Wireless plc 21, 63,
  64, 66, 69, 70, 72, 83,
  104, 110
Cameroon, public enterprise
  reform 347
Capital Asset Pricing Model
  108
capital-market effects 112-
  5
capital markets 10
Cardboard Packaging,
  Nigeria 93
Caribbean Community
  (CARICOM) 378
Caribbean Development
  Bank (CDB) 378
Central Africa Republic
  331, 348
Ceylon Extraction Co. Ltd
  92
Ceylon Oxygen Ltd 40, 92,
  207-8, 211
Ceylon Plywoods Corporation
  92
Ceylon State Hardware
  Corporation 92
Chad 347

China 250-67, 411-2
  Assets Responsibility
    System 257-61, 263,
    264-5
  competition 262, 264
  Contract Responsibility
    System 261-5:
    problems 264-5
  debureaucratisation 266
  decentralisation 254-5
  denationalisation 266
  enterprise autonomy
    254-5
  enterprise shares 257
  entrepreneurial atratum
    266
  ownership structure 250-
    3
  privatisation 250-67
  public enterprise 250-5:
    characteristics of 253-
    4
  public shares economy
    256-7
civil servants 14
clawback 66, 112
coach services, UK 126
Colombo Commercial Co.,
  Sri Lanka 92
Committee of Public
  Accounts, UK 25, 26
Companies Act, UK 32, 33
comparative advantage 14-
  17, 38, 48
  in developing countries
    33-4, 48, 429
compensation payments 8
competition 7, 26-7, 55-6,
  125-32
  economic constraints on
    127-9
competitive auction 108
Congo 331
Conservative Manifesto,
  1987 20

contracting out 8
co-operatives 6
    India 191
    Sri Lanka 200
core industries 50-1
crowding out hypothesis 95
current losses 36-7

DAB 64, 65
denationalisation 4, 11-17,
    42
    criteria for 38-40
    in developing countries
        33-4
    in Nigeria 291, 292-3
    in Pakistan 148-9, 152-3
    in UK 18, 24
deregulation 4, 7
    in developing countries
        99
    in Jordan 244
    in Pakistan 157, 158-9
    in UK 18, 129
developing countries,
    privatisation and 34-53,
    98-101, 118-19
developing countries, and
    UK, privatisation 24-34
development strategy 51-3
disinvestment, India 183
disinvestment, Pakistan 147,
    152, 159-60, 169-77
distribution 97-8, 139, 424-5
distributional equity 420-5
divestitures 428-31
Divident Discount Model
    108

economic concentration 41
efficiency 25, 26-7, 141
    of private enterprise 49-
        51
    socio-political climate
        on 24
Electricite de France 7

electricity industry, UK
    121-2
employees' shares 22, 28-9,
    45-6, 71-5
Enterprise Oil plc 21, 63,
    66, 69, 73, 83
enterprise shares 257
equity investments 50
Essential Oil (Ceylon) Ltd
    92
Ethiopia 352-7, 416
    Department of Public
        Enterprise Admin-
        istration 355-6
    privatisation 352-7:
        financial objectives
        353; social objectives
        354; strategy 354-7
    World Bank and 357
exchequer (UK), privatisation
    and 54-5

Fairey 63
Ferranti 63
financial restructuring 30,
    36
fiscal impact of public
    enterprise 95-7
flexible clawback 112
foreign buyers 46
Francophone West Africa
    347-50, 416

Gabon 347
Ghana 43, 122, 303-21, 415-
    16
    Agricultural Develop-
        ment Corporation
        (ADC) 308
    cocoa and coffee 318-19
    Cocoa Board 318-19
    divestiture 307-8, 312-16:
        problems 316-21
    Divestiture Fund 315
    Divestiture Implemen-

tation Committee
314-15
foreign investors 319-20
holding companies 305
Industrial Development
Corporation 308
Industrial Holding
Corporation 305, 308
joint ventures 46, 47,
305, 314
plantations 318-19
privatisation 303-21:
necessity for 310-11;
problems 316-21
public enterprise 303-8:
finance 306-7
Public Enterprise
Project 312
redeployment and
redundancy 320-1,
427-8
government control of
public enterprise 10
Guinea 416-17
public enterprise reform
347, 348
technical assistance
project 330
Guinea Bissau 331

Hall Russell Ltd 64, 65
Himal Cement, Nepal 40, 45
holding companies 6-7
Howe, Sir Geoffrey 18

IMO Modern Poultry Co.,
Nigeria 93
incentive payments 8
income concentration 41
income distribution 13-14,
97-8, 139
India 24, 38, 40, 43, 178-98,
407-8
accumulated losses 35,
90-1

Arjun Sen Gupta
Committee 181, 184
Bureau of Public Enter-
prise 181, 184
co-operatives 180, 191
disinvestment 183
efficiency 49-50
electricity 180-3
employment 192
equity issues 187-8
financial issues 189
financial sector 180-2
Institute of Public
Enterprise 182
irrigation 180-1
joint ventures 47-8, 180,
185, 186
legal issues 190
macro-economic aspects
188-9
management contract 53
manufacturing 180-2
monopolies regulation
189-90
privatisation 178-98:
opposition to 40
public enterprise 178-83,
193-7
radio 180-1
railways 180-1
regulation 189-90
share ownership 41, 46
Sick Industries Act 188
social issues 187-8
Standing Conference of
Public Enterprises 185
state level enterprises
182-3
telecommunications 180-
1
television 180-1
transport 180-3
Inmos 63
Integrated Aluminium
Products, Nigeria 93

International Aeradio 63, 65
International Glass Industries,
    Nigeria 93
International Monetary Fund
    11, 12, 97, 99
investment criteria 8-9, 10
investment of privatisation
    proceeds 429-30
Istel 21, 64, 65
Italy, share ownership 28
Ivory Coast
    foreign equity 30, 46
    joint ventures 46
    public enterprise reform
        325, 347

Jaguar plc 31, 63, 66, 69,
    70, 73, 83, 104
Jamaica 378-401, 417-18
    agriculture 383
    banks 380, 383
    communications 380, 383
    deregulation 387
    divestitures 383-4
    National Commercial
        Bank (NCB) 394-5
    Nutrition Holdings 379
    privatisation 378-401:
        problems 393-5;
        thinking on 386-9
    public enterprise 379-84
    State Trading Corporation
        379-80, 381
    Structured Adjustment
        Programme 388
    television 388
joint ventures 46-7, 93
    Ghana 305
    India 185, 186
    Nigeria 293-5
Jordan 236-49, 410-11
    agriculture 238-9
    airlines 240, 241-2, 245-
        6
    autonomous private

    investment 243-5
    autonomous public
        institutions 237, 241-2
    communication 241-2
    deregulation 244
    electricity 240, 241-2
    financial services 241
    land transport 240
    manufacturing 239-44
    mining 239
    mixed enterprises 237
    ports 240
    private sector enterprises
        237
    privatisation 236-49:
        problems 248-9;
        strategy 243-9
    public enterprise 236-42:
        size of 238-41
    public investment 238
    railways 240, 241-2
    telecommunications 240,
        241-2, 247-8
    trade 241
    transport 240-2, 246-7
    water 241-2
Joseph, Sir Keith 18

Kenya 24, 122, 268-82, 412-
    13
    accumulated losses 36
    agriculture 272
    banks 278-9
    holding companies 275
    indigenisation 280
    joint ventures 46
    manufacturing 274-6
    Meat Commission 278,
        279
    National Construction
        Corporation 278, 279
    Parastatals Advisory
        Committee 279-80
    privatisation 268-82:
        criteria for 39;

problems 280-1
public enterprise 268-76
share ownership 28
Task Force on Divestiture
    of Government
    Investments 39, 277,
    279
Working Party on
    Government Expend-
    itures 39

leasing assets 7
Leyland Bus 64, 65
liberalisation 4, 51-3
    developing countries 99
Liberia 331
liquidation 6
Littlechild, Professor
    Stephen 130
losses 34-7
    accumulated 35-6, 90-2,
        162
    current 36-7
    reasons for 11-12
loyalty bonus 21, 22, 76

Malawi 331, 352-7, 416
    Parastatal Commission
        355
    privatisation 352-7:
        financial objectives
        353; social objectives
        354; strategy 354-7
    World Bank 357
Malaysia 24, 122, 216-35,
    409-10
    agriculture 227
    aircraft maintenance
        225-6
    airline 223-4
    Bumiputera Investment
        Foundation 234-5
    Central Information
        Collection Unit 219
    construction 226-7

contract privatisation
    222
health and medical
    sector 222-3
holding companies and
    subsidiaries 232-3
leasing privatisation 222
management privatisation
    222
National Equity
    Corporation (PNB)
    219, 220, 228-9, 234
partial privatisation 222
ports 223
privatisation 216-35,
    427: concepts of 221;
    forms of 221-2;
    objectives of 220-1
public enterprises 216-
    20: profitability of
    220; public equity
    ownership of 217; size
    of 217; supervision and
    monitoring of 218-19
public utilities 227
railways 223
selective privatisation
    222
shipping 224
telecommunications 224-
    5
television 225
water supply 227
Mali, public enterprise,
    financial restructuring 326
    public enterprise reform
    project 330, 347
management 134-5
    buy-out 6, 21, 22-3
    contract 53
managerial autonomy 10
managerial compensations 8
market surrogates 30
marketisation 31, 121
Mauritania 329-30, 347, 348

Mercury Communications 26
Mexico, foreign equity 30,
  46
monopoly 41, 424
  natural 116, 127, 128: Sri
    Lanka 212
  regulation of 129-31:
    India 189-90; Sri
    Lanka 201-2
Morocco, joint ventures 47

National Audit Office, UK
  25
National Bus Company, UK
  64, 65
National Enterprise Board
  24
National Express 26
National Freight Corporation
  plc 23, 29, 30, 63, 65,
  84-7, 104, 125
national interest 115-16
National Paper Corporation,
  Sri Lanka 92
National Textile Corporation
  Ltd, India 50
National Textiles
  Corporations, Sri Lanka
  92
nationalised industries, UK,
  statistics 17-18
nationalised industry policy
  1, 105-6
natural monopoly 116, 127,
  128
  Sri Lanka 212
Nepal 40, 41, 43, 51
  accumulated losses 35,
    92
  Capital Development
    Fund 45
  Industrial Development
    Corporation 45
  policy statements 38
  privatisation, criteria

  for 39
  Securities Exchange
    Centre Ltd 45, 49
  underwriting 45
Niger 416-17
  public enterprise,
    financial restructuring
    326
  public enterprise reform
    347
Nigeria 43, 44, 45, 122, 283-
  302, 413-14
  agriculture 292-3
  airports 288
  Airways 286-7, 288
  denationalisation 291,
    292-3
  development companies
    284
  divestiture 284, 291
  electricity 288
  holding companies 284
  indigenisation 296
  investment corporations
    284
  joint ventures 46, 47-8,
    93, 293-5
  losses 34-5
  management contract
    53, 294-5
  parastatals 284, 287, 297
  petroleum 293-4
  policy statements 37-8
  ports 288
  privatisation 283-302:
    buyers 300-1; civil
    service and 298-9;
    criteria for 39;
    political support for
    298; price 296-7, 300;
    public reaction 299;
    workers' reaction 299
  public enterprise 283-4:
    divested ownership
    companies 286;

federal 285; ownership
pattern 285
Securities and Exchange
Commission 44, 291,
293, 296, 297, 300
Structural Adjustment
Programme 289-91
Study Group on Statutory
Corporations and
State-owned Companies
287-8
Technical Committee on
Privatisation 297, 298-
9, 300
telecommunications 288

operational privatisation 8-
10
organisational privatisation
6-8
overall deficit 95-6
ownership 6

Pakistan 40, 43, 44, 50, 51,
122, 145-77, 406-7
accumulated losses 168
Banking Council 155,
174, 176-7
denationalisation 148-9,
152-3
deregulation 157, 158-9
disinvestment 147, 152,
159-60, 169-77
Industrial Development
Corporation 152, 154,
173, 174
Investment Corporation
of 44
joint ventures 46
liberalisation 157
National Development
Finance Corporation
44-5, 173
Oil and Gas Development
Corporation 158

privatisation 145-77:
criteria for 38-9;
1983- 153-5
public enterprise 145-7,
164-77: performance
of 145-7
share ownership 28, 41
underwriting 44-5
Water and Power Develop-
ment Authority 43,
158
parastatal organisations
284, 287, 297, 323
partial tender 112
Peru 358-77, 417
banks 375
cement plants 365, 374,
375
denationalisation 374
divestiture 363-6, 374
fishing industry 374
joint ventures 374
media 365, 374, 375
privatisation 358-77:
political opinions on
366-73; problems 375
public enterprise 358-66
state owned enterprises
359-63: accumulated
losses 364; adminis-
tration 360; legal
framework 362;
performance 360-2;
profitability 364
planned losses 11
policy statements 37-8
Post Office, UK 18
price control 31-2
price determination 43-5,
107-9, 423
Nigeria 296-7
pricing principles 9, 10
private enterprise
civil servants and 14
comparative advantages

of 14-17
efficiency of 49-51
private sales 65
privatisation
    aims of 121-2
    buyers 42-9
    capital market effects
        112-15
    case for 11-17
    concept of 4-10
    criteria for 38-40, 135
    definitions of 4
    developing countries and
        34-53, 98-101, 118-19
    development strategy
        51-3
    distributional implications
        138-41
    the exchequer and 54-5
    financial processes of 55
    implementation of 40-2
    joint ventures 46-8, 93
    legal processes of 55
    legislation for 32-3
    levels of 120
    macro issues 54, 94-8,
        103-17, 188-9
    modalities of 55, 103-24
    national interest and
        115-16
    objectives of, developing
        countries 419-20
    objectives of, UK 25-6
    operational measures 8-
        10
    opportunities for 120-2
    opposition to 40-1
    organisational
        implications 133-41
    organisational measures
        6-8
    ownership measures 6
    policy on 121-2
    preparation for 30-1, 49
    price determination 43-

    5, 107-9
    proceeds from 428-31
    programme for 42, 105-7
    public offers 68-9
    sales proceeds 63-4
    sales, size of 421-3
    senses of 62
    social and cultural
        context of 140-41
    stages of 121
    steps to 88-9
    strategy for 122-4
    successful 107, 111-12
    underwriting costs of 44-
        5
profit status 421
Progress Bank, Nigeria 93
public enterprise
    civil servants and 14
    comparative advantage
        of 14-17
    deficits 95-6
    distributional impact of
        97-8
    fiscal impact of 95-7
    income distribution and
        13-14
public offers under
    privatisation 68-9
public regulation 23, 55-6
public sale, techniques of 21
public sector, size of 94-5
public sector borrowings
    requirement 12-13

RPI minus X formula 32,
    130-1
Raisin & Peanuts Co.,
    Nigeria 93
rate-base regulation 130-1
rate-of-return regulation
    130
redundancies 30
redundancy payments 431
refuse collection, UK 126

regulation 23, 55-6, 125-32
  India 189-90
restructuring 7-8, 425-8
Retail Price Index 32
Ridley Report 19
Rolls Royce plc 21, 22, 64,
  66, 69, 70, 73, 83
Rover Group 65
Royal Nepal Film
  Corporation 36-7
Royal Ordnance 64, 65

SOCFINCO, Nigeria 93
Schroders 110
Scooters India Ltd 40-1, 186
Sealink UK Ltd 31, 63, 65,
  83
Senegal 416-17
  foreign equity 30
  public enterprise reform
    325, 347
  technical assistance
  project 328-9
share ownership 27-9, 41,
  423-4
  employees 22, 28-9, 45-
    6, 71-5
  joint ventures 46-7
  restrictions on 33, 45, 70
share prices 44, 423
shares, marketing techniques
  29-30
special share 6, 21, 22, 32,
  33, 77-83, 115-16
Sri Lanka 24, 40, 199-215,
  408-9
  accumulated losses 35,
    92
  airline 203
  banks 203
  co-operatives 200
  Gem Corporation 201,
    203
  'government owned
    business undertakings'

(GOBU) 208, 211
  imports 202
  insurance 203
  joint ventures 46
  land 203
  liberalisation 201-4
  management contract 53
  manufacturing 202
  monopoly, regulation of
    201-2
  natural monopoly 212
  nationalisation 199-200
  Paddy Marketing Board
    202
  privatisation 199-215:
    Commission 49, 207;
    criteria for 39-40;
    opposition to 209-10
  public enterprise 199-
    200, 204-6, 212, 215
  redundancies 202
  road passenger transport
    201
  share ownership 41
  State Distilleries
    Corporation 40, 92,
    207, 210-11
  State Mining and Mineral
    Development Cor-
    poration 92
  telecommunications 207,
    211
  unemployment 209
striking price 108-9
Swan Hunter Shipbuilders
  Ltd 64, 65

Tanzania 331
target setting 9, 10
tax evasions 50
tender offer 108-9, 112
Thailand 25
Tobago 378-401, 417-8
  divestiture 385-6
  privatisation 378-401:

problems 393
public enterprise 384-6
Togo 416-17
public enterprise reform
325, 347-8
Treasury, privatisation and
105-7
Trinidad 378-401, 417-18
divestment 389-91
divestiture 385-6
privatisation 378-401:
problems 393; thinking
on 389-93
public enterprise 384-6

Uganda 352-7, 416
privatisation 352-7:
financial objectives
353; social objectives
354; strategy 355-7
Public Enterprise
Commission 355
World Bank and 357
underwriting 21, 109-11
arrangements 66-7
costs 44-5
Unipart 21, 64, 65
United Kingdom
and developing countries,
privatisation 24-34
electricity industry 121-
2

nationalised industry:
statistics 17-18
privatisation 17-34, 103-
4
refuse collection 126
water industry 18, 19-20
United Motors Ltd, Sri
Lanka 40, 92, 207-8, 211
United States, as aid giver
11

Vickers Shipbuilding and
Engineering Ltd 64, 65
Vosper Thornycroft Ltd 64,
65
water industry, UK 18, 19-
20
wealth concentration 41
workers' shares 22, 28-9, 45-
6, 71-5
World Bank 11, 99
in Africa 350
in Ethiopia, Malawi and
Uganda 357
write-offs 35, 36

Yarrow Shipbuilders Ltd 63,
65

Zambia, public enterprise 98